D1880804

FACES OF GOA

FACES OF GOA

A Journey Through the History and Cultural Evolution of Goa and other Communities Influenced by the Portuguese

KARIN LARSEN

GYAN PUBLISHING HOUSE
NEW DELHI-110002

FACES OF GOA

(Arts, Culture, Education, History, Linguistics, Religion, Sociology, Tourism, Women's Studies)

ISBN : 9788121205849

© Karin Larsen

All rights reserved. No part of this book may be reproduced in any manner without written permission.

Published in 2015 in India by
Gyan Publishing House,
5, Ansari Road, Darya Ganj
New Delhi-110002

Laser Typesetting at A.S. Printers, Delhi.

Printed at Mehra Offset Press, Delhi.

Contents

Part III

PORTUGUESE INFLUENCE

Acknowledgements

With deep gratitude, wholehearted love and sincere thanks, I would like to acknowledge the following people and institutions who have been instrumental in my life and who have made it possible through their love, encouragement and faith, the publication of this work.

- *My loving parents* and close family, who have always been a source of inspiration and support in all of my endeavours;
- *Dr. Anthony Dias*, my fiancé, who has been the wind beneath my wings and lasting joy in my life;
- *Mr. Bob Dillon*, my High School teacher and long-time friend who gave me the courage to search within myself and strive for excellence;
- *Dr. Satti Khanna*, who encouraged me to explore the unknown and break down barriers of understanding;
- *The Menezes family*, who cared for me and made me feel at home and at peace in Goa;
- And my best friends, who stood by me and who will always remain in my heart, no matter how far away I may be: *Maryann Carrino, Laurie Sickmen, Marissa Perry, Lindsey Tyler, Julie Knight, Hallie Harper, Jennifer Gonzales, Kim Rostan, Pam Cosse,* and *Jennifer Orthouse.*
- My most sincere thanks go to Duke University, and the class of 1996.
- A special reference to: The Goa University, the United States Educational Foundation, the Fulbright Foundation and the Fulbright Committee in India who provided financial and logistical support for this project.

  Also thanks to Gyan Publishing House who have made possible the publication of this book.

Introduction

When I first began 'Faces of Goa', I had two particular themes in mind that I wished to juxtapose and convey to my readers. The first was the idea that culture is a process and one which evolves over time, incorporating, reinterpreting, and reinventing a myriad of elements which come together and manifest at a particular moment in time. The second theme suggests that while there are several overlapping characteristics which characterise a larger group of people and place in any one moment, within that group there also exist many different communities who for a variety of reasons, (i.e., socio-economic and educational levels) absorb their *general* environment in *particular* ways to produce some strikingly different mental realities.

But even within those themes the very notion of 'culture' stirs up some heated debates. Just what exactly is culture has been debated for centuries and many of us when probed would come up with different definitions, based on what should be included and/or excluded from the notion of culture. The more historical definition of culture has defined it as the fine arts and refined tastes and talents of a community in addition to its language, religion, tools, customs, and legacy. This gave rise to the definition of a 'cultured' person, i.e., one who knew the fine arts, literatures and sublet mannerisms of his/her particular society. Within the last several decades, however, that definition has come increasingly under the microscope as other elements of society called for inclusion into classical notions of culture. Today, this debate still continues as people attempt to determine which of those elements should be included in this new definition. Because this is an issue which faces contemporary academics as well as the larger community, I have devoted Chapter 1 of this book to 'culture', therefore, defining it in a more broad and open way to reflect these current modes of thought. Chapters 2 and 3 then explore the culture and history of Goa through this perspective. Culture, when seen as a continuous process, eliminates the need to include and exclude various elements, but rather views culture as all of these various elements undergoing a constant process of change and evolution, including not only the fine arts and field-labourers but also the current outside influences fuelling evolution and the historical processes which make possible the present moment.

Often the notion of 'culture' is confused with 'cultural identity', which can be a dangerous mistake. What is professed by individuals as 'Goan culture' is usually *cultural identity,* i.e., those elements existing or historically existing in the culture which have been chosen to represent the society. Chapter 4 of this work explores the formation of 'Goan Cultural Identity' as it exists today while Chapter 5 examines the different communities which exist and flourish under the blanket 'Goan cultural identity', at times overlapping only briefly between wide diversions in experience, religion, perception, and even language. Chapter 6 then explores migration as a process, while Chapter 7 documents the migration of a particular community from Goa to a major Indian city and the effects that this process has had both on the city, Goans themselves and on the solidification of 'Goan Cultural Identity.' Chapter 8 then demonstrates an unusual case where a migrated community cast off its former identity and in its place developed a new cultural identity which differed, at least in name, from that of the old 'Goan' identity.

The aim of this book, therefore, is not to tell the reader what Goan culture *is,* but rather to explore the historical evolution of the land known today as Goa, including the major events in her history which have shaped the cultural patterns and communities existing today. This book also has the larger aim of bringing to light the difference between Goan culture and cultural forms as they exist in society today and 'Goan Cultural Identity', which is a selection of particular elements in the culture which do not represent all individuals and communities within the larger society. Often throughout my research I was asked the question, 'How can Goan identity and culture be preserved?'

Again we are brought back to the very question surrounding identity and culture, and the question of which elements are included and which are excluded, certainly a value judgement and easily a political one as well. Yet the question is an important one for social scientists as wars are fought and thousands of lives are lost because of this notion of cultural identity and preservation (including religion).

What does it mean to try and 'preserve' one's culture and is that merely a human illusion of possibility or can communities successfully 'preserve' their culture and compete in the modern world? What are the sacrifices that accompany such attempts? And for what purpose? This book attempts to examine this contemporary social problem in Part III, which applies concepts from Chapter 1 to other areas along the West Coast of India where communities were 'culturally' influenced by the Portuguese. In Chapter 9, the community in Kerala into which the cultural elements (Portuguese influence) were introduced, was a society whose social intricacies and barriers were such that the element did not permeate deeply into the fabric of society. The history explored in Chapter 9 also discusses the initial entry of the Portuguese and their culture and religion on the Indian soil, and the results of that impact on later generations of Goans who attempted to migrate and settle in Cochin. In Chapter 10, the cultural permeation was to such an extent in Daman that the community involved lost its touch with its mother tongue from India and identified itself wholly with the Portuguese. Today, that community is struggling to preserve its perceived identity against the normal course of evolution, a struggle which brings to light the very debate regarding 'cultural preservation'. Chapter 11 describes the cultural evolution of Fort Bassein, a place which rose to greatness and international prominence during the height of the Portuguese empire, and likewise fell into obscurity once the power of the Portuguese disappeared. These simple people, who have followed the flow of cultural evolution in that small place, demonstrate a real blending of elements whose origins are unknown to them (although readily identifiable to the trained social scientist) and each is carried out in succeeding generations based on what their father's before them have done. Part III, thus, highlights various attitudes towards cultural 'preservation' and cultural evolution, demonstrating how various societies have dealt with one particular time-marked cultural element; the Portuguese.

The question of 'cultural preservation' is really quite relative, depending upon which era in history, which group of people, and which particular elements should be considered 'Goan culture'. At what point do we cease travelling back in time to find the elements which should be preserved, and who determines at which point in history elements should no longer be considered 'candidates for preservation'? Shall proponents of cultural preservation look to the Portuguese Era, when the city of Old Goa was thought to be the Rome of the East? Many argue that this should be the starting point for Goa. But what about the 65 per cent of the population who follow ways of life which roots existed prior to the Portuguese?

Others, therefore, feel that Goan cultural heritage should initiate much farther back, prior to 1510, when Rajas and Ranis dominated the scene. During this long era Hinduism arrived in Goa as well as the Brahmanical caste system and other rituals practised by the Aryan races. Likewise, what about the pre-Hindu aboriginal tribes who inhabited the land known today as Goa? They too had a religious system, folk art form, language-dialect (Konkani), and village arrangement. Shall we begin 'preserving culture' at this point in history? What about the pre-recorded history and the current argument that the migration from the African continent to the South of India formed the Dravidian ethnicity and culture which also found its way to Goan soil? Shall we then trace the history of Goa from the people who may have migrated there from Africa? The question of cultural preservation, therefore, opens up a host of other issues, many of which can become quite esoteric.

Rather than examining culture from a 'preservationist' point of view, this book examines culture from an evolutionist point of view, tracing the evolution of the culture as far back as it is known, until the present day. This work does not seek to place a value and/or a premium on any one particular time period or element, rather demonstrates that the forceful and/or peaceful introduction of cultural elements from outside sources is a process which has occurred throughout recorded history. Most things and ideas, at one point in their history, were novelties. Thus, what we think of today as part of 'tradition' and history had to evolve and/or originate from somewhere and had to be introduced into a pattern of previously existing cultural elements.

In our time, as communication links have increased and more people and things have come into contact with one another, cultural borrowing will intensify. Yet throughout history we can see that cultural borrowing, especially in terms of trade, has occurred throughout the centuries. China's silk trade with Arabia, her spice trade with Indonesia and her gold trade with India have their roots in ancient times. In a larger sense then, it is only the medium of exchange which has changed the ways and degree to which new ideas are brought into a different society. We can see this today in Goan society, or any society for that matter, as ideas migrate from place to place and are subject to both absorption, reinterpretation and rejection. The concept of democracy is one such idea which has been absorbed by a variety of modern-day nation-states, yet each state has its own version of 'democracy' when all are compared in fine detail. Similarly, some attitudes and behaviours which have filtered into Goa from the American and European nations are much criticised in Goa and are often prevented from entering into the fabric of Goan society and social relationships.

Whether or not these ideas are positive or not, whether the Portuguese conquest was a good moment in history or not, whether wars were just or not, is *not* the purpose of this work. Those value judgements I will leave each reader to decide for himself, as the aim of this work is to inform and explore. The term 'culture' will continue to be debated as individuals and communities aim to 'include' and 'exclude' various elements for ulterior motives, whether those motives be political mobilisation or preservation of a set of beliefs valued by society's constituents. It is crucial that the reader understand that this author views culture as a dynamic process, not as a particular entity or set of elements and tools. *The only thing which we know with certainty is that things will change.*

Seasons change, countries rise and fall, flowers bloom and wilt, tides ebb and flow, relationships evolve, people change, ideas change, money changes, even religion and language change.

Cultures also change. What becomes of these successive changes in a particular place over a long period of time in the realm of human behaviour can be thought of as cultural history. It is the nature of culture to evolve and change, as it is the nature of culture to be reproduced through successive generations. If we now have an understanding of the push-pull, attractive-repulsive, innovation-obsolete, conservative-liberal forces which are simultaneously and constantly in motion throughout the human social experience, we can now enter into this work ready to understand 'Faces of Goa.' Those faces, therefore, become more than those of different people; they are also the faces of different historical eras, civilisations, philosophies, religions, values, ethnicities, languages, art forms, communities and events. Ever evolving, ever changing, yet ever repeating, they are the cycles which describe events in human cultural history the world over. They are the 'Faces of Goa'.

PART I

CULTURE

CHAPTER 1

Exploring the Nature of Culture and Cultural Dynamics

Culture as a Process

Before attempting to explore the cultural evolution and identity of a place and people, it is important to discuss and develop a thorough understanding of the very concept and nature of 'culture'. Many circulating definitions exist which may or may not be wholly or partly consistent with this research. Thus, this introductory chapter is designed to familiarise the reader with the concepts which are assumed, explored, and/or developed throughout this work. Therefore, it is a crucial chapter and one that need be read because it relates across cultures, nationalities, languages and centuries. It is in a sense timeless in its approach, stressing the cyclical patterns, blurred lines, and continuous evolution which describe the nature of all cultures and societies. In the history of the human world, civilisations constantly rise and fall, societies grow and stagnate, people live and die, and these processes repeat themselves at different locations on earth, at different historical moments in time, and among different communities. *The aim of this chapter is to develop a deeper understanding of culture, and also to foster the idea that people are very much embedded in their cultures.* The first chapter, thus, forms the foundation for the research which follows, placing Goa in a perspective as a microcosmic case study of the macrocosmic dynamic processes which characterise many other cultures and societies. Seen in this light, Goa is not marginalised and isolated as a separate entity but rather interlinked and connected to the same forces the world over whose effects manifest in a myriad of forms, locations, and individual realities. What are these assumptions and processes?

Foremost is the recognition that culture is universal in the lives of men, yet each local variation is unique. Every culture has a philosophy of life or religious system, as well as a set of laws and rules (political system) to which people must adhere to avoid punishment. Each culture has devised a variety of tools and 'technologies' which are used to obtain from the environment that which is necessary for survival. Every cultural system has given formal expression to family, kinship and other associations not based on blood relation. Universal to cultural systems is some form of distributive system, or economics. Language, sanctions, and goals which give meaning and purpose to life are cultural universals, as well as some form of artistic expression either through oral means, dance, song or the 'plastic' arts. Some form of humour and patterned control over emotion are also cultural universals, except in a very few, isolated instances. But while culture is universal and the experience of every man, it is also unique owing to the different experiences of its population, past and present. Each culture has developed from the skeleton of these cultural universals which found their expression in a multitude of forms which evolved over time according to social forces. The present state of a culture cannot, therefore, be separated from its past, as it is the cumulative effort and experience of generations of people over hundreds if not thousands of years.

Culture has many definitions. In layman's words, culture is taken to be the language, literature, habits, dress, and cuisine of a particular community; in short all the observable elements which manifest in a particular group of people. Classical anthropologists have taken this a step further to include social institutions, mannerisms, world views, values, and interactions between people. The linguist, Gulherme of Humbold writing in 1836 defined civilisation as "all that helps to soften the lot of human beings in the context of material interests and development of customs and as a consequence that help to arouse individuals or people towards sentiments of reciprocal benevolence."[1] Psychiatrists define culture as that which comprises "inherited artifices, goods, technical processes, ideas, habits, and values."[2] Culture creates a common world-view which enables people to communicate. Culture guarantees survival of the human race by formulating ways of passing on knowledge, accumulating information, and facilitating adaptation.[3] Culture provides human beings with a way to communicate, to understand each others' needs, and to be understood. Some theorists argue that following in Freud's theories, culture is merely "a defence against man's primordial instincts (Id) which wish to be satisfied now (socially illicit impulses) without regard to cultural norms".[4] Culture therefore, helps to lessen the anxiety caused by the Id (Super Ego) conflict by allowing certain expressed behaviour.

While all these are true, it is also important not to underestimate how very deeply culture affects not only society but individuals acting within that society. It shapes not only our patterns of speech but also our patterns of desire, goals and aims. It determines how we react to a given situation, with whom we interact, and even how and in which situations we invoke defence mechanisms, which are again conditioned by society. *We cannot separate culture from ourselves, and neither can we argue that we act independently of our culture.* Deviant forms of behaviour are conditioned by culture, and even many mental illnesses are a product of excessive tension created by culture. If we look merely around our living quarters we discover that everything, from beds and books to clothes and computers, are products of our culture whether diffused from outside or invented from within. *Our emotions, hopes, dreams, attitudes, sexual habits, dislikes, in short even all basic human needs are all in some way heavily conditioned by culture. Even primary, biological motivations are susceptible to cultural influences. Hunger, thirst, sexual behaviour, fatigue and pain all these experiences are cultural modifications according to a particular social milieu.*

An individual's culture, therefore, patterns his very mode of being. In Goan society, for example, the desire for particular food (Goan sausages, fish-curry-rice, ginger-lime water, etc.) is culturally conditioned as is the need for rest period following the lunch in a rural village. Similarly, an expression of pain is culturally conditioned. Light pain such as the hearty back-smack of a friend is responded with exaggerated cries of pain, but major accidents or painful (physical) experiences are expressed with as little outward display of pain as possible. In some instances, self-inflicted pain (tattoos, brawls) is likewise faced with courage and outward displays of strength among the younger male members of the lower social strata in Goa.

Culture is stable, but also dynamic and in a constant process of evolution and change. Goan culture, like all cultures, embodies both stability (tradition) and change (transformation). The very nature of culture allows for change while simultaneously maintaining limits around those changes. Two major types of changes are existent in Goan society; the slow, normal evolutionary change from within, (characteristic of Hindu culture prior to foreign domination) and the drastic, and rapid change often imposed from the outside (the Portuguese colonial era). The forces of conservatism and transformation are present in every culture, though some cultures look more favourably on change while others view change in a negative light. American culture, for example, is often considered to be the one most susceptible to the forces of change, owing to the high value placed on individualism, success, economic movement, and technological development. Yet even American culture is stable in such fundamental concepts as religious freedom, democracy, freedom of expression, the ideal of equal rights, and the persue of the aforementioned concepts. Goan culture is likewise both stable and subjected to transformation. Traditions such as the institution of marriage, religious faith, the fulfilment of motherhood, and the importance of ascribed social status remain as powerful stabilising forces in the society. However, the introduction of western technological advancements, opportunities for women in gainful employment, emphasises on economic and social development, as well as an increasing importance on achieved status are powerful forces changing the face of Goa in her social interactions, underlying motivations and formal occupations.

Enculturation in early life is how stability and perseverance of a culture are formulated; only later in life once embedded in this culture do avenues for change arise through the process of rational decision-making. Thus, culture is both tradition and transformation simultaneously in process, each influencing the other and members of society.

Culture guides people, yet, individuals remain largely unaware of its pervasive presence in their decision-making processes. Goals, aims in life, perceived opportunities, moral values, ways of social interaction, and desired character traits are so deeply internalised resulting from years of early enculturation that people become products of their surrounding environment and owe even their patterns of thought and emotional reactions to that environment. Yet, these effects remain out of our conscious minds most of the time. This is true even for those who rebel against the norms of their particular society. This rebellion and emphasis on one's own thought and action are themselves ways of thinking induced by a culture which encourages free-choice. By deviating from the mainstream behaviour they in fact fulfil a cultural ideal which extolls uniqueness and individuality. Rebellion against a mainstream culture often results in the creation of a sub-group which is even more conformist than the previous mainstream culture. Any formation of a gang creates this seeming paradox, where membership is exclusive and dictated by a series of rituals, behaviours, and beliefs which must be adopted as one's own prior to acceptance into the group. Even then, most gang-members never truly 'free' themselves from early acculturation, instead forming defensive reactions directed against their mainstream culture and making constant comparisons to the former. Though beyond the scope of this research, the study of gangs and gang mentality demonstrates, often tragically, that early acculturation[5] remains imprinted in the minds of individuals and cannot be erased even by adherence to a deviant social group.

Culture is both beyond man yet paradoxically forever dependent on him. An individual is born into a culture from which he extracts the systems of values, beliefs, norms, etc. These then become an integral part of his being, even if he later chooses to disregard them.[6] However, culture exists only as it is recreated by man in successive generations. Experiments conducted by B.F. Skinner demonstrated that a child kept isolated from society does not develop or cultural behaviours characteristics of that society nor the capacity for language. Culture, therefore, shapes human beings as it is simultaneously shaped by them. The former process occurs in the early acculturation phase, the second in the later acculturation phase. In these processes, though big changes are noticeable, it is more often the small and subtle changes which add up over time resulting in the transformation of cultural manifestations, patterns of behaviour, and thought.

Let us take the example of making of curry in a typical village household in South Goa. Possibly one morning a woman is missing a particular ingredient and substitutes it with a different one or changes the concentrations of the other ingredients. The resulting curry, now slightly modified, may be preferred by the other family members and become habitual in the household. When her daughter comes of age and learns to cook, she may be taught only the newer method which then becomes the traditional method, resulting in a very subtle change in a very specific element of the Goan culture. Possibly this change occurs in a restaurant's preparation and over time becomes known as the 'traditional' Goan curry preparation, though it may not be more than 10 years old! Technology also creates subtle changes in small cultural elements. Using the same example, suppose the housewife or restaurant cook utilises a blender instead of the traditional stone grinder when making curry. The result is a curry with a different consistency which may be praised by guests resulting in the diffusion of this technique to other families within the area.

Culture, therefore, is that part of human behaviour which must be learnt in order to pass from generation to generation.[7] This learning occurs on both conscious and subconscious levels owing to the very nature of infancy whereby rational decision-making is absent and a child must learn to make his desires known to his providers in the language and symbols that they understand to ensure his own survival. Later as young children, they learn through rewards, sanctions, pleasant and unpleasant experiences which behaviours are acceptable and desired and which are unwanted. This learning occurs because as children and throughout life we seek approval, recognition, love and attention. We also devise successful strategies according to cultural patterns to obtain that which we desire (which is again a function of the goals and values we internalise from our culture). This learning is known as cultural conditioning and effects even minute character traits like ways of walking, behaving in a crowd, addressing one's elders, gesturing for emphasis (notice the Italians!), dealing with the range of human emotions, and enjoying leisure time with friends.[8] All find their expression based on cultural forms which are first imitated, then internalised, and finally adopted (and even slightly modified) as our own to become a part of our unconscious repertoire.

These traits become readily apparent to the casual observer who observes an individual or group of individuals in a foreign country. Even if the group's ethnicity is hardly distinguishable, initially they are easily noticed as foreign by manners, gait, expression of emotion and social behaviour. After several months, however, if one observes the individual, he may demonstrate certain forms of acculturation such as dress, mannerism and food habits following a healthy and normal desire for social approval. His behaviours and attitudes, after prolonged immersion, may also begin to resemble that of his surrounding culture, though this varies among individuals based on their abilities and desires and desire to adjust. Some of these attitudes will change forever, while others will remain as they existed prior to immersion. Others will undergo the process of synthesis whereby a combination of two conflicting systems of belief is created by establishing a compromise between the two. The results of such immersion depend on a number of variables, such as the flexibility of his culture, his individual psychology, and the values of the host country. However, it is important to clarify that this occurs in the second stage of acculturation, when a functional, rational mind is at work to find acceptance in society. This stage differs from the first in that a rational individual has the ability to selectively adopt various habits and beliefs whereas an infant/child does not.

Culture affects every part of human life, yet man is not merely a creation of his culture. Though experience is determined, defined and perceived through a particular lens, culture also provides an individual with the decision-making power to question his environment and the behaviour of others when necessary.[9] Every culture allows for some degree of variation and choice. The way one individual will perceive and absorb his culture is slightly different from everyone else owing to his unique historical experience and interactions with others which give shape to his ideas and self-perceptions. A man's position in society also determines the options to which he is exposed to in early childhood and the way in which culture will be imbibed in the second stage of enculturation. In the end, culture is more than any one individual who lives within its boundaries, yet it is not separable from men and does not exist as an entity in itself.[10]

Culture moulds individuals in two distinct but interrelated phases.[11] *Phase I* occurs in early childhood, while an individual is constantly being conditioned to conform to the desired behaviours pre-existing within an established society. He learns consciously and unconsciously, verbally and non-verbally, those behaviours which will lead to the satisfaction of his needs and wants and those which will result in disapproval. A child's gender mediates the way that society will react to him/her and how adults will condition the child to win approval. In the case of a Goan male toddler, self-assertion and curiosity will be rewarded while among young girls obedience and manners will earn them praise. *During Phase I, a child has no discriminating powers; he absorbs his culture without selective rejection and cannot tell the difference between right and wrong if both are condoned by his/her parents.*[12] It is Phase One which establishes cultural stability because culture becomes internalised within the new generation and these cultural patterns will continue, though perhaps modified, throughout adulthood.

Phase II occurs after the age of reason where selective absorption and creativity are most apt to manifest.[13] This phase is marked by cultural evolution which is a by-product of cultural stability. It is mature individuals which start new traditions, import new technologies, and devise economic development plans. It was during Phase II of acculturation that many Goans in the Portuguese territories decided collectively to convert to the religion of their rulers. Either out of a desire for economic gain, an increase in social status or out of a fear of loss surrounding the existing privileges and village structure, people felt compelled to change their religion *in order to maintain other cultural institutions.* Some converts were so poor at the time of conversion owing to famine and other economic hardships that they were ready to sell their children as slaves to the Muslims and could be brought into the Christian fold with a mere meal or two. Thus, we can see how conversion, because it took place in Phase II of the acculturation process, could not possibly remove all the cultural patterns and forms learned during infancy. In our example, the first generation born from Catholic converts in Goa, thus, incorporated both Phases (I and II) of their parents' development into Phase I of their cultural development, creating the first real 'Goans' (as traditionally defined, a matter to be addressed in later chapters). In those times, they were considered both Indian and Portuguese as defined by the culture and belief system which they absorbed as children during Phase I of development.

Culture is reinforced by a system of formal and informal sanctions. These sanctions reveal the conscious and unconscious system of meanings and values that govern the responses of a society. They are often formal in terms of laws and punishments to which everyone must abide or face imprisonment and fines. Stealing, homicide, vandalism, physical abuse and violence are only a few behaviours upon which formal laws are wrought to keep individuals in line with acceptable behaviour. These are similar throughout many Western and Eastern societies where democracies exist and are put in place by a certain political regime. During the heyday of Portuguese missionary zeal in Goa, politics and religion went hand in hand in order to impose formal sanctions on behaviours that were contrary to their desires. Even as late as 1736, an edict was published which forbade by law certain Hindu customs among Christian converts. (see chapter on social history).

This process of informal sanctions shapes daily behaviour and gives rise to specific cultural patterns. The emphasis on achieving a good character and on maintaining an untainted reputation in Goan society are examples whose results are determined mostly through informal sanctions. Heavy informal sanctions are imposed on women in Goan society who have a number of pre-marital relationships with men. At times it is enough to provoke questions regarding the reputation of that girl, which can have drastic consequences when a prospective husband's parents do a check on her. If she is found to be morally lax or unchaste according to hearsay, the boy's parents may decline the proposal of her parents. At times sufficient money from the girl's side is enough to compensate for a 'black spot' on her character, but in other instances the decision remains final. These sanctions are employed not so much in order to suppress women but rather to preserve the institutions of marriage, family, and the ideals of fidelity, chastity, and loyalty in women. Protecting one's reputation has become so emphasised and the informal sanctions so overwhelming that those women who do dare to engage in a pre-marital relationship do so only under cover and away from the public eye. This attitude is more prevalent in the lower classes and among the Hindu communities, but even wealthy Goan Catholic girls who are allowed to have an overt relationship must be very careful to keep their reputations clean in all other respects. These women are, therefore, not likely to engage in possibly damaging relationships as such unless they foresee marriage with that individual.

Culture has a focus and in Goa this focus is first on religion and then on social status. That which characterises a particular culture also tends to dominate the lives of its individuals and communities. Feast days and religious celebrations structure the time-concepts of people as much as the rhythms of nature and the monsoons. In Goa we find that religion is a major cultural focus which shapes the lives of peoples whether Hindu, Christian, or Muslim. Not only does Goa demonstrate three very distinct religions with their own institutions, but of late some of her people have been patronising various charismatic Christian groups and other philosophers such as those of Jehovah's Witnesses, Sri Aurobindo, and Deepak Chopra. In Goa, religion has also undergone the most changes, including the introduction of these new groups as well as the alteration of rituals and traditions in Goa's pre-existing religions.

Belief, when focal, encourages innovation and experimentation because within it lies an incredible source of creativity and stimulus to thought.[14] Thus, we find in Hindu-Indian society the highly scientific and brilliantly ingenious sacred religious books (Vedas), including the Puranas, the Upanishads, the Mahabharata and the Ramayana. On the flip side, however, when religion is the cultural focus *and* people experience domination by another culture wishing to impose its changes within that same cultural focus (as in Goa), retention of traditional forms occurs in often underhanded ways. Thus, we find that while the majority of converts changed their religion, they did not all necessarily change their culture and many have adopted styles of religious ritual and worship similar to those of their Hindu brethren subsequent to Liberation in 1961. The use of flower garlands, incense and food offerings in Catholic religious ceremonies are such introductions most observable in close-knit village communities. Likewise, many Catholic girls in villages have returned to wearing the Salvar Kamiz in public and wearing 'tika' on their foreheads for ornamentation.

Culture occasionally experiences what social anthropologists have coined an 'historic accident'.[15] A historic accident, unlike cultural drift, cannot be predicted from evidence within an existing culture. The Portuguese conquest of Goa is such an historic accident whose antecedents were not pre-existing in the culture of Goa, even though a rising discontent was apparent under the Bahmani rule owing to its oppressive tax structure. An historical accident significantly alters and/or diverts the original cultural drift which was in process prior to the accident, creating an altogether different evolution of culture than from what would be expected.[16] In Goa, for example, the creation and isolation of a neo-Catholic society in the three coastal talukas resulted in a new evolutionary path which has since separated these communities and provoked animosity in earlier years. Such conquest as was in the case of Goa may lead to an interchange of cultural ideas and a synergistic effect which revitalises a declining culture. An imposition of a culture by a dominant group such as the Portuguese on those living a different lifestyle might also serve to "rally them to forbidden earlier ways and result in those contra-acculturative movements that often mark the course of foreign rule."[17] For example, Hindu temple feasts that were forbidden within the conquered territories after 1540 were still conducted in secret and celebrated with great pomp and splendour in the neighbouring territories by both new converts and Hindu devotees. This counter-culture did rise in the early years of Portuguese cultural domination. The continued consultations with astrologers prior to births and marriages, prohibited by the Catholic clergy, further proves that a dominating culture cannot fully have its way with the culture of another people. This is primarily owing to the first phase in the acculturation process which, as mentioned before, occurs during the early years of child development before the powers of discrimination and selective absorption can develop. This early phase, thus, allowed cultural stability in the face of massive social upheaval. In our example of Goan society, both cultural innovation and cultural resistance resulted from the 'historic accident' of the Portuguese conquest.

Cultural Patterns

Culture also manifests through patterns and sub-patterns. These patterns exist in every known society and are recognised among members within that society. They exist as the form which institutions of a culture characteristically tend to manifest and the psychological patterns observable in behaviours, speech, inter-relations, and value-orientations.[18] Both types of patterns coincide with the attitudes and behaviours prevalent among a certain group or sub-group, the former originating from the latter. Patterns regulate and sanction behaviour including marriage, birth, death and all the activities which individuals in a culture perform in their daily lives in a similar manner. Cultural patterns are the "designs taken by the elements of a culture which, as consensus of the individual behaviour patterns are manifested by the members of a society, give to this way of life coherence, continuity and distinct form."[19]

Cultural patterns vary according to age, gender, established role, social status, size of subgroup, and economic class. Thus, it is difficult to establish one pattern as defining a particular society and only when all are active together can one see the differences between them as well as their similarities. Let's use the example of Goan roadways, which at first glance appear lawless but on closer examination employ a host of widely-known informal rules, laws, sanctions, and expected behaviours. First, the bigger the vehicle, the more dominance he assumes on the road. The behaviour of large trucks and buses on the road, dominates the scene, and other people are forced to comply and mimic their behaviour in order to avoid accidents. Following heavy vehicles, cars are next in line in the rank and file, followed by motorbikes, bicycles, bullock carts, and finally pedestrians. Each assumes dominance over the other and, thus, the man found stopping short and dodging most vehicles are usually those on bikes and scooters. Pedestrians have to wait until all is clear before they dodge the incoming traffic. A car driver is not expected to stop for a pedestrian, who must submit to all those above him. Overtaking a vehicle is commonly practised by trucks and buses, and can occur anywhere, anytime, regardless of curves, blind hills, or incoming traffic. Selfishness is the way of life on the Goan roads. The belief is that once space has been secured, others will have to slow down to accommodate. This is the dominant cultural pattern which exists on the roadways and upon closer examination belongs to the blue-collar working class society. The men driving heavy vehicles and buses invariably belong to this community and express sentiments on the roadways which arise owing to their general lack of education, lower position on the social scale, frustration due to scarce economic resources and need for social power and dominance in at least one aspect of their lives.

This same example also points to the psychology behind such driving which is reflective of other behavioural patterns pervasive in society and provides insight into the cultural sub-pattern of the blue-collar working class male. As author Herskovits writes, "the pattern phenomenon in culture is a reflection of the common elements in the individual behaviour of those who live in that culture."[20] The driver's attitude symbolises the general psychology in Goan culture which awards recognition and privilege to those who demonstrate ascribed and achieved social status while marginalising those communities (the low working class) who possess neither. Truck drivers often openly resent those individuals with cars and private transportation in a reckless demand for recognition, while at the same time enjoy anonymity behind the wheels of heavy vehicles. In this case because truck drivers have 'absolute power' on the roadways, a complex set of informal life driving laws has evolved which favours their positions and allows them to continue to abuse that power. These men are, therefore, mimicking those who they perceive to have absolute power over them and are reacting in a way which demonstrates their perceived positions in society in relation to those who are economically and socially sound.

Cultures within Culture

Culture is, thus, variable and is not a homogeneous, integrated whole. Individuals within a society perceive it differently and behave according to their perceptions in a variable manner.[21]

While a general pattern does exist to distinguish it from other cultures, this pattern is flexible and demonstrates many deviations and exceptions. These differences have many sources, but not limited to individual choice, changes in time, place, situation, or different reactions owing to different communal perceptions and sub-patterns.[22] The elements of a culture, therefore, are variable over time and place and depend on the limits defined by a particular culture over a period of time. They also depend on the distance between ideal and actual behaviour which gives the breadth of a particular cultural element's variability. For example, a pious Goan, (Catholic or Hindu), would attend mass/go to temple everyday; though we find that many attend only once a week and a few only once a month. On closer examination one discover that certain age-groups follow certain trends; those still attending mass everyday are usually senior citizens who have passed the age of retirement and have little other activities. Those attending once a week are usually families, middle-aged working people and children of the families whose elder relatives still go to mass everyday. Those going only once or twice a month are usually young urbanites, who are not only working and enjoying the weekends but can also escape the sanctions that would normally occur in the village owing to lack of attendance. The actual collective behaviour of any culture, therefore, depends on the observer, the natural bias through which he perceives his surroundings, as well as the sub-community within which he lives and interacts with others.[23] "Every individual will behave a bit differently from others; this is an accepted fact in human experience even within a culture whose members do not question cultural norms."[24] (An attempt to characterise and describe the culture of Goa, however, necessitates that some deviant behaviour or that falling outside the normal limits will be ignored or considered as the possible origin of a future cultural drift, depending on the example.)

Culture, therefore, has a variety of levels and sub-levels in its patterning and behaviour. Even then, cultural patterns are not entirely homogeneous among people and upon further examination one discovers that socio-economic classes or specific communities (castes in Indian parlance), each have some of their own traits and cultural patterns which are unique to that particular sub-group. In this work the recognition of various sub-communities and cultures is paramount and the remarkable characteristics which define a particular group to other members of Goan society will be referred to throughout this study when examples are used from field research to explain more general and abstract concepts.[25]

Personality within Culture

Culture, however, is more than the patterns of behaviour that govern an existing system; it also encompasses the encouragement or suppression of various personality traits which are considered desirable/unwanted within a particular culture.[58] Thus, in a discussion on Goan culture and cultural identity, the concept of personality must also be considered. While each person is an individual in a particular society, he is to a great extent moulded and shaped by the particular culture into which he is born. Personality, therefore, is a product of culture and exists within its realms. However, while culture serves to shape individual personalities, those same individuals demonstrate wide variations amongst themselves and amongst sub-communities within a larger culture.[26] The degree of variation among individuals greatly depends on the observer and the comparisons to which they measure the difference.

Culture, also encourages the expression of certain personality types. "In every generation personalities develop through utilising previous generations' experiences that have been symbolically stored in memory or in its extensions (computers, literary works, folk-lore, etc.)".[27] Thus, over generations a cultural system selectively chooses advantageous personality/character traits and promotes them as the desirable qualities which everyone should attempt to embody. Early social relationships and interactions are the means by which these values and desirable traits are consciously and/or unconsciously transmitted. Children during Phase I are subsequently raised in ways which foster the expression of these traits and discourage others through rewards and sanctions. As a consequence, these cultural values and culture-orientations heavily influence an individual's desires, tastes, private meanings, and the way in which those goals are realised or abandoned.[28]

Moreover, sub-cultures (Kunbi tribal community) within a larger culture (Goa) embody similar cultural patterns differently, depending on their socio-economic and power status. For example, those communities who are politically powerful often have a greater role in shaping 'national' or 'regional' traits than do those in menial jobs and they tend to exude more confidence and capability than do members of repressed or socio-economically limited communities. These traits further differ according to occupation, caste, social class and other divisions.[29]

Culture, therefore, conditions personality traits, the vast majority of which are learned at home and during human interaction. These traits continue into adulthood and can be witnessed in all aspects of life and social interaction from business meetings to child rearing practices.[30] People learn similar ways of responding to a situation and link them with common ways of acting, thinking, and feeling. Individuals derive their social personality from others who have conditioned it both at home and in public interaction through rewards and sanctions as well as verbal and non-verbal signals.[31] Manifestations of anger, frustration, hostility, and sadness, even in private domains, are likewise socially conditioned and influence expressed personality traits.

Personality is, therefore, a function of culture that varies in response to cultural conditioning. The continuance of specific cultural elements and practises must, therefore, begin in Phase I of acculturation as an individual matures and assimilates social values and expected responsibilities. Culture (specifically those people who live in and have been moulded by it) conditions through encouragement and sanction the expression of certain personality traits which differ among age, gender, and sub-community. In Goan Hindu culture, for example, the maintenance of 'traditional values' is highly encouraged by the community and has survived years of onslaught under the Portuguese rule which threatened the community with a variety of sanctions in order to compel them to conform. Thus, today we find that the adherence to the traditional family structure, expected social roles and personality ideals for men and women, and a strong attachment to religion and religious rituals characterise most individuals among the Goan Hindu community. Many of these values are likewise strongly promoted within the Gaon Catholic culture, though a more positive attitude towards change is apparent among this latter community.

The psychology of Christianity has also played a formative role in the religious personality of the Catholic community. Achieving the grace of God through personal piety and the avoidance of sin, both practices whose actions were established by the church, has formed the typical 'Goan' characteristics that are still recognised in Bombay school children such as honesty, respect for elders, pious attention to matters religious and the maintenance of the institution of marriage. In general, however, "people fashion their cultures largely unconsciously following their motives and values, which are of course, products of the very culture into which they were born."[32] This results in a circular relationship between the two, each actively influencing the other and consequently affecting individual personalities.

Culture influences personality especially in the expression of gender and age roles.[33] That personality develops within and is heavily influenced by culture is visible by examining the common gender personalities which a Goan society promotes. Among women, aggression, ambition and curiosity in matters already male-dominated or those that endanger one's 'reputation' are discouraged in the expression of personality. In contrast, self-sacrifice, contentment, understanding, orthodoxy, piety, obedience servitude and goal-orientation towards motherhood and family are highly encouraged personality characteristics in traditional Goan society, both Hindu and Catholic. For young girls, identification with mother is expected and harmless mischief during childhood and an interest in education are also often rewarded. Male members of society, in contrast, are encouraged to express curiosity, bravery, dominance, aggression, sociability, ambition and intelligence. Sensitivity, surprisingly, is not a discouraged personality trait, but rather a man who is capable as well as understanding and considerate is often thought to be ideal. Men in Goan society are discouraged from experimentation with drugs, sexual exploits, and other wayward behaviour, though a brief indulgence in such activity does not leave on their reputation the same social stigma as it would were it to occur amongst members of the opposite sex. Identification with father is expected and goal-orientation towards family and fatherhood are also encouraged personality characteristics. In addition to family, male members are also expected to be the bread-winners in society and to adopt the social roles characteristic of their professions both in and out of the office during casual interactions.[34]

Culturally-defined gender roles naturally evolve and change within a particular culture and within its sub-cultures. Of late, changes in these social roles have begun to manifest amongst the middle and upper-classes in both communities, especially as regards the position of women. This gender-role evolution began with the Portuguese missionaries who first encouraged education for girls and most recently through the mass media which unintentionally elucidates the varying position of women in other world cultures. As a result, Goan women are increasingly encouraged to put their efforts towards education and employment, though family and motherhood are still considered the highest ideals. Education is thought to improve a woman's mind and make her capable of better communication with her husband. In some communities it is looked upon as an unaffordable luxury, while in others it is considered a productive past-time for women between childhood and motherhood. Women are encouraged to value an education and a career, but not over and beyond the traditional values of family and motherhood. Little encouragement is placed on independence and Goan culture still creates in women a degree of dependence in matters social and material. Men's roles have also changed in accordance with the acceptance and/ or discouragement of male dominance and female suppression. Thus, in an upper class society where men and women enjoy a near-equal position, wayward behaviour is less tolerated and aggression against females is likewise socially sanctioned. In lower socio-economic communities, however, where education is less and gender differences are more distinct and observed, women and men participate in society in markedly different ways which more closely resemble the aforementioned gender stereotypes.

Culture and its component values must be examined taking into consideration the underlying psychological motivations of individuals and communities.[35] Motivation accounts for both normal and abnormal social behaviour and is influenced by cultural values and a culture's value orientation. In Goa, for example, both ascribed and achieved status are highly valued in today's society. The community (caste) into which an individual is born in addition to the education, profession and salary he earns are important considerations in determining self-identification and consequent motivation. An individual with a higher status with meagre resources, will place more emphasis on his ascribed status and attach his feelings of pride and superiority in relation to others in accordance with this quality that he possesses. Similarly, an individual from a low socio-economic background who has come into money through overseas employment in the Gulf, for example, will emphasise his financial status more than his ascribed status in his conception of self and superiority over others.

Cultural and religious conversion are additional examples which can be explained by examining the underlying personal motivations which influenced the decision of large segments of the Goan society to convert to Catholicism under the Portuguese regime. Economic incentives definitely motivated individuals to enrich themselves converts were offered employment and financial help to further motivate this decision. Privilege, power and an increase in one's 'lawful' social status were further motivations which encouraged conversions. Under the Hindu system, one could not increase one's social status and people were likewise prohibited from moving up in the economic realm as well. Under the Portuguese administration, all Catholics were granted special privileges and superior status over all Hindus, the latter group whom were relegated to the lowest rung of society regardless of education, rank or other former caste qualities. Also, basic human necessities motivated many to abandon their former religion and embrace Christianity. Fearing persecution, loss of family finances property and the disruption of family and social life, many families chose basic security and possible prosperity over probable famine, loss of property, prestige and even life. Conversion, thus, reduced many sources of stress by reducing poverty, improving sense of self-esteem and offering converts encouragement and support.

Religious conversion is also one way to change identity and self-perception. When this is the case, conversion is often carried out with great ceremony and publicity to ensure that others become aware of an individual's new social being and treat him accordingly.[36] The very poor Catholic converts, normally marginalised by larger society, enjoyed the attention they received from the authorities who praised them as changed, 'saved' beings following conversion. During the early years, they also began to perceive themselves as superior to those who would not embrace

Catholicism. Religious conversion, therefore, was a cultural adaptation which ensured the survival of communities, families and individuals in a way that coincided with the underlying motivations of the Goan community *at the time of the Portuguese conquest.*

Values and Cultural Orientations

A culture's value orientations influence the common world-view which most individuals in a particular culture adopt over time.[37] In Goan society, for example, man's relationship with nature is one wherein men recognise their reliance on the vicissitudes of nature owing to their dependence on natural cycles. Still a primarily agricultural society (80%), the success or failure of each harvest depends heavily on the weather, which is then reflected in subsequent bumper crops and financial gain or poor harvests and consequent economic distress. For example, the production of mangoes and tropical fruits necessitates a cool winter during which months the temperature drops sufficiently as to allow for the flower buds to remain on the trees. Monsoon season also dictates behaviour during the months between June and October, postponing many outdoor social events and dampening the tourist season. As a consequence, Goan society does not view nature as separate from life and activity but rather views nature as an integral part of life and as domina over man.

Culture also influences the importance which individuals place on the dimensions of time; past, present and future. Those cultures which value the past and or the present tend to be averse towards directing their futures. In Goan society a gradation exists wherein the past, the present and the future are valued in varying degrees according to various cultural elements. A woman's reputation (i.e. her past) is very important and can often limit her desirability as a life partner. Once a woman's past is tainted, it is usually never recovered no matter how noble her actions are in the present. Likewise, tradition is highly valued among both Catholic and Hindu communities, especially among those of lower socio-economic status. Here, traditions of one's forefathers are maintained even when the majority of the participants have little knowledge of the original purpose of such a tradition. For example, very few participants in the Igiton Chalne Hindu Festival understand the symbolism behind the ritual actions in which they take an active role. Respect for elders and the wisdom of the ages is another indication that the past is highly valued in Goan culture. The present is also valued in Goan Society and 'the moment' is relished.

The Goan society places a high esteem on current human relationships and hours spent on to discussions, outings, and/or other activities with friends and family. Planning ahead is, therefore, not as emphasised as in European countries, as the roads and infrastructure in Goa will attest. Of late, however, following the Five-year government Plans which have given importance to education, family planning, health/child care, and economic development, this orientation is slowly changing and additional foresight is beginning to characterise the time-orientation of the Goan community among are levels of society.

Culture colours the lens through which people perceive themselves and others in their environment.[38] Most people conceived themselves as they are perceived by others and this latter is determined by comparison to cultural ideals. In Goa this is especially true as Goans are highly aware of and psychologically influenced by their surrounding society. Women are encouraged to marry and fulfil the ideals of motherhood which in its highest ideal envisions the birth of at least one child of the male gender. If an individual measures up to society's ideals, he/she is awarded social approval and develops a sense of pride and self-confidence. If an individual cannot 'measure up', he/she feels inferior and develops a sense of shame and negative self-consciousness. This can produce psychological stress leading to strain because the goals and ends that an individual seeks (in accordance with the social ideals of society) can be thwarted by cultural arrangements and socio-economic conditions. Thus, in the Goan society the image of a doctor is idealised by many, but is only attainable by a few whose social and financial circumstances encourage and enable the realisation of such a profession.

Culture also colours the lens through which individuals perceive various occupations. Inequalities in the socio-economic strata of Goa and certain values placed on some professions creates certain occupational trends in the society. Trends in the Goan society reveal that office, business, professional, and/or other generally 'urban' jobs are given a higher social value than rural economic activity. This is owing to Goa's history, wherein certain occupations (toddy-tapping, fishing, farming) were the domains of particular communities belonging to the lower Sudir (Sudra) caste. Of late, however, social mobility has increased owing to the reserved seats in professional institutions which encourage members from lower socio-economic communities to strive for urban employment and professions formerly restricted to the higher castes. As a result of this government policy, the goal orientations of individuals from these communities has shifted towards an emphasis on urban employment and a sense of shame has been attached to traditional, caste-bound occupations. Adopting office attire and 'commuting' to work enables village youths to experience the 'modern world' and perceive an improvement in their social status by moving from a rural to an urban work environment. Such individuals, predominantly those from the Shudra and middle-class Kshyatria communities, leave behind traditional occupations and take up jobs in offices which pay less but offer individuals perceived social prestige and achievements.

Cultural critics may argue that this trend in Goa is due to the introduction of western education by the Portuguese and later British, but this is only on the surface of the situation. Prior to the Portuguese, the Hindu caste system kept people in their fathers' occupations and prevented both social movement and occupational mobility to preserve the vested interests of the higher castes. Consequently, a child grew up learning the occupation of his father and performed it later in life regardless of the social prestige or shame with which it was accompanied. If these were not true, how can history explain the continuance of such despised occupations such as leather tanners, which were slated to the outcast communities in the midst of a culture which placed a high value on social prestige? Economic necessities do not entirely explain the persistence of such occupations when in former days the necessity to maintain social prestige often resulted in the impoverishment of families. Following the Portuguese (1510-1961) and post-Liberation eras (1961-present), both which strove to abolish the legal/political ramifications of caste by adopting progressive government policies, an explosion of social mobility resulted. "In their egos, lower-class communities incorporate community-wide values exemplified by more successful and prestigious fellow members,"[39] and thus in their attempts to achieve these cultural values they often mimic those whom they perceive to embody such social ideals. As a consequence, individuals from the lower socio-economic communities were for the first time able to leave those 'shameful' occupations which for so long carried oppressive social stigmas.

Culture influences both normal, stable society and individual mental illness as well. For example, in Goa the use of alcohol among men in particular Goan sub-cultures, whether sanctioned or not, has resulted in distinctive communal patterns regarding the use and consequent misuse of the substance within these same communities. Among the working class of low socio-economic status, alcoholism within the male members reaches around 70 per cent. Consuming alcohol at small one-room taverns in both communities (Hindu and Catholic) is encouraged by particular social groups and has become the patterned 'escape route' of the blue-collar working class. Among the Gowda Saraswat Brahmans (GSBs) and other educated communities, however, the use of alcohol is religiously sanctioned and the substance is considered impure and one which pollutes both mind and body. Drinking as a way of escape is not socially sanctioned among peer groups and consequently statistics show a very low rate of alcoholism among members of these communities. In addition to religious sanctions among the GBS Community, a form of 'cultural exclusiveness' exists among members which fosters the maintenance of these standards. Similarly, in most communities the use of alcohol among women is socially sanctioned and consequently the cases of alcohol abuse in the female gender are correspondingly low.

Dynamics of Culture

Culture is dynamic and is marked by the processes of reinterpretation and syncretism. Reinterpretation is the process through which any element of culture undergoes a marked change.[40] It is the process whereby old and new thoughts, beliefs and values are reconciled with each other. Among the uneducated converts in the Goan society, successful adaptation to the Christian religion prompted a reinterpretation of value-orientation whereby it became more important to save ones land, economic livelihood and gain social privileges and status than to maintain one's religion. This resulted in the conversions of villages en masse where all strata of society converted together to maintain the system that they had, not foreseeing the extent to which they would have to change. Subsequently, many of those converted attached old meanings to new forms, thus, establishing the saints either as reincarnations of their former gods and goddesses in Portuguese language or as in the case of African slaves in Brazil, they merely reinterpreted the Christian saints to be embodiments of their former gods. Syncretism was another strategy employed by people to harmonise the outer cultural changes imposed on them in Phase II of their lives with the culture internalised during Phase I. When the Aryans first imposed their religion on the tribal communities in Goa, the former were compelled to include one or two gods of the latter into their original pantheon. Thus, today in Goa we find the goddess Laira among the Hindu agricultural labour class, a goddess which owing to the nature of the fire worship ceremony seems to be an aboriginal Goddess which became incorporated into the Vedic religious pantheon. The syncretism between the two forms of worship is apparent in the first half of the ritual whereby for an entire day (and previously several days) men and women walk up and down the hill in penance and devotion to the temple gods, bathing after each climb and performing a tribal dance within the temple in dedication to the goddess. The second half of this religious festival-ritual involves the circumambulation around a bonfire over 20 feet in height. Following this ritual, all those who participated in the morning's treks and evening's temple dances, now line up to run across hot coals raked from the smoking bonfire in an act of penance, purification and bravado. Likewise, among the Catholic converts the former annual village feast days became synchronised with those of the Church Feast days in honour of patron saints, whereby the same customs such as a mela and theatre were performed.

These principles are fundamental to an understanding of the stability which characterised the Goan society while under foreign cultural domination. By attaching old meaning to new forms, for example, many customs among Goans were retained under their changing conditions. For example, we find the religious practices of the Catholics similar in both custom and form to those of their Hindu brethren. Catholicism in Goa, therefore, reflects the earlier cultural pattern of worshipping several deities among a pantheon manifested by the attention paid to the worship of various saints as well as celebrating particular deities with special attention (the cult of Ganesh versus the Catholic veneration of St. Francis Xavier). Further, we find the practice of veneration of a family deity in the Hindu religion reflected in the village patron saint of each church. Though some of these practices were instigated by the Catholic clergy in recognition of the spiritual customs and habits of their new converts, in the first generation of converts these practices had a stabilising effect among the converts whereby they could insert old meaning into new forms.

Culture is never static, even within areas which have a great propensity towards conservatism. In Goa, Konkani is the local language which has survived through thousands of years, following repeated onslaughts and attempts at extinction. Though, the language has survived, significant differences have evolved across sub-cultures and regions in Goa. For example, Catholic Konkani is infused with Portuguese, while Hindu Konkani has borrowed more extensively from Marathi. Similarly, the Konkani spoken in the villages is different from that spoken in the urban centres, the northern Konkani differs from the southern and the coastal dialect varies from that prevailing in the in-land regions.

Likewise, even between single generations there are differences in attitudes and opinions known in popular terminology as the 'generation gap'. Among the young urban generation, in Goa, for example, there is a desire and increasing ability to go out in mixed sex groups to discos, parties and other non-chaperoned functions. Those engaging in this social behaviour are still a relatively small young minority among the upper classes, and it is behaviour in which their parents did not participate. This trend seems likely to continue, moreover, as education, economics and social freedom of women continue with increasing upward momentum.

Culture evolves from the 'differential selectivity of a people faced with a cultural innovation.'[41] That which is perceived to increase status, prestige, wealth or character will be accepted, whereas those traits which may upset the stability of the culture will be rejected. Cultural evolution, therefore, involves both processes surrounding cultural stability and cultural change. Those diffused incoming elements which are similar to and in accordance with previous cultural patterns (religious piety and devotion) will find acceptance, whereas those which deify the traditional foundations of society (pre-marital/extra-marital relationships) will be strongly rejected and sanctioned when they occur. Change of this type usually results from the discussion of individuals who actively choose to alter their modes of thought or reorient their values.[42] In Goan society we find that the decision to convert to Catholicism was often a collective decision wherein the conversion took place en masse. As a consequence, "these ever-changing historic streams at once reflect and shape the attitudes and points of view of societies that, in the final analysis, determine the degree to which each will be hospitable or hostile to innovations."[43] Benedict, who belongs to the configurationist school of thought writes: "the cultural pattern of any civilisation makes use of a certain segment of the great arc of potential human purposes and motivations just as any culture makes use of certain select materials and cultural traits. Without selection, no culture could even achieve intelligibility and the intentions it selects and makes its own are a much more important matter than the particular detail of technology or the marriage formality that it also selects in similar fashion."[44]

Culture can change to result in a new identification with a different social group following an historic accident. Unquestioning belief in Catholicism, Portuguese superiority and the importance of good manners and honest dealings are some of the new qualities absorbed by children in the Catholic school system. Along with the new culture, and consistent with the former social patterning of the caste system, these first generation children absorbed not only the religion and outward cultural symbols of the Portuguese but their attitudes and beliefs as well. They were told they were superior to their Hindu brethren in religion and culture, the latter which was the mark of a 'backwards' society. The clergy awarded lavish praise to those converts who could most nearly mimic Western culture, encouraging them to strive towards these ends. In the end, a variant of the master-slave relationship evolved whereby the Catholics of subsequent generations were rewarded for striving to be like their subjugators. The converts identified with the Portuguese in varying degrees, those having more contact and enjoying more privileged positions identified to a greater extent with the new culture. The upper class even identified with them politically, further consolidating the Portuguese rule and for many years even those who might seek to undermine the regime were brought under the Catholic fold.

The difference was owing to the Jesuit educational system whose priests studied Western thoughts and thus, developed their minds along those lines. In the end they became imbibed with the ideals of liberty and equality in theory but could not attain it in reality, at which time they finally became aware of their subjugation, a realisation marked in Goan history by the Pinto Revolt. What makes this revolt so significant was that it originated with a parish priest who was by definition strongly identified to the Portuguese and the Catholic religion.[45] In contrast, this political consciousness did not arise in the Daman society as we can see from their sombreness and nostalgia following Liberation. Even after the freedom the people of Daman maintained their identity to the Portuguese and can even be heard singing 'Viva Portugal' during some of their functions.[46] The example of Daman illustrates that the "earlier conditioning level is the instrument that gives to every culture its stability; that prevents its running wild even in periods of most rapid change"[47]. In the later phase where enculturation operates on the conscious level, it facilitates change and reconditioning to new modes of thought and behaviour patterns.

Cultural elements introduced into a society are most often borrowed from outside sources. The people of Goa have been exposed continuously to cultural elements from outside the region since its beginning as an important point along the international trade route. Architecture in Goa illustrates this assumption following the arrival of the Portuguese. Initially Goan houses were constructed from mud walls and thatched roofs and later tiles were used in the wealthier homes. Under the Portuguese administration, houses of both native converts and Portuguese nationals were constructed in the traditional Portuguese villa style complete with front porch, long high windows, and high, cooling ceilings. The trend since liberation has been to construct houses modelled after those found in Gulf countries which are made of cement and have flat rooves.

In some instances, however, borrowed elements are absorbed so completely into a society and the life of a people that their origins are difficult to ascertain. Cashew nut is one such introduction in the Goan society whose distillation has become a traditional occupation among the Goans. Cashew nut trees are found in abundance in sparsely populated wooded areas, the new conquests and other in-land forested areas. Those involved in the production of Caju feni comes from both Hindu and Catholic communities and collect fruits from trees on land which is still auctioned annually as in pre-Portuguese village society. History reveals that the cashew fruit was introduced into the Portuguese colonies from Brazil and was imported in Goa after 1510. Thus, even borrowed elements can take on traditional forms when absorbed fully into the society.

Cultural borrowing occurs not only among foreign nations and religions but within regions as well. Carnival, for example, has significantly altered the expression of Shigmo, which at one time was a Hindu folk dance paying respect to the gods. Today's Shigmo festival is absolutely unique to Goa and one whose pattern was borrowed from the Carnival floats and lively street parades in Panjim (which were earlier borrowed from Portugal). Like Carnival, modern-day Shigmo involves street dances, bands and culminates with an all-night parade whose final floats depict in graphic life-size sculptures of ancient mythological stories. Beyond a simple folk dance, the Shigmo parade has more grown to encompass all the folk arts and historical eras existing in Goa and is very popular. The Konkani theatrical form borrowed from that of Marathi is another instance where regional borrowing occurred within Goa (see later chapters).

The extent of human interaction likewise determines the cultural diffusion between regions. Communities that live in close proximity will have more shared similarities, whereas those separated either by natural boundaries or by force (as in the case of Goan Catholics and Hindus) will have less in common as time progress.[48] Those cultures in close contact have more opportunities for diffusion and borrowing from one another (border of Goa and Maharashtra) and are less likely to adopt elements from outside sources. Regardless from where these elements originate, each is absorbed selectively into a new culture and nothing is absorbed by accident.

Cultural contact can result in a minimum amount of borrowing with or without external pressure or it can range to almost complete acceptance and regulations of the ways of life of another people.[49] All are the result of a particular historical experience which influences the psychological motivations underlying the selectivity of specific cultural elements.

Cultural elements undergo change and are absorbed at different rates and in different places. At any given moment a variation is "the expression of change in process" and may not occur consistently throughout a culture but may show a large adherence in urban areas or in specific regions.[50] Conservative and/or progressive attitudes towards cultural change are the result of the interplay of environmental, historical and psychological factors. Remote areas of Goa which have the least contact with outside influence may demonstrate resistance towards change, whereas heavily trafficked areas often show a very high acceptance of change. This does not necessarily mean that isolation from outside influence creates a conservative culture. A culture may be conservative in one area and be very progressive in the other. For example, in Goa there is heavy resistance to change regarding the institutions of family and marriage. Both are considered the foundations of Indian society and changes are heavily sanctioned. However, Goa is quick to absorb economic and technological changes such as the introduction of computers, a trend towards studies in the fields of engineering and an increase in industrial development. This change is welcome and considered positive and good for many. Also, education and opportunities for women in gainful employment have increased and Goa has several women doctors and other professionals. More than mere physical changes, the increase in technological developments in rural Goa points towards an evolution of attitudes and value-orientations among members of this society. Though the 'sussegard' lifestyle may still characterise many village communities, for those in contact with urban areas and international employment, the desire to 'come up' and display material forms of wealth have infiltrated the society.

Cultural drift is the natural evolution which occurs from within a society and in accordance with the goals, interests and motivations which characterise a society.[51] Drift results from the variations which are allowed in normal behaviour and create an inner dynamic which directs a culture towards change. These can usually be predicted and tend to be slow relative to the lifetime of any one individual. As these undergo subtle changes according to various diffused elements and ideas, they crystallise from ideas into reality and manifest in institutions. Discovery and/or invention also falls within this category of cultural change from within. Also "important in readjustment are the drives that have motivated individuals toward re-adaptation and how these drives are rewarded."[52] For example, the freedom struggle in Goa was actually a process lasting nearly one hundred years by which few individuals first realised their subjugation and then diffused these ideas into the larger society in order to garner support. These ideas then became ideals, translated into institutions with the goal of realising the ideals of self rule, freedom and a democratic state. Thus, anyone studying the changes in the psychology of Goans at the turn of the 20th century would have realised that the seeds of rebellion had begun and according to the psychological trends which were in conflict with the existing system, that a confrontation would eventually result. Freedom as well as economic and political control were the motivating forces underlying this struggle.

Culture establishes the limits wherein certain deviant behaviour will not be accepted or result in a cultural drift. Rather, a deviant form of behaviour may incur harsh sanctions and further define the limits of acceptable behaviour in a particular society.[53] In the Goan society, the western tourist often runs the risk of playing the role of the extreme deviant. At times tourists' behaviours, though acceptable in the western society to a limited extent, are considered beyond the limits in Goa. Walking shirt-less through town in the afternoon for men and sunbathing in bikinis for women are considered deviant behaviours. Approaching a stranger in the street to engage in casual conversation and/or wearing shorts, short skirts, or sleeveless shirts in public is considered deviant behaviour and is rarely found among members of this society. Physical displays of affection between a man and a woman in open public, even a married couple, are often considered deviant and are cause for unusual stares. A western woman who smokes or takes more than one drink at a pub is also considered deviant in this society and is ascribed a host of other qualities which characterise her as 'morally lax', regardless of whether she otherwise merits such a characterisation. The informal sanctions imposed on western tourists can often be severe; they become the butt of jokes, are stared at and photographed on the beach and are often the victims of unwanted sexual advances. Yet, like the village alcoholic, the western tourist is in many respects needed by the society to point a finger and establish certain boundaries. The role of the extreme deviant in society is, therefore, crucial for the maintenance of cultural stability.

Cultural convergence was the social principle at work among the new Catholics under the Portuguese rule and cultural laws in 1540, owing to the latter's attempts to create a 'mini-Portugal' on Indian soil. When these two cultures came into contact and the Portuguese assumed cultural domination over the other, the culture of the converts was not allowed to evolve as it would under normal circumstances, but rather was limited and directed by the formal and informal sanctions placed on it so that it would most closely resemble that of the dominating power. Any changes in the accepted form of behaviour and ritual among the converts were grudgingly accepted by the clergy, but those who identified completely with the new administration developed cultural habits and forms which mimicked those of the Portuguese. Thus, one finds that in most classes of Catholic Goans, the rituals which determine 'proper' worship, attention in church, observance of feasts and other religious functions 'converged' more closely to resemble those of the Portuguese at the time of conquest.

Cultural convergence among Hindu and Catholic Goan communities is the latest trend in the society, following Liberation and reintegration in 1961. If cultures in collision exchange attributes with one another, than it should follow that upon reintegration, Goan society of both Hindus and Catholics should undergo change which ultimately will lead them towards each other in a process of convergence. This follows from an earlier argument which assumes that when two neighbouring cultures come into contact, they will exchange much more from one another than from an outside source. Thus, the cultural fusion and synergy which one would expect to find following a realignment and a political identification with the Indian nation would result in a cultural drift towards becoming 'more Indian' and towards a greater identification with India rather than Portugal. Thirty-six years after Liberation this is indeed what we find, especially among the age-group under thirty. Among them few finds an identification with Portugal and even their parents (with few exceptions in the upper class) have begun to identify with the larger sub-continent. This is furthered by outside pressure from the current pro-nationalist government. In Goa today, the increasing contact among these two communities whose ties were severed 450 years earlier is compelling individuals to adjust and adapt to the culture of each other and sort through the prejudices against one another which they were taught since the time of their separation.

However, common threads exist and as the liberated community attempts to reintegrate itself, those common threads will be emphasised and cultural convergence will take place. "Wherever a wider range of variability in origins and developments coexists with a limitation of end results, there will be a reduction in variability, a decrease in dissimilarity and an increase in similarity or convergence."[54] Beyond religion, studies find similar goals, attitudes, styles of dress, social discourse, educational levels, and professions along three distinct lines: upper, middle, and lower socio-economic class divisions. A Hindu Brahmin and a Catholic Christian have much more in common with each other than do a Brahmin and a Koli though they may follow the same religion.

Culture Revisited

What is culture? *Culture is the evolution of social history, including such processes as historical accident, diffusion, drift, convergence, synergy, reinterpretation, and constant and continuous variation. Culture is an expression of people's behaviour, psychology and motivations which underlie that behaviour.* The behaviour and belief of no two individuals is identical owing to the nature of human experience and in terms of culture must be considered variable, not rigid and fixed. Culture, therefore, is the complete range of variation in individual belief and behaviour found among members of a given society at a given point in time and characterises that society and its sub-cultures. These variations are not random, but rather diverge around established norms within society. These norms are established from communal consensus regarding beliefs and behaviours and create the patterns visible in any cultural system. The size which defines a particular group determines the homogeneity of behaviour; thus, to use an example in Goa, a study of the Catholic working class will uncover more similarity in behaviour among individuals than will an examination of the Hindu community as a whole.

This chapter has intended to explore the definition, dynamics, sub-cultures and patterns within culture in general; utilising Goa as an explanatory case example. Subsequent chapters of **Part I** outline the political, social and economic history of the Konkan region known as Goa in an attempt to deconstruct the various layers of history, including the Portuguese 'historic accident' and its subsequent repercussions in the cultural evolution of the Goan society. Later chapters discuss the liberation of Goa and the consequent formation of 'Goan' identity, representation of Goan cultural identity, and related issues. **Part II** is devoted to the major communities from Goa which migrated to various urban areas and the cultural evolution which followed owing to larger cultural influences in their new environment. **Part III** is devoted to the examination of other areas which had significant historic relevance with the Portuguese and their subsequent cultural evolution following the removal of the Portuguese administration. These final chapters can also be viewed as possible precursors to the historical evolution which Goa will follow in the future; parallel albeit unique to other communities formerly under the Portuguese Indian empire.

Thus, this book is a humble attempt by this scholar to weave together Goa's history and cultural evolution of the past, present and possible future while at the same time broadening the readers' understanding of the nature of culture, migration, cultural identity, and evolution.

REFERENCES

1. Herskovits, Melville J., *Cultural Dynamics,* New York: Alfred A Knopf, Inc., 1964, p. 25.
2. Leland E. Hinsie, MD and Robert Jean Campbell, MD, *Psychiatric Dictionary,* 4th Ed., p. 174.
3. Honigmann, John J., *Personality in Culture,* New York: Harper and Row Publishers, 1967, p. 67.

4. Honigmann, John J., *Personality in Culture,* New York: Harper and Row Publishers, 1967, p. 67.
5. Acculturation defined as it is to be taken throughout this work means 'the implanting in children of the customs, beliefs, and ideals held to be important by adults of the culture group: a process of cultural indoctrination of children, much of which is carried out by educators (parents, teachers, media, etc.) without a formal plan, as an unconscious attempt at disseminating their own beliefs': *Psychiatric Dictionary,* p. 8.
6. Herskovits, Melville J., *op. cit.*, p. 7.
7. *Ibid.*, p. 11.
8. *Ibid.*, p. 12.
9. *Ibid.*, p. 13.
10. *Ibid.*, p. 14.
11. *Ibid.*, p. 151.
12. *Ibid.*
13. *Ibid.*
14. *Ibid.*, p. 186.
15. *Ibid.*, p. 151.
16. *Ibid.*
17. *Ibid.*
18. *Ibid.*, p. 109.
19. *Ibid.*
20. *Ibid.*, p. 118.
21. *Ibid.*, p. 196.
22. *Ibid.*
23. *Ibid.*, p. 197.
24. *Ibid.*, p. 202.
25. Certain rituals and observances common to certain communities will also be mentioned in accordance to their various adherents, but I must admit that an exhaustive study of each of the many sub-cultures existing in Goa went beyond the scope of my research. I will try to include as much as possible regarding these various communities and to interrelate them as often as I can. At times the sub-cultures of various communities overlap owing to similar socio-economic levels or religious beliefs, and these will be examined in due course, especially in the section on current trends in Goan culture. There is still much scope for study regarding various specialised communities, and I hope that someone interested in the study of Goan culture will build from my work and further the understanding of Goa.
26. Honigmann, John, J., *op. cit.*, p. 25.
27. *Ibid.*, p. 69.
28. *Ibid.*, p. 75.
29. *Ibid.*, p. 41.
30. *Ibid.*, p. 97.

31. *Ibid.*, p. 80.
32. Honigmann, John, J., *op. cit.*, p. 41.
33. *Ibid.*, p. 63.
34. There are deviations to this 'rule'.
35. Honigmann, John, J., *op. cit.*, p. 77.
36. *Ibid.*, p. 82.
37. *Ibid.*, p. 78.
38. *Ibid.*, p. 79.
39. *Ibid.*, p. 82.
40. Herskovits, Melville J., *op. cit.*, p. 190.
41. *Ibid.*, p. 194.
42. *Ibid.*
43. *Ibid.*, p. 151.
44. Honigmann, John J., *op. cit.*, p. 122.
45. See Chapter 4, Liberation: Causes and Consequences.
46. See Chapter 10, Daman.
47. Herskovits, Melville J., *op. cit.*, p. 151.
48. *Ibid.*, p. 155.
49. *Ibid.*, p. 164.
50. *Ibid.*, p. 165.
51. *Ibid.*, p. 180.
52. *Ibid.*, p. 165.
53. *Ibid.*, p. 203.
54. *Ibid.*, p. 157.

CHAPTER 2

History of the Konkan Territory known as Goa

Recorded History as Interpretation

Before entering into a discussion of the Goan history, it is important to explore the concept of 'recorded history', because this very concept has evolved over centuries. For instance, during the vast majority of recorded human history, importance was awarded to the rulers of kingdoms, their wars and conquests, their political exploits, etc. Later the history of trade relations was given its due importance, the rise and fall of great international ports and the economics of regional politics. Because most history had been written by scribes (scholars employed by their kings), importance was concentrated on the lives of individual men and their administrative policies, rather than on society as a whole. History in the past was, thus, seen entirely through the perspective of the ruling families. Thus, we have 'glorified' battles and other such instances where the historical records paint a very subjective picture of what has occurred.

The life of the common man was rarely a matter of historical concern for any given ruler and neither was it left to posterity in the annuls of scribes. People as such were documented in historical memory only when detailing the body count after a war, uprising, epidemic or famine. Thus, we know a lot about wars, a lot about regional economics, too much about politics, but very little about the life of the common man. How did common people of ancient times think, feel, and/or behave in their worlds? How was their culture influenced by that of their rulers? It was only after the 'common man' began to receive an education and discover his own potential for action that the 'social history' of man came into being as a subject worthy of scholarship. And only very recently in recorded history, within the last 200 years, has attention been paid to what I will call 'the common man'; his trials and tribulations, customs, lifestyle, rituals, etc. Increasing numbers of people becoming educated must have wondered where they belonged in the annuls of history. *Gradually the 'voice' of the common man emerged and, thus, we have some of our first great writers which introduced into literature the feelings, philosophical queries, successes and failures, loves and enmities, and a myriad of other issues which confronted man in his daily social environment.* Minds were awakened and having few empires to run or people to control, they turned to pursuits of a more intellectual nature, eventually questioning the whole foundations of society and transforming the evolution of thought in an unprecedented way. Thus we have our Marxists, our Ghandhis; and so many others who, upon finding a voice, began to exert themselves in a way which brought the life of the common man into importance and in a way, into recorded historical existence.

Thus, began a new evolution of the historical process itself as well as 'historical importance' and 'historical perspective'. No longer were historians merely the scribes who had ingratiated themselves to their kings. Soon poets, novelists and researchers started asking questions and left these discussions in written forms to posterity. As more and more 'educated common people' had their own stories to tell, the 'historical perspective', (any particular lens through which history is written), evolved over the centuries. Issues surrounding daily life, religious faith, humanity, identity, culture, love, treachery, and basic human emotions began to get their due place in society. Even then, however, the social history of mankind was left seriously incomplete.

Of late, with the education of women and otherwise marginalised communities, issues surrounding the 'interpretation of history' were again opened and space was created by those communities to enable themselves and others to hear 'their voice' and view issues from their perspective. American history is an excellent case in point regarding these latest trends. Today students read about what it was like to be a slave in American society, not just a wealthy landowner. We can discover the trials and tribulations regarding Spanish-American migrants, questions regarding their identity, and what it feels like to be a marginalised member of society. In India as well we are beginning to hear the voice of women, how they feel within their culture and how 'out castes' were treated by those believing themselves superior. Thus only in recent years have many segments of society formerly ignored begun to find their voice. Sadly, much has been lost in our history owing to this filter which prevented most groups in society from participating in both the making and the retelling of their own history. But to lament is pointless, to rectify is the key.

The point I wish to make is that 'recorded history' is 'an Interpretation'. It is defined, at least under the American Educational System, as 'an objective description of facts, names, dates, and places.' Only in high school and university do students begin to hear the words 'interpretation of events', to mean facts, which is often ignored and history is again taken for granted. Yet history is a collection of generally accepted truths which circulate among members of a society and are interpreted in a way consistent with the characteristic modes of thought within that society. Thus in American society during the 1600's to 1700's, wars won against the native American Indians were looked upon as glorious and deserving of merit. In the 1900's these wars are now viewed as atrocities committed on one race by another thinking itself superior. To site another instance, British writers of the 19th century discussing Indians would refer to people of the Hindu faith as "heathens" and in other instances as 'debased creatures'. While scholars of today recognise this as a grossly subjective and ethnocentric description, during the time when such research was written this was the generally accepted set of attitudes among the British community. Even the question of sovereignty arises when attempting to find an 'objective' historical representation. How many dynasties over the centuries recorded a particular territory as theirs, only to be faced with war when this 'fact' was contested by another kingdom?

Why bother to study recorded history at all, then, if everything is subjective and dependent on the political, economic, and social climate of the times? For several important reasons, the most important of which is to fully grasp that everything we know, think and feel regarding history has been and will be subject to these boundaries. It will be subject to the current political sentiment in our era, the current value-orientation, prevailing economic conditions and the current perspectives which arise to examine again the annuls of history. That which we interpret as 'such' today will tomorrow be interpreted as a different 'such'. Thus, in today's society we define an Indo-Portuguese war as a 'massacre', when through the lens of that age it was a completely justifiable war based upon current beliefs which were prevalent in that society. Tomorrow that same war may be interpreted in a different manner, depending upon the prevailing social climate. Thus, how we as individuals come to understand history is in truth an 'interpretation' of an 'interpretation'.

Two broad categories of 'interpretative history' are in vogue today. The first involves the collection of many 'facts' with the intention to explain certain social phenomena. The second involves the creation of an explanation using only certain 'select facts' which best agrees with the current social sentiment and/or attempts to influence that sentiment by directing the flow of thought within a community. In either case, the results show that though the first may be a better 'interpretation' of a situation, the latter is often more persuasive because it is designed to affect one's emotions. Consequently, the latter often becomes generally accepted as correct, thus, fulfilling its aim to shape mood and/ or create a particular type of behaviour and/or thought. This is in fact one of the most fascinating evolutionary trends in the interpretation of the Goan history and its discussion indeed has something to do with the current 'crisis of identity' within which some Goans found themselves in the post-liberation era.

What we find in the annuls of history today is that until the Portuguese made their presence felt and were respected in Goa, there were very few accounts of the social history of people in that region. We know about them in relation to their economic activities, political leadership, and one or two folk arts and temple zatras. We know that they were Hindus and tribals owing to the prejudice against them by the Muslims and the lives which were lost on account of cultural differences. Still, what we know about the pre-Portuguese era in Goa has been obtained through the observations of travellers, missionaries and records within the temples such as taxes, population, numbers of marriages, satis, etc.

However, scholars were able to determine some particular aspects of a community's culture and identity through historical records. During the Middle Ages when the Muslim armies imposed their religion and customs on the people, for example, the position of women in Goan society declined. Likewise, more the battles that occurred in a region, the less their rulers worried about cultural differences and the more they tried to create an identity which would cause men to take up arms in defence of their ruling dynasty. Politics, it is soon discovered, plays a significant role in the formation of regional and subsequently cultural identity. In the early days the highest point of secular identification was centred around dynasties and local chieftains. Later some individuals in Goa identified with Portugal and following Liberation the common man was asked to identify with his state and nation. Given that much of a community's 'cultural identity' is both political and economic at the core, much can be inferred from the political and economic history of people as seen through the ruling administrations. Generally, the less certain communities were in contact with any particular ruling power, the less the customs, language and lifestyle of those people were influenced. However, the more dominating and pervasive the ruling power, the more culturally conditioned the people would become.

The aim of this chapter is to examine the basic political history of Goa beginning from the first conclusive records in 300 B.C. to the most recent political developments leading to the creation of Goa, a state in the Indian nation. Knowledge of this ancient political history is necessary in order to more fully understand the various cultural, economic and political forces that arrived in Goa and exerted their control and influence over the region and its inhabitants. It helps to place in proper perspective the advent of the Portuguese along the time-line of Goa as well as set the backdrop for the events which culminated in Liberation. In addition to helping to discover the past and explain the present, an outline of classical Goan history enables the scholar to predict what may happen in the future course of events in Goa.

An Outline of Political History of Goa

	Era of Hindu Dynasties: Earliest known records:
300 B.C.	Bhojas of Chandrapur: Goa as a province of the Mauryan empire
200 B.C.-300 A.D.	Satavahanas (under Bhojas)
249-250	Kalachuri Era (Abhir King)
420	Kadamba Kings of Goa declare independence from Pallavaś, their overlords
500	Maurya's (under Kalachuris): Kadambas as feudatories-rule over Goan province
540-757	Chalukyas of Badami (onset of reign): Kadambas as feudatories
753-973	Rashtrakuta Dynasty (Chalukyas as feudatories): Shilaharas rule the Goan province
980	Chalukyas of Kalyana (Konkan as feudatory province ruled by Shilaharas)
	First Muslim attacks
750-1020	Shilaharas in Goa
945-1042	Shilahara/Kadamba conflict
1008-1300	Kadambas reign in South Konkan and Goa as feudatories of Chalukyas
1198	Death of last Chaluka King; Kadamba territory of Goa vulnerable to attack
1209-1247	Kadambas as feudatories under the Yadavas of Devagiri

Middle Ages

1300-35 A.D.	Goa invaded by Malik Kafur, military general of Alauddin Khilji
	Years known as a time of disorder, Muslim invasions and rise of petty chiefs
1350 A.D.	Arrival of Bahmanis

1347-1489	Empire of Alla-ud-din Hassan (Bahmanis);
1355-60	Persecution of Hindus and consequent uprisings against Bahmani rule
1445-1472	Muslim control contested by Vijayanagara and Naik chiefs in Goa
1472	Bahmani Muslims control all of Goa including Belgaum. Frequent uprisings
	Capital shifted to Ela Goa
1498	Ain-ul-Mulk (administrator) surrenders Goa to Bijapur Crown
	Adil Shah's power established in Goa
	Portuguese arrive off the Coast of India at Calicut and later Cochin

Portuguese Era in the Old Conquests

1498-1510 A.D.	Portuguese concentrate on establishing trade centres in Malabar, i.e., Cochin
1505, 1508, 1509-1515	Portuguese attack the city of Old Goa, and build strategic forts
1510	Goa surrenders to Portuguese on second invasion on November 25th
	Islands under effective control: Goa Island, Chorao, Divar, Vamsim and Jua
1511	Muslims renew attacks
1543	Portuguese gain control over Bardez, Salcette and Tiswadi
1570	Formation of Muslim alliance against Portuguese
1580-1640	Portuguese overtaken by Spain, Inquisition established in Goa
1604, 1636-41, 1652	Dutch enter competition for spice trade; attack Portuguese vessel
1659	Shivaji (Maratha leader) extends territory into the Konkan from the north and establishes a Navy base
1660-66	Shivaji attacks Ponda to oust Adil Shah

1664	Shivaji conquers Kudal (Maharashtra), Pernem, and Bicholim from Adil Shah
1667	Shivaji attacks Bardez (dies in 1680)
1683	His son, Sambhaji, invades the Bardez taluka under the auspice to liberate Goa
1689	Mughal army takes Ponda from Sambhaji
1698	Bhonsles capture Bicholim, Pernem, and Sanguem from the Mughal armies
1702	Marathas invade Ponda currently under the Mughals
1706	Portuguese attack and capture the Bhonsle Northern territories
1707, 1717	Marathas attack Salcette, Daman
1737-39	Marathas invade and seize territories/forts of the Portuguese between Goa and Daman, i.e. Bassein
1739	2nd invasion of Bardez by Ramachandra, the ruler of Kudal (Maharashtra)
	Margao, Sanguem, Ponda, Supem, and Bassein fall to the Marathas
	Bardez attacked, all but two Portuguese fort captured;
1741	British reinforcements arrive to help defend Tiswadi, Bhonsles repelled
1746	Portuguese capture Tiracol, Reddi, and Alorna from Bhonsles
1754-56	Bhonsles regain control of Alva, Reddi, and Neutim
1762	Portuguese and Bhonsole alliance attack the Marathas
1763	Hyder Ali's forces attack Ponda which was then ceded to Portuguese by Marathas
1764	Canacona, Quepem and Sanguem ceded to Portuguese by King Sonda for territorial protection against Hyder's army., followed by Bicholim and Sattari

Struggle for Freedom from Portuguese

1776-82 A.D.	Period of general dissension in Old and New conquests
1781	Chhatrapati of Kholapur invades territories held by Bhonsles
1782	Pinto Revolt (sowing the seeds of dissatisfaction in Goa)
1788	Portuguese obtain land in the New Conquests (Sawantwadi to Karwar)
1740-1897	Rebellions by Satari Ranes helped by common people, (esp. in 1822)
1851	Dipaji Rane liberates Quepem, Canacona, Hemad Barshe and Bhatagrama
	Strict laws clamped on Satari by Portuguese;
1895	Hindu soldiers rebel against Portuguese, Martial Law Proclaimed in Goa
1928	Dr. T.B. Cunha founds the Goa Congress Committee, the 1st nationalist body
1937-46	Portuguese impose restrictions on Goa, Daman & Diu
1946	Dr. Lohia (freedom fighter) arrested
1954	Portuguese authorities seal Goan borders to prevent Satyagraha of Aug. 15th
1955	Series of Satyagrahas undertaken along Goa's Eastern border, attacks on police outposts, customs houses, Economic blockade undertaken by the Indian Government

Independence

1961 A.D.	Operation Vijay to liberate Goa (December 19th)
1961-87	Struggle for Statehood
1987	Goa gains Statehood under the Indian Confederacy
1987-91	Government adopts 5-Year Plan for infrastructure, schools and economic developments

Political History of Goa

The above outline was created to give the reader an overview before delving into the more detailed aspects of the history of Goa. Goa's history has been well-documented from the information available and an exhaustive study of this subject is not undertaken in this work. However, in order to understand the Goan culture and identity it is necessary to have at least fundamental knowledge regarding the political and economic history of a region. Goa as its current size and statehood is a new construction dating only from 1987. Prior to that it was under the Portuguese administration from roughly 1510, and only four of the 11 talukas experienced her culture directly. The other areas were occupied by the Portuguese much later in the late 1700's and were used as a 'Buffer Zone' between the British and the Portuguese imperial powers. Prior even to the Portuguese, the region of Goa was ruled by petty chiefs, Hindu dynasties and Muslim army. The history outlined below is that of political history, which is important in the understanding of identity and culture. Chapter 3 examines the socio-cultural history of Goa in greater detail.

The earliest known records of the Bhoja empire date from the 3rd century B.C. (time of Ashoka), and were found in the town of Shiroda, 41 kilometers from Panjim.[1] However, human communities had been living in Goa for many years prior to the Bhoja empire, and were predominantly tribal leading a semi-nomadic existence as herdsmen, fishermen and early farmers. Theirs was an oral language and culture, however, and few records have been left to posterity. Their religion combined elements of animism and belief in spirits and many of these early beliefs are still visible in the religious rituals of these communities today.

According to Pauranik tradition, the Bhojas belonged to a sub-group of the Yadavas of the Aryan race of Kaikeyas and settled in the Konkan during the 3rd century B.C. Two copper plate grants were also unearthed in the village of Bandora in Ponda taluka, written by King Bhoja Prithiuimallavarman. Another copper plate of the Bhoja dynasty dated from the late 5th and early 6th centuries A.D., was found in the Hire Culti village near Karwar (South of Goa)[2]. From the 4th to the 7th centuries A.D. historians have concluded that the Bhoja rulers of

Chandrapur were ruling over a region that included Goa, Belgaum and North Kanara. These records are sustained by the current Christians of Chandor (modern-day Chandrapur) known as Charddos, who claim their ancestors were the original Ksyatriyas of the ancient Bhoja empire.[3]

By the 2nd century B.C., Krishna Śatakami of the Satavahanas annexed the region of the Konkan, including the territories of the Bhojas.[4] The Satavahanas had been ruling in areas in the South of India and claimed that they belonged to the clan of Manavyasa. Under them, Kolhapur was the capital and Chandrapur remained as a major commercial city ruled still by the Bhojas, who had since become the feudatories of the Satavahanas. Their reign lasted until the 4th century A.D., when their territories in the Konkan and western Maharashtra were conquered by the Abhir King Ishvarasena.

Thus, began the Kalachuri (Chedi Samat) Era in the years 249-50 B.C.[5] The Traikutakas established themselves as the feudatories of Abhir. His rule was effective until the mid-400's A.D. when King Dahrasena performed the Ashvamedha sacrifice and afterwards declared himself independent from his overlord Abhir by 416 A.D. The former's son Vyaghrasena ruled over the Konkan from 465-92 A.D. Until the mid-6th century, the Kalachuris were ruling over the Konkan, though their rule was contested by the Chalukyas of Badami on several occasions. Eventually the Kalachuris placed the Mauryas in charge of the south Konkan and the Mauryan Kings, Chandravarman and Anirjitavarman, were the only Kings known to have ruled over this territory during the 6th and 7th centuries.[6]

The reign of the Chalukyas of Badami dates from 540 A.D., and they are thought to be princes belonging to the Manavya Gotra (family line). In 543 A.D., Pulakeshi I, the first prince of the family, established his capital at Badami. He defeated the Maurya King Aninjitvarman and gave his lands to Swamiraja, also of the Chalukya family. The latter established his headquarters in Rewatidwapa (modern-day Reddi) just across the northern border of modern-day Goa.[7] He had two sons; Mangalesha and Kirtivarman, the former who ruled from 597 to 610 A.D. During his reign he ousted King Buddharaja (son of Samkaragana) and conquered the Northern territories up to the Kim River in 602.[8]

Mangalesha was also responsible for the death of Swamiji who betrayed him and sided with King Buddharaja right before Màngalesha entered his territories to defeat the King. He also uprooted the Mauryas in the North part by the early 600's. Kirtivarman, Pulakeshi's second son, expelled the Mauryas by 578 A.D. in the South Konkan.[9]

Mangalesha's son, Pulakeshi II, helped expand and consolidate the Chalukya empire. In 610 A.D. he began his reign and annexed the North Konkan after defeating the Konkan Mauryas. In 613 A.D. he defeated Harshavardhana who was the Lord of North India and was attempting to expand his empire to the Deccan.[10] Upon his defeat, Pulakeshi II acquired the title of Parameshwara (Lord Paramount) and became the ruler of three countries. His fame spread far and wide and an ambassador from Persia was sent to establish trade relations. Pulakeshi's second son Vikramaditya succeeded him from 654-81 A.D. He was known for stopping the rebellion of three Kings on different occasions.[11] His son, Vinayaditya, advanced to the throne of the Chalukyas at Badami from 680-96. Vijayaditya succeeded his father from 696-733-34 A.D., whose empire at that time extended as far north as Gujarat. He ruled for 37 years, was awarded the title of Niravadya Sahasarasika (conquest in Chalukya history) and promoted art, culture and learning throughout his kingdom. He was succeeded by Vikramaditya II (733-34-745 A.D.)[12]. During his reign, the Tajakas (Arabs) invaded the region of Gujarat in the Chalukya territory.

In 742 A.D., Rashtrakuta Dantidurga defied Kirtivarman and the Chalukyan forces, defeated their armies, and placed the Chalukyan princes as his feudatories.[13] He laid the foundation for the Rashtrakuta dynasty of Manyakheta, which had effective control over the Deccan, Karnataka, and Gujarat from 753 to 973 A.D. He reigned supreme in Malkhed and Maharashtra. In 980 A.D. he was overthrown by the Chalukyas of Kalyani and the Deccan was once again came under the control of Chalukyas. The Konkan, including Goa, was considered a feudatory province and as far as the Goan people were concerned, they were ruled by the Shilaharas from 750 A.D. to 1020 A.D.[14]

Under the Shilaharas, a succession of rulers exercised control over the region including Goa. Shanaphulla had lordship over the territory from 765 to 795 A.D., followed by Dhammiyara from 795 to 820 A.D.[15] Aiyapa, a Vigigishu ruler, invaded Chandrapur and held sway over these territories from 820 to 845 A.D., before being usurped by Avasara I who ruled for the next 25 years. Under his command, the power and influence of the Shilaharas increased and they held sway over the whole of the Konkan from Goa to Thane. He was followed by Avasar II (895-920 A.D.) and then by Indraraja between 920-945 A.D.[16] Under the former the empire expanded, but the latter was content to rule the region and did not engage in expansionary battles. During the reign of Bhima (945-970 A.D.), attempts began by the Kadambas to become feudatories of Chandrapur. He was forced to invade the city to stop the Kadamba insurgence. Avasara III (970-995 A.D.) was the next in the line of succession, and his son Guhalladeva (980-1005 A.D.)[17] also seemed to be ruling at this time. With Rattaraja (995-1020 A.D.), the reign of the Goa Shilaharas came to end. Jayasimha II, brother of Chalukya Vikramaditya V, invaded the Konkan in 1024 A.D. and helped to capture the territories under the Shilaharas. The Shilaharas had been faithful feudatories of the Rashtrakuṭas, but owing to a war over the Deccan which divided the two Shilahara families, they were susceptible to attacks from outside forces.

The Kadamba Dynasty

The Kadamba Dynasty ruled over Goa and the south Konkan as feudatories of the Chalukyas of Kalyani from 973-1162 A.D., and later under the Yadavas of Devagiri. They had made common cause with the Chalukyas of Kalyani for the overthrow of the Rashtrakutas, which was a successful venture. Under the Kadambas, the main capital was shifted from modern-day Chandor to Vodlem Goem (Velha Goa). The Kadamba Dynasty is considered by historians to have begun in 1008 A.D., owing to unearthed records of their dynasty found in Goa and other outlying regions which date back to that year.[18] Shasthadeva I was the founder of the Goa Kadambas and his reign coincided with that of the Chalukya King Taila II, who overthrew the Rashtrakutas and established his new empire at the city of Kalyani in the Deccan by 973 A.D.[19] In 1020 A.D., during the reign of Shasthadeva II, the Bhojas tried to recapture the North Konkan, but were unsuccessful in their attempts. Records indicate that the

Kadambas and the Chalukyas may have been in collusion to oust the Rashtrakutas, thus, enabling the Kadambas to solidify their rule by 1042 A.D.[20]

The next Kadamba King was Jayakeshi I who reigned from 1052-80 A.D. He was very influential and appointed the Arab merchant leader Chhaddama as governor of Gopaka, the then prosperous mercantile city on the mouth of the Zuari River. Jayakeshi I created a powerful navy at the city's Port (Velakula) to protect the Arab traders and their merchandise. He further developed that city and made it Gopakapattana, the capital of his Kingdom.[21] Under his administration many Arabs were appointed to high official positions. In the later years of his reign he defeated King Mummun of the Thana Shilaharas (1045-70 A.D.) which was the result of another civil war between the two Shilahara families. His successor, Guhaladeva III, took over in 1081 and was the first Kadamba King to be titled "Gopakapura vardhishva" (Lord of Gopaka, the best of the towns).[22] His younger brother is also mentioned in early records dating from 1081 to 1104, and historians surmise that he might have shared power with his elder brother Guhalladeva III. The latter is remembered as a pious ruler who promoted the establishment of monasteries, patroned the arts and gave financial grants to centres dedicated to Vedic instruction. Guhalladeva III also encouraged the settlement of Brahmin communities into Gopaka. A copper plate grant of 1106 A.D. refers to the 'establishment of a Brahmapuri of 12 Brahmin families and an image of the Goddess Saraswati' in Gopaka, the then capital of the kingdom.[23] (Hence, the probable origin of the Gowda Saraswat Migration). During his reign the maritime power of the Kadambas declined and their rule was again contested by rising powers from all sides.

Thus, when Jayakeshi II succeeded Gulhadeva III in 1104 A.D., the power of the Kadambas reached its zenith. Their rule was attacked from all sides and by 1122 A.D. the Kadambas were compelled to recognize the supremacy of the Chalukyas.[24] Jayakeshi II held out, however, and during his reign peace, prosperity, and progress were the defining characteristics. The next ruler, Shivachittapermadideva (1147-81 A.D.) promoted arts and learning. His wife Kamaladevi instigated the construction of two temples; the first dedicated to Kamalanarayana and the second in reverence of Mahalakshmi. As the Kadambas hailed from the South, Kannada was their official language and most records from this period were written in that language, a few in Sanskrit. During the Vijayaditya II (1180-88 A.D.), several attempts were made by outside powers to subdue the Kadamba dynasty.[25] Jayakeshi III took the reigns from his father and ruled from 1186-1216 A.D. He was succeeded by Sovideva from 1212-38 A.D., the latter who coined the Royal symbol of the Kadambas in the raised palm of the lion's left foot.[26] He ruled independently from his brothers, but the Kadambas generally were feudatories of the Kalyani Chalukyas.

During the reign of Sovideva, the Yadavas were busy gaining control over the Deccan under the Emperor Singhana II (1209-47). Their Royal emblems were the golden eagle and the God Hanuman and they controlled a total of 84 fortresses with their capital at Devagiri. In 1020 A.D., during the reign of Shasthadeva II, the Bhojas tried to recapture the north Konkan, but were not successful in their attempts.[27] In the years 1218-19 A.D. he conquered the Bhojas and acquired their territories. Ramchandra was the 9th Yadava King whose territories included the Deccan, Konkan and Karnataka by 1294 A.D. His reign coincided with that of the First Khilji Emperor of Delhi (1288-94 A.D.) and within a few years the two met and forever changed the evolution of history on the Western Konkan coast.

The Medieval Rulers

The period between 1294 and 1335 A.D. was characterised as a time of chaos and confusion owing to Muslim invasions and the rise of petty chiefs. Though the succession of the Delhi Sultanate seemed inevitable owing to their growing power and compulsion for territorial expansion, the Kadamba King Ramchandra was able to prevent the imposition of their rule even after they defeated him in 1294.[28] Alla-ud-din (nephew to the first Khilji emperor) gained control over the capital city of Devgiri in a surprise attack against the Kadambas. The Yadavas, who served as their overlords, had been weakened by the Muslim invasions and the ancient conflict between the Kadamba and the Hoysala houses ended only in 1301 in favour of the Kadambas. Ramchandra worked along side of the Muslim conquerors to maintain the kingdom, but his son Shankar fought against this new dominating power. In 1312 A.D. he withheld tribute (tax) from Malik Kafur, who in retaliation attacked and looted the main cities of Shankar's territory and murdered the ruler himself.[29] Gopakapattana was also burned and looted at this time, after which the Kadambas retreated to their old capital at Chandrapur (Chandor). In 1315 A.D. Harpaladeva succeeded Shankardevi, but by this time his was merely a puppet administration. When he also slighted the Delhi Sultans in 1318 A.D., the Emperor Mubarik (1317-21 A.D.) invaded the Deccan and killed Harpaladeva.[30] In 1325 A.D. Muhammad Tughluk was given the task of subduing the distant provinces, and under the Muslim armies again invaded the Konkan and destroyed the Kadamba capital of Chandrapur. From 1327 to 1336 A.D the Muslim invasions ceased and the Kadambas again regained control over the Konkan territories. King Bhimabhupal ruled Pernem as a feudatory of the Kadambas and Govapuri in Pernem became the administrative centre. By 1347 A.D., Malerajya and Palasige, which formerly belong to the Kadambas, now fell under the empire of Vijayanagar from the South.[31]

Muhammad Tughluk set his aims towards making Devgiri the capital of his empire, which by now included all but the Southern portion of India. By the end of 1358, the Kingdom of Alla-ud-din Hassan Shah, from the Bahmani family, extended from Mandu in the North to Raichur in the South; from Bhongir in the East to Dabul and Goa in the West.[32] Due to its size, he was forced to divide his kingdom under four separate governments. From 1358 to 1375, he followed a policy of Hindu persecution which was also felt in Goa. As the persecution of Hindus reached its peak around 1360, many were compelled to migrate to north towards Sangameshvar or South to the Kanara district and beyond. The GSBs formed a part of this migration wave and formed the Chitrapur group of Saraswat Brahmins.

Rebellions against the Muslim invasions were common, and in 1365 a battle between Muslims and Govindadev (the Maratha chief of the Naiks) supported by other petty Naik chiefs occurred. The latter collusion was defeated decisively, and in 1380 the Muslims gained absolute control over the Konkan and part of the Vijayanagar empire.[33] They regained some of their empire and by 1390 the Araga-Gutti province was separated and Mallap-Odey became the Vice-Royalty of Goa in 1391. In 1396 under the Wodeyar empire, Barchanna-Wodeyar extended the boundaries of the kingdom of Goa-Gutti and continued as Vice-Viceroy of Goa until 1406. Barchanna is thought to be the last Viceroy of the Goa-Konkan empire under the Wodeyars (Vijayanagar Kingdom). Savana (1412-13), was the first to rule among the later Vijayanagar administrators of the Goa-Cutti Kingdom.[34] In 1415 Trimbakadev was appointed as the administrator of Goa and was given the title of Immadi Deva Raya. In 1422, during the administration of Mallarasa, Chandra-Gutti was separated from Goa and annexed to the province of Hampi.[35]

After 1445, there are no records or names of Viceroys' in the annuls of history, and it seems likely that Goa was administered by local chiefs (Naiks) from that time. Similarly, those territories to the immediate North and South were also ruled by independent Chalukya chiefs. Goa was probably under the jurisdiction of Bankapur at this time, whose Appaji Chiefs were administering the territories when they were conquered by the Bahmani Sultans in 1472.[36]

Era of the Bahmani Sultanate

During the 1460's, the Bahmanis attempted to dominate the territories in the Konkan. The Marathas who were in possession of those lands defended such invasions, however, and retaliated by pirating the vessels of the Muslims which called at the Port of Goa Velha. In 1469 this piracy reached its height and the result was a serious decline in the commercial activities and revenue of the Arab traders. Consequently, the Bahmanis invaded Goa and the Konkan coast for three years continuously, after which time all the forts in Goa and surrounds were completely subdued in 1472. The Bahmani army then invaded the city of Goa and acquired it for their empire in that same year. The Marathas tried in vain to recapture their territories, but by the end of that year both Goa and the Belgaum regions were annexed by the Bahmani empire. Fakr-ul-Mulk became the governor of the forts in Goa and Belgaum.[37]

In 1490 Bahadur Gilani, the governor of the Konkan under the Bahmanis, openly revolted and declared the territories of Goa and Belgaum as his independent kingdom. He was easily defeated by the Bahmani army who annexed his territories and took his life.[38] In 1500 the three most powerful Bahmani nobles agreed to divide the kingdom which had reached such extensive limits. The Commander of Goa agreed to acknowledge Yusuf Adil Khan of Bijapur as his Sovereign and the whole of the Konkan south of the Bankot river came under the domain of Bijapur. However, the administration was such that the villagers experienced relatively few of these changes. They were under the supervision of the village Gaonkars, who were chiefs by inheritance and were of the Dessai, Sardessai and Mahal families. The latter in turn owed their allegiance to a succession of overlords which eventually made its way through the ranks until finally reaching Yusuf Adil Khan himself.

From Voddlem Goem to Old Goa

Owing to the silt which had collected in the harbour of the Zuari river as well as the devastating attacks on Voddlem Goem by the Bahmani armies, the capital of Goa was moved to Old Goa (Ela village) during the Bahmani administration.[39] This new city was located on the Mandovi river which also had the topographical advantage and easily defensible harbour. Owing to the international traffic and trade brought by the Arabs, the city of Old Goa soon gained importance as the main centre for international commerce. By 1510 it was an entirely Muslim city inhabited by Moors, Hindu gentry, foreigners and a standing army. They maintained a roaming sea fleet which protected ships from piracy and the construction of ships from Oak wood was a city speciality.[40] Horses from Ormuz, muslin, spices, betel and areca nuts, food stuffs and a variety of other items from emporiums around the world were traded from here.

Arrival of the Portuguese

It was this city which the Portuguese discovered and coveted when they landed on the island of Anjediva off the coast of modern-day South Goa and built a fort there in 1505. They were helped in their aims by Timoja, who was the brother to the King of Honawar, Malharrao. The latter was a well-respected King by the Naiks (chieftains) in Goa and belonged to the Vijayanagar empire.[41] The latter had been trying unsuccessfully to oust the Muslims from the Konkan territories, and hoped that the Portuguese would come to their assistance. The people were against the Bahmanis as well, for their administration imposed a heavy tax burden on the villages and trade activity. In addition, recent victory the Portuguese had over the combined forces of the Sultans of Egypt and Gujarat had boosted their morale to an unprecedented level.

Thus, with Timoja's help, the Portuguese defeated the troops of the Panjim Fort on 1st, March 1510. The armies of Adil Shah did not go quietly, however and they gathered in the forts of Banastarim, Cortalim, and Dhavje to launch a counter-attack. Meanwhile, to discourage the Muslim troops, Albuquerque burnt down the Muslim city of Old Goa and beheaded some well-known Muslims who had been held prisoner in the fort.[42] A naval battle followed, and the islands were recaptured. Not until their second attack on November 25, 1510 did the Portuguese gain control of the islands of Goa, Chorao and Divar. This time, Adil Shah surrendered peacefully and the majority of Turkish and Egyptian residents left Goa to escape the clutches of Albuquerque. Timoja , as a reward for his services, was made the chief magistrate over all of Goa's citizens and was given revenue from the islands of Divar and Chorao.[43]

Once Goa fell to the Portuguese, the Samorin of Calicut and the Sultan of Gujarat made their peace with the Portuguese, at least for the time being. Consequently, from 1509-15 Afonso de Alburoeque solidified his control over the recently conquered Goa Islands, and further gained control of Malacca in 1511, whose port was considered the key to trade with China. In that same year, however, Puladh Shah, who had been gathering an armed force at Banastarim, again tried to recapture Goa from the Portuguese.[44] The Vijayanagar emperor offered help against Shah's forces in return for a regular supply of Arabian horses. Together they routed the Muslim forces but again in 1534 war broke out to contest the Portuguese acquisition of Salcete and Bardez, which Ashad Khan had demanded them to return to his territory.[45] In this first battle, Khan attacked the Rachol Fort with a force of 10,000, sorely defeated the Portuguese and destroyed the Fort. In 1540 the Muslim armies again attacked Salcette, destroyed the newly constructed church of Salcette and burnt and looted several villages.[46] Vijayanagar again assisted and in the final outcome by the end of 1543 the islands of Salcette, Bardez, and Tiswadi (Ilhas) were firmly under the control of the Portuguese. That same time period also witnessed the capture of Bassein, Chaul, Honavar, Bassur, Mangalore, Cannanore, and Quilon, details of which are mentioned in later chapters.

In 1570, however, those rulers displaced by the Portuguese formed an alliance to oust the latter from their possessions on the West Coast of India. The Adil Shah of Bijapur, Nizam Shah of Ahmednagar, the Samorin of Calicut, the Queen of Gersoppa (N. Kanara), the Queen of Ullala (S.Kanara) and the King of Achin (East Indies) attacked on the Portuguese but were successfully defeated under the captaincy of Luis de Ataide.[47]

Annexation by Spain

Between 1580 and 1640 Portugal came under the sovereignty of the King of Spain, Phillip II. He annexed the Portuguese territories and as a result the latter's attention was diverted towards issues pertaining to the mother country, specifically the recapture of lands annexed by Spain. Troops were needed in the mother country, thus, the Spanish monarchy also contributed to the neglect of Portugal's eastern empire. Meanwhile, the Dutch, who were at war with Spain, thus entered into war with Spain's annexed territory with whom they were no longer permitted to trade. Consequently, the Dutch set sail for India and rounded the Cape of Good Hope in 1597. In 1604 they established an alliance with the Samorin of Calicut with an aim to obtain spices and oust the Portuguese from their possessions.[48] Between 1636 and 1641 the Dutch effected a blockade at the mouth of the Mandovi River in Goa which proved detrimental to the Portuguese colony. In 1639 the Dutch burnt three Portuguese places of worship in the Mormugao harbour and caused an estimated loss of 1,500 men and 155 ships in total between 1580 and 1640.[49] In 1640 the territory of Ceylon fell to the Dutch and in 1641 Malacca was also lost by the Portuguese to the Dutch. Between 1641 and 1644 the Dutch naval fleet again blocked the Goa Port, causing considerable financial loss to the latter. Even after a treaty between the Spanish and Dutch was established in 1648, the hostilities between the Portuguese and the Dutch on the Western Coast of India intensified. The Dutch continued to attack on the Portuguese forts and by the end of the rivalry in the late 1660's the Portuguese had lost most of their Forts except for Diu, Daman, Bassein, Chaul, and the three talukas of Goa (Tiswadi, Bardez, and Salcette). An alliance between the English and the Dutch had resulted in the cession of Bombay Island to the British in 1661 and in the end the commercial relations of the Portuguese had been substantially affected.

The Era of the Marathas

Just as the Dutch attacks diminished, the Marathas led by Shivaji began to prepare for territorial expansion. The Portuguese became concerned with their activities once Shivaji extended the domain of his territories into the Konkan region and began to establish a naval fleet. By the end of 1659 he had amassed a fleet of 20 warships and had erected forts at Bhivandi, Ralyan and Panvel.[50] The Portuguese, fearing that the Maratha troops would attempt to capture Goa, refused to allow his fleet to enter the Portuguese ports. Caution is the word which best describes the Portuguese attitude towards the Maratha leader during this time, because although they had a superior naval fleet, the Marathas had more territory and able-bodied men in their domains.

Shivaji requested help from the Portuguese to defeat his bitter enemy, Adil Shah. The latter declined, however, not wishing to upset the balance of power which had stabilised in the Deccan. Shivaji continued with his plans, however, and captured Kudal (north of Goa), Pernem, and Bicholim from Adil Shah.[51] The Dessai family gave assistance to Adil Shah as they were his feudatories and were provided asylum in Goa after the successful capture of their territories by the Marathas. In 1665, fuelled by his conquest, Shivaji signed a treaty with Jai Singh, against his rival Adil Shah. Their combined forces defeated Adil Shah's general, Khawas Khan, on the Konkan coast, yet throughout the war the Portuguese kept a neutral stance. In 1666 Shivaji besieged Ponda, a territory still belonged to Adil Shah, and at that point the Portuguese decided to enter the war on the side of the Adil Shah latter.[52] In retaliation, the Maratha troops attacked Bardez in 1667, burnt and plundered many villages, took hostages, and caused sporadic violence for three days in succession. Shivaji justified his invasion on the grounds that Goa was harbouring the Dessais who were heavily involved in activity directed against the Maratha leader, and for helping Adil Shah by sending Portuguese troops to man the garrison at Ponda.[53] Other reasons for the invasion were less obvious; the Maratha leader needed finances to continue his invasions and the Dutch encouraged hostilities against their European enemy. On 5th December, 1667, a treaty was established between the two rivals which involved the return of captives, the expulsion of the Dessais from Goa if they made further incursions into Maratha territory, the payment of tax in commercial dealings, the sale of arms to the Marathas if necessary, and the decision to negotiate before entering into formal war.

The treaty was short-lived, however, for in October 1668 the Portuguese discovered that Shivaji had amassed 8-10,000 troops and was planning to invade Goa.[54] Because the Portuguese made it known that they knew of the secret attack, the battle did not occur. In 1672, however, Shivaji attacked the King of Ramnagar, the latter who had ceded some territory of Daman to the Portuguese in exchange for a regular payment of tax. Shivaji then demanded that the tax be paid to him, whereupon the Portuguese entered into an alliance with King Ramnagar and assisted him with resources and troops in battle against Shivaji. In 1677 King Ramnagar was defeated and the Marathas, to punish the Portuguese for assisting the former, planned to attack Goa.[55] Preparations for war started on both the sides, but owing to Shivaji's sudden death in 1680, peace was established for two years.

This was again short-lived, for Shivaji's successor Sambhaji, was as determined as his predecessor to expand his territories beyond those which already existed. In 1682 Sambhaji for the time being requested for peaceful relations with the Portuguese to enable him to attack and defeat his other rival Rajaram, but the Portuguese had already concluded that they could not trust the Marathas. In 1682, upon learning that the Mughals planned to attack Sambhaji, the Portuguese agreed to allow them safe passage through their territories. In 1683 Sambhaji captured Chaul and destroyed the Ponda Fort.[56] On 11, December 1683, Sambhaji's troops entered Bardez and attacked, plundered, and burnt several villages. Tivim Fort fell to the Marathas and the Chapora fort fell without firing a single shot. Concurrently, the Maratha army attacked Goa from the South, entered Salcette and destroyed the churches in Margao. The villagers of Assolna and Cuncolim agreed to become Maratha subjects[57] and the troops stationed themselves in Salcette to prepare for an attack against Tiswadi.

The Mughals Descend on the Konkan

At this point of time, the Portuguese were in an extremely vulnerable position owing to the loss of many men, resources and the lack of necessary reinforcements from other colonies. Sambhaji's forces could have easily routed the Portuguese in Tiswadi while they were in such a depressed state. Yet, before the Marathas could realise their goal, a massive Mughal army descended from the Deccan led by Shah Alam (son of Aurangzeb) and arrived in Bicholim ready for war with the Maratha forces.[58]

The Mughal forces captured and plundered Bicholim, defeated Sambhaji decisively in 1684. They established a friendship with the Portuguese, the latter whom allowed them a safe passage through their territories through the Chapora River. In that same year, Sambhaji signed a treaty with the Portuguese which restored to the latter all lands, forts, armaments and provisions taken as the spoils of war. Sambhaji also pardoned his bitter enemies, the Dessais, and agreed not to construct forts along the borders of Portuguese territory. The Portuguese, in return, agreed to pay them the tax from the territories of Daman on time and in full.[59]

Though the Portuguese seemed to have established peaceful relations with her neighbours at this point in time, the events which followed proved quite the opposite. Neither party lived up to the treaty and the Forts of Bardez remained in the possession of the Marathas. They again began stationed troops at Ponda with the goal to capture Tiswadi and the Marathas continued with sporadic attacks until 1689. The friendship established with the Mughals similarly proved negative and Aurangzeb instructed his son Shah Alam to capture Goa by force while maintaining a facade of alliance. As the Portuguese discovered that their allies were truly enemies, they entered into an alliance with the Dessais of the Konkan in 1685 against Sambhaji.[60]

In March 1689, however, the Mughal forces raided Maratha territories, killed Sambhaji. This outraged and united the Maratha forces and further led to the Dessais joining in against the Mughals. Sambhaji's successor Rajaram, however, was unprepared to continue where Sambhaji had left off and immediately offered to form an alliance with the Portuguese before retreating to Jinji. The Portuguese decided to keep a neutral stance, however, Goa soon became a place of political asylum. They remained neutral and peace existed between Rajaram and the Portuguese administration until the former's death in 1700.[61] His successor was not as peace-oriented and in October 1702 the Maratha army invaded Ponda which had been under the control of the Muchals since 1689 (when it was captured from Sambhaji). It was again recovered by the Mughals in 1705, and given in 1707 by the Mughal army to the care of the King of Sonda who was a feudatory of the former.

The Rise of the Bhonsles

Meanwhile, a new local chieftain was making an appearance on the Goan stage and in 1698 the Bhonsles captured Bicholim, Pernem and Sanquelim (modern Sanguem) from the Mughals stationed in those territories. In 1705 the Portuguese invaded the Bhonsle territories and destroyed the forts erected at Amona and Volvoi. In 1706 the fort of Bicholim was likewise captured, and in 1707 Panelim and Corjuem were captured by the Portuguese armies. Ponda was offered to the Portuguese in 1716 by the Mughals, but they declined the offer preferring to consolidate and fortify their existing areas.[62]

After 1707 the Portuguese relations with the Marathas steadily deteriorated and in 1717 the latter attacked and plundered many villages in Salcette. This southern taluka was again invaded on 23rd January 1739 and owing to the weakness of the Portuguese, fell to the Marathas three days later on the 26th,[63] following Margao. Soon all of Salcette, excepting the Forts of Rachol and Mormugao came under the domain of the Marathas forces. The Marathas also took Sanguem, Supem, and Ponda, the latter territory which helped them in their invasion. That same year Ramachandra and Jayaram Sawant, rulers of Kudal, invaded the neighbouring territory in the South, Bardez, with the encouragement of the Marathas. Following their invasion, the entire region excepting the Forts of Aguada and Reis Magos came under the sway of the Bhonsles. In 1739 the Portuguese opened negotiations with Peshwa, wherein the Marathas demanded the end of the Inquisition and the right of the Hindus to live by their own moral code and way of life.[64] A second treaty signed in 1740 in Bombay ceded Chaul and Morro (Korle) to the Marathas. The latter agreed to withdraw from Cuncolim and Assolna in return for the cession of the territories adjacent to Daman and those of Bassein.

The Bhonsles would not leave Bardez and except for the aforementioned Forts of Aguada and Reis Magos under the Portuguese, they controlled all of the region. The treaty of 1740 gave the Portuguese back the Bardez region, but in 1741 the Bhonsles again waged war against the Portuguese hoping to capture all of their possessions.[65] Were it not for the unexpected arrival of a British fleet off the coast of Goa, the Portuguese may not have been able to defend themselves against this latest attack. In May 1741 the Viceroy Marques de Lourical arrived in Goa with reinforcements which together were able to expel the Bhonsles from Bardez.

In 1746 war again broke out between the Portuguese and the Bhonsles, the results of which put the Fort of Alorna in the hands of the Portuguese. The latter also entered into an alliance with the King of Sonda, the Ranes of Sanguem, Quepem, and Manerim, whereby all transferred their loyalties to the Portuguese.[66] On 23 November of that year, the Tiracol fort was captured from the Bhonsles and on 20 December the Reddi fort (on the Northern border of present-day Goa) also fell to the Portuguese.[67] In 1752 the Portuguese again attacked the territory, including Ponda and made incursions into Canacona with 2,000 troops. During the monsoons of 1756 the then Viceroy Conde de Alva attempted to seize Mardangad from the Marathas and lost both his life and territory in the ensuing battle. Confusion resulted in the Portuguese administration owing to the power vacuum left behind from the Viceroy's unforeseen death and their defeat at Ponda. The Bhonsles used this time to their advantage and attacked the Portuguese in Pernem, Sanguem, and Maneri. They besieged the Forts of Bicholim and Tiracol, and waged war until a new treaty was signed on 24 December 1761, which ceded the lands once again to the Bhonsles.[68] In 1762, to counter the Maratha invasions, the Portuguese joined forces with the King of Sonda to regain control of Ponda for the King. In 1763 with assistance from Naraba Naik and the Dessais of Ponda, the Portuguese troops attacked the Ponda Fort (Mardangad) which surrendered two weeks later. The nominal sovereignty of Sonda over Ponda was subsequently recognised.

The Arrival of Hyder Ali

Hardly had the Portuguese and the King of Sonda had time to celebrate their victory when Hyder Ali of Mysore in that same year attacked Ponda and declared himself sovereign of all the lands owned by King Sonda. The latter took shelter in Goa and gave his territories of Ponda, Quepem and Canacona to the care of the Portuguese until he was capable of regaining them. In so doing, he saved the lands from Hyder Ali who wished to remain in friendship with Portugal. The King was given a yearly maintenance subsidy by the Portuguese and as he was unable to regain his lost lands, ceded them permanently to the Portuguese in 1771.[69] This did not occur without argument as both the Peshwa Madhav Rao (overlord to the Sonda King) and Hyder Ali claimed ownership of the lands. The contestors also happened to be arch rivals and as their territories came into close proximity each solicited the aid of the Portuguese for help in defeating the other.

Thus, followed a general period of dissention and chaos between 1776 and 1782, in which the Portuguese took full advantage. Specifically, they coveted the land between Bardez and the Tiracol River to its North (Pernem) which belonged to the Kem Sawant, a Bhonsle of Sawantwadi. Consequently, when the Bhonsles asked the Portuguese for assistance in repelling the invasion from the North by the Chhatrapati of Kolhapur, they readily agreed. However once they ousted the invaders and seized the Forts of Bicholim and Sanguem, they claimed these territories for the Portuguese empire. In 1782, war ensued to recover these lands from the Portuguese and in 1783 they hoisted the Portuguese flag over the Alorna Fort.[70] In 1785 the armies of Kolhapur again descended into the territories of the Bhonsles, and the Bhonsles were again compelled to seek assistance from the Portuguese. In 1788 the latter agreed to help repel the Kolhapur armies in return for the remaining lands of Pernem, thus succeeding in their original mission.[71] Thus, by the end of 1788 the new conquests were complete and Pernem, Bicholim, Satari, Ponda, Quepem, Sanguem and Canacona all came under the domain of the Portuguese empire.

Conclusion

Goa's political history prior to liberation, therefore, is hardly the tale of a homogeneous, integrated society. Rather, history demonstrates that the territories of Goa remained divided, ravaged by a series of political conquest and reconquest throughout most of its history. While in the early years and medieval ages, these periods of rule were longer and more stable, the era ushered in by the Bahmanis a period of confusion, chaos, and rapidly changing administrations vying for control of the Konkan region. Under the Portuguese administration itself, the people were hardly united in their political and cultural identification. While many people in the old conquests felt compelled to identify with the policies and aims of the Portuguese colonists, those in the new conquests were busy fighting in the armies of the Marathas, the Bhonsles, the Dessais, and the Satari Ranes. Yet the events which took place in the new conquests had serious repercussions in the old, even though the people were isolated from each other in the social sphere. At times the Portuguese were compelled to form alliances, in other instances they provided assistance in wars beyond their territorial boundaries.

With various layers of the ruling administration came also the high culture advocated by these individual administrations. These influences, though top-down, did influence the cultural identity of the people to a certain extent. During the rule of Ashoka, for example, Buddhism flourished in Goa and many institutions (monasteries) and cultural practises (meditation, non-violence, etc.) were advocated as socio-cultural ideals. Later under the Kadamba dynasty, the culture and literature of south Kanara was patronised and as a result Kannada became the official language and Hinduism the ideal religion. During the rule of the Bahmanis certain Muslim practises were in vogue such as the use of slaves, the practise of polygamy, and the seclusion of women from the public eye. Following the latest historical administration the Portuguese language, religion, and culture were imposed upon and eventually accepted by the people with the result of a large Catholic community flourishing in Goa today. After Liberation and the realisation of 'freedom', all of these various cultural layers surfaced within particular communities. Today Muslims, Hindus, and Catholics practise their religions and lifestyles freely with little fear of persecution or economic insecurity.

Throughout these successive administrations, the ways of life of the tribal communities and their original mother tongue have survived and resurfaced among the Goan tribal communities of the present day. This continuance of tribal cultural forms despite constant persecution and condemnation is a remarkable example of cultural resilience in Indian society. Despite being labelled as 'backward' among all of the successive administrations, the communities of the Kunbis, Gaudes, and Dhangars have remained intact, a bit worn down, for thousands of years. This is most likely because theirs is a culture born from within and based upon the cycles of life and nature rather than one borrowed, imposed, or otherwise adopted by a people from a ruling administration. The existence of the tribal culture in modern-day Goa, thus, exposes the paradox surrounding the origins of cultural identity. While a ruling administration has the ability to impose its laws, language, religion, and economic structure on the ruled society, the foundations of that particular human culture arose from within and have the ability to withstand the most powerful of destructive forces.

REFERENCES

1. Gune, V.T. (editor), *Gazetteer of the Union Territory of Goa, Daman and Diu*, Parts I-III. Bombay: Government Central Press, 1979, pp. 67-68.
2. *Ibid.*, p. 68.
3. *Ibid.*
4. *Ibid.*, p. 69.
5. *Ibid.*, pp. 69-70.
6. *Ibid.*, p. 71.
7. *Ibid.*, p. 72.
8. *Ibid.*, p. 74.
9. *Ibid.*, p. 77.
10. *Ibid.*
11. *Ibid.*, p. 78.
12. *Ibid.*, p. 80.
13. *Ibid.*, p. 82.
14. *Ibid.*, p. 84.
15. *Ibid.*, p. 85.
16. *Ibid*, p. 86.
17. *Ibid.*, p. 87.
18. *Ibid.*, p. 93.
19. *Ibid.*, p. 94.
20. *Gune, V.T., op. cit.*, p. 97.
21. *Ibid.*, p. 99.

22. Gune, V.T., *op. cit.*, p. 102.
23. *Ibid.*, p. 104.
24. *Ibid.*, p. 106.
25. *Ibid.*, p. 110.
26. *Ibid.*, p. 112.
27. *Ibid.*, p. 113.
28. *Ibid.*, p. 120.
29. *Ibid.*, p. 121.
30. *Ibid.*, p. 122.
31. *Ibid.*, p. 124.
32. *Ibid.*, p. 125.
33. *Ibid.*, pp. 126-27.
34. *Ibid.*, p. 129.
35. *Ibid.*, p. 130.
36. *Ibid.*, pp. 130-32.
37. *Ibid.*, pp. 134-38.
38. *Ibid.*, p. 138.
39. Abram, David. *Goa: The Rough Guide*, London Penguin Books, 1995, p. 190.
40. Gune, V.T. *op. cit.*, p. 139.
41. *Ibid.*, p. 140.
42. *Ibid.*, p. 142.
43. *Ibid.*, p. 143.
44. *Ibid.*, p. 147.
45. *Ibid.*, p. 148.
46. *Ibid.*, p. 149.
47. *Ibid.*, p. 150.
48. *Ibid.*, p. 152.
49. *Ibid.*
50. *Ibid.*, p. 166.
51. *Ibid.*, p. 167.
52. *Ibid.*
53. *Ibid.*, p. 169.
54. *Ibid.*
55. *Ibid.*, pp. 170-71.
56. *Ibid.*, p. 172.
57. *Ibid*, p. 172.
58. *Ibid.*, p. 173.
59. *Ibid.*, p. 174.
60. *Ibid.*, p. 175.
61. Gune, V.T., *op. cit.*, p. 176.

62. Gune, V.T., *op. cit.*, p. 177.
63. *Ibid.*, p. 178.
64. *Ibid.*, p. 179.
65. *Ibid.*, pp. 179-80.
66. *Ibid.*, p. 181.
67. The latter was returned to the Bhonsles during 1754-56.
68. Gune, V.T., *op. cit.*, p. 183.
69. *Ibid.*, p. 184.
70. *Ibid.*, p. 185.
71. *Ibid.*

Chapter 3

Evolution of Social History and Political Economy of Goa

The evolution of the social history of Goa is one of the most relevant topics for discussion on Goan culture and identity. Prior to the advent of the Portuguese, the Konkan region, including that of Goa was primarily a part of the same loosely-defined cultural system which was manifested throughout India. Aryan-Hindu and Muslim cultures were predominant, and Goa also had its share of Buddhism and Jainism. Later the latter were patronised by the Kadamba dynasty whose rule oversaw the construction of caves and monasteries devoted to religious purposes. Thus, until the consolidation of the Portuguese power around 1540, the region known today as Goa was interconnected religiously, politically, economically, and socially with her neighbours. The predominant socio-cultural system was, of course, Hinduism. The Muslims had compelled many to convert and follow the belief in Allah and they had destroyed many temples in Goa which were constructed under previous administrations. However, different their religious philosophies, they had some similar beliefs and practices such as the inferior position of women, the necessity of purification rites/ablutions, the marriage of girls at a young age, the dominance of the male in many matters and the denial of education to girls. Generally, the people of Goa prior to the Portuguese shared a similar socio-cultural history with people in the rest of the Indian subcontinent, excepting regional variations which evolved owing to cultural drift, innovation and borrowing from Dravidian and aboriginal cultural forms. Her people also witnessed all of the major religions on

Goan soil; animism, Hinduism, Buddhism, Jainism, Zoroastrianism/Judaism, Islam, Catholicism and most recently Protestantism. Her people have likewise passed through the Vedic age, the age of the Puranas, Arab mercantile trade, the Muslim and Moghul empires, the imposition of European rule and ultimately the struggle for freedom which resulted in the unification of the major regions of India under one sovereign, parliamentary government.

Following the arrival of the Portuguese in the history of Goa, the politics of the region become completely intertwined with the social history of her people. Political events are indeed crucial to the understanding of the 'historical accident' which took place on 25 November 1510, but it is the social history of Goa in the first 100 years of the Portuguese rule which truly illuminate the changes which occurred in the lives of the local people. Structure, cultural forms and administrative policies underwent massive changes which resulted in the enculturation of a segment of Goa's population into a new faith and identification with an alternate authority. For the majority of converts, this occurred in Phase II of the enculturation process, whereby the locals made the conscious decision to switch to the faith of their rulers. Because this occurred in Phase II, they had already learnt in Phase I all the cultural forms and patterns of their society which existed prior to the Portuguese conquest.[1] As discerned in earlier chapters, this Phase I provides cultural stability of old forms even in the face of significant social upheaval and change. In addition, various sub-cultures and communities among the native Goans absorbed both the Portuguese culture and its forms in a variety of ways and some, like the upper class natives, identified more readily with the Portuguese culture and adapted with less difficulty to these new cultural norms.

Alfonso de Albuquerque correctly realised from his own and others' experiences along the Western Coast of India that the Portuguese needed to garner local support in order to maintain control over the islands of Goa. Merely lowering the tax rate from its previous position under the Muslims would not be enough to maintain a trading centre in Goa. He needed a loyal community which would support the Portuguese administration as well as serve in the army and navy. He realised that religious and cultural divides disadvantaged them greatly in regard to their trade aspirations, so he made it a personal aim to colonise the islands and establish the Portuguese presence 'permanently' in the Goan islands. As a consequence of his landmark decision, the evolution in the social history of Goa would undergo lead to significant changes in the areas of education, language, religion, leisure, social position, power relations, migration, gender relations, the role of women and modes of thought. Thus, when Christianity came to Goa, it caused a momentous change in the social history of the people living in the three coastal talukas of Salcette, Bardez and Tiswadi. This chapter is designed to describe the culture which existed prior to the advent of the Portuguese and the layers of cultural evolution which occurred in Goa since the time of the first Aryan settlers.[2]

Culture of Pre-Portuguese Goa and Caste System

The Kolis, Mundas, Kharwas and Shabars were the aboriginal tribes which inhabited Goa during its pre-historic era. The Kunbis and Guades of today are thought to be the descendants of these ancient settlers and were themselves tribal communities with animistic religious beliefs and rituals of their own. As in animism, these early people believed that spirits inhabited most forms of nature. They practised hunting, gathering, fishing, and crude forms of agriculture. Some were nomadic tribes and others had taken to sedentary settlements. They followed certain 'superstitions' and had their own style of dress and adornment. They practised child marriage, and learnt the occupations and traditions of their fathers. Their language was anoial one and formal education did not exist as we think of today.

The Aryans are thought to have first migrated to Goa beginning in 600 B.C. and continuing in several waves until 400 A.D. owing to harsh conditions in their native environments. Most historians agree that they descended into India from the area from present-day Iran and some came by themselves while others came with their leaders who were in search of territorial expansion. By 250 B.C. under emperor Ashoka both Jainism and Buddhism had filtered into Goa. Buddhist caves which have been unearthed in Bandora, Kudvem, Aravale and Rivona which date back to this era. Prior to the Saraswats, the Chitpavan and Desatha

Brahmins from the Southern regions of India had also settled in the Konkan region. GSBs are believed to have migrated to Goa in the latter part of this era, around 300 A.D. from the Saraswati River settlement in Bengal. This accords with their own documented history as well as their linguistic heritage (Konkani), which has a similar structure and sound as the Bengali language. The Saraswats came as philosophers and scholars and brought, 'enlightenment' to the animistic tribal communities, bringing them into the Vedic fold. These Brahmins believed themselves to have descended from a superior Aryan race owing to their fairer complexion, lighter skin, advanced knowledge and literacy forms in Sanskrit. Thus, when they re-structured the social system in Goa, they did so according to race and ethnicity. Placing the Brahmins at the top of the social ladder and the aboriginal tribes on the bottom. In order to accommodate the pre-existing culture of the aboriginal, the Brahmins incorporated a few of the native gods and goddesses into the Hindu pantheon. Even in Goa today one finds a few of these regional gods and goddesses which have their origins in the native spirits of the aborigines. As the system evolved, the Aryan races achieved the 'twice-born' elevated status whereas the aborigines became outcast. This most likely resulted from the refusal or inability of the tribal communities to adjust their customs and behaviours to those dictated by Vedic doctrine, resulting in rejection as full-fledged community members. Even in Goa today several ancient tribal communities exist which still maintain distinct religious beliefs and customs.

During the Kadamba and Vijayanagara ruling dynasties, Goa had extensive cultural contacts with the Kannada language and culture of Karnataka. The administrative system, tax collection, distribution of land grants for religious and educational institutions and official language paralleled those of Karnataka under these dynasties. As early as 1209 A.D. a copper plate inscription from the rule of Jayakeshi III mentions the existence of a heavily trafficked road which connected Goa and Karnataka.[3] In addition, trade and agricultural activity were linked to that of Karnataka and regular trade convoys between the two regions continued throughout these years and even under the Portuguese. Cultural consistencies also existed between the two regions, such as the veneration of heroes who perished while protecting the kingdom, women and cows. The patterns of religious worship paralleled those of Karnataka; and the Advaita, Dvaita and Jain philosophies are thought to have diffused into Goa from its southern neighbour. Yakshagana, the famous folk art of Karnataka, is though to have been influenced by the 'Jagar', popular in Hindu Goa.[4]

As in the majority of India, the caste system dominated the social structure in Goan society. The Brahmins figured at the top of the social order followed by the Kshyatrias, the Vaishyas, the Sudirs (Shudras) and finally the Untouchables. The top-most social position was occupied by the Chitpavans, Gowda Saraswats and Desastha Brahmins who were further divided into Vaishavites and Shiavites.[5] The Desastha Brahmins migrated to Goa from the Kolaba district in the 1300's upon invitation of the ruling administration. Records indicate that during the rule of the Bahmani Sultanate in Goa, twelve Brahman families were given land and invited to settle in the commercial capital of Goa (Gopakattam). Among the Kshyatrias, the Ranes of Goa occupied a prominent position and claim to be descendants of the Rajasthan Kshatriyas (Rajputs). Little is known about the other sub-groups because following the Portuguese invasion, many either converted or else migrated to the Deccan in search of employment. The third social strata, the Vaishyas, consisted of the business class engaged in commercial trade. The sub-group of the Vanis were well-off, but many of these groups, such as the Daivajnas, Sutar, Lohars and Kansars claim the status of Brahmins. These first three classes were considered twice-born and enjoyed special privileges in society. Beneath the Vaishyas on the social hierarchy came the Sudirs (Shudras), who were the toddy-tappers, milkmen, fishermen, carpenters, washermen, potters, blacksmiths and other artisans. Agricultural labourers also came under this social division and the whole group performed the services of the upper-class. At the bottom of the social scale were the untouchables who performed services considered 'impure' such as leather work and sanitation removal. The tribal communities such as the Dhodia, Dubla, Nayaka, Siddi and Varli also fell under this category.[6]

As mentioned earlier, almost all of the major religions to touch Indian soil also arrived in Goa. The most dominant and socially determining, however, was the religion brought by the Aryan settlers. Once this Vedic religion arrived in India with these migrants it evolved quite uniquely from its original form once taking root on Indian soil. Though an entire description of the evolutionary process of the Hindu religion is beyond the scope of the study, it is worth mentioning that the initial system designed to create self-sufficiency and importance to all occupational fields eventually evolved over the years into a rigid caste system. Another important religious evolution in Goa was the joining of the two formally rival sects of Shiavites and Vishnavites with a subsequent neglect of Brahma in the Hindu trinity. The 'cult of Ganesh' was another local development in Goa which saw thousands of people flocking to the sacred waters of Naroa in late August in honour of this God of fortune.

Though caste and caste relationships dominated the stage in pre-Portuguese society, the restrictions placed on interactions between different communities do not seem to have been as strict as those in other areas such as Kerala.[7] Their are no records which mention that the sight of an untouchable, for example, caused pollution to a Brahman and many of the Sudirs performed a variety of services for the upper castes. This relaxation on caste restrictions is probably owing to the close-knit village communicates flourishing in Goa where each endogamous community performed vital functions necessary for the economic, political and cultural survival of the village. During the medieval period historians document that some Brahmans in Goa began leaving their traditional occupations and instead became men of trade and commerce, a lucrative decision. They belonged to the community of Saraswat Brahmans, who today are known as noted traders as well as doctors, priests, engineers and other notable professions.

Slavery in Pre-Portuguese Goa

Slaves were also a part of pre-Portuguese Goan society. Most of the outcasts and landless labourers were virtual slaves to the upper castes and under Muslim rule during the medieval period, slaves were commonly used as soldiers and as domestic servants. In the Hindu socio-economic caste system, the Shudras were virtual slaves for the twice-born castes and were kept away from education so as to keep them ignorant of their exploitation. Under the Muslims, slaves were well clothed, fed and educated. They were usually prisoners of war whose lives were 'spared' in exchange for a lifetime of servitude and they performed a host of duties from domestic chores to military service. They were allowed to improve their lot in life through demonstrations of bravery and loyalty and the Slave Dynasty from 1206 to 1290 was known as such because the rulers of that dynasty were one-time slaves. Malik Kafur was one such slave in history who rose to pre-eminence under the Muslim system of slavery.[8] Slaves in medieval times were also status symbols and the more slaves a noble or merchant possessed, the better off he was deemed to be. In addition, under the empire of Adil Shah, eunuch slaves were used in Goa to guard over a wealthy Muslim's harem. Thus, prior to the advent of the Portuguese, both domestic, military (typical of Muslims) and feudal slavery (typical of Hindus) were practised in Goa.

Economy and Administration

On the eve of Portuguese rule in Goa, 80 per cent of the local population was actively engaged in agriculture. During this time the Arabs carried on a brisk trade with Arabia, Persia, China, Ethiopia and East Africa whereby they imported slaves, horses, gold, silver and carpets into Goa.[9] These luxury items circulated mostly within the Arab communities and a few wealthy Hindus and did not reach down to the average village household. Goa also carried on trade with the in-land regions; exporting food grains, textiles, spices, diamonds, rubies, pearls, slaves and art crafts to the aforementioned countries.

In addition to commercial trade, of which Goa was an international hub, ship building was also a major industry of pre-Portuguese Goa. The ships which originated from Goa were almost equal in quality to those of the Portuguese in tonnage, mast, sail, speed and navigational equipment. Blacksmiths were also in high demand as the producers of weapons, agricultural tools and household implements. The talukas of Bicholim, Pernem and Sattari were famous for their brass work, owing to the abundance of natural elements used in the formation of this metal. Craftsmen such as potters, weavers, masons and tanners were all part of the self-sufficiency which distinguished village Goa from its Indian neighbours. Jewellery was an important craft of the goldsmiths and the local gold, silver and bronze items were admired by the Arab traders in the region.

The village administration in Goa dates back possibly as far as the pre-historic Kolis and Gaudas and was certainly in place subsequent to the Aryan immigrants. At the top was the village assembly, which was made up of all the 'Gauncars', village founding fathers. It was a hereditary position for male family members only and could not be gained by Culacharins, later settlers in the village. Beyond membership in the village assembly, the gauncars enjoyed other exclusive rights and privileges such as the collection of 'jon', the left over produce from a successful harvest.[10] The assembly was in charge of political, administrative, social, economic, religious and cultural issues of the village and they met on certain dates to discuss any or all of the above issues. Tax collection, further development of land for the purpose of agriculture, land distribution and property rights were some of the main concerns of the assembly. They would meet openly in the village square or else under a Banyan tree and call for unanimous vote. Every village assembly had its chief gauncar, who enjoyed the highest village position. Unlike other village positions which were hereditary, the privilege of chief gauncar could be purchased by any of the gauncars.[11]

Under this administrative system, lands were parcelled out to the various village sub-groups as long as they performed their required functions. In this way, the priests, washermen, potters, barbers, cobblers, goldsmiths and witch doctors were each provided with plots of land. The various sub-communities within the casts lived in distinct 'vaddos' or wards and the village or the 'gao' was the cluster of these wards. Under this communicate system which was a unique feature of village administration in Goa, the villages were self-sufficient and self-contained entities. All of the needed services could be found within each village and accordingly sanctions were enforced against accepting or offering one's services to members of another village.[12] At times a village would be without a particular community and would offer land and privileges to those providing that service who were willing to leave their village and migrate to another. Thus, as the people owned the village, the village also owned its people. The Muslim rulers did not disturb this communicate system, but instead utilised the gauncars as tax collectors for their own purposes.

Language in Pre-Portuguese Goa

Konkani has been the language spoken in Goa since recorded history, although it seems to be linked with the Gaurian languages of the North, therefore, coinciding with the migration of the Saraswat Brahmins. It is the mother tongue of the Saraswats and all migrated groups, from Varansi to Cochin, maintain Konkani as their mother tongue even though the Kashi-Mutt sect of Saraswat Brahmins did not migrate to Goa but rather came straight from Varanasi to other areas outside of the Konkan region. It is most likely, therefore, that the aboriginal had their own oral language along the Western Coast of India some of whose words and intonations mixed with that of the ruling Aryans to eventually form several dialects of Konkani such as the Portuguese discovered in both the Bombay island group and the Goa and Karnatakan coastal areas. Though the exact origin of Konkani remains debated, most historians agree that Konkani has been an entirely oral language up until the advent of the Portuguese.[13] This does not suggest that the Konkani language was simple or primitive in any way. Rather, the Konkani language showed a high degree of development in its oral grammar and its figurative language. This is because Konkani, as an oral language, was the means by which people passed on knowledge from one generation to the next and story-telling became, as in most oral societies, the way through which this was accomplished.

During the Kadamba dynasty, whose origins lie in the regions South of Goa, Kannada was patronised as the official language in Goa from approximately 1,000 A.D. to 3,000 A.D. Their successors, the Vijayanagara empire, also came from the South and patronised the Kannada language and literary forms throughout their rule in Goa from 1366 A.D. to 1472 A.D.[14] Thus, for nearly 500 years in the three coastal talukas, Kannada was the language in vogue among the literate classes and all 'high' culture was related to it.

From the 8th and 9th centuries onwards until the advent of the Portuguese, the Arab traders began to settle in Goa in order to perform their commercial activities. Under the Kadamba dynasty, for example, many Arabs were employed in high official positions and mosques were constructed throughout the Konkan territories to cater to their religious needs. During these early years they were a small minority, but the culture and language (Persian) which they brought with them must have diffused to some extent among the educated locals who also occupied official positions or carried on trade relations. In later eras, when Goa was annexed by the Bahmani Sultanate, Persian became the official language in government and the people assimilated these new cultural forms to some extent. Those wishing to secure high government posts needed knowledge of this language and the Muslims had set up Ulemas (educational monasteries) whereby to impart such knowledge to students.

The north-east talukas of Pernem, Bicholim, Sattari and Ponda had, throughout this history extensive ties with Maharashtra and had exchanged many cultural forms from neighbouring territories. Education was imparted in Marathi and forms of entertainment peculiar to that region also found a devoted audience in Goa. It is of little wonder then, that with the arrival of Shivaji concurrent with the Portuguese rule in the Old Conquests, the new conquests would identify with the culture and language (Marathi) of Maharashtra.

Role of Women

Prior to the arrival of the Portuguese, the society in Goa was connected historically, economically and socially with the larger Indian subcontinent and consequently the practices and customs relevant to women were also present in Goa. Before entering into a discussion about the role of women in society, it is important to take into account that these roles reflected the beliefs and common practices of both men and women in the society. From today's modern perspective, the situation of women then appears as an injustice. However, for those enculturated into this system and having no recourse to conceive of a different way of life, the role of women was accepted and remained unquestioned until the Hindu reformists of a much later era. Thus, most historians write about what women did not have, as it is difficult to know what life felt like from their perspective. Even the women who still undergo severe subjugation in today's society may have some awareness of the freedom allotted to others of their same sex owing to media and information technology. Yet learned men note that the status of women in society determines its overall development and progression and this status has undergone significant alterations upon the arrival of the Portuguese and in the post-Liberation era. Therefore, a brief examination of the status of women in pre-Portuguese society is an important component of this study.

Among the Hindus in the Vedic age, women partook of education, participated in society and enjoyed freedom. However, as society evolved and the Puranas came to reinterpret Hindu society, women in the later ages were virtually devoid of freedom, rights, choice of a life partner, education and public participation.[15] Women were considered inferior to their male counter-parts and the birth of a girl child was an unwelcome family addition. She was bestowed inferior status and accepted it as truth, just as she accepted her betrothal without having a voice in the matter.

Sati, self-immolation on the funeral pyre of one's deceased husband, was also widely practised in Goa during the age of the Puranas. As Pires writes: "In the kingdom of Goa, all the Hindu women burn with their dead husbands; this act is considered sacred."[16] A woman understood that Sati was the ideal act of a woman following her husband's death and that this act of love, loyalty and sacrifice would gain her family great honours. According to current belief, Sati ensured the safe passage of both man, woman and family into a higher incarnation in the next life, whereas refusal to commit Sati resulted in a lifetime of virtual slavery and abuse at the hands of her in-laws. The practice of Sati fulfilled the Hindu woman's ideals of self-sacrifice, piety and undying love. This practice was also prevalent among child-widows, though at times those who escaped could find recluse in temples and spend their lives in its service as devadasis, i.e., temple dancers.[17]

The Devadasi (dancing girl) institution dates back to the era of the Puranas and through it young maiden girls would dedicate or be dedicated to the temple. They would perform various needed services of the temple and lived in secluded villages near to the temples. Before being given to the service of the temple, a young girl would undergo a mock wedding ritual wherein she was married to another girl dressed in male clothing.[18] The devadasi system was a form of sanctioned prostitution whereby the women were given to priests and to important temple guests on occasion. Some became wealthy as consorts of merchants who would spend some weeks or months with a particular dancing girl and provide for her welfare. The offspring of the alliances between priests and or laymen resulted in three separate communities; the Kalavants, the Banvis and the Kulambinis. The Kalavants were the highest caste among the three and learned to read, write, sing, dance and perform a variety of arts in the temple. The sons from such alliances could marry and settle down; they often sought employment as temple and/or village musicians. The young girls would continue as their mothers in the service of the temple. These devadasis were considered a necessary part of society and were not held in contempt by other members of the community.[19] Besides performing in temples for important guests and on religious occasions, they also performed during the annual village festival for the community and heralded village weddings.

Hinduism advocated monogamy (though polygamy was allowed in theory) and a wife could not remarry after the death of her husband, no matter her age at the time of her husband's death. Women were not allowed to inherit landed property, though at the time of their marriage they were given a dowry which was in proportion to her parent's wealth and the demands of the grooms' family. Dowry could take the form of gold, clothing, money, household items and/or other moveable values. Once a woman married, she left the house of her parents to live her remaining days in the home of her husband, where she was further instructed by her mother-in-law. Women were considered less as individuals and more as family property.

Though denied social equality with men, women were often idealised and worshipped in divine forms.[20] An unmarried girl was considered a good omen and 'woman' was worshipped in Goa in the forms of Shantadurga, Parvati and Mahalaxmi. Women were well-protected by male members of their households and they led virtuous lives in relative innocence. They were taught that their greatest aim lie in fulfilling the ideals of womanhood: purity, chastity, self-sacrifice, family and motherhood. Though they were prevented from attending formal schooling, the girls were 'cultured' by their parents at home, especially those from the highest classes.

During the medieval era, the social movement of women became further restricted owing to the Islamic culture which gave even fewer privileges to women. In Muslim society, women were totally secluded and confined to inner rooms; those who did venture out did so in complete purdah. The Koran considered women the absolute property of men (as interpreted) and were told not to question the decisions of male family members and relatives. The practice of keeping a harem among wealthy Muslim nobles and merchants also arose in Goa during this era.[21] The harems of these men consisted of women bought and imported from all over the world and was a formalised and sanctioned institution. Women under Muslim law were able to inherit family property and both divorce and remarriage were permitted according to the doctrines of the Koran.

Education in Pre-Portuguese Society

The Portuguese did not find an uncultured, uneducated society in Goa when they conquered Tiswadi province. Rather, they soon discovered educated Brahmans who were fluent in several languages and were literate as well. According to Vedic philosophy, education was the first of life's four stages through which every Hindu should pass in order to realise self-fulfilment. In the Goan society, two types of education existed, formal and informal. In the latter, children would learn their occupation from their parents, whether toddy-tapping, fishing, or cooking and keeping house. Formal education was conducted under the shade of a Banyan tree or in some shaded spot in the village square. Girls were denied formal education and were not instructed to read, write, nor solve arithmetical problems. Primary education was taught through the local language medium and came to be known as 'parishads' and 'pathasalas'.[22] To impart higher education the Brahmans created several institutions throughout Goa known as 'agraharas' and 'Brahmapuris'.[23]

Under the Muslim system, education was divided into primary 'maktab' and secondary 'madrasa' sections. Islamic education was very oriented towards Islamic philosophy and the subjects taught were of a religious nature. Tasfir (exegesis), Hadis (Islamic traditions) and Figh (Jurisprudence), along with grammar, logic and mysticism were subjects taught throughout one's education.[24] Arabic and Persian were taught at the secondary level for those pupils who desired government office employment and education in general was aimed towards securing employment.

These institutions were controlled by the 'Ulemas' (headmasters) and financially supported by tax-free gifts of land and wealthy Arab merchants.

Family, Housing, Habits and Leisure in Pre-Portuguese Society

Prior to the arrival of the Portuguese, the houses in Goa closely resembled those of its neighbours all along the Western Coast of India. They were usually one-storey with small doors and windows, whose floor was made of dirt and stones pressed firm and coated with cow dung. The house was built around a small open-air courtyard within which was situated the tulsi plant in its mandapam. This open square was used by the women to husk and pound rice and was a characteristic feature in Hindu homes.[25] Surrounding the inner courtyard was a covered veranda where the men would gather in the afternoon and evening to pass the hours in discussion and/or leisure. Radiating outwards from the inner veranda were the bedrooms, kitchen and sitting room. This type of house can still be found among the wealthy Hindus in the inland talukas of Goa, such as the Dessai family house in Bicholim. This inner courtyard is also found in the village of Chandor in some of the oldest, largest and most opulent Portuguese villas in Goa.[26] Houses of the Sudirs and outcasts were usually thatched or made from split bamboo and coconut leaves, covered by a thatched roof. In all homes, shoes were removed upon entering an abode. Before the construction of any house, a Hindu consulted an astrologer who would decide an auspicious day and time for such a major undertaking.[27]

Food habits were also highly ritual in pre-Portuguese society, especially among the Brahmins. Kanji, a rice gruel made by boiling rice and retaining a certain portion of the water and adding sugar, was the average breakfast of a Goan Hindu. In the wealthy homes fish, vegetables (bhaji), pickles and chutney were included as well. Lunch consisted of rice, fish, curry, bhaji, pickle and papad (a thin crisp cake which is made of several kinds of pulx, sago, potato, etc.). Poorer homes would cook only curry, rice and bhaji.[28] Dinner was the same as the day's lunch. The eating habits of the Brahmans were extremely ritualised, including bathing prior to food consumption, speaking mantras, wearing only a light white cloth and refraining from all meats and alcoholic drinks. The Saraswat Brahmans were the only exceptions in that they permitted the consumption of fish with their meals. Fresh fruits and sweets also accompanied meals. The consumption of liquor, specifically coconut feni, was popular among the lower castes though soma (the juice of hallucinogenic mushrooms), was used by Brahmans during some special religious rituals and was considered the drink of the gods.[29]

Habitual forms of dress also identified the Hindus in Goan society. All males excepting those in the highest classes wore very little clothing in public and certain tribes like the Gaudas had their own special form of crude sari created by tying a knot in the fabric below the left shoulder and allachey a strip of cloth which crossed the left shoulder and was fastened on the back. In the example of the Kunbi tribal community, women wore a red and white checked sari-style dress which is still occasionally seen in the rural Kunbi villages. The Brahmans and wealthy upper classes would wear a dhoti, duparta and turban while out in public and most persons prior to the Portuguese would have caste markings located somewhere on their bodies. Often unmarried daughters of Brahmans would have their caste markings tattooed on their foreheads and other twice-born classes also took up this trend.[30] The custom of tattooing originated in Goa amongst the Gaude tribe, where it was a popular custom from ancient days.[31]

In addition to caste markings, Hindu girls wore brightly coloured saris, gold jewellery from head to toe, scented flowers in their hair and vermillion paste in their hair if betrothed or married. A married woman also wore a mangalsutra, which was a necklace made of black beads strung on a gold wire as either a single chain or a double chain with a connecting pendant. Jewellery, like caste markings and clothing, reflected the wealth and status of the family and was a sign of prestige. The more wealth a family possessed, the more jewellery the women wore including earrings, anklets, bracelets and nose rings.[32] With the advent of the Muslims, jewellery continued as an important status symbol for women, though Muslim men were not in the habit of ornamenting their bodies. The educated and highly cultured also began to use jewellery more moderately. The culture which Islam diffused into Goa also affected the styles of dress in that era.

Wealthy Hindus wishing to imitate and/or identify with their political authorities adopted the long coat (caba) and tight-fitting pants characteristic of Arab attire, while some women began to wear the salwar Kameez.[33]

Goans enjoyed certain amusements prior to the Portuguese intervention, most of which were shared with their neighbours in Maharashtra. Marathi theatre-dramas depicting scenes from the Puranas, and popular epics especially the Mahabharata and the Ramayana, were a popular source of entertainment amongst the Hindu population in Goa. Village musicians and dancing girls also entertained in villages on certain occasions and weddings were a week-long village affair. The musical instruments in vogue were the veena, sarangi, dolak, cymbols, gumhot, madlem and the tasha and these were used to accompany most dances, theatres, festivals and folk arts.[34] Prior to the Portuguese, a Goan variety of Marathi music was in vogue in the region. The music was heavily influenced by its neighbour, excepting the *talas* of *vittras* (Dhamar, Savari, Tappa, Zumra, Hori, Tilwada), which are unique to Goan musical forms.[35] Each village also had its own Zatra, which consisted of a feast in addition to certain religious rites. Zatras lasted for several days during which time dancing, singing and the display of crafts were popular sights. Goa also had its share of folk art which took place on a separate space reserved for this purpose (a mand) and was centred around religious themes. Some examples of that period are the Perani Jagar, Musalam Khel, Ghodemodani, Goph, Phugdi, Khel and Tonyamel.[36] The Kunbi tribals also performed a special circle dance following a successful harvest in thanks and praise to the gods. All of these latter folk arts were performed in Konkani and were living reminders of the various historical forces which gave shape and colour to the Hindu society in Goa.

Family has always been the corner stone and nucleus of society. Family in Goa is more than a social grouping; it is a recognised institution. It is here where the first phase of enculturation takes place and where the morals and fundamental values in life are imparted. Most Hindu families were characterised by the joint-family system, whereby an extended family of parents, grandparents, children and sons' wives occupied the same living quarters. The eldest male member of the family managed the finances, religious rituals and attended any functions where family representation was required. The decision of the father was binding and final regarding all family matters and this patriarchal system continued throughout the ages among Hindu families. Hindu law permitted the sale of children owing to disobedience or famine and were usually bought by Muslims as slaves.[37]

Hindu Samskaras

The Samskaras were the Hindu sacraments important for the twice-born castes (*dvijas*) in Goa. They constituted the milestones in the life of an individual and were designed to incorporate the Hindu religion into all aspects of life. They also served the dual purpose of refinement, acculturation and acceptance of formal and informal laws. The Hindu Samskaras begin prior to birth and continue post-mortem. Garbhadana is a ceremony which expresses gratitude to God when the first signs of pregnancy are noticed.[38] This ushers in a period of confinement during which time the pregnant wife returns to her mother's house until the birth of the child. During the 7th month of pregnancy, the Simantonnayana Samskara occurred. On this occasion, a young (future) mother would be gifted with flowers, jewellery and sweet meats during a gathering of women who would then ask God to bless the woman and her unborn child. With the onset of labour pains, the expectant mother would be given to the care of a midwife for a period of 10 to 12 days. Following a successful delivery, the next Samskara in the life of a Hindu in Goan society occurred on the 6th evening following birth and was called 'Sathi'.[39] On this occasion, an all-night vigil was kept over the child as it was believed that on this night gods would come down to 'write' the future of the child on its forehead. On the 11th day after the birth of a child, both woman and new-born were ceremoniously bathed (Jatakarma) and the house cleaned following a period of impurity (contamination). During this period, which lasted for eleven days, no one could approach mother and child except the midwife and neither could perform other samskaras within this period. The Namakarana, Samskara (naming ceremony) was often performed at the same time as the Jatakarma, at which time the child was cradled.[40] Subsequent ceremonies included the Annaprasana, or first feeding ceremony, followed by the Chvdakarma (chaula) ceremony at which time a child's head was shaved as the first hair of a new born was considered impure.

The next Samskara was very important in the life of upper caste boys. Known as the Upanayana ceremony, this marked the beginning of Vedic studies and formal education, the first stage in life for a Hindu. Education was deemed necessary in the life of upper class boys as it developed an individuals's mental and spiritual capacities and prepared him to lead an upstanding life infused with religion. For Brahman boys, they could begin this stage of life as early as eight and as late as 16. For male members of the Kshyatria community, they could begin starting at the age of 11 but not after 22. For the Vaishyas, they begun their Vedic instruction by the age of 12 but not after 24.[41] Regardless of the age in which studies began, all boys would leave home and spend 12 years in the care and instruction of their particular teacher (guru). During this first stage celibacy was mandatory and it was known as the Brahmacharya stage. Once the Portuguese destroyed the temples, Brahmapuris and Agraharas in Goa existed though the true significance of this ceremony was lost in the coastal talukas of Goa.[42] Now this ceremony occurs only among young Brahman males who are endowed with the sacred thread at this time after having learned the various mantras which they must repeat on this occasion.

The second stage of marriage, was ushered in through the ceremony, a duly important Samskara in the lives of Hindus. Marriages were considered fixed by the stars (heavens) and indissoluble.[43] Monogamy was the preferred form of marriage alliance among the Hindus, but owing to the Muslim domination whose culture viewed more than one wife as a sign of status and prestige, some wealthy Hindu men had also taken more than one wife. In most cases the parents of the groom would make a proposal to the bride's parents and proposals were brought to women within the same caste but not within the same family as that of the groom. Prior to final marriage arrangements, an astrologer would be given the prospective couples' horoscopes to determine their compatibility and recommend an auspicious date for marriage.[44] Under this system a wife could not divorce her husband regardless of any atrocities he committed against her, but he could divorce her if she committed adultery, came down with a terminal disease, or did not bear him a son after 10 years.

Dowry (*stridhana*) was also part of this system whereby a daughter was given a portion of the family's wealth in movable property. Originally this took the form of gold jewellery, clothes and money; in later years furniture and other household items were included. The amount of dowry varied depending on the status of the bride and or groom. A groom earning a high salary would ask for a larger dowry and a bride with a deformity or other vice would have to provide a larger dowry in her marriage proposal. Among the low-caste masses the dowry system was not as widely observed, though parents made gifts in the form of money and clothes to the bride.

After an agreement was reached regarding dowry and the date of the marriage, preparations would begin for the wedding ceremony. On the first day of the ceremony, both bride and groom would be bathed according to tradition, which usually included being first doused in coconut water and then covered in sandalwood paste.[45] Throughout the wedding preparations which lasted from 2 to 3 days, the devadasis would dance and sing to herald the coming wedding. The groom on the day of marriage would visit the brides house and offer gifts, after which the bride would be given away formally (*kanya pradana*). The ceremony lasted between five and six days and from that point onwards the young bride, until she became pregnant with her first child, would remain at the home of her newlywed husband.

Last Rites for a Hindu, performed during the Anteya Samskara, lasted as long as 13 days. Following a Hindu's death, the corpse was bathed and placed on a bamboo/wooden pyre covered with a white cloth. The funeral procession began at the house of the deceased and proceeded to the cremation ground, led by the eldest son of the family. The latter then lit the funeral pyre and all would watch until the fire died. Sati would also be performed at this time. On the third day following the cremation ceremony the ashes were collected by the eldest son and placed in the sacred Naroa River or immersed into the sea. For ten days, the family of the deceased was considered in a state of 'death impurity' and confined themselves to the house.[46] On the 11th day the house was purified by sprinkling it with Panchagavya (milk, curd, ghee, urine and cow-dung) and the family members had ritual purification baths. On the 12th day, Varshantika, the relatives and friends of the deceased were invited over to the house for a feast. This date marked the Shrardha, which became the death anniversary for the deceased.

These customs were codified in 1526 under the administration of Albuquerque, however with the coming of the inquisition and the repressive regime in 1540, these customs were prohibited in the conquered territories of Ilhas, Bardez and Salcette.

Developments in Hindu Culture during the Portuguese Regime

The culture flourishing in the Konkan region prior to the 'historic accident' of the Portuguese arrival was, thus, a rich and vibrant one; literate, cultured, organised and economically viable. They had a very structured, ordered and religiously founded society complete with ancient philosophies, traditions and institutions. Though the Hindus suffered much destruction of their temples at the hands of the Muslims and some were forced to embrace Islam, the majority of the customs and traditions among the Hindus were left unaltered by the ruling administration of the Bahmanis. Though looked down upon as inferior, the Hindu people were capable of continuing in their ritual celebrations and customary traditions. The administration's main preoccupation was the collection of taxes, the domination of foreign trade and the maintenance of law and order.

However, when discussing the events which took place *following* the advent of the Portuguese, it is important to first remember that the talukas which compromise today's state of Goa did not all experience this enculturation process as they were under the authority of different administrations. Adil Shah's forces effectively controlled the region of Ponda, the Dessais of Bicholim and Sanguem talukas were his loyal feudatories, Pernem was under the Sawants of Wadi, the King of Sonda administered the talukas of Canacona and Quepem under the Mughal empire and the Sattari Ranes were the dominating force of that taluka. Thus, until these regions came under the effective control of the Portuguese in the late 1700's, they were not answerable to these new laws which were transforming the cultural identity of Christian converts in the old conquests. By the time they did become answerable to these new laws, the seeds of rebellion had already been sown in both the new and old conquests which effectively prevented any further talukas from identifying with the Portuguese administration. They continued in a socio-cultural evolution contiguous with the neighbouring regions until the Portuguese imposed their laws and sanctions, to which a variety of rebellions arose. These talukas experienced classic forms of cultural diffusion and borrowing and their cultures evolved along the lines continuous with their past history.

Prior to the Portuguese, the language and culture of Marathi had been an integral part of the Goan culture. Marathi and Sanskrit religious texts were widely in use among the Brahman and other 'twice-born' communities and most youth in Goa went to Marathi-medium schools. A Konkani-Marathi dialect was the first used by the Portuguese missionaries to educate the native population in Catholic doctrine and Marathi was the medium of dramas, temple performances and all aspects of Hindu high culture in Goa.[47] Upon the advent of the Portuguese, Marathi schools, texts and all forms of the performing arts were banned by the European authorities. They felt that the Marathi language harboured anti-Portuguese feelings and pro-Indian sentiments which was, therefore, detrimental to the administration whose goal became the complete Lusitanisation of the local Catholic converts.

The majority of Hindus in the Goan society was not subject to the Portuguese administrative regulations until 1788, when the New Conquests were firmly in the latter's hands. By this time also, the Portuguese administration imposed mostly their laws and social hierarchy on the people and the zealous proselytisation which had been undertaken in the Old Conquests did not reach the same feverish pitch in the New Conquests. Thus, the Hindu-Marathi culture in Goa continued to evolve throughout the early years when the Portuguese possessed only the Old Conquests and even following the annexation of the New Conquests the culture continued to evolve. While Christians were educated in Portuguese parish schools or English-medium institutions, the Hindu community preferred to establish their own schools in the

Marathi-medium for the first five years of formal education. Subsequent to those five years, their children would attend either Portuguese or English-medium schools. In this way, they kept alive their mother tongue and maintained the traditions of their ancestors.

While the new converts to Catholicism were cut off from their heritage and encouraged to assimilate the Portuguese culture, the Hindu community in Goa looked towards the neighbouring State of Maharashtra for their identification and cultural cues. The Marathi language consequently became the main link whereby the two communities, so alike in culture and history, could exchange ideas and develop along similar lines. These links manifested in many facets of Goan Hindu life, including cultural programmes, music, theatre, religious rituals, festivals, newspapers and journals, all of which were transmitted through the Marathi medium. The Hindu culture of Goa not only survived but even flourished despite its ban in the New Conquests and the administration's attempts to abolish Marathi in the Portuguese possessions. D.V. Pai, editor of the *Hindu*, wrote in 1938: "If the creek of Marathi language had not flowed in Goa, the small lake of its Hindu society would have been permanently isolated from the mainstream of Maharashtran Hindu society and consequently it would have stagnated or would have merged into the powerful lagoon of the nearby Christian society. The Goan Hindu society feels indebted to Marathi which has enabled them to preserve their Indian roots."[48] Thus, as Konkani was the binding force which kept alive the roots of Indian culture in Catholic Goa, Marathi and its time-honoured literary heritage bound the Goan Hindus to his culture even through times of oppression and distress.

The region of Goa had opted for the North Indian Hindustani styles of artistic expression rather than the Karnatakan styles which flourished in Goa's Southern neighbour. Goan Hindus excelled as court singers, classical dancers, accomplished vocalists, composers/performers of Bhajan (devotional song) and as instrumentalists skilled in the playing of tabla, sitar, sarungi, shehnai and other North Indian classical instruments. This music continued to evolve in the New Conquests throughout the Portuguese period in India, producing talented individuals such as Mohana Palkar (court dancer-singer), Morarba Pednekar (vocalist - instrumentalist), Babay Palkar (shehnai) and

Pandharinath Nageshkar (tabla). Hundreds of other accomplished musical artists arose from the region of Goa, all of whom devoted much time and effort to the classical Indian forms of artistic expression.[49]

In addition to the cultural heritage which identified itself with Maharashtra and its native language, the events and discourses which pervaded the Marathi journals in that State of British-India also permeated into the Goan Hindu society. Through newspapers and journals from Maharashtra, ideas of 'nationalism' diffused into Goa, which educated the Goan Hindu community politically and fostered an identification with the issues and concerns which the locals in the Indian Union discussed. Changes which occurred in Maharashtran society, therefore, had a profound influence on subsequent evolutionary trends in Goan Hindu society. In a similar manner, when Maharashtra set forth a series of reforms dedicated to the abolishment of child-marriage and untouchability, the Hindu community in Goa addressed such issues in their society as well. Shunned and condemned by the Portuguese administration, the local Goan Hindu society did not look to Portuguese culture for fresh innovations into its culture; rather they began to take cultural 'cues' from the neighbouring state of Maharashtra. As a consequence, Goan Hindu society under the Portuguese repressive administration evolved along lines similar to the neighbouring State of Maharashtra from which it took its cultural cues and from where ideas both political and cultural diffused into Goa and enabled evolution to continue according to the direction taken by traditional Hindu India.

THE WAKE OF PORTUGUESE RULE

Acculturation into Catholicism during Phase II

Before entering into a discussion concerning the laws and customary practices which the Portuguese imposed on their new subjects, it is important to place their activities in the proper historical context lest the reader conclude that the Portuguese were domineering racists whose behaviour will forever go down in the annuls of history as atrocious and inhuman. Were it not for the Portuguese arrival in Goa, the people would have continued to suffer under the heavy tax burden of Adil Shah, which demanded 1/2 to 2/3 of the village agricultural produce.

Some historians even argue that by defeating the Muslims and weakening their hold in the coastal areas, the Portuguese acted as a catalyst which saved the Hindu religion and various kingdoms from complete domination by Muslim forces. It is difficult to say decisively what course the events in history would have taken, but it is certain that the Portuguese broke the trade monopoly of the Arabs in the Indian sub-continent which weakened the Arabs economically continued to check the Arab advancements throughout their time in India. In addition to their activities directed against the Arabs, the Portuguese also should be remembered for improving the position of women in their territories, a practice which eventually diffused throughout the upper classes of Hindus who had contact (commercial or otherwise) with the Portuguese and Christian converts. And finally, the activities of the clergy had the effect of loosening the rigid barriers between the different castes, awakening the creativity among the people and establishing educational institutions which benefitted many classes of people, not only the upper castes.

The Portuguese, especially the religious authorities, felt that both spiritual and temporal conversion to Portuguese Catholic ways of life were necessary to establish a colony faithful to the Portuguese interests. Though Albuquerque originally allowed religious freedom of the Hindus and allowed them to live by their own set of codified laws, by 1540 a new administration arrived which significantly changed the status quo. As a result, every one of the aforementioned traditions underwent significant change among both communities. Though the changes most deeply affected the new converts to Christianity, even the Hindus could not escape these new laws which forbade such practices as Sati and temple celebrations in the Old Conquests. Converts were forced to abdicate all of their former customs and traditions following conversion to Christianity and were prohibited from studying in the Hindu literary traditions. This was done with the intention of creating a colony in India loyal to the Portuguese crown, whose people would transfer their sense of political identity and martial sacrifice to Portugal.

The 'historical accident' in the Old Conquests, therefore, resulted in the eventual decision by many to undergo a second major enculturation phase wherein the Portuguese culture was imitated and absorbed. What resulted following 100 years of Portuguese cultural dominance was in fact the successful establishment and formation of a native Christian colony identified, at least superficially if not entirely, with Portugal. The imposition of the Portuguese laws and ways of life on the Christian converts ushered in major changes in the three coastal talukas which altered the evolutionary path of social history. By offering government jobs, land grants and other privileges to those communities who converted, combined with repressive legislation against those who refused, the Portuguese were able to convert thousands of natives to Christianity. It is to these talukas that this work now turns, to examine first the laws and ways of life of the Portuguese in Goa and then to an examination of the synergy between old and new cultural forms which eventually resulted after 100 years of Portuguese rule.

Social Structure of Portuguese Goa

The slave enterprise and the society into which it arose resulted in significant changes and alterations in the social structure of Goa. 'On top' of the existing caste structure, the Portuguese attached their own class structure which included the various ethnic mixtures they produced. At the top of this new social stratification were the *Reinois*, the Portuguese nationals who served a specific term in government office in Goa and were not permanent residents. These were further divided into the higher nobility, *fidalgos* and the lesser nobility, *nobres*. The *Casados* occupied the second rung of the social hierarchy and were Portuguese nationals who married native women and settled in Goa. They were given money, privileges, landed property and government jobs upon announcement of their engagement. This second tier was further sub-divided into the *Casticos* of pure Portuguese blood and *Mesticos*, the offspring of married Portuguese men and native women. Below the mesticos came the *Mulattoes*, the offspring resulting from the Portuguese slave masters and their female African slaves. After these new segments of society came the native neo-Christian system with all of its sub-castes and communities. The Naturais, as they were called, consisted (in descending order) of the Brahmans, Kshatryias, Vaishayas and Shudras. Slaves and outcasts (tribals) occupied a much lower rung on this ladder. The bottom-most position on the scale of social privilege belonged to the non-Christians, Hindus and Muslims alike, who were denied most of their rights and lost many of the privileges they once enjoyed. This was the new social order following the annexation of Bardez and Salcette and the adoption of new, discriminative policies which occurred concurrently between the years 1540 to 1543.[50]

However, among the old social order which placed Hindu Brahmans at the top, the policies adopted by the Portuguese were not considered valid. From their perspective, the Hindu civilisation was far superior to that of the new administration in terms of literature, social behaviour, personal hygiene and tradition. When their brethren left the Hindu fold to adopt the religion and consequently the privileges of the Portuguese administration, they were outcast by the Hindu community and lost all rank and privilege which they had hitherto enjoyed. This defensive reaction served to alienate the new converts from their culture and probably inadvertently bonded the converts more securely to their new rulers, knowing that they could never again rejoin the Hindu fold as rightful citizens. Thus, the year 1540 marked the beginning of a new social system arising in Goa and a new community of natives who began to identify with the Portuguese. The Hindus were forced to recognise the authority of the Portuguese, however, when the non-Christian converts were prohibited from completing their functions as village Gauncars.

Slavery under the Portuguese

Slavery had existed under the Muslims prior to the Portuguese and in the Hindu system whereby the Shudras and outcasts lived in virtual servitude to the upper, twice-born castes. Under the Portuguese, however, the system of slavery took on an even greater dimension and came to affect not only the social structure but the economy and ethnic identity of the Portuguese in Goa. Under the Arabs, spices and Arabian horses had been the most lucrative traded commodities in Goa. With the introduction of African slaves by the Portuguese, however, the slave trade became the most lucrative business in Portuguese Goa. Slaves were bought and sold in the Praca de Leilao, where they were carefully examined and forced to demonstrate their strength, dexterity and other skills required of a slave. Slaves had absolutely no rights and were not considered as human beings. They were encouraged to procreate by their masters and the offspring were considered the property of the slave-owner. Slaves were left uneducated and their sole purpose was to perform the agricultural labour and menial household tasks considered unfit for the Portuguese nobles and wealthy merchants. The wealthy converts also adopted this attitude and bought slaves to tend their fields and perform the household chores.

As the years went by and the population of slaves in Goa increased, priests and members of the clergy encouraged Catholic slave-owners to uplift their slaves by educating them in the Christian doctrine and encouraging them to act in civilised ways. The wealthy were asked to take better care of their slaves and consider them at least as human beings though inferior in intellect. They also created an ordinance whereby a slave who converted to Christianity would be freed after eight years of service to his master, an act which encouraged the conversion of many slaves.[51]

Such stipulations were set by the Church owing to a growing concern among the clergy regarding the treatment of slaves and the latter's public behaviour. Portuguese men often had illicit sexual relations with their female slaves which resulted in numerous mestico children. Male slaves were let out to roam the streets at night and seek vengeance on their master's enemies.[52] The city of Goa became notorious for such night-time brawls and robberies which slave masters encouraged. Word of such atrocities spread as far as Portugal and eventually a decree in 1869 abolished the institution of slavery. It nonetheless continued in the Portuguese colonies for several decades following the decree and only after 1900 was the practice fully arrested in Goa.

Economy and Administration

Until the 1540's, the people of Goa were allowed to continue in their customary practices even while conversion began. Upon the arrival of the Portuguese in Goa, Albuquerque reduced the heavy tax to which the natives had been subjected and gave political amnesty to all followers of the Hindu religion who had been persecuted under Muslim rule. Albuquerque renovated the summer palace of Adil Shah in Panjim and fortified the city with the construction of walls and fortalezas. He expanded the number of dockyards from one to three and hired many skilled natives to construct Portuguese warships. He further established a mint in 1510 with which he began to produce coins specifically for Goa and imported a printing press to facilitate the publication of books and other administrative documents.[53] In 1511 he founded the municipality of Goa which consisted of ten Portuguese officers, a captain major and a feitor (to oversee commercial operations), as well as an official scribe (escrivao). In what became known as the 'House of 24', the craft guilds and artisans were represented and delegates were assigned to advocate their interests. He maintained the communicate form of village administration and kept the Thanadars as his tax-collectors.[54] The Gauncars were also permitted to keep the 'jon' (village surplus) for themselves as they had done under previous ruling administrations.

The economy under the Portuguese continued to flourish. It was fundamentally a feudalistic society and large landowners emerged in the upper classes whose fields were tended by slaves. The Goan textile industry flourished in a marked comparison to what had happened to the artisans and weavers under the British rule. Usury became another lucrative business among the rich who would lend money with a monthly interest of 6-8 per cent.[55] Agriculture was also utilised to its fullest extent and the Portuguese found they were forced to import rice and other food grains from the coast of Karnataka owing to a shortage in Goa. Trade continued to prosper from the sale of Arabian horses, spices and other commodities previously traded under Arab rule and slaves were an addition to this commercial traffic.

In the Goan society there was also a social stratification based on wealth, although in both Hindu and Portuguese Goan societies finances did not matter quite as much as ascribed status. The merchants and nobles enjoyed the most material wealth and as was customary in society, they displayed their wealth in a variety of forms. Imported luxuries, travel by palanquins, escorts of slaves, fine clothing and large palatial homes were some of the more ostentatious forms of wealth in which the nobles indulged. Within the Portuguese society the traders, large land holders and those in high military/government positions lived their lives in great luxury.

Position of Women under the Portuguese

The Portuguese administration did much to improve the social position of the native converts, through both informal and formal regulations. Polygamy was prohibited among the Christian converts and divorce was only allowed under extreme conditions. The Cannon Law prohibited child marriage among the converts, insisting that girls reach the age of 14-16 and boys the age of 16-18 before getting married.[56] Christian women could inherit property and widows who converted to Christianity were allowed to remarry. The practice of Sati was abolished and those families who were caught practising this custom were fined and their lands were confiscated. Sati was perceived by the Portuguese clergy as a practice designed to rid in-laws of an unwanted female burden, adopt the deceased couple's children and make them slaves and as a way to regain the properties and jewellery of the newly deceased. Though critics argued that this prohibition was motivated by a desire to gain more converts and the lands which these women could now inherit, there certainly was a humane underlying force as well which felt sorry for the young brides who had to offer up their lives as well following the death of their husbands.

Women were permitted to converse openly with strangers as did their Portuguese counterparts and were not considered morally lax if they smiled in public. Under the Cannon Law, first cousins could not marry as was the custom among Hindu families to keep the property within the family.[57] Women were expected to participate in social and religious functions, including attending banquet functions where they were asked to dance with men. Whereas Hindus separated themselves by gender in nearly all walks of life, the Portuguese society, though gender-conscious, requested the presence of women at social functions and did not exclude them as much from participation in social life. They were considered as individuals and consulted prior to the taking of some important decisions.

Converts were asked to imitate and dress like the Portuguese women under western influence. These were usually calf-length dresses in vibrant colours consistent with the styles in vogue in Europe. Jewellery was also used by the Catholic women, though more for decoration than as a display of wealth. Elaborate designs and different varieties were available following this new administration and the goldsmiths began to craft designs such as crosses, Jesus and Mother Mary to cater to the needs of the Catholic community who still supported the system of 'stridhana' (dowry). The women converts also began the practice of wearing rosaries around their necks or holding them in their hands while in public. An ordinance of 1644 prohibited women from wearing nose rings and this custom fell out of practice among the natives.

Upper-class Portuguese women moved about in palanquins covered by parasols accompanied by slave girls while going to church or on other outings. The upper class Portuguese women used a separate entrance when going to church and sat in a secluded section of the hall.[58] Though they were denied formal institutionalised education, women learned a variety of arts at home such as musical instruments, singing, reading, writing and embroidery. These arts were not considered the domain of devadasis, as in the Hindu system, but were marks of high culture and refinement. The middle class and the converted natives tried to imitate the upper class through similar displays of wealth. At times they resorted to borrowing suits and employing slaves only on Sundays to give the pretence of wealth.

Social Welfare Institutions

In addition to the Seven Sacraments administered by the clergy in Goa, the Portuguese established several educational and social institutions whose underlying motive was to create a loyal, educated Portuguese colony of natives in Goa and thereby attract more people into the Catholic fold. The Santa Casa de Misercordia (Holy House of Mercy), was initially founded by 100 Portuguese men and open only to Portuguese citizens who were poor, wounded from battle, widowed or disabled. In 1545 the role of the institution expanded to caring for orphan girls sent from Lisbon and seeing that they were given dowries land and government jobs for those Portuguese citizens who would marry them. Owing to this expansion, the institution was later divided in 1605 and a recluse house for widows and orphans was established.

The Portuguese also constructed hospitals in Goa which eventually replaced the Hindu system of shamans, pandits, mid-wives and exorcists. The first hospital was completed in 1542, though a make-shift one had existed in Goa since the time of the conquest. The impetus for this institution came out of concern for the wounded soldiers and ailing sailors who needed special treatment and care. In addition to war injuries and sickness arriving from the sea, Goa was a host to a variety of epidemic outbreaks related to sanitation problems and on several occasions major outbreaks of dysentery and cholera would cause significant human loss in the Portuguese overseas colonies. In addition to the first Royal Hospital (House of Mercy) established in 1542, the hospital of St. Roque arose in 1551 to treat the locals and even the non-Christians. Two additional hospitals were founded to help the poor converts and were known as asylums.

The Portuguese rule, thus, affected not only culture, education and social structure, but also the concept and treatment of illness. The Portuguese introduced the allopathic system of medicine which used drugs and knowledge of the body based on scientific experimentation and physical examination in order to cure illness. Previously homeopathic and ayurvedic medicine was used for treatments by the Vaidyas who enjoyed respected positions in Hindu society.[59] Brahman priests were also consulted owing to the belief that evil spirits had visited the homes of ill people. Exorcists were often called to remove the evil spirit from within an individual who was believed to have fallen ill owing to such spirit possession. Under the Portuguese administration, all of these earlier forms of healing were discarded as false and scandalous and the native converts were prohibited from seeking the help of such 'false' doctors when they were afflicted with disease. Under Catholic thought, illness resulted from the will of God but could be treated with medications by a doctor. Likewise, a patient's survival and/or untimely death was also considered to be in the hands of God and 'of His will'.

Education

The Portuguese constructed many institutions for the education of children and in 1514 Alfonso de Albuquerque established the first school in Goa.[60] The impetus for the institution arose from the growing number of illegitimate Portuguese children in the city of Goa who were in need of education and training so as not to become wayward youth. Most schools in Goa were, in fact, initially designed to admit only Portuguese children, but most eventually admitted those native children from the upper classes who were capable of advanced studies. By 1567 a law was established which prohibited the functioning of Hindu schools in the New Conquests, thus, an individual could go out of the colony to get an education or he could convert to Catholicism and join the Portuguese-Catholic religious institutions. The language of instruction was Portuguese and the natives had to first attend the Portuguese primary schools in order to learn the language fluently. This they did in the village parish schools, which unlike the Hindu system which admitted only the upper class, enabled converts from any class and caste to send their children for an education. Girls were not admitted into these formal institutions during the early years of their inception, but they received an informal education at home and later were allowed to attend the parish primary schools. The goal of Christian education under the Portuguese was to develop mature students who had developed in the areas of intellect, morality and social behaviour.[61]

In the initial years following the conquest, the Indian children were denied access to the educational institutions of the Jesuits. Other educational institutions of the Hindus and Muslims having been banned in the New Conquests the natives at first had few chances of securing education under the religious orders. Mesticos were accepted in the schools, but others were denied access because of the staunch racial prejudice of the Portuguese. Owing to a Royal Decree of King Joao III in 1545, primary education at parish schools for the native converts became mandatory. By the 1600's natives were finally admitted into the educational institutions, but even then the Jesuits retained the practice of racial discrimination until 1758.[62]

In 1541 the Jesuits founded the Seminary of the Holy Faith with its attached College of St. Paul. The college was designed to educate the young converts, who were taught Portuguese, Latin, Christian doctrine and music. The secondary aim of the institution was to help in the 'character formation' of the boys in terms of manners, respectful customs and proper social behaviour according to the western culture. The school system began with language studies in the early years, then broadened to humanistic studies (grammar, rhetoric, poetry and western literature). Once passing through the humanities, the student went on to the arts (philosophy, logic, mathematics, science) after which time he received a Bachelor of Arts degree.[63] The final faculty and one intended for those wishing to be ordained as priests, was that of theology. The school lasted for nine years, three at the elementary level and six at the collegiate level. The student body was international and contained youth from Ceylon, Java, Malaysia, Burma and China.[64]

To encourage the establishment of schools and colleges were given maintenance funds from the administration and free land endowments of lands formerly occupied by temples and Hindu institutions.

In 1560 the Jesuits were given permission to Christianise the southern taluka of Salcette. They founded Holy Spirit College in 1574 in Margao and taught students Konkani (in Kannada script) and Catholic moral theology. In 1578 following a Muslim invasion, the college was attacked and set to flames. It was rebuilt in the Rachol Fort in 1610 and included a primary school where Portuguese, Konkani and simple arithmetic were taught. Several Konkani schools also emerged during the early years of Portuguese rule, but following an ordinance in 1754 by the then Archbishop of Goa, Portuguese was deemed the necessary language of the people and it, rather than Konkani, became emphasised in the school systems. The prestige of Konkani then quickly deteriorated and it became a 'second class' language in Goa.[65]

Through this system, the Dominican College was established in 1554 which matriculated only Portuguese and mestico students. This Colegio Academico instructed its all-male student body in reading, writing, arithmetic, Christian theology and sacred music at the elementary level.[66] In a similar manner, the Franciscans were given permission to Christianise the taluka of Bardez and they established the Monte de Guirim seminary and the College of Santo Boaventura. Likewsie, the Augustinians Order established itself in Goa in the year 1572. In 1622 a school and convent were founded in Neura village, dedicated to St. John the Baptist.[67] Both Portuguese and native Catholic students were admitted into these institutions, where they studied reading, writing, Portuguese grammar, Catholic doctrine and Western music. In 1633 the

Colegio de Nossa Senhora de Populo was constructed in the city of Goa which admitted students who had passed out of the Neura school and wished to continue in higher studies. In 1630 the Carmelites arrived in Goa and constructed an elementary school, monastery and College of Carmo and the Convent of St. Monica; all of which were patterned after the existing parish schools of other Catholic orders in Goa.[68]

At the parish level native Christians were admitted into the village schools. Children of all castes within the Catholic fold could attend and Portuguese, Konkani, Christian doctrine and sacred music (hymns, etc.) were the subjects taught at these village-level schools.[69] A rigid structure of inculcating the Catholic doctrine into the children was followed and all classes were infused with religion. Natural science was ignored and young minds were encouraged to absorb the said doctrines of Catholicism rather than question the world around them. At these schools the Portuguese began infusing their culture into the young minds of children while they were still in Phase I characterised by undiscriminating, subconscious absorption.

Here, then, is where the most important and lasting efforts at 'cultural conversion' took place. Everyday children would learn the basic tenets of Christianity, the 'proper' moral values to hold dear (honesty, love of God, respect for elders, etc.) and the importance of Confession and other Catholic sacraments. They grew up under the supervision of teachers dedicated to this enculturative effort and these same youth began to internalise the value-orientation and culture idealised by the Portuguese. This had long-reaching effects on the character formation of Goan children as well and reached down into all community levels whose parents had sent their children to school in this system. First, the children grew up 'protected' and 'privileged' by the ruling administration and were rewarded according to their likeness in behaviour and mannerisms to those of the upper Portuguese classes. Because of their constant exposure to social role models (teachers, priests) who further embodied the Portuguese ideals, the children also began to identify with them and internalise their value systems and religious beliefs. Good manners, respect for elders, honesty, contentment, obedience and unquestioned love of God and Jesus were the ideals imparted to the young minds of native converts.

Thus, the children of this first generation represent the first 'real' cultural products of this acculturation process because only they were introduced to the doctrine and ways of life of the Portuguese before they had developed the processes of discrimination which heralds Phase II of enculturation. But school, as even educators come to realise, is only one of the major aspects of early acculturation. Home life and family are also big influences which leave even deeper imprints in the psyche of an individual social being. Thus, the Catholic child absorbed both styles of behaviour and both cultures; that of their parents who underwent Phase I of acculturation in their pre-Portuguese environments and that of their new social role models who advocated the Portuguese culture. The children exposed to these two environments absorbed both equally and did not recognise the 'duality' which both sides separately may have felt. These children harmonised both lifestyles and cultural ideals within their own psyches and merged the two cultures fluidly. While they identified with the Portuguese owing to their presence as ideal social role models, they naturally imbibed many of the cultural patterns at home which were consistent with the pre-Portuguese culture in Goa.

The Provincial Councils

The 1560's heralded serious changes in the existing laws and stipulations in Portuguese Goa. By order of the Provincial Councils which were the law-making body of the Inquisition, formal rules and ordinances were enforced in the Portuguese overseas possessions. These Councils set forth laws in 1567, 1575, 1583, 1592 and 1600.[70] The law of 1560 went so far as to banish the Hindu Brahmans from the Goan islands for disturbing insubordination and harassing the converts. The Provincial Councils asked the King of Portugal to protect the interests of the new converts in both social and economic concerns. In 1560 alone, 12,000 Hindus from the villages of Daugim, Batim, Movla, Mercondim and Carambolim converted en masse to the Catholic religion. In that same year 2,270 people from the single village of Agassaim also converted under pressure from the Portuguese administration and the Inquisition[71]. The majority of these conversions were among the low caste communities, the results of which made them exempt from taxes which they could not otherwise afford.

An edict ordered in 1736, summarised below illustrates the extent to which the laws of the Portuguese administration attempted to permeate into the culture and lifestyles of the native Catholic converts:[72]

- Neo-converts should not use Hindu musical instruments during wedding celebrations;
- Biddies (areca nut and beetle leaf) should not be given out during ceremonies;
- Ovios (a form of Marathi poetry) should not be recited during ceremonies;
- The milling of rice or grinding of cereals during wedding ceremonies was discouraged;
- The tel (anointment in oil) ritual should not be practised during wedding ceremonies;
- Pandals "with festoons of leaves" should not be erected in front of the houses of bride and groom;
- Footwear should not be removed by those who serve food at banquets;
- Feasts following the death of relatives should not be arranged;
- Rice should be boiled using salt;
- Hindu and Catholic feast days must not coincide on the same day;
- Males should not wear dhotis, females should not wear cholis and saries;
- The tulsi plant should not be planted near a Catholic house;
- Betel and areca nut should not be planted and harvested;
- Bride and groom must not have rice placed on their foreheads on the wedding day;
- Bride and groom must not distribute edible gifts to the houses of relatives;

- The all-night vigil observed following the 6th day of a child's birth should not be practised;
- Catholic labourers must not seek employment from Hindu landlords;
- Hindu converts to Catholicism were exempted from the payment of land tax;
- Widows and daughters of a deceased Hindu could inherit the latter's property if they converted;
- A son/daughter who converts to Catholicism is entitled by the law to 1/3 of his/her father's property; and
- Hindus residing in Goa must attend Catholic mass regularly.

The Councils also put restrictions on the converts interaction with their Hindu brethren. New converts could not remain living in the house with their Hindu relatives, as the latter were thought to cause a relapse in the behaviour of the former. This effectively ended the practice where one member of the family would convert to Catholicism in order to protect the family property and privileges. This restriction also served to further isolate the converts from their old ways of life and associations so that they could better adapt to the Portuguese way of life. They were forbidden from having any type of relationship with Hindus; familial, mercantile, occupational, or otherwise. In 1644 an order issued by the Councils forbade natives from wearing anything of Hindu origin, especially among the women. They were also discouraged from richly adorning themselves in jewellery and other ornaments. Through these restrictions and laws, the Portuguese administration succeeded in moulding many of the converts to the Portuguese ways of life, at least on a superficial level.[73] Many of these same laws pre-date the visible cultural differences still present today. For example, Catholics women in Goa today do not wear nose rings and the tulsi plant is not planted by the house as it is in Hindu houses.

Catholic Sacraments

The sacraments followed by the Catholic church replaced the Hindu sacraments of old for those who joined the Christian fold. Baptism, Confession, Holy Communion, Confirmation, Holy

Matrimony, Holy Orders and Extreme Unction were the seven sacraments which were integral in the lives of Catholics and became the traditions followed by the native converts. The first sacrament, Baptism, was the process whereby a child or new convert became admitted into the church. White garments were worn to symbolise purity and innocence and the converts were annointed with holy oil by the officiating priests. This sacrament also functioned as a naming ceremony for the child. In the case of new converts, during the baptism ceremony they were given new names which were of Portuguese origin to replace those which designated one's Hindu caste. This is how Portuguese surnames were adopted by native Goan Catholics. Confession was the next sacrament performed by a baptised individual once he reached the age of logic and reason. Converts were required to confess their 'sins' committed intentionally or not, which were then absolved by the officiating priest. This sacrament continued throughout one's life and was not a single affair such as Baptism. Holy Communion followed the first confession and subsequent to receiving this sacrament a child could receive communion following the mass service. The Portuguese and wealthy native converts would celebrate this sacrament with a banquet followed by a dance.[74]

Confirmation was the next important sacrament in the lives of young Catholics and was preceded by a series of classes designed to strengthen the faith of a Catholic and help him to lead a pious life. The important doctrines of the Catholic faith were taught prior to this sacrament, when an individual became 'confirmed' into the Catholic religion. Holy Orders were reserved for those wishing to devote one's life to the service of the Church as a priest or a nun. Special educational institutions were developed in Goa for this purpose and they involved ten years in dedicated study of Latin, philosophy and moral theology. Upon completion of the ten years, a student could be ordained to become a priest or could join the clergy as a Lay brother.[75] Those who became priests were asked to take vows of poverty, celibacy and obedience to the Catholic church.

Matrimony was the sixth sacrament whereby a man and woman were joined in holy union by an officiating priest in the church witnessed by family and friends. The exchange of gold rings replaced the tying of the Mangalsutra and the wedding celebrations were shortened to two or three days rather than the customary five or six. The final sacrament (last rites) was known as extreme unction in the Catholic religion and was given to a person on the verge of death. The individual about to expire was anointed with holy oil and was asked to repent for his sins whereupon the officiating priest would ask God to forgive the individual and receive him into his kingdom. Following the death of an individual, his body was placed in a wooden coffin and carried in procession to the burial ground. With close friends and family gathered, the priest would through handfuls of earth onto the coffin as it was lowered into the earth.[76]

The first four sacraments were compulsory among Catholics in Goa and were designed to enculturate the converts into the new methods and rituals followed by the Portuguese. Each sacrament was followed by a social gathering of relatives and friends which usually took the form of a feast. Converts were expected to follow these sacraments and other Portuguese cultural traditions and were not allowed to celebrate their weddings in the traditional Hindu-Indian style. These sacraments replaced those of the Hindu religion and by the time the children of the converts had passed through all of these sacraments, they were full-fledged Catholics who knew no other faith. Prohibited from associating with anything reminiscent of the pre-Portuguese Hindu culture, these sacraments indoctrinated the young in a new belief system which became their very own within one or two generations.

Family, Food, Housing, and Leisure

Besides changing the administration and customs of the territory known as Goa, the Portuguese also altered the landscape with the construction of churches and bungalows. The houses were built in the Iberian style with long, high windows conducive to ventilation and verandas which lined the front of the house. The houses had large and ornate doors and most had two levels. Imported home furnishings were in vogue among the wealthy natives and upper class Portuguese nationals, who brought carved wooden tables, chairs and beds, brass lamps, wine glasses, Chinese porcelain and embroidered linen[77]. The sitting room consisted of rows of wooden chairs and sofas lining the walls of the sitting room. Surrounding the house was a garden of plants and fruit trees, whose maintenance was the domain of the slaves.

The Portuguese also encouraged the native converts to adopt food habits similar to their own. The major difference between the two groups was the consumption of meat especially beef. Under the Hindu religious code, the cow was a sacred animal, thus, its consumption was strictly prohibited. Under the Portuguese, however, this meat was cherished as a culinary delight and the converts too began to adopt the practice of eating beef and pork. A typical Portuguese breakfast would consist of porridge, jam and bread, butter, cheese, eggs, milk, coffee or tea and fresh fruit.[78] Following breakfast the Portuguese had served with sweets. Soup, salad, pork, beef, chicken, fish, rice and fruits was the usual lunch served in a variety of combinations. Dinner was served between 7 and 9 p.m. and consisted of the remaining food from the lunch meal. Dining tables, chairs and elaborate place settings were in vogue and port wine was a standard accompaniment to the meal. Women dined with their families accept in the presence of guests and slaves served the upper class in the houses of nobles and fidalgos.[79]

Amusement in Goa took a variety of forms under the Portuguese rule. All the leisure activities formerly enjoyed such as the devadasis, Marathi theatres and temple feasts were prohibited in the Old Conquests and attendance by native Christians was forbidden. In their stead, other amusements were established which supplanted the old forms of leisure. The Church feast replaced the former village feast and in addition to high mass the church surrounds held a mela and arts competitions. As each village was given a patron saint to replace family deities, these annual feasts grew in importance and became big affairs where natives would come dressed in suits and fancy dresses for the occasion. In addition to various Church Feasts, each village celebrated a Christmas feast and an Easter feast, following the 40-day lent period characterised by fasting. In later years the festival known as Corpus Christi was celebrated in July and was celebrated by all the churches.[80]

Thus, those who were able to identify with the Portuguese culture and administration usually belonged to the upper castes and enjoyed privileged positions in government service. Often, they had been educated entirely by the Catholic missionaries and had internalised them as social role models within the context of Portuguese culture. As converts were praised for their likeness to the Portuguese themselves, they began to derive their source of pride from their ability to most closely resemble their rulers in all but skin colour. It became a vicious cycle in favour of the Portuguese culture wherein the more the converts resembled and identified with the Portuguese, the more they were encouraged to do so and to experience their pride as a product of this resemblance. Thus, beyond adopting the customs, dress and mannerisms of the Portuguese, they attempted full identification with them, including leisure pursuits, women's many social roles, language patterns and social interaction. Even today aspects of Catholic Goan culture which differ substantially from Hindu culture are primarily the results of these laws and codes put in place during those early years.

War: Casualties Failed Assimilation of the Gauda Community

Some groups, however, could not acculturate to the habits and customs of the Portuguese. Specifically, some tribal communities such as the Gaudes and other lower class natives could not give up their former ways of life. Most had converted owing to impoverished conditions and a desire to increase their social rank and privileges, but were neither educated nor able to fully grasp the requirements which such conversion entailed. Many were former outcasts and still adhered to some traditional beliefs and worshipped special spirits unattached to the Hindu pantheon. Owing to the upper class converts who were dogmatic about adhering to the social hierarchy, these lower communities were often excluded from Catholic religious life, education and experience and, therefore, did not identify with the Portuguese. Because they had converted, they were now also outcast from the Hindu community and suffered extreme alienation. Neither community seemed willing to accept them and with the coming of the Inquisition, communities like the Gaudes found it even more difficult to extricate themselves from their predicament. Consequently, many moved from South to Karwar and coastal Karnataka during the 1560's, where the Inquisition would not bother them.

For those Gaudes who stayed in Goa and survived the inquisition, the majority of the community could not identify fully with the Catholic religion to the Portuguese satisfaction, nor understand its often complex doctrine. These were the aboriginal tribes of Goa and had come into the Hindu fold following the Aryan settlements in the region. Thus, in 1927 a swami (spiritual leader) by name of Vinayakbuva Masurkar came to Goa from Karwar with the aim of establishing a 'religious consciousness' among the Hindu people.[81] He became particularly interested in the plight of the Gaudes, who suffered from alienation and wished to rejoin the Hindu community with which they felt a stronger identification. Masurkar gathered support from other Hindu communities in Goa and in other regions and asked the Hindu community to accept this 'backward' community into the Hindu fold. On the 26th of February, 1928, a total of 1,150 Gaudes were reaffirmed into the Hindu faith of their forefathers. The total number of reconversions which took place between 1927 and 1930 are 7,815, out of a total population of 1,05,000 (both Hindus and Christians).[82]

Following this attempt at reconversion, acceptance into the Hindu fold did not occur as promised. The Hindus who had not converted during the Portuguese refused to allow them back into their community and the Catholics now alienated them even further. They developed into a separate community (caste) among the Hindus which until today only encourages marriages among itself and has restricted relationships with other communities. Alienated from other social groups, immobilised by an inferiority complex and now ignored by those same forces which instigated their reconversion, the Nav-Gaudas could be considered the true 'casualties' in the war for socio-religious dominance in Goa, following the stirrings of Liberation.

SYNERGY

Synergy in Religion

To achieve some form of psychological harmony, the clergy compromised on a variety of customs and practices which the new converts seemed unable and/or unwilling to discard. The synergy came about owing to two motivating factors. The first was prestige; those converts from the higher classes considered themselves as superior and insisted to be recognised as such. They were 'superior' by classical notions of the definition' including education, manners, economics and comprehension of abstract religious doctrine. The second motivating factor was the original culture in which early converts were raised since the time they were children. This phase I occurred within the Hindu religion and lifestyle and the results were ingrained habits, rituals and leisure which were difficult to erase. In order to minimise the psychological destabilisation which might accompany such a major change in religious orientation and ritual observance, the church allowed certain practices which differed from the normal church customs. The use of brass oil lamps, flowers and the extensive worship of saints are some such practices which evolved from this synergy.

Within the social structure of Goa, caste distinctions were initially discouraged and converts were compelled to adopt western dress and Portuguese surnames which removed the major marks which distinguished among castes. Still the upper castes would neither dine, sit in close proximity nor fraternise with those converts from the lower castes during the church feasts and other activities. Moreover, initially these feasts were restricted to the upper three castes alone and Confraternities developed which were exclusive to the two upper castes of Brahmans and Kshyatrias.[83] The church was also compelled to allow the use of the sacred thread among the upper-castes and reinterpreted such a practice as a sign of nobility. Following complaints from the native converts, the church passed an order which permitted only those natives from the upper classes to join the seminary and aim for priesthood. This was also owing to the lack of respect which the early priests hailing from the lower classes were shown by their peers.

In a similar manner, the converts were permitted to keep small alters in their houses as was common practice among their Hindu brethren. These new altars contained statues of Mother Mary, Jesus on the Cross and other pictoral images which replaced parallel Hindu deities though they could still burn incense and candles as offerings to the Catholic deities. As they were accustomed to taking the Hindu deities in procession around the temple on annual feast days and important religious occasions, so the Saints and other statues (Infant Jesus in Colva) were displayed in similar processions. In the latter example, the statue of the infant Jesus is taken in procession from the church and brought to the nearby river where it is immersed, a symbolic bath done in much the same manner as the Hindu community performs with their revered deities. Christians also celebrate November 2nd as a day dedicated to family ancestors, which is akin to the Hindu 'Shradhanavami' on the 9th day of the 7th month in the Hindu calendar year.[84] Navaratri is another 5-day 'female' Christian hybrid festival in Goa beginning on the 25th of October which is parallel to the nine-day Hindu festival which precedes Dassera.

Synergistic Evolution of Language

In the early years of the Portuguese administration and attempts at conversion, the Konkani language was promoted by the Catholic church. As Konkani was the native tongue of the people, all priests stationed in Goa were given a maximum period of one year to learn this language. During the early years of the Portuguese rule the Konkani language flourished and the first written forms of the language appeared. To facilitate the learning and understanding of the language by the Portuguese clergy and laymen, Konkani eventually was transferred into the Roman script. Though it was an oral language at the time of conquest, it was nonetheless a very rich and descriptive language which had several borrowed words from Marathi, Kannada, Sanskrit, and Persian.[85] This was owing to the successive administrations which claimed lordship of Goa and brought in their own linguistic preferences to be used in the administration.

The Portuguese made many attempts to impose their language on the local converts. Soon it became mandatory for education to be through the Portuguese medium and all Catholics were expected to read and write the language. While promoting both Portuguese and Konkani languages, the Portuguese administration discouraged the study of Marathi and Sanskrit, literary languages in which the religious doctrines of the Hindus were written. They banished all the schools which taught these languages in the Old Conquests and effectively separated the new converts from their previous literary tradition. With this separation, the Konkani of the Old Conquests began its historical diversion and evolved into a distinct dialect with borrowed words from Portuguese and of late English. However, the common man was not able to educate his children as they were needed to work in the fields, and as the Marathi language and its mediums were banned, the children of the labour class had few opportunities to learn the language. They remained illiterate, and would even sign their names with a thumb-print rather than written signatures.

The church medium of instruction for all intensive purposes was the Konkani language. The priests understood that language was the key to transmitting religion and cultural values, and a population that did not understand Portuguese would likewise have difficulty in grasping the meaning of Catholicism in a foreign tongue. Thus, Konkani, which up to the advent of the Portuguese had been kept within the oral realm, was now established in a written form using the Roman alphabet. Owing to its oral form, knowledge of the Konkani language did not enable the reading of the Vedas or other Hindu religious texts, a practice which the Portuguese administration was adamant to prevent. Through Konkani language the clergy were able to transmit a large amount of Portuguese cultural information, and the local Goan priests whose native tongue was Konkani could likewise propagate the Catholic faith and cultural values. Thus, though the Portuguese failed in their attempts to establish their own mother tongue in the region of Goa, they were able to transmit their culture through the Konkani language which every new convert understood. The Konkani language, therefore, flourished under the Portuguese whose clergy formalised the language albeit in a script foreign to Indian soil.

Those who were able to become fluent in Portuguese, roughly 5-10 per cent of Goa's population, used the language for official transactions during their employment in the Portuguese administration or during social occasions when knowledge of the Portuguese language was required to demonstrate social position and status. As Portuguese became the official language and Konkani that of the masses, those converts seeking to identify with the Portuguese would adopt as many Portuguese words into their oral vocabulary as possible.

Prior to the Portuguese, the local people had listened to the Puranas and stories from the Mahabharata and Ramayana read by Brahman priests in Marathi. Following the banishment of any literary forms related to that language, the priests decided to substitute these old forms with new forms which related to Christian theology. Consequently, Father Thomas Stephen wrote the 'Christa Purana' which was written in Konkani and depicted the life stories of various Saints.[86] This work then served as the literary foundation for a new form of theatre which replaced the old Marathi theatrical form. The religious plays offered again the stories of Saints, Jesus Christ, and other prominent figures from the Bible. In later years these plays took on a secular nature where a typical village story would evolve in a classical western theatrical form with the character and plot introduction, conflict description, rise, climax and resolution. Elaborate costumes were prepared and they were a favourite leisure activity of the village community, especially the working class. These Konkani dramas, as they were called, were both religious and secular and the music was likewise a creation which adapted western musical forms brass bands, C-major scales, musical composition, lyrical structure to the Konkani language and the vocal capabilities of the people. The Konkani cultural forms which evolved, thus, were not products of high culture, which had been expressed through Marathi, but rather were forms reflective of the common man of the region of Goa. As Marathi and other Indian 'high cultural forms' were banned among Catholic converts, the culture of the masses was elevated and issues relevant to the average man appeared in artistic expression. Issues confronting the average Goan, thus, found their way into artistic expression and this tradition has continued until today.[87]

In the Old Conquests, which were still under their former rulers, the Konkani language evolved under a different sequence of events. Marathi, Persian, and Sanskrit continued to influence the North and north-eastern talukas while Kannada remained an important linguistic influence in the Southern talukas of Quepem and Canacona. Thus, today in Goa alone we find several dialects of Konkani which demonstrate these different historical sequences. For example, the Panjim Konkani has incorporated many Portuguese words and adopted those words directly when no other word from the Konkani language was available. The Northern and Eastern dialect of Konkani is infused with Marathi words and phrases and has continued along those evolutionary lines owing to the primary studies in Marathi and most literary forms continuing to flourish in the Marathi language. In the South, Kannada had the greatest influence on the development of Konkani prior to and during the early years of the Portuguese rule. Now, however, this evolutionary trend has been rapidly replaced and these Southern talukas have been much removed from their Kannada-speaking neighbours.

Of late, English words have been incorporated into the vocabulary of Konkani. This is occurring throughout the North, South and West owing to the introduction of many English schools throughout the state of Goa. Many students have begun their early studies in the English medium and Konkani is taught only as a single subject throughout the school system in Goa. English has assumed great importance because it is the international language which facilitates employment overseas, in the local tourist industry, government jobs, and is the language through which higher education medicine, law, engineering is imparted.

Synergy in the Arts

In addition to synergy among the forms of worship and the system of communal hierarchy, several new forms of folk art arose during the Portuguese times. The Mando was one such dance performed at Christian wedding ceremonies. Though its origin is thought to date back only as far as 1840, other historians believe its origins originate in the first one hundred years of the Portuguese rule. In its current form it is a mixture of native Christian folk and Western church music, sung in Konkani and performed in the villages at Christmas. The Carnival celebrations in Goa also show a mixture of native and Portuguese cultural elements. The Carnival of the West is demonstrated by the street parade, the fancy costumes and the Portuguese songs. The Carnival evoking within Goa has been mixed with earlier customs such as throwing water and coloured powder during Holi and village plays which have their origins in the ancient Khel from Karnataka.[88] In all the Folk Arts of Goa, Konkani was the language used. In addition to folk art, Portuguese songs like the 'corridinho' and 'serenades' serenades were also popular among the urban dwellers, natives and Portuguese nationals alike.

Following the ban on all sorts of Hindu artistic expression, the parishes became the centres of music in the villages. The priests would train young boys and girls to sing church hymns, which would then be performed during the high mass and on feast days. In addition to the choir, the clergy also instructed village youth to play musical instruments to accompany church activities such as the harp, organ, violin, fiddle, trumpet, and the drum.[89] In addition to learning instruments and hymns, two important psychological changes had to work their way into the young minds of native converts. The first was the audio adaptations the children had to make in order to grasp the foundations of western music. Whereas classical Indian musical forms are on a sliding-note scale, western music makes concise distinctions between each note which a singer must strike in order to maintain the fluidity of the piece. In a similar manner, Indian music tends to be performed in a 'minor' key, whereas Western music is usually performed in a 'major' key.[90] Another significant psychological change which had to follow the performance of church music by village children occurred in the attitudes of Goans regarding the 'cultural context' of musical performance. In the Hindu culture music existed in the realm of the devadasis and the temple musicians born of these liaisons. In the Portuguese culture, however, musical performance was considered the domain of the cultured upper class and ladies were expected to attain proficiency in one or more forms of music, including singing. Dancing in Portuguese culture was also the domain of the culturally refined, and women were expected to join their men on the dance floor at social functions.

In addition to social functions and musical forms, art in Goa was also influenced by the Portuguese. The Portuguese admired the work of the craftsmen in Goa, but wanted designs which were more to their liking. Consequently, some goldsmiths took to the task of designing gold crosses, faces of Jesus, and other Catholic religious jewellery which then became part of a brides dowry. Art that evolved from the interaction of these two cultures came to be known as Indo-Portuguese art; a blending of the two cultures whereby Portuguese subjects Jesus, Mother Mary would be incorporated into the current Indian artistic forms, or less often the reverse, whereby Hindu-Indian subjects would emerge in western forms.[91] Like other Indo-Portuguese synergistic forms, this artistic expression evolved in the coastal talukas of Goa but diffused into other areas as well. Thus, we find Catholic icons carved from ivory and sandal wood Portuguese subject into Indian form/substance as well as lacquer work in Cucolim and brass-making in Bicholim Indian subject into Portuguese form. This hybrid art emerged also in furniture, embroidery, gold, silver, and iron work, sculpture, and tapestries.[92]

Jewellery also underwent some cultural evolution, not merely in the forms which evolved but also in the psychology which motivated those who adorned themselves. The Hindu community in Goa used jewellery to demonstrate the wealth of the girls' families and the social and financial status which they enjoyed. The Portuguese women, like other Western women, did not use as much jewellery and considered such objects as mere decorations for their bodies. From the contact of these two perspectives, jewellery adopted both psychological symbols; a demonstration of wealth as well as decoration for the body. Consequently, the jewellery which was at one time heavy and weighted evolved into new lighter and more intricate forms. The use of stones, both precious and synthetic, also came in vogue following the introduction of the Portuguese culture in Goa. These changes occurred mostly among the Christian converts whose jewellery underwent significant evolution. The Cordao is one such hybrid form consisting of one or two black-beaded chains reminiscent of the Hindu mangalsutra and also worn by women as a sign of marriage.[93] The black beads were interspersed with roughly 20 gold coins beads which formed a gold pendant normally in the shape of Jesus or the Cross. Though jewellery is still an important part of dowry for both Catholics and Hindus, it has continued to evolve in its lighter forms and delicate patterns and is perceived as both a sign of wealth and cultural refinement.[94]

Synergy in the Changing Roles of Women

As discussed in detail in the introductory chapter of this work, people in Phase II of enculturation who decided to accept cultural changes did so selectively, not only from within cultures but from within elements as well. Thus, we find that the converted native women, while they attended social functions and received an education, still retained many of their pre-Portuguese beliefs and values following conversion to Catholicism, resulting in a evolved role available to women. For instance, the institution of marriage still bound women to the choices made by their parents, and most of their activities were confined to their homes. Motherhood remained a cherished ideal towards which women should strive, and sons were still the preferred offspring. Self-sacrifice, obedience, and humble submission were still considered the marks of an excellent female character, and modesty in dress and behaviour continued as accepted norms. The consumption of alcoholic beverages as was practised among Portuguese women was still taboo, and illicit affairs were punished with severe sanctions. The selfishness, pretentiousness, and vanity which characterised the Portuguese ladies in general was not permitted to infiltrate deeply into the fabric of native Catholic society.

Yet while the native Catholic women maintained many pre-Portuguese values and traditions, the progressive attitude of the church and state regarding the position of women diffused into the Hindu community as well during the latter years of Portuguese. In 1933 in the city of Margao, some concerned members of the Hindu community met to discuss the need for Hindu women's education in Goa. The results of this first meeting generated the formation of the Seva Samiti for the upliftment of women.[95] The Adarsha Vanita Vidyalay Marathi School for girls opened in 1934, and the subjects taught included standard courses like geography, history, literature, mathematics, in addition to special subjects such as tailoring, nursing, cooking, gardening, domestic finance, and child-care. The languages of English, Konkani, Marathi, and Portuguese were also taught in this school. Though the school became co-educational in 1945, it remained dedicated to the upliftment of women from poor and disadvantaged communities, and was particular to help the girls from the Kalavantin caste, which had arisen from the offspring of Devadasis.[96] Thus, the progressive spirit which characterised the Catholics in Goa was not strictly maintained within that community, and efforts among enlightened men of the Hindu community to improve the status of their women has significantly altered the status of middle and upper-class Hindu women in modern-day Goa.

Conclusion

The Portuguese church and administrative authorities attempted to erase the Indian identity of the new Catholic converts through a series of laws, sanctions, and educational activities.

Under the Portuguese, the Hindu and Catholic communities were in fact alienated from one another and the Catholic population became estranged from the religious and literary traditions in Marathi of their forefathers. Thus, the Portuguese did succeed in isolating a portion of the Goan population from some aspects of Marathi high culture, but even this isolated community maintained its mother tongue and much of the ancient wisdom and tradition of the past. When in later years education through the Portuguese medium was made compulsory, those converts who were unable to get an education learned neither Portuguese nor Marathi 'high' cultures, but rather developed the folk-traditions in the Konkani language. Konkani, thus, became the professed mother tongue of the local Catholic population and folk-arts in Konkani were continued, revised, and or created depending on the religious content. Konkani, thus, gained a new status under the Portuguese administration because it was the only native language allowed and moved from the status of an oral dialect to that of a written language. Similarly, many of the art forms which had formerly been expressed through Marathi, likewise, became translated and reinterpreted through the Konkani, language producing new varieties of artistic expression which gave recognition to the common man. Beyond folk arts, Konkani was also one of the first very regional, entirely oral languages in India to be given a place in the artistic expression of people.

In the New Conquests acquired in 1788, however, the areas were occupied mostly by Portuguese soldiers within the forts rather than with lay Portuguese and zealous missionaries. Though some Catholic churches were erected and some natives converted, the New Conquests, in effect, acted as a 'buffer zone' between Portuguese Goa in the Old Conquests and the invading Muslims, Maratha troops and later British aspirations originating in larger India. These regions, therefore, had relatively little contact with the culture of the Portuguese and the laws which now applied to both New and Old Conquests were not strictly enforced in these rural areas. They were, thus, able to maintain their pre-Portuguese lifestyle, religion, and cultural forms. Owing to the constant wars, which pitted several different rulers against each other, this area was also not able to make significant advancements in education, technology, and infrastructure. The old system of land tenancy and caste occupations continued, keeping the common man in the fields and away from the realisation of his own exploitation by wealthy landlords.

The difference between the regions of the Old and New Conquests in Goa is quite marked, therefore, in part owing to the latter's late occupation by the Portuguese and the maintenance of prior administrative and social forms. Consequently, the cultural forms, practises, and identity of the majority of Goa's interior population more closely resembles the pre-Portuguese society described in the first half of this chapter. Sati, the Devadasi system, and women's exclusion from formal education are no longer practised, but the descriptions of the Samskaras, folk-arts, language, literature, housing, family relationships and clothing have undergone only slight modifications from their pre-Portuguese forms.

The evolution of social history of Goa following the advent of the Portuguese, thus, had significant effects on the subsequent history of Goa. The question still remains whether or not the Goan Catholic community evolved a separate 'cultural identity' from that of their Goan Hindu brethren. The social history of Goa demonstrates that certain changes did in fact occur within the traditions, ways of life, and psychology of the Goan Catholic converts. It is also true that most members belonging to this community inhabited the Old Conquests 1510 which were under the Portuguese administration and laws for over 450 years. The Hindu community by contrast, especially those in the New Conquests 1788 neither identified with nor absorbed the culture of the Portuguese community. Rather, they identified with Maharashtra whose culture was akin to theirs, and the cultural identity, cultural evolution, and political awareness of this community followed along lines similar to that of Southern Maharashtra. They maintained their Indian cultural traditions and were unable and unwilling to identify with and assimilate the Portuguese culture, even during times of considerable pressure which resulted from the zealous missionaries followed by the Salazar dictatorship.

The result of the historical accident of the Portuguese is that two powerful societies evolved in the region of Goa. The first was the traditional Indian caste system with its twice-born members assuming powerful positions in society, and the second was the new 'assimilated' Catholic community which enjoyed privilege and prestige under the Portuguese administration. Following the inception of the latter community in 1510, these two groups diverged in two distinct ways; the Hindu community retaining its former traditions under persecution and identifying instead with Maharashtra and the Catholic community looking, both voluntarily and forcefully, to the Portuguese from which to receive their cultural cues. Yet even among the Catholic converts who assimilated much of the outward forms of Portuguese behaviour, the basic psychology of Goan Catholics surrounding family, marriage and religion has remained Indian in character. The process of Goa's liberation, to which this research now turns, illuminates these real and perceived differences in communal social evolution which occurred in Goa following the advent of the Portuguese and which gave rise to different political, economic, and cultural identifications.

REFERENCES

1. See chapter 2, History of the Konkan Territory known as Goa.
2. *Unfortunately, there are significantly fewer available historical records which document the momentous changes among the aboriginal Dravidian tribes, for example, who had been living in Goa prior to the Aryan migration which brought the Hindu religion. The available evidence suggests, however, that they also experienced much of the same religious subjugation and racial segregation.
3. Xavier, P. D., *Goa: A Social History from 1540 to 1680*, Panjim: P. D. Xavier, 1993, p. 34.
4. *Ibid.*
5. *During a later era they united and incorporated both gods into temples and rituals.
6. Xavier, P. D., *op. cit.*, p. 36.
7. *See chapter 9 Fort Cochin: for descriptions of pre-Portuguese social stratification in Kerala.
8. *Ibid.*, p. 158.
9. *Ibid.*, p. 20.
10. *Ibid.*, p. 68.
11. *Ibid.*, p. 69.
12. *Ibid.*, p. 70.
13. *Some argue that prior to the Portuguese Konkani in the Kannada and Marathi scripts existed but were destroyed during the Inquisition. This seems unlikely, however, as history demonstrates that the missionaries coveted knowledge of the Konkani language and would probably have

used and translated these written works to aid them in their proselytization of the local people. Thus, a few such works would have been saved had they existed in written form.

14. See chapter 2, History of the Konkan Territory known as Goa.
15. Xavier, *op. cit.*, p. 163.
16. *Ibid.*, p. 164.
17. Some historians argue that Sati arose during the Medieval era possibly as a way to keep young widows from being captured by Muslim invasions or sold by relatives into Muslim harems.
18. *Ibid.*, p. 215.
19. *Ibid.*, p. 217.
20. *Ibid.*, p. 166.
21. *Ibid.*, p. 169.
22. *Ibid.*, p. 175.
23. Prior to the Portuguese a well-known agrahara was functioning on the Tiswadi island, and Queen Kalamadevi of the Kadamba dynasty established a Brahmapuri in Belgaum. These institutions attracted scholars from around the country and imparted free education to qualified students in exchange for gifts and donations to the institution. In all Hindu centres for higher learning, Sanskrit was the medium of instruction.
24. *Ibid.*, p. 177.
25. *Ibid.*, p. 202.
26. *In April of 1997 this author visited the Dessai family and was given a tour of the house.
27. *Such practises still occur in Goan Hindu homes and some occur in Catholic village homes as well.
28. *Ibid.*, P.D., p. 202.
29. *Ibid.*, p. 204.
30. *Ibid.*, p. 209.
31. *Ibid.*, p. 210.
32. *Such customs and practises are still practised by the Goan Hindus today and are elaborated according to socio-economic status; those being able to afford to will wear gold jewellery in proportion.
33. *Ibid.*, P.D., p. 213.
34. *Ibid.*, p. 227.
35. *Ibid.*
36. *Ibid.*, p. 230.
37. *Ibid.*, p. 56.
38. *Ibid.*, p. 59.
39. *Ibid.*, p. 60.
40. *Ibid.*, p. 61.
41. Xavier, P.D. *op. cit.* p. 61.
42. *Ibid.*, p. 62.

43. *Ibid.*, p. 52.
44. *These practises are still customary among Hindus in Goa today.
45. *Ibid.*, P.D., p. 58.
46. *Ibid.*, p. 60.
47. *Marathi dramas and theatre are still widely performed today in the taluka of Ponda and Bicholim and are also of late sponsored by the Kala Academy in Panjim.
48. Angle, Prabhakar, S. *Goa: Concepts and Misconcepts*, Bombay: Goan Hindu Association, 1994, p. 77.
49. *Ibid.*
50. Xavier, P.D., *op. cit.* pp. 27-29.
51. *Ibid.*, p. 19.
52. *Ibid.*, p. 20.
53. *Ibid.*, p. 7.
54. *Ibid.*, p. 19.
55. *Ibid.*, p. 9.
56. In the early years, however, before this custom became effective, the converts continued to practice child marriage by betrothing a young child years prior to the wedding ceremony and by conducting illegal marriages behind closed doors.
57. Though successful in maintaining material wealth, these marriages often resulted in mentally deficient or otherwise deformed children. The Catholic Brahmin families of Margao continued this practise owing to their desire to maintain their property and Brahmin status which prevented them from inter-marriages with other communities even while their own community substantially decreased in numbers. As a result, many of their offspring following liberation have been plagued with a variety of mental illnesses, including schizophrenia, mental retardation and Down's syndrome.
58. *This was also the custom in Bassein where a large concentration of Portuguese ladies lived.
59. Gracias, Fatima da Silva, *Health and Hygiene in Colonial Goa 1510-1961*, New Delhi: Concept Publishing Co., 1994, p. 153.
60. Xavier, P.D., *op. cit.* p. 177.
61. *Ibid.*, p. 179.
62. *Ibid.*, p. 178.
63. *Ibid.*, p. 179.
64. *Ibid.*, p. 181.
65. *Ibid*, p. 183.
66. *Ibid.*, p. 189.
67. *Ibid.*, p. 190.
68. *Ibid.*, pp. 190-91.
69. Xavier., P.D., *op. cit.*, p. 192.
70. *Ibid.*, p. 133.

71. *Ibid.*, p. 134.
72. Angle, Prabhakar, S., *op. cit.*, pp. 19-23.
73. *These same laws were enforced in all of the Portuguese possessions including Bassein, Daman, & Fort Cochin.
74. Xavier, P.D., *op. cit.*, pp. 125-30.
75. *Ibid.*, p. 130.
76. *These sacraments continue among the native Catholic population today.
77. Xavier, P.D., *op. cit.*, p. 203.
78. *Ibid.*, p. 206.
79. *Ibid.*, p. 207.
80. *Ibid.*, p. 225.
81. *Goa: Cultural Trends—A Collection of Scholarly Essays*, Panjim: Goa University, 1995.
82. *Ibid.*
83. *The Confrarias were elite social groups within the church designed to cater to the upper-class Catholic converts who wished to distinguish themselves from their brethren. The Confrarias were responsible for the social upliftment of the village community, sponsoring church feasts, and helping poorer church members. They took part in religious processions and wore red and/or purple capes over their white church gowns to identify themselves as a member of the organisations. These groups still exist in Goa today though their importance has diminished and now it is viewed more as an honourable status.
84. Angle, Prabhakar S., *op. cit.*, p. 34.
85. *Ibid.*, pp. 30-36.
86. *Ibid.*, p. 181.
87. In 1997, to take just one moment in time, a Konkani theatrical performance will express not ancient stories but rather modern difficulties, such as the attitude and behavioural changes which result when youth return from employment in the Gulf countries.
88. *The Khel is a folk dance-drama with dialogue in prose and verse.
89. Xavier, P.D., *op. cit.*, p. 226.
90. The intricacies in both musical forms are remarkable each in their own right, but those accustomed to hearing music in an Indian style had to make the necessary tonal and audio adjustments in order to perform the Western church music as required.
91. *Goa: Cultural Trends—A Collection of Scholarly Essays*, Panjim: Goa University, 1995.
92. *Ibid.*
93. *Ibid.*
94. *Ibid.*
95. *Ibid.*

    Members also contributed financially to the purchase of a plot and construction materials for such a Dharmasala going back to pre-Portuguese educational institutions catering to the education of women. In 1938 the first two Hindu women joined the association which stood out owing to the culture which normally denied women such participation. Mr. N.D. Naik was the main support behind this proposal and he gained the support of both Hindu and Catholic communities.

96. *Ibid.*

CHAPTER 4

Liberation: Causes and Consequences

The First Awakening: Liberation as Realisation

The rebellious attitude among the Hindu community following the annexation of Sattari and the New Conquests could not have shaken the Portuguese while they had a loyal Goan population behind them identified with Portuguese interests. *The true awakening first began in 1787 when several native priests rebelled against what they viewed as racial discrimination and injustice amongst the clergy.* They contested that owing to their ethnicity, they were bypassed for the high offices of the clergy even though they had rightly earned such positions. Father Pinto, joined by Fathers Caetano Francisco Couto and Jose Antonio Gonsalves, plotted a revolt with the aim of establishing an independent republic in Goa. The revolt was planned for the 10th of August, 1787 and those involved in the execution of the plot numbered 47; 17 priests, 7 army officers and 23 lay men.[1] Planning went on in the house of Father Pinto but word of the revolt leaked out and was foiled by the Portuguese authorities. *This rebellion, though never fully executed, marked an historic turning-point in the history of Goan society. It was through this rebellion that those people who had most identified with the Portuguese began to realise the extent of their repression, thus, breaking the age-old 'master-slave' mentality which kept the Goan people bound to their oppressors.*

"Liberation becomes possible only when one recognises that he has collaborated in his own subjugation...that the 'master' has done nothing to him that the 'slave' has not also done to himself."[2]

This realisation must, therefore, precede any type of full liberation. Even if a colony or subjugated people have been set free, they are not truly free unless they release their minds from the master-slave relationship which was imprinted on their conscious and unconscious from an early age. Full liberation, therefore, requires confrontation rather than escape, because only with confrontation those subjugated realise their own internal, *psychological* liberation. In the case example of Goa, the Hindu community already knew, because they had suffered under the discriminatory laws of the Portuguese, that they were subjugated. It was the Catholic community who had identified politically, culturally, religiously and emotionally with the Portuguese and who now had to 'liberate' themselves. Owing to generations of people who had been inculcated with the Portuguese culture, values, etc., their proverbial 'master' had inhabited their own minds, incapacitating them from realising their subjugation. These people had, therefore, not only to realise their subjugation, but re-capacitate themselves and understand that they were psychologically capable not merely of fighting against, but also of 'killing' those who oppressed them.

At the same time, in order to actually *be* subjugated, an individual or a community has to recognise that they are *in* that condition. Without this recognition or *awakening*, the 'condition of subjugation' does not exist as it is not actually experienced from the perception of those individuals who are under such conditions. Through this lens, therefore, the Catholic converts considered themselves free, owing to the voluntary internalisation of the constraints placed on them by the administration of the Portuguese. This acceptance, in addition to the many social welfare institutions created by the Portuguese administration, created a certain institutional 'opacity' wherein the underlying motivations of the Portuguese were not apparent to the native converts. In Goa, therefore, the Catholic converts in the upper rungs of the Portuguese power structure had to realise their oppression for what it was and decide to take affirmative action against the existing policies. Once the situation (in this example, Portuguese subjugation) is fully realised *by those subjugated (Catholic Goans)* for what it is, then that institution (the Portuguese colonial rule) can no longer exist and must be abolished.[3]

This is usually marked by an historic moment and in the case of Goa can be marked by Pinto's Revolt. Upon closer examination we fully understand just how critical was this revolution. Those who revolted, in particular three native Catholic priests, had advanced as far as any natives were able to under the existing power structure. These same leaders had also fully internalised the Portuguese culture and identified with them in all aspects other than ethnicity. They were men who had been raised in the Portuguese educational system and were fluent in a variety of Latin languages. They had fulfilled their socially desired roles by devoting their lives to the service of the church and even strove to reach higher among the existing social structure to become bishops in Goa. Thus, these men, more than most others in society, were both consciously and unconsciously identified with the Portuguese and their administration. They were the perfect examples of the slaves in the 'master-slave' relationships described by socio-economists Hegel and Marx.[4] Slavery consists of unconsciously internalising the 'master' and who more but a native Catholic priest in the Portuguese colonial system could internalise their 'master' to such an extent.

What is striking and illuminates the full extent of this new psychology is what followed from their realisation that under the current system they could not get beyond this glass ceiling. The glass ceiling, in this context, is taken to mean a position to which one can strive and that one can see clearly in front of him, but owing to some invisible barrier he is prevented from reaching that very thing. What is striking is that the native priests who realised this did not simply urge for internal reform. This would seem to have been the likely course of events owing to an unconscious identification which would have prevented them from entertaining the idea of liberation. Instead, what history demonstrates is a virtual psychological revolution whereby these men decided to revolt with the aim to establish a separate republic. They were virtually risking everything because they already enjoyed power and significance, albeit only within the established structure.

However, the punishment which the Portuguese dealt out to the leaders of Pinto's revolt was severe enough to inhibit further uprisings among the Catholic population for many years to come. All were tried under the Portuguese law courts; 3 priests were released, 14 were banished to Portugal; 5 rebel leaders were exiled and 5 were sent to the gallows. The rest, especially the laymen, received the sentence of 'pena ultima', which under the Portuguese regime was terrifying indeed. A man sentenced as such was dragged from the back of a running horse from the court to the scaffold, where his hands were cut off before he was hung. His head was then stuck atop a pole and placed in a place visible to the public and other parts of his body were displayed atop similar poles throughout the coastal talukas and in his home village.[5] Such harsh repercussions were enough to dissuade any further rebellions among the 'loyal' population for quite some time. Yet though the revolt was harshly repressed, the sleepers had awoken.

In order to understand why the Portuguese were able to maintain control over the colony for almost another 200 years, one also has to realise that the people were not initially united in their struggle for freedom. The converts who had left the Hindu fold knew they were outcast according to the Hindu law and would never again enjoy the same positions and privilege they had enjoyed under the Portuguese. This caused them to seek out group identification under the Portuguese rule and to identify themselves with their rulers. This situation, coupled with the repressive laws which favoured the adoption of Portuguese culture and persecuted that of the Hindus, further resulted in an identification with the ruling power. Second, the Portuguese practised the policy of divide and rule which severely isolated the new converts from their Hindu brethren. Catholics were forbidden to communicate and hold relations with Hindus and were unable to discuss relevant issues with them.

Therefore, to successfully execute a freedom struggle, the people would have to unify across caste and religious lines, a concept which was not yet appealing to the majority of Christian converts. If the Christian community was to become independent, they had no intention of giving up the rights and social status which they currently enjoyed. Thus, though the Portuguese converts were subjugated under their rulers, they perceived their situation under the Portuguese as better than what might transpire if they were to allow the Hindu or Muslim community to regain control. Consequently, the freedom fighters from within the system (the high-caste, powerful converts) were not initially in collusion with those from outside the Catholic community. Thus, the Rane revolts and other mass-Hindu rebellions were not entirely supported by the Catholic community who rather reasserted their identification with the Portuguese.

Furthermore, the majority of native Catholics were unable to realise the extent of their subjugation because they had been born and raised to accept the current social environment without question. As can be seen from the 450 years presence which the Portuguese were able to maintain in Goa, the attitudes of the Portuguese had affected the native converts more than superficially. In fact, they had internalised the attitudes and beliefs about themselves and their heritage which the Portuguese held to be true. These included but were not limited to the beliefs of racial, cultural, religious and linguistic superiority of the Portuguese. The result was a native Catholic community that was incapacitated by the feeling of inherent inferiority, which they tried to recover by imitating the Portuguese to the best of their capability.

While they simultaneously were taught to feel ashamed of their former ways of life, converts were rewarded for their assimilation of Portuguese culture. Converts were told they were citizens of Portugal and were not part of the Indian nation. They were taught to believe that they were special and superior to their Hindu brethren because of their assimilation of Portuguese religion and culture, statements which subsequent generations accepted blindly. To be considered 'Portuguese' was to be paid a very high complement indeed. Catholic natives internalised the ideals of equality, liberty and justice which were impregnated in the church sermons. Thus, the Catholic Goans grew up as honest, well-mannered and good-hearted individuals who were not at first aware of the hypocrisy of the clergy and their less than stellar behaviour behind closed doors. They were taught that anyone who studied hard and had the motivation could reach as high as was possible; but they were not taught that there was a glass ceiling which prevented them from reaching beyond a certain level of power and prestige.

Thus, during early acculturation, converts internalised the goals and values of their rulers and strove valiantly to attain those coveted positions, be it in government office, as members of the clergy or as officers in the Indo-Portuguese army. The various segments of society, therefore, found their various niches within the power structure. The upper class Catholic Goans had found theirs in the administration and clergy, both areas where power prevailed. The mesticos and mulattos had found their power niche and accepted social role through participation in the Portuguese Indian Army which was active until 1871. The lower class had continued to perform their prior functions, only with an increase in social status over their Hindu brethren and a few economic benefits and tax reductions which they also gained.

Thus, Pinto's revolt demonstrated the historic psychological turning-point among some members of the clergy, but owing to the aforementioned reasons, most Catholic Goans continued to identify culturally, politically and emotionally with the Portuguese administration for the next 100 years following the rebellion. It would take another 100 years before some enlightened men from the Catholic community would rise to the occasion and take up where Pinto's rebellion had left off. In 1852, for example, Father Jeremias Mascarenhas in a speech before the Portuguese Parliament, cited the liberation of Brazil as an inspiration for the people of Goa.[6] In 1862 Francisco Luis Goes, a famous Goan author, advocated liberation in his popular novel, *Os Brahamanes*.[7] In 1870, the journal *O Brado Indiano* was founded by Father Alvares with the aim of exposing the hypocrisy and corruption rampant in the Portuguese administration in Goa.[8] Beginning in 1885, a national consciousness arose in India which questioned the foreign British administration. This was institutionalised by the creation of the Indian National Congress and their ideas found a voice in the *Kesari* and the *Maratha*, newspapers which also circulated in Goa. In addition to the neighbouring ideas which diffused into the Goan hinterlands, Goan migrants in Bombay, both Catholic and Hindu, also got caught in the rising tide of nationalism.

Early Discontent: The Sattari Ranes

The Portuguese had hardly any time to enjoy their victory before the seeds of discontent sprouted in both the New and Old Conquests. The north-eastern Taluka of Sattari, the last to come under the Portuguese dominion, harboured rebellious activity directed against foreign rule. In 1746 the taluka had been conquered by the Marquis of Alorna, but in 1756 it was recaptured by the Bhonsles from Sawantwadi. In 1781 Sattari was captured by the Portuguese and seven years later the battle ended with Sattari in the hands of the Portuguese (1788).[9] But along with the territory came the Ranes, descendants of the Rajputs who were insistent upon self-rule.

Between the Treaty of Annexation in 1788 and the year of 1912, the Ranes of Sattari made known their discontent through a series of attacks and incursions of the Portuguese conquests. In 1822 alone no less than 12 rebellions broke out in the Sattari region and they made it their goal to liberate the New Conquests from the laws of the Portuguese. The first organised attack occurred in 1848, but was quickly suppressed by the Portuguese. The rebellion strengthened, however, owing to the imposition of new taxes by the Portuguese in 1851 which burdened the agricultural labour class in Sattari. Supported by the agriculturists under the leadership of Dipaji Rane, forces were gathered and the Fort of Namus on the bank of the Madevi river (Sattari) was taken in a surprise attack the following year. For three years the attacks continued using guerrilla war tactics and Dipaji Rane conquered and liberated Sattari, Quepem, Canacona, Hemad Barshe and Bhatagrama from the clutches of the Portuguese. In 1855 the Portuguese government was compelled to enter into a treaty with the Ranes which withdrew the religious restrictions on the Hindu community and protected the rights of the village councils. Following the treaty, however, the Portuguese further repressed the Sattari taluka creating widespread dissension among the people.[10]

In 1895, following a concerted effort to oust the Portuguese, the city of Mapsa in the taluka of Bardez (Old Conquests) fell to the Rane armies. The Hindu soldiers in the Portuguese military service had revolted weeks earlier following an order which would have sent them to Africa to suppress another insurgence in a different Portuguese colony. The major season was because the Hindu religion sanctioned overseas travel with the loss of caste and the Hindu soldiers did not want to loose theirs. Regardless of the underlying motive behind this caste rule, the people ardently believed in its negative consequences and would not obey their military commanders. As a consequence, they revolted and joined forces with the Ranes and the peasantry in Sattari, the latter who were against the Portuguese owing to the monopoly they had on the agricultural produce of the taluka. The soldiers captured the Nanus Fort and made serious incursions into Bardez and the number of freedom fighters topped 6,000.[11]

As the forces under Dada Rane approached Panjim and occupied all but the island of Tiswadi, the Governor of Goa signed a document through which the soldiers would be exempt from overseas military duty and they would be pardoned for their revolt. The Portuguese declared Martial Law five days later in all of its colonies to stop the spread of the revolt.

The New Republic

However, in 1910, significant events in Portugal altered the course of history in Goa, for the time being. Inspired by the egalitarian concepts of the French Revolution, civil leaders in Portugal overthrew the monarchy and established a democratic republic in Portugal. Their new conception of government enabled autonomous self-rule in Portugal and her overseas possessions and the Church and State separated formally five months following the Revolution. The Republic in Portugal began to hear of the religious oppression in Goa under which the Hindus lived. Soon there emerged from the new Republic the impetus to stop the activity of the Catholic zealots in Goa, who had taken religious conversion and cultural assimilation to extreme levels, abusing their power.

In 1911, leaders of the Republic voted in a new constitution whereby all the inhabitants of the Portuguese territories were to be considered Portuguese citizens with equal rights. This was welcomed in Goa and gave the Hindu and Christian populations equal rights and priviledges under the Portuguese law. 'Political freedom', as described by Hegel,[12] had been granted. The new Republic also favoured provincial autonomy and the distribution of power among the native population. Following this new Constitution which guaranteed religious freedom to all of Goa's people, the banner under which the Ranes had united with the common people quickly faded. The people were seemingly tired of war and turmoil and were content to resume their normal lives as politically free citizens of Portugal. The impetus which had fuelled the Rane revolts was removed and the Hindu community, for the time being, seemed satisfied. The year 1912, thus, marked the last year of the Rane revolts.

From 1919 to 1926, a general optimism surrounded the Portuguese province of Goa. With the onset of political freedom, the Hindu community began widespread efforts to improve their depressed condition. Most of the religious, educational and cultural forms which had been banned under the repressive Portuguese rule were created anew, including political parties, schools (*dharmasalas*), newspapers and journals in Marathi and religious celebrations. Following the announcement of political freedom in Goa, the spirit of the Hindu community was ignited and a flurry of activity resulted in the arts and social areas. During the second decade of the 20th century, the two communities in Goa, previously segregated, began to interact with one another. By doing so they began to recognise their ancient cultural ties and similarities, but the Goan Christians were still impregnated with the idea of Hindu inferiority and the native Hindus still considered the converted Christians to be outcast.

Throughout the Portuguese administration, much cultural diffusion occurred between the territory of the New Conquests and the neighbouring British territory of India. Thus, as the freedom movement gained importance on the Indian sub-continent, people in Goa felt its repercussions as well. In 1905, when Lokamanya Tilak propagated the idea of Swadeshi (an autonomous Indian nation), his ideas spread into Goa from Mahararshtrian patriots who sought asylum for their 'subversive activities'.[13] The idea of an independent Indian nation was new to Indian soil, as prior to the British, the sub-continent had been controlled by a variety of princes and petty chiefs who each had their own administrative policies.

When Tilak died in 1920, Gandhiji appeared on the scene to uplift the peoples' spirit and revive their fight for civil liberties. With Gandhiji came the true awakening whereby the Indian administrators and masses realised they had collaborated in their own subjugation and from this day forth would cease to do so, thus, crippling the British administration. This movement, which began to emanate strength by 1921-22, also effected the people and psychology of Goa, who, like other Indians, had suffered under a repressive regime and whose majority Hindu population was not willing to allow Portugal to overstay its welcome. The Hindu population in Goa had suffered the most and identified the least with the Portuguese administration and were, thus, most taken by the ideas of Gandhi and the spirit of Liberation.

Goan Catholics, however, appeared more identified with the Portuguese. Having been given a degree of autonomy never before felt in Goa and sharing the religion of their rulers, the Goans were relatively content with their current status under the liberal Republican regime. It is not surprising, therefore, that the large majority continued to identify with the Portuguese and were considered 'de-nationalised Goans'. The idea of nationalisation, it must be remembered, arrived only in 1905 following Tilak's call for Swadeshi. Prior to that the Indian sub-continent had been under foreign British rule and prior to the British it had been administered by a variety of sub-regional political regimes which had been in constant war with one another over territory and the subsequent economic gains. Thus, when some Goans were called 'de-nationalised', what had happened was that they had not answered the 'call' of Tilak to unite under a single new Indian Republic. This was to be expected, and considering the history of Goa and the optimistic, liberated social atmosphere during which time the 'call' came, it does not seem abnormal from a psychological standpoint that the native Catholics in Goa, having just been granted full citizenship in the Portuguese nation and a degree of autonomy previously unseen in all of Portuguese history, did not respond as did other Indians.

Portugal under a Military Dictatorship

However, when in 1926 a military coup resulted in the instalment of a military dictatorship in Portugal, the power and freedom which the natives in Goa had gained was taken from them suddenly. Chaos prevailed in the Lisbon administration and the revolution turned into violent skirmishes throughout Portugal. Finally in 1928, Carmona assumed the Presidency of Portugal and the position of Finance Minister was given to Salazar. The coup marked the end of the sixteen-year Democratic Republic in Portugal and the Goan people awaited the effects which this rule would have on Goa.

Though the Hindu community had been appeased for a short while under the New Republic, following the dictatorship in Portugal efforts began again among political parties, newspapers and revolutionaries to arouse dissatisfaction among the local population. Once again the ideas were to free the land from foreign rule. An identity was, thus, fostered which linked Goan Hindus with larger India and specifically with Maharashtra, whose political leaders were actively involved in garnering support for Goa's merger to that state along cultural, historical and linguistic lines. For those who entertained these political views, they felt that the borders between Goa and larger India were superficial political boundaries erected in the interests of the foreign rulers and not in line with existing cultural boundaries. They further believed that the future of Goa was inextricably linked, as was its past prior to the Portuguese, with that of larger India. Journals, newspapers and political rallies kept the Goan community briefed on all events taking place in India and the success of India's freedom movement was presumed to have a domino effect which would result in freedom from colonial rule.[14]

Riding the wave of this new identification with Indian nationalism, a section of the Gaude community in Goa were persuaded by a Swami from Karnataka to convert back to Hinduism in 1928.[15] They did and had they been accepted back into the Hindu fold as they had been previously, other re-conversions en masse might have followed, thus, further eroding the loyalty of the native population towards Portugal. But as the other Catholic communities soon realised, the Gaudes were segregated from other Hindu communities once they returned to Hinduism. The other Gaude whose forefathers had not converted isolated these new converts and relegated them to an inferior caste known as the Nav-Gaudes. This treatment effectively stopped other reconversions and resulted in the virtual alienation of these community members from both Hindu and Catholic communities.[16]

In 1927, the Indian National Congress was established with the aim of complete Independence of India. With nationalism increasingly on the minds of all, the forces which separated Hindus and Catholic began to erode with the call for unity of the native population against foreign domination. Subsequently, Dr. T.B. Cunha founded a branch of the National Congress in Goa, which was initially supported in Bombay and Delhi. In 1928 at the Calcutta National Congress, the Goa Congress Committee, represented by T.B. Cunha, was officially recognised and given representation in the all-India Congress committee.[17] This was first official political link between Goa and the Indian National Congress. In January of 1930, following Britain's refusal to grant the concessions laid out by the Indian National Congress, a 'pledge of Independence' was taken all over the country and satyagrahas became the official disobedience policy of the 'Independent India.'

In May of 1930 events in Portugal took a turn for the worse and the Colonial Act became the official policy under the new dictatorship. This new martial law forbade the organisation of any rallies or politically subversive meetings. In sum, this new policy virtually nullified the policies set up by the Democratic Republic and reinstalled the colonial policies of segregation between Hindu natives, assimilated Catholic natives and Portuguese nationals. The Constitutional Charter of 1826 which had given the overseas possessions the status of 'provinces' was voided and in its place the provinces were newly termed 'Colonies', or possessions of the Portuguese. The policies of Christianisation and Lusitanisation were again deployed from the top and all the privileges and political freedoms which the natives had enjoyed were fully revoked. Compulsory conscription in the Portuguese Indian army was another unpopular stipulation of the Colonial Act (Acto Colonial).[18] Thus, these new government decrees erased most of the progress and autonomy which had evolved in the overseas provinces, once again relegating them to an inferior status under the Portuguese authorities. However, as history demonstrates, power and freedom once gained are sorely lost and the natives in Goa, both Christian and Hindu, reacted accordingly to their new inferior status.

The Colonial Act and the Pledge of Independence coincided, thus, creating major psychological tension in Goa between that which was ideal (full liberation) and that which was real (foreign colonial rule). Owing to this tension and the people's earlier sense of freedom, it seemed foolish to expect the people to accept this new repressive regime while India, now in communication with progressive leaders in Goa, headed towards freedom.

Yet it would be another 30 years, 1961 precisely, before Goa became liberated and another 55 years, 1987, before she would fully integrate herself into India. And this time, those who would eventually help to realise the freedom struggle in Goa would hail from both the powerful Catholic elite as well as the repressed Hindu community which had extensive socio-political contacts with the neighbouring States, especially Maharashtra. *What would happen between 1928 (the creation of the Goa Congress and 1987 (Indian statehood) would result in the question of identity coming to the forefront of Goan politics and raising many heated issues that would take time to resolve.* Looming large were the differences between the two major communities inhabiting in Goa; the Catholic converts from the Old Conquests and the Hindu community from the New.

Meanwhile, the Goa Congress Committee set about the task of political education, or as Hegel and Marx would describe realisation of subjugation-among the people of Goa and Bombay. They combined political awakening not only with realisation, but with a call to activate the fulfilment of civil liberation. While newspapers, pamphlets and village rallies helped people to accept that they were in fact dominated by the foreign rule, these media flows also channelled such emotionally charged energy into active involvement in the communal goal to liberate Goa. True enough that those political parties who held the majority vote stood to gain tremendously as heirs to the Portuguese colony, but all felt they justified their actions owing to the repressive regime which had taken control in Portugal and hence in Goa.

Political Mobilisation

Under pressure from the Portuguese government, the Indian National Congress was compelled to disaffiliate itself with the National Congress (Goa). In October of 1938 the Provisional Goa Congress was established in Bombay and created links with Goa.[19] The Goans in Bombay were still considered Portuguese subjects and both Hindu and Catholic Goans had been influenced by the wave of nationalism sweeping the Indian nation. In 1944 this same Goa Congress Committee in Bombay published a booklet entitled 'Denationalisation of the Goans' which condemned the colonisation attempts of the Portuguese administration and their attempts to create a culturally 'European' community on Indian soil. It was also published with the aim to 'awaken' the Catholic Goans from their situation and make them aware of their own subjugation.

In 1946, following Cunha's arrest, a meeting of over 100 Goans across the border in Londa was organised and A.G.

Tendulkar, became the president of the new Goa Congress Committee. Tendulkar identified Goa and her people with the larger Indian sub-continent and sought support in Goa's attempt to align herself with the Quit India Movement which he hoped would apply to all the foreign administrations currently in India. The Goan Hindu population, it seemed, was hoping to ride the wave of India's liberation movement and identified completely with this movement, feeling confident that the Portuguese would leave once the British were compelled to evacuate. The Portuguese, however, maintained their stance, arguing that Dr. Lohia and other agitators were disturbing the 'peaceful' people of Goa.

Though Martial Law had been declared, thus, banning political organisation in Goa, the events which were occurring in Goa were widely discussed and political identification among the Goan Hindus with her Indian neighbours had occurred despite the government's attempts otherwise. On the 18th of June, 1946, Dr. Ram Manohar Lohia instigated the Civil Disobedience Movement in Goa,[20] which would further rally the people towards an understanding of their subjugation. From October until December, 1946, a series of Satyagrahas in Goa were executed to demonstrate overtly the peoples' desire for their civil liberties.[21]

The year 1946 also witnessed the development of several political parties, each with its own agenda and assumptions as to where the land and people of Goa owed their greatest allegiance. Some political leaders argued that Goa should integrate herself as a part of Maharashtra, owing to the predominance of the Marathi language and culture in the Goan Hindu hinter-lands. Others harkened back to the Kadamba and Vijayanagara dynasties to demonstrate how close socio-cultural ties existed between Karnataka and Goa. Still others argued that the formation of an independent Republic was the only solution to the 'Goa question'. Finally, those leaders arising from within the native Catholic community promoted the creation of a Union territory functioning autonomously yet still linked to Portugal.

Thus, the people were pulled apart according to the private agendas of political parties, each of which tried to garner support for its own political position by creating an identification within the masses to these larger ideals. The people were veritable pawns in the political power play to determine which party would control the distribution of economic resources and power in Goa. As a result, the 'identity of Goa' came under fire and the people became confused and divided as to where they belonged. With all the politicised hype surrounding 'cultural heritage', 'imposed assimilation' and 'denationalised Goans', the question of 'Who am I ?' became a heavy psychological burden, especially for the native Catholics who inhabited the Old Conquests.

To help the Goans unite in their movement, Gandhiji suggested that all should unite under one platform i.e. the goal for the attainment of civil liberties.[22] He correctly realised that the encouragement of several different identifications would lead to social disintegration and even violent confrontation. In June of 1947, all the political parties in Goa met in Bombay and requested the Portuguese government to 'Quit India' and her possessions in the sub-continent.[23] The Liberation leaders assumed that as Britain was on the verge of leaving India, Portugal would soon follow. But on August 3, 1947, just prior to the Independence of India, Dr. Lohia made it public that Goa would have to continue her own freedom struggle and that contrary to popular opinion, the freedom of Goa would not coincide with that of India.[24] He also encouraged the National Congress (Goa) to fight not only for civil liberties but also for freedom and independence. His statement seemed to arise from the mixed sentiments emanating from the top levels in the New Delhi government, who were at odds in trying to resolve the 'Goa Question'.[25]

India gained her independence in August, 1947. Disillusionment among the people set in when the liberation of Goa was not followed by that of India's. The freedom fighters had put their faith in the new all-India government who now seemed to turn their backs and remove their support. This, in addition to the harsh repressive measures employed by the Portuguese government and the imprisonment of prominent freedom fighters in Goa resulted in a lull in the pace of activity. Meanwhile, the Indian Independence Act came into existence and ended the British empire in India, forming two nations along religious lines; India and Pakistan. The massacre, which followed as hundreds of thousands crossed the borders to relocate according to their respective religious alliances occupied the new Indian government. Thus, the events in Goa took a back seat to the more pressing problems resulting from partition. The massacre must also have frightened the Goan community, who were also somewhat divided along socio-religious lines.

Reactions in Portugal

Meanwhile, the dictator Salazar had delivered a speech in 1947 in Portugal which spread throughout Europe the image of Goan people as 'European' ; culturally, socially and religiously connected to Portugal.[26] This further discouraged the freedom fighters who had placed both their hopes and identities in the hands of the new Indian Government. The Catholic Goans continued to question their own heritage, identity and rightful place in society. If larger India seemed unwilling to address their concerns, to whom could they turn to? No doubt within the minds of the Goans both of these diverging views were entertained within various communities. In the 'war for identification' which followed in the wake of Indian liberation, people actively sought out an identity with a larger political entity and community. Those who were Catholic no doubt felt somehow 'different' from their Hindu brethren and if 'different' was understood to mean 'European', than it was towards Europe where many placed their hopes. The upper class Catholics who had even taken on Portuguese as their native language continued to identify with the Portuguese. In contrast, those Goans who followed the Hindu way of life and had only of late come under the Portuguese administration, felt identified with larger India and especially with Maharashtra. Likewise, communities from the Southern talukas of Goa (Quepem, Canacona) felt more aligned with Karnataka as they had throughout most of their history been connected politically and culturally with North Kanara.

In December of 1947, India and Portugal began to establish very weak diplomatic ties.[27] In January of 1948 the Portuguese Consul met the Indian Prime Minister and the question of Goa's integration into the Indian Union was again raised. The Portuguese, however, were unwilling to negotiate as they intended to retain their possessions of Goa, Daman and Diu. By 1948 the movement for Goa's liberation had come to a virtual standstill and on the 30th of January Gandhiji was murdered. People all over Goa and the world lamented the assassination of one of India's greatest men of all time.

In January of 1953, the Indian Legation in Lisbon sent a letter to the Portuguese Ministry of Foreign Affairs which clearly elucidated the Indian impression of the 'Goan situation'.[28] While the Indian government foresaw the eventual integration of Goa into the Indian union, the Portuguese administration was not ready nor willing to accept the 'inevitable'. Again the offer of a direct transfer was broached to the Portuguese administration, which was again unquestioningly refused.[29] In May of 1953 Diplomatic relations deteriorated and the Indian Legation in Lisbon closed down its office. In July of that same year, Prime Minister Nehru openly stated that the French and Portuguese possessions in India should be integrated into larger India, thus making known publicly the Indian government's position.[30] Reports circulated that the people in Goa were also receptive to the idea of integration, except for approximately over 200 families who were totally culturally assimilated to the Portuguese ways and enjoyed high political positions in the Goan administration. They were the Brahmin and some Ksyatria families who had converted to Catholicism and felt they had the most to loose if Goa was transferred to India.

The Involvement of India and the International Community

Consequently, two polarised camps propagating their political (and therefore economic) interests and using the issue of 'cultural identity' evolved to back up their claims. For the Indians and pro-Nationalist Goans, ample evidence existed in human form which demonstrated that Goa was really a part of India no different in culture, religion and language from that of her neighbours in the Indian Union. Other evidence also pointed out the existence of a Luso-Indian community which was markedly different culturally and religiously from larger India. Thus, while the western world came to understand Goa through the eyes of Portugal and Dr. Salazaar, larger India began to see the situation through the eyes of the freedom fighters and the Indian Nationalist government.

Beyond political considerations, however, there also appeared to be an emerging truth about Goa; that there were in fact two communities existing side by side, one which was identified to larger India and another whose culture, language, religion and society had evolved under the influence of the

Portuguese. Both Portugal and India believed they were in the right, consequently and that justice would prevail on each one's side. The Portuguese felt they had territorial sovereignty over Goa by rule of law and by the existence of a Luso-Indian community in Goa. Dr. Salazar also criticised the Indian government for propagating false statements regarding the Goans' opinion of their current situation. He further argued that the Luso-Indian community in Goa was markedly distinguishable from other Indians owing to the 'inter-penetration of cultures' which emerged following over 400 years of Portuguese rule.[31] The Indian Government and freedom fighters felt they were right in insisting that India must integrate into one nation and rid itself of foreign rule.

In 1954 Dr. P.D. Gaitonde, a prominent Goan surgeon and recognised freedom fighter, was arrested and jailed following an overt protest against the notion that Goa belonged to Portugal. When the complaint of Dr. Gaitonde's arrest reached the Indian government, the Nehru administration was reluctant to take action against Portugal. The reason for the Indian government's reluctance to take action regarding Goa becomes clearer in the context of the world situation. Portugal had formed an alliance with NATO, in which the latter countries (Great Britain, France, the USA, etc.) had agreed to offer each other assistance in the event that any country's territorial sovereignty was threatened. This agreement did not apply to colonies, however, but in Portuguese Law their overseas possessions in Goa were officially considered 'part' of Portugal and, therefore, any threat to them was considered as if it were a threat to mainland Portugal.[32] Thus, Portugal had the backing of some of the most powerful nations worldwide and had already alerted them to the situation in Goa. The Indian government, therefore, had to act cautiously and diplomatically in order to keep the situation under control and not risk the involvement of other international forces.

In 1954 the Goa Vimochan Sahayak Samiti (All-Party Goa Liberation Committee) was establishe to continue the civil disobedience movement and help the Satyagrahis financially and politically.[33] The Maharashtra and Gujarat Praja Socialist Party, for their own reasons, also took an active interest in the liberation of Goa and its integration into the Indian union as part of

Maharashtra. In 1954 and 1955 these political parties organised several Satyagraha movements in Goa inspired by Gandhiji and his demonstrations of non-violence disobedience. As a result of these organised movements, the Portuguese government charged the Indian government with propagating such activities and seeking to obstruct the territorial sovereignty by executing a Satyagraha along the Goan border.[34] They made it clear that action would be taken against the satyagrahis as their activity could hardly be seen as peaceful as it was intended to rouse the people to rebellion.

The Portuguese then appealed to various international powers and subsequently, Prime Minister Nehru announced that the Indian Government disapproved of the Satyagrahas.[35] His announcement, unexpected by the Satyagrahis who assumed all along that they had the Indian government's support, effectively stopped the impact of the Satyagraha. On the day when thousands were to instigate a Satyagraha only a small portion of the original five-hundred freedom fighters crossed the border. The Terekhol fort was seized but, it was captured by the Portuguese less than 24 hours later. Following the disapproval of the Indian National Government, the freedom movement lost its momentum, though it was kept alive by occasional small Satyagrahas across the border and the continued activity of the All-Goa Political Party Committee.[36]

In 1955 several organised Satyagrahis continued and were met with harsh treatment by the Portuguese army and government officials. The violent action of the Portuguese armies against the unarmed Satyagrahis gave the Indian government the ammunition they needed to justify a forceful entry into Goa and the liberation of her people.[37] Borders were sealed and all those stuck on either side were forbidden from crossing into their native territory.[38] The 'Goa question' gained further recognition within India and additional political organisations and even individual politicians in Parliament began overtly supporting the idea of Goan liberation. Still not everyone identified with the liberation from Portugal, especially the educated Goan Catholics who were anxious regarding the outcome of Goa's integration with India.

By 1955 the attitude of the Indian Government towards the Portuguese in Goa was clear: It supported the freedom fighters and intended to liberate Goa.[39] As a result of the nationalist movements gaining force around the world, tiny Goa became a symbol of the old colonial regimes and a territory which needed to be free in keeping with the spirit of the times. Between 1955 and 1961 no less than 6 political parties were found in Goa working towards the fulfilment of these aims namely the Azad Gomantak Dal, the Rancour Patriota, the United Front of Goans, the Goan People's Party the Goa Liberation Army and the Quit Goa Organisation.[40]

In 1958 elections were held in Portugal, following which Admiral Thomas, Salazar's chosen successor, was installed as the new dictator. Salazar , meanwhile, was under the impression that all was well in Portugal and Goa, owing to a period of peace which saw few Satyagrahas and arrests in Goa.[41] It was not long, however, before opposition began following the election. Within Portugal itself, the military dictatorship became increasingly unpopular and insurgencies in the African colonies further eroded the strength of the Portuguese empire.[42] Yet confusion still existed within the international community regarding the cultural identity of the Goan people. The Portuguese regime had presented a falsified picture to the world community which effectively portrayed Goa's population as entirely Luso-Indian and 'Portuguese.'

To correct this misconception, Dr. P.D. Gaitonde, now released from prison, presented a series of lectures around the world which addressed the 'problem of Goa in the context of Portuguese colonial policy'[43] and was instrumental in bringing Goa to the attention of the international community. Her plight became connected to that of the colonies in Africa which were similarly struggling to be free from foreign rule. While Portugal still threatened India with the use of NATO (North Atlantic Treaty Organization), world opinion regarding Goa was slowly shifting in favour of India and the liberation of Goa.

In 1961, the Government of India reasserted her position and determined that Goa would be liberated either with full peace or with the full use of force. The nationalist Goans and many non-Goan Indians, considered this change in official policy an enormous success.[44] The Luso-Indian community in Goa, however, was not thrilled with the idea of Goa being integrated into larger

India. Priviledged and praised by the Portuguese administration, they had been fully acculturated under the Europeans and felt pride in their current cultural heritage and shame towards that of the Hindu-Indians. Yet the Indian nation was calling for them to join in the fight to free Goa. However, the word 'peaceful' liberation was stressed and India's commitment to the maintenance of world peace took precedence over the use of force to liberate a Portuguese colony. Portugal, on the contrary, was refusing to accept that her colonial empire had to end and showed no qualms about throwing the weight of NATO into the areṇa in order to maintain its hold on the colonies.

The War for Liberation

In August of 1961 the Indian military began preliminary preparations for a three-pronged attack on Goa, Daman and Diu. With the international community favouring the Indian perspective, Prime Minister Nehru on December 1st, 1961 publicly announced that India would not remain silent regarding the 'Goa situation'.[45] Following that announcement, Indian military troops were concentrated in various cities on the periphery of Goa such as Belgaum and Karwar. By mid-December, European women and children, the families of military and official personnel, were evacuated from Goa, Daman and Diu.

As troops built-up along the 180-mile border between Goa and India, the USA and Great Britain urged India not to use force but rather to seek a negotiated settlement.[46] Portugal remained defiant, however, insisting on her absolute right over the territory of Goa. Final preparations were made and Operation Vijay, a simultaneous attack on Goa, Daman and Diu, was scheduled for December 18th, 1961. On that morning, Indian troops entered Goa and without any resistance occupied the southern stretch from North of Karwar to the city of Margao. The North and East were taken in a similar fashion and the invasion was over in less than 48 hours. In Goa the Portuguese armies had installed roadblocks and blown up bridges, buying a few days time from in UN for a ceasefire.[47] They also expected reinforcements from Portugal and Pakistan, which never arrived owing to the expediency of the invasion. In all, less than 50 casualties were reported and all three former Portuguese possessions were occupied by the Indian military forces.[48]

The Indian occupation had been quick and relatively peaceful and the native population was grateful that virtually no fighting had occurred. By the end of the month, the majority of Indian forces had left Goa and over 20,000 employees of the former Portuguese administration took an oath of loyalty to the President and Constitution of the Indian Union.[49] Following this oath, they were then reinstated in the same posts to which they had been ascribed prior to the Indian occupation. Thus, the concern which the Catholic community had held regarding the possible loss of their status and occupations was alleviated and religious freedom was further guaranteed to both Catholics and Hindus. The Portuguese citizenship which Goans had hitherto enjoyed was still recognised and eventually those citizens who wanted and were able to secure passports migrated from Goa to Portugal.[50] Following the liberation of Goa, Daman and Diu, Dr. Salazar continued to insist that the people in his colonies were Luso-Indian that the culture of Goa would conflict with that of larger India.

POST-LIBERATED GOA

On the 20th of December, 1961, Goa, Daman and Diu were integrated into larger India under the designation of Union Territories. The territories would remain as such until the people reached a decision as to how they would like to integrate into larger India. They were also assured that their cultural uniqueness would not be affected by their merger with India and that all were free to practice their religion and cultural traditions. Following the replacement of the military administration with a Civil Administration in June of 1962, the new government decided to promote economic and social development schemes akin to India's Five-Year Plans. In October of 1962, the first democratic elections were held in the villages and in December of 1963 the first general elections were held to elect 30 members to the Goa, Daman and Diu Assembly created by the Government of the Union Territories Act of 1963.

The Maharashtrawadi Gomantak Party won these first elections, demonstrating that many of the people of Goa now identified with Maharashtra politically, culturally and linguistically.[51] Though this demonstrated a strong identification with Maharashtra, it is also important to realise that several of the main political parties hailed from that region and had launched massive compaign in an attempt to gain Goa for Maharashtra. However, the majority vote kept Goa in its status quo, though from these figures it could be seen that this status quo would not be accepted for long. Daman and Diu similarly rejected unification with Gujarat and all three for the time being remained as Union Territories.

Following the economic planning and human resource development policies adopted by the Goa government, the statistics gathered in 1986 showed a marked improvement in the social conditions of the majority. The infant mortality rate had gradually declined from approximately 13.5 per cent to 6.8 per cent, the literacy rate had increased from 31 per cent to 57 per cent and the number of villages with electricity had increased from 4 to 411.[52] The number of combined middle and higher secondary schools had increased from 4 to 32 and in 1985 the Goa University was founded to provide for higher education. Other polls showed that situation of women in Goa was far superior to that of other

Indian States and that most women in Goa were receiving at least a basic education. Family size had decreased owing to the supportive attitude taken by the government towards the practice of family planning. Health awareness and education had been established in schools and the roads and infrastructure were likewise undergoing improvements.[53]

Though the liberation was greeted with enthusiasm among the Hindu community who had long suffered from oppression under the Portuguese, the Catholic community was not as ecstatic following Goa's integration with India. No longer would the Catholic Goans enjoy the same degree of power and prestige which they had enjoyed under the Portuguese administration and no longer would their religion and culture, within the context of larger India, be regarded as superior. Rather, many feared they would be reduced to the status of a minority community and would face reverse persecution as had the Muslims following the partition of India and Pakistan. From the experience of the Gaudes, it became clear that reconversion in order to adapt to the new socio-administrative environment was not a viable option. More than that, the Goan Catholics, especially the women, enjoyed their relatively 'progressive' social environment which enabled education attendance at social functions like dances. Thus, among the average Goan Catholic who had neither power nor prestige to gain from the Liberation, the event was greeted more with passive acceptance than with jubilation.

REPRESENTING GOAN CULTURAL IDENTITY

Liberation created both a political power vacuum and an identity crisis for the Catholic Goans who had identified themselves with Portugal and Portuguese culture. The question of how to fully integrate Goa into larger India remained. The removal of the dominant Portuguese power also created a vacuum of concrete political identification in the early post-Liberation years. As a result, different political groups began vying for the popular vote, hoping to mobilise the masses towards a particular political party which served its own agenda. Neither Maharashtra nor Karnataka could garner enough support to vote to evoke a merger, however, political rivalries began again. Both neighbouring States felt they had the 'right' to claim Goa as their territory, though Karnataka's cultural ties with the Goan people had lessened owing to the influence of the Portuguese in the coastal talukas and the influence of the Marathas in the in-land talukas during the Portuguese rule. Goan society was again pulled apart, forced to divide itself rather than work towards integration. Once again in the history of Goa, communities were asked to identify themselves politically on religious and linguistic lines.

Those communities wishing to keep Goa as a Union Territory were strongly identified with the Portuguese and had reluctantly acceded to the transfer of Goa. Among this community, namely the upper-class Catholics, an 'identity vacuum' was created owing to the removal of the Portuguese administration with whom they had for so long identified. This group, having been enculturated in a different environment, could not imagine a merger with a neighbouring State whose majority might completely alienate the Catholic community. They feared that merger with Maharashtra would result in the marginalisation of both Goa and the Catholic community. Although 40 per cent of the inhabitants in Goa had chosen to identify with Maharashtra, the elite community of Catholics raised a voice of strong opposition when this possibility was posed. They proposed separate Statehood based on their real and perceived differences in religion, language, culture and lifestyle. Separate Statehood also satisfied the problem of an identification void created by the removal of the Portuguese administration. The Catholic community could identify themselves politically as Goans, therefore, maintaining their separate identity while simultaneously adjusting to their new status as part of the Indian Union.

The Hindus of Goa, however, did not experience a similar identity crisis. They felt united and integrated into the Indian Union and did not manifest symptoms of psychological strain following Liberation. The Goan Hindus easily identified with larger India and felt proud to call themselves 'Indians' after so many years. Most were very content following the events which brought in the Indian Army and were gifted with a new freedom of cultural expression. Yet in the final outcome the idea of a separate State was offered as a way to fully integrate Goa while simultaneously recognising and supporting the idea that part of Goa had, in fact, evolved for 450 years under different socio-historical circumstances. This resolution seemed to please the majority and in 1987 Goa entered the Republic of India as a separate State.

Even then, however, the question of the State language was raised and hotly debated among communities. Konkani was spoken by most, but was an oral language whose only alphabet had been given by the Portuguese in Roman script. Marathi was offered as it was the literary language of the Hindu population, but the Catholic majority rejected this proposal on the grounds that they had neither attachment nor knowledge of Marathi whatsoever. English and Portuguese were briefly proposed by some, but as they were foreign languages, these proposals were soon dropped. After considerable discussion, it was decided to adopt Konkani in the Devnagiri script as an adequate compromise which not only satisfied both communities but which subsequently recognised Konkani as a separate language rather than a mere dialect of Marathi, which many had presumed it to be.

As the Hindu Goans had identified themselves with the Indian nation and had readily accepted the term 'Indian' to describe themselves, the Catholic community, sensing its difference, was not ready in those first post-Liberation years to fully embrace the self-label 'Indian'. Therefore, they monopolised the term 'Goan' which had a dual meaning as 'part Indian, yet actually different from Indians'. While the Hindu Goans cheered their identification with larger India as Indians, the Catholic population was busy defining 'Goan' identity in accordance with their own culture. This new 'Goan' identity, created following integration as a Union Territory, which replaced their now obsolete identification as 'Portuguese'. The Catholic community quickly defined 'Goan' so as to mean their way of life, was both Indian and European, ignoring the 60 per cent Hindu population which inhabited the tiny State. This explains Perceva Naronha's perception of 1993 in which he states, "We Goans have a different mentality, a different language, a different culture. Although we are now under Indian occupation, I feel awkward when I cross the old border into India...suddenly everything changes; the food, the landscape, the buildings, the people, the way of life.."[54] Goa here is presented as a place altogether different from the rest of India. Though misleading when the entire community and State is taken into consideration, it does speak frankly about the perceptions that Catholic Goans, especially the upper-class, shared about themselves and their State.

Consequently, when the decision had to be made as to whether Goa should become a State or be integrated into Maharashtra, the Goan community had already defined and elaborated upon this cultural identity which, they argued, necessitated separate Statehood. Proponents of Statehood promoted this different cultural identity far and wide to garner support for the establishment of a separate State. The entire State of Goa, as a consequence, became represented by the Catholic community and their different cultural identity was used as political justification for the creation of a new State.

The people of Goa from both communities at first chose to represent the cultural identity of Goa as different. Educated members of the Hindu community also saw the chance for Goa to improve and become economically viable if she were given the status of statehood. They feared that Goa would be neglected under a merger with neighbouring States or that a major migration would occur which would destroy Goa's natural beauty and over-populate the region. Many elite members of both Hindu and Catholic communities were also lured by the possibility of power and political control, which, as an Indian State, would involve both Hindu and Catholic communities according to the voters. Thus, it was initially in the interests of all communities involved to represent Goa as having a cultural identity linked to larger

India yet unique to Goa as well. It was this 'unique' cultural identity which garnered support for the creation of the State of Goa. Officials in New Delhi could justify the move because of their previously stated intention not to disturb the existing cultures in Goa and, thus, appease all of their constituents (except Maharashtra). By integrating Goa as a separate State, political, economic and social decisions would be made by both communities, giving them a sense of autonomy and responsibility for the welfare of the people. Communities which had been previously marginalised under the Portuguese administration would be able to actively participate in the administration of government and the Catholic community would continue to hold high offices as well. Reverse persecution was avoided and events such as these had occurred between Pakistan and India were also avoided. Thus, Statehood, justified by the different 'cultural identity' of Goa, was perceived by both Hindu and Catholic communities alike as the best outcome for all those concerned.

Promoting the cultural identity of Goa as 'different and unique' served the tourist industry as well. Western tourists, for example, began arriving in Goa in the 1960's immediately following Liberation. Mistaking Goa's 'live and let live' attitude for permissiveness, many back-packers and followers of the so called 'hippie' culture also began making Goa their home and soon she had earned a worldwide reputation as a popular tourist destination. Hotels, restaurants and many tourist attractions were created and within less than 20 years Goa's economy came to rely heavily on the industry of tourism. Goa, thus, needed a gimmick, something to make this tiny Indian State stand out among other popular tourist destinations. Again the 'East meets West' and old colonial legacies were harnessed to service such needs. Tourist brochures flooded Europe with descriptions of Goa as the 'Rome of the Orient', a true blending of Occident and Indian and 'India's Last Paradise.' Tourism catered to Western countries, whose people had been taken by the idea of travel and had the money to spend on such luxuries. Therefore, to improve business the image in Goa was further crafted according to what people in Goa thought would appeal to the western countries. The cities were highlighted for their old Portuguese-style villas and the restaurants which served Goan food listed it separately from Indian food. 'Goan' again was taken to mean 'different' but 'related' to India and such cultural representation continued to enlarge the audience which accepted these representations as absolute reality. Goan cultural identity came to be represented worldwide as the Eastern Orient, an image which appealed to the western tourists and brought them to Goa in droves, especially from various countries in Europe. This image was confirmed by the travellers who came to Goa and stayed mostly in the three coastal talukas of Salcette, Bardez and Tiswadi of the Old Conquests where the most tourist facilities and incidentally the most Catholic Goans, reside. The preponderance of white-washed churches, western dress and public functions (dances, feast days, etc.) in the most heavily touristed areas further contributed to the propagation of the Goan cultural identity as mostly Luso-Indian. Even in major tourist guides written entirely about Goa, there is hardly any mention of Bicholim Taluka. Sanguem, Sattari and Quepem are likewise virtually omitted. Goa tourism seems to have determined that with all the temples and Hindu religious cites publicised throughout India, visitors to Goa were looking for something different, something unique and the Portuguese legacy in Goa offered just that.

Though the Catholic population in 1996 was only 30 per cent of the entire population of Goa, it has been an important segment of the population from a cultural and historical perspective. It was this population which helped to consolidate the Portuguese control over the three coastal talukas and it was this population whose majority remained relatively loyal to the Portuguese crown and culture throughout their rule. Only when the Catholic Goans themselves began to question their own situation, marked in Goan history by the Pinto's Revolt, did the Goans begin to realise the extent of their subjugation. Also, it was this community whose cultural identity became an issue both in political circles and within their own psychology. Had this community not existed in Goa, then it surely would have been integrated into Maharashtra following Liberation. Thus, the existence of the Catholic community is responsible for Goa's attainment of statehood as its cultural identity was considered justification for such a political decision. In the case of the Goan Catholics, the majority seemed to react with an attitude of passive acceptance towards the liberation of Goa from the Portuguese. Though they were subjugated, they were given a better position in society and were praised for their loyalty and cultural assimilation. When the troops came into Goa, many Catholics feared for their lives and some fled to off-shore boats during the first freedom wars. Following Liberation, the Catholic community was able to salvage its identity and social status by redefining 'Goan' in a way which satisfied their identity crisis and incorporated both Indian and Portuguese elements into a description of their 'unique' culture. The question remains, however, if the Goan Catholics ever liberated themselves psychologically from the internalisation of Portuguese attitudes.

The Hindu community, albeit persecuted by the Portuguese, has since Liberation been able to identify with larger India and regain some of the confidence and pride which had been suppressed by the Portuguese. As is characteristic of repressed communities, the Hindu population in the Old Conquests had suffered under some prejudicial laws which kept them from advancing their position. Those Hindus who kept to their religion were forbidden from taking part in the life of the Catholic community while at the same time were prohibited from establishing their own. Yet Marathi schools still flourished in Goa and the Hindu community still celebrated its religious festivals at the temples in the talukas of Ponda, Bicholim and Quepem. Upon liberation this community, 60 per cent of Goa's population, finally won its freedom. They knew they were repressed and consequently were able to realise their own liberation. Later on, a form of subconscious repression arose from the omission of the Goan Hindu culture in definitions and descriptions of Goan cultural identity. Members of both communities seem to be in the process of rectifying this development.

Following the creation of the State of Goa in 1987, this 'cultural identity distinct from larger India' remained attached to Goa and marginalised the Hindu population. Statehood, thus, solved a variety of problems, but also created some in its stead. Goa became identified with the Catholic community which was only 30 per cent of the entire State of Goa and few people outside the State even knew that there were Hindus living in the State. Goa quickly became known both regionally and internationally as a State which was 'different' from the rest of India and as a culture comprised of 'Catholic, Carnival and Curry'. This purposeful misconception brought in many tourists looking to 'get a taste of the good life'. In national demonstrations of the Goan cultural heritage the Portuguese dances and songs are often invoked and an international dance tour which visited Portugal in July of 1997 performed Mandos, Dulpods, the Dekhni and the Kunbi as the cultural folk-dances of the State.

The Hindu community, as a consequence, became marginalised in descriptions of Goa both nationally and internationally. The 'element' of Goa which fought for her freedom and liberation consisted mostly of Goan Hindus and it is to them where the most gratitude is owed for Goa's liberation from a repressive regime and integration into India. The majority of freedom fighters and Satyagrahis were of Goan Hindu origin and most of those who lost their lives also hailed from the Hindu community. It is only of late that small voices, mostly within the academic circles, are calling out for recognition. *Goa: Concepts and Misconcepts*, for example, is a scholarly work published by the Goan Hindu Society in Bombay intended to expose the misleading representations of Goan cultural identity and simultaneously bring to everyone's attention the existence of the Goan Hindu community in the State of Goa. Thirty-six years after Liberation, brochures have begun to include the Saraswat Temples of Goa and other Historic sites in the taluka of Ponda. No longer a crisis of identity but rather a call for inclusion, the Hindu community in Goa is also desiring recognition as an active, dynamic element in society seeking to share the 'Goan' identity.

State-identification has become an important part of an individual's self-definition in our modern age, even more important than national identification for those who will never travel outside of their own country. Consequently, a modification of the definition of 'Goan cultural identity' seems to be necessary in order to allow all of Goa's inhabitants to be recognised in the identity of Goa. How to achieve this while still maintaining a strong tourist industry lured by the promise of 'East meeting West' is the latest challenge to politicians, business interests and individuals who seek to incorporate both Hindu and Catholic communities into one which identifies with Goa and with 'Goan cultural identity.' This is a necessary challenge, however, in order to create a State whose residents recognise and are recognised by the State as important to the larger community and culture. Psychologically, this will also ease the tension which still exists between both communities. For a while Goan Hindus are able to fully identify with larger India, they are yet to identify with Goan culture and the identity of their state.

Changes in this direction are already apparent in 1997. Goan *Shigmo,* an ancient religious celebration in Goan Hindu society, has evolved into a street parade akin to the carnival following the Portuguese era. This year, the crowd, the participants and the gaiety of Shigmo surpassed that of the carnival street parade of February for the first time. Several folk-dances of the Goan Hindus, bands resembling those of the Maratha armies and night-time floats depicting scenes from the *Mahabharata* and *Ramayana* wound their way through the main streets in Panjim and continued pleasing the crowd until past midnight. The Zatras (temple festivals) are widely celebrated in the in-land talukas and during Holi even the capital city of Panjim comes alive with people throwing coloured particles. In addition, large tourist brochures printed by the Goan Tourism Department are now mentioning the Saraswat temples as among the sites worth visiting in Ponda taluka and the history of Goa prior to the Portuguese conquest is also included. Slowly, changes are taking place in the collective attitude which will allow for modifications in 'Goan cultural identity'.

The Goan Catholics of today's generation are also changing in this direction. Identification with larger India is generally part of the self-definition among most of the educated youth population, even among those whose parents adhere to their post-Portuguese identity. Hindi is known among many in the community, although, it is not spoken in Goa amongst locals. Konkani is still a widely spoken language among all communities and English is also very popular among the educated classes. The Cultural Festival of Miramar is the larger community's attempt (beyond obvious economic gains) to integrate the various forms of musical enjoyment and cultural styles into a programme which gives recognition to them all. During this festival which lasts for 5 nights, folk-dances and classical Indian music are presented alongside rock bands and fashion shows. Konkani theatre, Classical Indian dance and Hindi pop songs are also part of this week-long event.

The Hindu community in the younger generation has also made steps in the direction of integration. Youth will sometimes attend Catholic-sponsored dances and public events and a few even make the sign of the cross as a sign of respect while passing the Bambolim shrine. Inter-dating between Hindus and Catholics is also on the rise and intermarriages, though still highly criticised, have also begun to increase in frequency. Members of both communities are now sharing the same work environment and are continuously influenced by each other, resulting in a slow but steady convergence of cultures. Individuals from the highly educated communities are finding that they have much in common and it seems that the most recent social trends point to the development of a socio-economic class system as opposed to one divided along lines of caste.

Research indicates that the socio-economic status of women in Hindu society also parallels that of their Catholic brethren. The communities in Goa were divided into six broad categories: low, middle and upper classes of Hindus and the same divisions among the Catholic community.[55] Among the low socio-economic groupings, much similarity was reported between both Hindu and Catholic communities. The girls start work between the ages of 13 and 15 and stop their education after the 10th standard at which time tuition is charged for higher studies. They usually find employment as saleswomen, selling in the local markets, or in some cases working in the fields. Most formal salaries earned range around one lakh yearly (US$ 3,500). Dating is very covert if it occurs at all and women are given little voice in their choice of a life partner. Full male dominance combined with full female suppression are characteristics in communities belonging to this socio-economic status and family size ranges from 3-5 children of late, 6-9 at the time of liberation. The frequent use of alcohol among male members of this community (70 per cent) which results in a corresponding rate of extramarital affairs among women, is also an unfortunate trend among members of this community.[56] Chamars, Gaudes, Kunbis and some Shudra communities (50 per cent of the latter) belong to this socio-economic grouping.

Among the middle socio-economic class, similar trends are reported between Catholic and Hindu communities with slight variation. Women in both communities usually continue their education until the ages between 18 and 22-23, often earning higher degrees in Masters' Programmes. Middle class Catholic women will seek out employment, but most middle-class Hindu women view it as a sign of prestige if their husband is able to support the family. Nursing, marketing and office employment in government jobs are often the domain of the middle class. Some engineering and medical professionals also emerge from the middle class and the average yearly salary ranges from 2 to 4 lakhs. Dating is covert among this community and women are given some voice in their choice of a life partner. Among the Catholics, partial male dominance combined with mild female suppression is generally recognised, while among the middle-class Hindu families significant male dominance and moderate female suppression occurs. Shudras (50 per cent), Kashatriyas (70 per cent) and some Brahmins (1 per cent) make up the majority of this community whose average family size is 2-4 children of late and 6-9 at the time of Liberation.

Among the upper class Goan Catholic and Hindu communities, parallel socio-economic trends are also emerging. Women are not expected to work at a young age and often seek advanced degrees leading to medicine, business and other highly skilled professions. They begin working by age 27-28 and often assist in the family business. Among the Catholics, women often do not work after marriage but take on social work in the church or other charity organisations. They often help out with their husband's business and manage the financial accounts or public relations. Dating occurs openly in both communities and women are given considerable voice in their choice of a life partner. Five lakhs and above is the expected salary for members of the upper class communities usually from the Kshatryias (30 per cent) and Brahmins (70 per cent). Today's family has from 1 to 3 children, a number which had decreased from 6 to 9 in 1961.

Trends indicate, therefore, at least a socio-economic convergence among the Hindu and Catholic communities of Goa today. The similarities in socio-economic status often create the same world view and cultural concerns as well. Personality development is also heavily influenced by socio-economic status and certain personality traits may be more attainable in one community where the socio-economic opportunities are greater than in other groups where finances present a constant obstacle to upward mobility. Government policies have also encouraged the deterioration of caste and the emergence of class by adopting affirmative action policies which recognise the economic disadvantages of the poor communities. Individuals in a similar socio-economic brackets aim for similar goals, expect similar experiences in life and demonstrate similar attitudes towards communities of higher and lower socio-economic status accordingly. An upper class Hindu and Catholic would most probably be able to develop a more genuine relationship with each other than would an upper-class Catholic with a lower-class individual from the same religious community.

Differences and prejudice between the religious groups do exist. However, young Catholic women are highly criticised for what people perceive as 'moral laxness', when in actuality both communities are relatively conservative and more closely resemble the behaviour of each other than that of the western community. Owing to the 'fun, food and fiesta' reputation that has been presented to tourists, Catholic women in Goa are often placed in the picture as part of that scene. If one travels to the tourist destinations, however, the Catholic Goan women are relatively few in number compared to the out of State tourists of both western and Indian origin. If there do exist avenues for carnal enjoyment, they arise from the tourists themselves and only very rarely from a native female Goan. The recent influx of migrants from other areas may also have contributed to the current stain on the reputation of Goan women. These migrants usually come from more conservative areas within India and are not used to the freedom and social movement which Goan women enjoy. The amiable, fun-loving Goan personality is viewed through a different lens that perceives these behaviours as deviant and unbecoming in the female character.

Likewise, the Hindu community is often thought to be backward and stuck in obsolete tradition by some Catholics. Female suppression is highly criticised by educated Catholics who feel that Hindu women do not enjoy the same social and psychological freedoms as do their Catholic friends. Likewise, the Hindu community is often considered hypocritical owing to their outward presentation which often does not match their covert action. On both sides, many of these prejudices are leftover from pre-Liberation days and will hopefully fade with time, education and greater efforts towards respectful understanding.

Thus, this chapter's is was to examine possibilities surrounding how and why the entire cultural identity of Goa came to be represented as that of the Catholic community and the elite Catholic community in particular. Initially, during the struggle for Liberation from the Portuguese, Goa was projected as socio-culturally linked to larger India and her people identified themselves with the Indian Union. Later, owing to economic, political and social interests, the separate and 'different' cultural identity of Goa was promoted both internationally and in the new administration of the Indian Republic following Liberation. Socially, the projection of the 'unique' cultural identity allayed fears that the Catholic community would become marginalised under the new Republic. Economically, the projection of Goa as the place where 'East meets West' brought thousands of tourists into Goa and created a new industry based on tourism. Politically, projecting Goan culture as 'different' and 'unique' from larger India justified the formation of a new State which appealed to both Hindu and Catholic communities. Statehood enabled the people to control their own economy and urged them to work together for the same goals of economic, social and infrastructural development. Subsequently, 12 years following the creation of the State of Goa, the two communities have come closer together and demonstrate similar socio-economic trends which surpass religious differences. However, differences are still widely recognised between the communities and it will take additional time before these differences are reconciled and both communities become fully incorporated into representations of Goan cultural identity.

REFERENCES

1. Gaitonde, P. D., *The Liberation of Goa*, New Delhi: Oxford University Press, 1987, p. 5.
2. Political Identity.
3. *Ibid.*
4. *Ibid.*
5. Gaitonde, P.D., *op. cit.*, p. 5.

6. Gaitone, P.D., *op. cit.*, p. 6.
7. Gaitone, P.D. *op. cit.*, p. 6.
8. *Ibid.*, p. 7.
9. *Ibid.*, p. 5.
10. *Ibid.*, pp. 7-8.; includes factual information of the preceding paragraph.
11. *Ibid.*
12. Whereby the individuals recognised Portugal and Portugal recognised them as individuals of the State.
13. *Ibid.*, p. 17.
14. *Ibid.*, p. 20.
15. P. P. Shirodkar, (Ed.) Goa: Cultural Trends- Seminar Papers. Panjim: Director of Archives, Archaeology, and Museum, 1988.
16. See Chapter on Goan Communities Today.
17. Gaitonde, P.D. *op. cit.*, p. 20.
18. *Ibid.*, p. 22.
19. *Ibid.*, p. 25.
20. *Ibid.*, p. 30.
21. *Ibid.*, p. 33.
22. *Ibid.*
23. *Ibid.*
24. *Ibid.*
25. *Ibid.*, p. 35.
26. *Ibid.*, p. 46.
27. *Ibid.*, p. 48.
28. *Ibid.*, p. 70.
29. *Ibid.*, p. 72.
30. *Ibid.*
31. *Ibid.*, p. 46.
32. *Ibid.*, p. 95.
33. *Ibid.*, p. 92.
34. *Ibid.*, p. 93.
35. *Ibid.*, p. 99.
36. *Ibid.*, p. 100.
37. *Ibid.*, p. 110.
38. *Ibid.*, p. 111.
39. *Ibid.*, p. 113.
40. *Ibid.*, p. 120.
41. *Ibid.*, p. 130.
42. *Ibid.*, p. 140.

43. Gaitone, p. 143.
44. Gaitonde, P.D., *op. cit.*, p. 143.
45. *Ibid.*
46. *Ibid.*, p. 153.
47. *Ibid.*, p. 166.
48. *Ibid.*, p. 168.
49. *Ibid.*
50. *Ibid.*
51. Angle, Prabhakar S., *Goa: Concepts and Misconcepts*. Bombay: Goan Hindu Association. 1994, Ch. 1.
52. *Ibid.*
53. Gaitonde, P. D. *op. cit.*, Conclusion.
54. Angle, S. Prabhakar, *op. cit.* p. 23.
55. The following information was collected during interviews at the IPHB Psychiatric Hospital in Altin, Panjim, in April of 1997.
56. *Ibid.*, Interview with Dr. Dias, IPHB, Altin, Panjim.

Chapter 5

Communities in the Old and New Conquests

The last chapters have examined the history, politics and social evolution of the people inhabiting Goa, thus, facilitating a better understanding of the many 'faces' and communities existing in Goa today. Placing the major sub-communities of Goa within their historical framework not only establishes the foundation which explains their current socio-economic, educational and cultural components, but also enables the student of Goa to more readily distinguish between the various communities as they interact and perform the tasks characteristics of their lives. The multilayered and ancient history of Goa manifests among the people who inhabit the land to such an extent that even the pre-recorded historical era of Goa lives in the cultures and ancestral beliefs of the tribal communities. Ancient ascribed professions such as toddy-tapping, buffalo herding and fishing likewise provide glimpses into the past as living examples because they have experienced only slight modifications over centuries and remain in tune with and dependent upon the rhythmic cycles of nature.

In order to get a glimpse of the communal variety existing in Goa, this next chapter outlines the major communities which colour the existing society as it is found today, from the upper-caste urban Catholics to the Dhangar buffalo herders. The economic, educational and traditional variety of communities in Goa attest to the various historical forces and cultural layers which have taken root in Goa and evolved accordingly. Though these social groupings vary significantly, there are some similarities which exist throughout the communities and subcommunities in Goa. Naturally, as the people of Goa occupy the same geographical space, they utilise common materials, experience the same climatic conditions and share an economic base. Communities in Goa likewise exist within the same social milieu which is comprised of 15 per cent Brahmans, 12 per cent Ksyatriyas, 9 per cent Vaishyas and 41 per cent Shudras.[1] Most people living in Goa consume rice on a daily basis and 75 per cent are non-vegetarian and take fish-curry-rice as their basic meal. All villagers have access to electricity[2], drinking water and most if not all have access to public transportation. Among society-wide trends, education for women has been accepted by most communities in Goa, though illiteracy still hovers around 20 per cent owing to the poor communities who need their children to work in the fields. Another trend in Goa across communities is the gradual erosion of the joint family in favour of the nuclear family system. This is more noticeable in Catholic families, urban-dwellers and families with a high socio-economic status. Many joint families are still found in rural areas where family income and property are less and financial need and extended family ties are stronger. Monogamy and marriage through negotiation are likewise practised among all communities inhabiting Goa, though the frequency of love marriages is on the rise among the upper-class urban educated youth. Migration from rural areas to urban centres is another society-wide trend; and the percentage of urban dwellers has markedly increased from 14.8 per cent in 1960 to 41.02 per cent in 1991.[3] Migration from the interior to the coastal urban areas is another cross-community trend owing to the facilities, employment and educational institutions available in these areas. Occupational mobility has increased among the youth in Goa. This is owing to both personal ambition as well as government affirmative action policies which have helped students from disadvantaged communities to attain new heights through the reservation of seats in government and educational institutions. All citizens of Goa also live by the same civil code of law which was first established by the Portuguese administration and has since been adapted following integration into the Indian union. Finally, religion in Goa, whether Catholic, Hindu or Muslim forms the backbone of society and structures most social and life-cycle events.

Until recently, most communities in Goa have been omitted from representations of 'Goan cultural identity'. While earlier chapters have pointed out the historical and political evolution which has led to such a misrepresentation, this chapter aims to include these 'forgotten' communities through an overview of their socio-cultural characteristics. Many inferences can be made from these statistics and characteristics which also reveal certain attitudes, community-wide beliefs and sub-communal social psychology. Education, political identification, economic resources, women's roles, traditional occupations, marriage rituals and religion are also examined as they are fundamental components of any community which determine the evolution of its culture and identity. Though the following chapter is not exhaustive, it does attempt to explore the more 'concrete' and visible differences between the various communities in Goa. These can then point to the more underlying psychological differences among Goans and open the possibility for further study in this regard.

The history, religion and cultural traditions of a society can be talked about with ease, but they often loose their meanings if no context is available in which to visualise such concepts. Goa's heart and soul lie in her villages and it is here where the values and traditions of the Goans are born, continued and celebrated. It is the village atmosphere and society which creates a sense of belonging and a set of attitudes which are transplanted along with rural-urban migrants in Bombay, Bangalore and other cities. Yet the question remains as to what does a Goan village look like? What does one feel like? History books and research works are often excellent producers of facts and figures but they leave the reader with little understanding of the daily life and character of Goan society. This chapter is intended to show glimpses of Goan village life within the Old and New Conquests within the State of Goa.[4]

The following village glimpses are meant not to provide the reader with facts, figures and descriptions of every celebration in a particular village, but rather to help the reader to develop an overall portrait of traditional village life in Goa. I have done this by highlighting specific aspects of particular villages which stand out as both unique and common features in order to demonstrate both similarities and differences existing within villages in Goa. Individuals in Goa would certainly agree that there are vast differences among villages and communities which scholarly generalisations often ignore, yet these ignored nuances are integral to the inner dynamics of village Goa as well as to a greater understanding of village life. Northern inland villages are different from Southern coastal villages which are different from suburban villages and remote tribal regions. A portrait of village life is also perhaps necessary to understand both prior and subsequent chapters of this book, including not only Goa and her past but also migrated communities and the future cultural evolution and identity that Goan society may experience. Rivona, Agonda, Galjibaga, Maulingam, Goa Velha, Anjuna, Ponda, Oxel-Kakra-Naxem and Panjim[5] are the villages under study in an attempt to gain a more regional understanding of the variety found in Goan villages.

RIVONA: A CASE STUDY

The village of Rivona is located on the border between modern-day Quepem and Sanquem talukas in the Southern half of the State of Goa. Located in the New Conquests, this area was one of the last to experience the Portuguese influence and one which only on occasion directly experienced the wars which raged in the northern New Conquests. It has remained a peaceful village throughout its existence, a serenity which manifests not only in the natural vegetation but in the village psyche as well. Rolling hills and lush green forest terrain dotted by small cultivated fields describes the landscape of this village which is watered by abundant flowing rivers and fresh springs.

Rivona is irrigated by the passage of the River Kushawati which runs through Quepem and flows into the Arabian Sea. During the 14th and 15th centuries the Arabs would sail through this river to reach Chandor. Prior to the Muslim invasions, during the Chandragupta and Kadamba dynasties, Chandor (only 12 kms from Rivona) was an ancient and prosperous capital city of successive generations. During that era the Rivona region was a sacred Buddhist hideaway owing to the fresh hot springs, abundance of rushing water and lush forests which made it an ideal place for meditation. It was also a sacred place for Rishis, ancient Hindu philosophers who went in search of enlightened knowledge through meditation and unity with natural elements. Within a span of 2 sq. kms, more than 20 perennial springs can be found in the Rivona countryside. Ancient rock-cut caves which were centres of Buddhist worship are found in the outskirts of Rivona and drawings of animals and birds on these rocks are dated from the centuries prior to the birth of Christ.

Today's town centre consists of few general stores, a daily market for fresh fish, fruits, vegetables and also houses the State Bank of India. Set aside from heavily trafficked roads, Rivona is a small, sprawling village which quietly merges into its neighbours with hardly any demarcation. Few tourists ever reach Rivona as there were neither guest houses nor restaurants to aid the weary traveller. But today, buses connect Rivona with Quepem, Margao and other nearby town centres which enable villagers to travel to work or places of higher education.

Rivona village is divided into 9 vaddos (wards) Addem, Zambaulim, Baga, Mott, Queri, Colomb, Ghantiwada, Rivona Market and Doirem/Fatima in which 75 per cent of the people follow the Hindu way of life and 25 per cent a Catholic way of life. Prominent temples are found in Zambaulim and Mott and ancestral caves and waterfalls are found in Mott and Ghantiwada. The wards are divided along both geographical and communal lines. Fatima ward, for example, is inhabited mostly by Roman Catholics, whereas Ghantiwada is inhabited mostly by tribal communities and their Brahmin landlords. In Fatima ward a church is situated of the native Catholics and in the Rivona market ward there is also a temple in addition to a shopping centre. Velips (Kunbi-sub-types), Gaunkars (Gaudes) and Charddo (Kshyatria) Catholics are the major communities inhabiting the village of Rivona in addition to a few Hindu Kunbis and Brahmins, the latter who are large landowners and temple priests.

The Gaude Community in Rivona

The Gaude community is believed to be the descendants of the aboriginal tribes of Goa and can be found in large numbers in Rivona and in the interior villages of the New Conquests (Ponda, Bicholim, Quepem, Sanguem, Sattari). They are thought to have migrated from the Bengal region due to similar linguistic terms and are thought to have brought rice, coconut and areca nut cultivation into Goa. They are over divided into three endogamous groups: the Catholic, Hindu and Nav-Hindu Gaudes. The first group converted to Catholicism around 1620, the second retained their former belief system and the third converted first to Catholicism in 1620 and then back to Hinduism between 1928 and 1935.[6] The Gaudes as a community are considered economically and educationally backwards and are labelled as scheduled castes by the Indian government. The Nav-Hindus are concentrated in Tiswadi, Salcette and Ponda, the Hindu Gaudes reside mostly in Tiswadi, Ponda, Canacona, Bicholim and Quepem and the Catholic Gaudes inhabit the talukas of the Old Conquests. The literacy rate among members of the Gaude communities is low; only a small percentage from every village will graduate from the 12th standard. The Hindu Gaude community speaks Konkani and reads and writes Marathi. Though non-vegetarian, they exclude beef and pork from their diets and consume fish-curry-rice as part of their staple diet. Neori (ground coconut, Bengal gram powder mixed with gur or jaggery), payasa (rice preparation) and ambil of Nachni cereal are special foods prepared by the Hindu Gaudes. Among this community, the Gaud Panchami (exclusively celebrated by this community) and Ganesh Chaturthi festivals are widely celebrated and common Hindu Samskaras and ritual practices are conducted within this community. Proposals, dowry, matching of horoscopes, tying of the mangalsutra and the exchange of wedding garlands are customary rituals in the marriage ceremony. During the ceremony, the newly-wed couples tie their dhotis and saris together and takes seven rounds around an earthen pitcher full of water and mango-tree twigs.[7] Women can inherit property and participate in economic, social and political activities, but they cannot take part in temple or clan deity religious rituals. Land ownership belongs to the klan (Kul) and members share the agricultural produce. The Gaude have special clan deities in addition to regular Hindu deities such as Naguesh, Mallikarjun and Mahadeo. Similar to the Nabhhanna festival in West Bengal, the first paddy produced is harvested and offered to Mallikarjun, when Payasa is prepared as a devotional offering. During the Dhalo festival in Jan/Feb, the Gaude women sing and dance the Dhalo while the male members of the community beat drums, play instruments and sing devotional songs. Upon the death of a family member, the dead is carried to the burial ground and the family observes rituals restrictions for 12 days after which the male members of the family shave their beards and head.[8] (Of late, this trend has resulted in the men shaving only their beard.) Following the 12th day, a ritual purification ceremony is undertaken and a feast is held for friends and family members of the deceased.

Village Administration

The village of Rivona has one Sarpanch, one deputy Sarpanch and seven panches, who are re-elected after three years. The duties of the sarpanch involve the issuance of construction licenses, the repair and maintenance of village roads and the development of irrigation for the fields. The Sarpanch is also responsible for settling down local disputes amicably so that the grieving parties do not need to enter into court proceedings. When a dispute first occurs in Rivona, villagers attempt to resolve the issue before it reaches the level of the Sarpanch, who is obligated to hear only those disputes of importance or extreme difficulty. Prior to the sarpanch, individuals within the Catholic community often solicit the help of the parish priests, especially when the dispute occurs between two Catholic families. A poor Hindu family will often consult their landlord when problems arise, who they look to for both sustenance and advice. If these measures fail, the dispute is forwarded to the civil court in either Sanguem and Quepem, where attempts are made to resolve the crisis. If everything else fails, the dispute reaches the Mamletber Court in Sanguem which is one of 11 taluka-based court houses. At this point the issue is usually resolved.

Health Concerns in Rivona

Health care in Rivona has improved over the years as more and more individuals with medical problems consult English educated medical doctors in rural outposts. Rivona has its own Out-Patient Dispensary (OPD) in the village which was created following Liberation by the government Directorate of Health Services. In close proximity to the dispensary, several sub-centres are located in the various wards where there doctors residence. There are roughly 14 sub-centres, as such, in Rivona and the outlying regions which are staffed on a daily basis by basic health workers. These sub-centres are, thus, the first link in a long chain of medical services designed to aid suffering patients. In a sub-centre the next closest medical aid centre is the OPD of the village. Following that, the nearest medical centre is the Primary Health Care centre in Quepem, which was upgraded when Quepem was made into a separate taluka. For larger medical problems patients are sent to the hospital in Marmagao or the Goa Medical College Hospital in Bambolim.

However, a patient who comes down with an illness would like to spend one or two days performing home remedies which he/she feels might cure the disease. Haldi (turmeric) powder and jeera (cuminseed) are often used in such home remedies. Some consult village priests when they feel that they have been 'cursed' by the evil eye or other spiritual disaster. If these fail, they go to the OPD believing that an 'injection' is a cure-all for diseases. Eventually they receive proper treatment and recover accordingly.

Dr. Anand Palekar is the current resident at the health clinic during the years 1996-97.[9] His clinic is open from 9 am to 1 pm and he sees an average of 50-60 patients a day. With the available equipment, Dr. Palekar with help from his two staff workers can perform minor surgery (stitching), drain abceses, inject medications, dress wounds and dispense with medicines. A villager pays Rs. five as registration fee after which they avail of their medications free of cost. Low incidences of malnutrition are reported in the village of Rivona and in Goa generally because most villagers have their own houses on small plots of land where they can raise food crops, vegetables and spices. Among the floating population of migrant labourers from Karnataka, however, malnutrition is common. The majority of patients who come to see him suffer from hypertension and respiratory problems such as bronchitis, chronic obstructive pulmonary diseases and other local infections. Most of these clients are above 50 and have worked in the nearby mines. There are 4 mines within 15 kilometres in the Rivona surrounds and many heavy trucks pass through the area, leaving behind dust and debris. Though much of the mining activity has diminished over the years, the village is still located in proximity to active mines which causes respiratory problems to the local inhabitants.

Health Education is likewise infiltrating into the village community owing to efforts by the government to increase such knowledge among the rural community. Owing to television broadcasting and other forms of mass media, the general knowledge existing in the rural communities has increased as they become linked to countries and cultural systems around the world. Government health education programmes in schools have also contributed to this effect. Most births are now performed in hospitals under hygenic conditions, whereas before they would occur in homes with the help of a midwife. When labour pains begin, the family of the would-be mother solicits the help of wealthy neighbours with transportation to escort the expecting mother to the nearest hospital, usually in Marmagao.

Hinduism in Rivona

Only one-fourth of Rivona's population adhere to the Catholic faith, while the rest follow the traditions of Hinduism. While the majority of the land-owners in Rivona belong to the Brahmin community, the Hindu population in Rivona largely consists of Gaunkars and tribal communities. These communities were incorporated into the Hindu-Vedic religion over centuries, but they have also maintained unique family and clan deities which are revered in addition to those brought by the Aryan religion. As a result during the weeks surrounding Shigmo (Goa's version of Holi), small local festivals occur in various regions, especially in the Southern New Conquests where the Portuguese cultural prescriptions and the Maratha invasions had little impact. The cultural traditions in these areas, therefore, have survived the historical evolution of centuries and maintain many of the characteristics of their aboriginal ancestors.

Rivona is dotted with many temples and their surrounding complexes (attached smaller temples), as the Hindu community in Rivona believes that gods like to reside together. Mahalakshmi, goddess of wealth and good fortune, and Ravanath, the protector God, are popular deities among the Hindu devotees in Rivona. Vimaleshwar is another temple which houses the Shiva Linga, whose stone was found in a paddy field by some Hindu farmers. During the Vimaleshwar temple ceremony of Dassera, a sacred stick (Tarang) is reported to remain perpendicular for over 30 minutes without support in front of the temple, owing to the power of the God.

The Zambaulim Zatra at the Zambaulim temple is another

large festival which draws thousands of devotees, including many from neighbouring regions in the Karnataka State. The celebration used to last for 4 to 5 days during which time the Mahajans (devotees) would bathe in the sacred Kusawati River to purify themselves before receiving the 'Darshan' of the God.[10] Though the festival takes place throughout the week, the majority of the crowd arrives on the last day. In the morning ritual baths are taken and by the afternoon coloured powder identical to that used during Holi celebrations cover devotees. Women are not coloured and it is mostly the men who take part in the ritual colouring of each other. The deity is also coloured by devotees in a caressing manner. In the night this Zatra, like others throughout Goa, involves the removing of the deity from its resting place and taking it out in procession around the temple for all to see. The idea behind the procession stems from the belief that the God/Goddess during special occasions likes to be in the presence of people and move about with them in joyous celebration. This temple Zatra occurs around the time of Holi and is similar in design. Holi is a celebration of Lord Krishna-Vatura which celebrates the joy of life and the coming together of people from all ages and socio-economic backgrounds. This celebration is not restricted to the wealthy and is an attempt to bring rich and poor, young and old together in a common bond of religious devotion and human kind.

During the week of Holi, the Shirvoi Shigmo is one such festival occurring within the agricultural community in Rivona. Like Holi and Zambaulim, this festival involves the smearing of colour on the faces and hair of male devotees and children prior to the ceremony. The religious celebration begins in the courtyard of Devmoll ward and by three o'clock a crowd of men, women and children dressed in their best clothes are forms. The Goddess Chamundeshwar Pai has already been removed from her normal resting place inside the small nearby temple and is relocated to a red velvet covered palanquin open on the sides to enable 'Darshan' of the deity. The goddess is showered with fresh flowers, fruits and the smell of burning incense. She is accompanied by the local God, Pike, who drives a horse and chariot. A metal bowl for offerings is set just inside the palanquin and following prayer devotees donate one or two rupees in reverence to the Goddess. Devotees approach the palanquin which falls on one side of the courtyard where they press their hands together in devotion and make silent prayers in front of the Goddess. They may ring a small metal bell to awaken the Goddess to their prayers while others may pass underneath the palanquin in a symbolic act of purification and asking forgiveness for ones tresspasses.

Once a large crowd has gathered, four men dressed in white dhotis and possessed momentarily of spiritual powers emerge from the inner recesses of the ward accompanied by assistants whose job is to restrain the men charged with spiritual energy. The four men believed to be blessed with spirit possession as well as the ability to predict the future are brought to the centre of the courtyard where people line up to receive their blessings and ask about issues troubling them. The four men, usually the elders of the community, are then prayed to as embodiments of the gods after which the men bless them and place red vermillion on their foreheads. Once all of the people have been blessed, the Goddess in her chariot (palanquin) and the four men proceed to the first house set back from the courtyard. There the owner of the house awaits outside his doorstep with offerings of fruit, flowers and a coconut in a ritual similar to most Goan Hindu communities. The chariot and the four men with their assistants and special 'umbrellas' line up in front of the offerings which are surrounded by white and blue chal, decorations drawn on the ground. As men arrive at the house, the male owner rings a small bell, performs *arti* with incense and a small fire from an oil-lamp and offers fruit and flowers to the men-gods while reciting prayers. As a final offering, a coconut is broken over the four umbrella sticks placed together and the milk pours over the bottom ends of the umbrellas. The procession then proceeds to the next house led by a small band with a drummer, the chariot and followed in the rear with the four 'spiritual' men who have embodied various gods and goddesses. The procession proceeds towards the town of Quepem stopping at all those houses who wish to be blessed. By the late evening hours the procession, now greatly diminished in numbers, returns to Devmoll and the Goddess and her consort Pike are once more placed within the walls of the temple, where they will wait for another year before they are once again brought into the daylight.

Catholics in Rivona

The Catholic population of Rivona belongs predominantly to the 'Charrdo' (Kyshatria-2nd order, Varna system) community spread throughout Goa.[11] The people are as pious in their beliefs as are the Hindus in theirs and the former's customs and traditions resemble those of the Catholics in Salcette and other coastal talukas of Goa. Christmas, Lent, Maundy Thursday, Good Friday, Easter and the seven Sacraments are celebrated there and Litanies also occur regularly. The caste system is equally stressed among both Hindus and Catholics and as such they are very endogamous regarding marriage rites. Interestingly but not surprisingly, the Catholic population is discouraged from observing the rituals and beliefs of the Hindu community and most have never seen a Hindu religious ceremony.[12] Many Catholic male youth have found employment in the Gulf countries and in the upper castes will continue their education beyond the 12th standard.

Education in Rivona

There are five government primary schools in Rivona which utilise the Marathi and Konkani mediums to impart primary education. There are two schools in Rivona which cater mostly to the youngsters within the Hindu community. The remaining Catholic population is given instruction through the parish primary school which teaches Konkani and English, bypassing the Marathi medium all together. Instructions given in Marathi from the 1st to the 4th standard, after which time instruction in English continues until the 10th standard. By the 3rd standard, the basics of English are learned in their written form, with the explanations and lectures in Konkani.

At the Uthkarsh High-School in Rivona, 350 students are enrolled, of which 90 per cent are Hindu and 10% are Catholic youngsters. "Utkarsh" means 'progress' in Marathi and the aim of the school is to educate the students from all socio-economic backgrounds so that they can improve their standard of living and their mental capacities. There are 30-40 students in each class and a total of 14 teachers, including the headmaster. Ninety percent of the students complete the 10th standard, the level of education which is free to all individuals regardless of socio-economic background. A.M. Pednekar has been this school's headmaster for 23 years and was just beginning his career when the new school building was erected in 1975. The money to build the modern structure was raised from the Kash Mandir (Rivona Society) and the government.[13]

The Kash Mandir was started in 1932 by 20 individuals concerned with the lack of education in Rivona. Before 1970, there were no facilities available for higher education beyond the basic primary level (1st to 5th). The closest schools were situated 10 kilometres away in Curcholim and Quepem at a time when no public transportation existed and only a few wealthy families owned their own transportation. Between 1961 and 1970, the majority of the Rivona villagers were without education. Following on the heels of Liberation, however, the State government started Marathi schools free of charge to the public and changed the medium of education from Portuguese to English. Prior to the establishment of these schools, girls in Rivona did not study beyond the 4th standard in Marathi, but following their inception, co-education was encouraged. In 1983, 87.5 per cent of students passed from the 10th standard and in 1996 that percentage was 80 per cent.

Of these who pass the 10th standard, 50 per cent continue directly on to higher education. Another 30 per cent continued in technical courses (ITI) while 20 per cent finished studies following the 10th standard and work as drivers, conductors, mine services, or traditional professions such as carpentry and pottery. The latter two are popular professions in the village of Rivona and are hereditary professions for various artisan communities. Education was free of cost until the 10th standard in Rivona, but those wishing to continue further studies were required to travel outside the village to one of the 70 schools in Goa allocated to higher education. Within the entire village Panchayat there are now five high-schools where in pre-liberation years not a single high school existed in Rivona village.

In addition to the schools run by the local Hindu community, Fatima High School located in Fatima Ward also caters to the educational needs of the community in Rivona. Father Carlos Fernandes, who received his education at Pilar Seminary and St. Charles College of Nagpur, has been the school headmaster for 8 years. Grades 5-10 are taught at Fatima High School and plans are underway to add the 11th and 12th standards. Currently, those seeking higher education must commute to either town of Sanvordem or Quepem. In addition to a co-educational High School, there is also a girls' convent school in Rivona. In both these schools English is the language of instruction while Hindi and Konkani are assigned one class period in each. There are a total of 340 students, 95 of which are boarding school students and 86 of which attend the convent school only. Ninety per cent of the student body adheres to the Catholic faith, while 10 per cent follow the Hindu traditions. Most of those students who pass the 10th standard go on to study in the Arts or in some form of vocational school.

As a result of the improvements in the educational system in Rivona, individuals are more conscious of their rites and duties. Prior to liberation, less than 20 per cent of the villagers were literate and even the parents of today's students are mostly unable to read and write. Following liberation, over 80 per cent of the community has become literate. Prior to Liberation, the Portuguese schools were open mostly to the children of Catholic converts in the Old Conquests. By the time the New Conquests were under Portuguese administration, the same proselytising fever which accompanied the initial conquests had died down somewhat. Though Catholic churches were erected and priests were stationed in the New Conquests, the area was viewed more as a buffer zone between the Marathas, Muslims and later the British empires than as an actual part of Goa and Indo-Portuguese culture. It was up to the individuals within Hindu communities to provide for their own welfare and as it was not in the interests of the ruling landlords to do so, the majority of the Hindu villagers remained uneducated. Those who converted to Catholicism were helped while those individuals following the Hindu way of life were barred from Catholic educational institutions.

In addition to advancements made in education, roads and other developments in infrastructure have improved the quality of life for the population in Rivona. Following Liberation, State banks, government offices, a telephone line, postal facilities and a health clinic all arrived in Rivona. The Land Tenancy Act as likewise redistributed village lands in a way which benefited small farmers and the middle income groups. Lifestyle changes were also noticeable among the villagers of Rivona. Roughly 50 per cent of the population is currently employed in agriculture, while others have diverted their energies to commerce, trade and more technical occupations. The aspirations of individuals has increased and people perceive a greater degree of autonomy in their lives regarding their careers. The population of educated voters has likewise increased, making the politicians more responsible for their actions and responsive to the needs of the village community. These progressive strivings are also manifested in the clothing change which has occurred among the villagers. Young women pursuing higher education started wearing salvar-quamizes rather than saris and men started wearing pants and shirt combinations rather than the dhoti worn in past generations.

However, this progress is yet to filter down among all the communities living in Rivona village. The scheduled tribes, known in government policy as the Other Backward Communities (OBC's) are yet to seriously reap benefits from the educational and technical advancements revolutionising village Goa in the post-Liberation years. Velips, Gaudes, Dhangar and Kunbi communities of Goa falls under this classification whose majority live in a poor economic and educational state, dependent on the land for their sustenance. Most are given small plots of land in areas 'reserved' by the State government and are often located in communities cut off from the larger environment. Some members of these communities have their settlements in Male Ward, near Rivona. The land on which they live is barren and unproductive, and they continue to be at the mercy of large landowners. Utkarsh school is hoping to take up a project whereby irrigation canals, bio-gas, solar energy and other inexhaustible energy sources are utilised for the development of these lands into productive plots. Health care and education likewise has had little impact on this impoverished population.

Rural Occupations in Rivona

Among the traditional artisan occupations in Rivona, pottery, carpentry and feni-production are popular in Rivona. Tucked away in a small community of 50, men still earn their livelihood by sculpting the soil of mother earth. The Kumbhar/ Kumar community are found among both Hindus and Catholics and live in their own distinct wards in certain villages located throughout Goa. Their traditional occupation is to make earthenware pots and jugs in addition to ceiling tiles. In Bicholim they craft big artistic urns and some also create idols of Lord Ganesh for use during the Ganesh Chaturthi festival in August. Men wear pants and shirts; women saris and blouses with gold ornaments and they speak Konkani and write and speak in Marathi in Devnagiri script. Kumbhars eat non-vegetarian excepting beef and pork and fish-curry-rice forms their staple diet. They have formed the Gomantak Vishvakarma Chakradhari Samaj to look after the welfare of the community.[14] Of late the educational level among this community has increased and both young men and women are attending college and a few are entering into engineering and law professions. Marriages are by proposal with girls entering into alliances around the age of 20 and boys entering into marriage around the age of 25. They follow the Hindu Samskaras regarding marriage rites and lifecycle rituals from birth to cremation. Their devaks are the Apta and Kadamba trees and they observe mhal and nami in the Hindu month of Ashvin (Sept/Oct) which are feasts held in honour of ancestors.[15]

In Shigoi Kumbar ward of Rivona village, the ancient art of hand-made pottery is still practised by a few men of the oldest living generation. The younger villagers have opted for more modern, 'prestigious' occupations, thus, this art in this place seems destined to become a historical memory. But the art is still alive for men like Vishnu Shetkar, whose skilled hands mould perfectly symmetrical clay pots using methods whose origins are lost in antiquity. In the morning the women go into the fields to collect special 'stones' used in the preparation of clay. These stones are pounded into powder, which is then mixed with water and then heaped into piles whose size depends on the final product. The men, using manual pottery wheels, spin the clay with dexterity to create pots and lids of various sizes which are then kept in the sun for drying. In the final step, the pottery is covered with hay and mud and baked overnight over a low fire. Once ready, the pots are taken to markets around Goa as well as the Zatras of special temples situated throughout the hinterland of Goa. Though a noble profession and one that brings in Rs. 200 per pot, the younger generation, craving a more modern lifestyle, has opted for education and office jobs in neighbouring cities.

Carpentry is another traditional occupation of some

communities in Rivona village. Teakwood, rosewood, jackfruit tree wood and neem are the most popular woods used in the construction of furniture and everything from doors to tables and elaborately-carved couches are constructed by carpenters. Some carpenters work in the front rooms of their houses, while others have been able to open their own showrooms in the town of Quepem. In Rivona, a sub-section of one small ward is inhabited by the Hindu Chari/Sutar community who are traditional carpenters, blacksmiths and woodworkers. They still perform such occupations and some have opened small businesses to make building materials or sell finished products. Konkani in the Devnagiri script is the mother tongue of this community and they eat non-vegetarian excepting beef and pork. Marriage alliances are formed through the proposal system when girls are between the ages of 22-25 and boys reach between the ages of 25 and 30.[16] An informal dowry is offered by the bride at the time of marriage and mangalsutra, red vermillion and bangles are traditional symbols of a married woman. During the marriage ceremony 7 circles are taken around the Holy Fire (Saptapadi) and the marriage is celebrated at a marriage hall officiated by a Bhatji (priest). This community observes most of the Hindu customs and Samskaras such as phulam maine (during the 7th month of pregnancy), 12-day birth pollution, mundan for male children, the sacred thread ceremony and Haldi-Kumkum to name just a few. Following the death of a family member, the body is carried in procession to the cremation ground according to traditional Hindu Samskaras and after three days the ashes are collected and immersed into a nearby river or the Arabian Sea. The Charis have a regional association in Mapsa, the Gomantak Vishwakarma Manumaya Brahman Samaj, which provides scholarships for students and concerns itself with the overall betterment of the community.[17]

Cottage Industries in Rivona

Mining is a major industry near Rivona and an occupation which many in the community, primarily those among the low socio-economic classes, have entered in place of farming and traditional craft occupations. Iron ore and magnesium are extracted from these mines, loaded into trucks and are taken to the city of Vasco da Gama where these products are exported to

Japan and other Asian countries. Among the Catholics, one youth from every family was able to find work in the Gulf on the ships or in other minor jobs. These jobs are coveted because with only a village 10th or 12th standard education, jobs can be secured which pay 10 to 20 times the salary which the same individual is capable of earning in Goa. Farming is the traditional occupation for the villagers in Rivona, who cultivate food crops such as wheat and rice as well as cash crops such as areca and cashew nuts. Those who are landowners hire landless or otherwise poor labourers to cultivate their fields as share-croppers while their own sons and daughters enter the more modern occupational sector.

The production of 'cashew feni' gave rise to one of many cottage industries in Rivona village and in this respect they are similar to other villages spread throughout Goa. For the families involved in the production of cashew feni, their work begins long before the trees show the first youthful budding of cashew fruits. In each season a particular landlord auctions his plot of land to those engaged in this trade for the use of the fruits and nuts from the cashew trees. In this case several families joined their resources together and purchased the use of the fruits for the season. During this time they were also permitted to remain on the land as tenants and to distill the feni on the property itself. Once the land has been bought for the season, in early March the families preparations for the feni production, three-month ardous stint.

The first step in the process begins early morning as the women and the menfolk hike into the forests in search of cashews. All morning they forage on the forest floor for yellow and red cashew fruits, piercing the fleshy fruit bodies with a pointed nail on the end of a long bamboo pole and collecting them in thatched baskets. When a basket becomes full, the cashews are dumped and piled up within a roughly carved rock-bottomed trough sloping downwards on one end and used in the pulverisation of the cashew fruits. All morning and afternoon men and women collect sizeable pile of cashew fruits from the forest.

During the second phase of urack and cashew feni production, the cashew nuts are removed from the fleshy bodies and collected for transport to a nearby cashew nut factory. The flesh of the cashew fruit is then pulverised by half-a-dozen men wearing knee-high rubber boots. Some of these workers hang on to an overhead wooden latticework to avoid slipping and draw the fruits from behind their heels and rhythmically tread on the flesh to squeeze out the juice. As the fruit emerges from their feet only the pulp remains and the juice slides down the sloped rock bottom through a low hole in the wall of the trough and out through a pipe into a container kept below. The pulp is then tied with a vine and squeezed again, then set out in the sun to dry and be recycled as fuel. The juice which collects into a separate basin is then removed and separated into smaller earthenware jugs buried in the ground and left to sit overnight covered with leaves and burning coals. By eight or nine in the night, the last of the fruit bodies are pulverised, the nuts sorted and the juice gets drained and stored in the jugs.

To begin the third stage, while the women returned to the forests at 7am, a meter-high earthenware pot is placed above a wood and coal fire. Forty litres of cashew fruit juice are then placed into this vessel and heated for several hours until the steam is produced. This steam escapes the tightly-sealed vessel only through a clay pipe which is placed a specific distance down from the top of the vessel. Because both water and alcohol vapours are formed during the distillation process, the pipe is situated at such a distance to allow only the alcohol vapour to escape due to its heavy weight. The pipe leads into a second, smaller earthenware jug cooled constantly by a man pouring water over it. The water gets collected beneath the pot and is recycled. The steam, after passing through the pipe settles into the second jug, then recondenses into urack and gets collected in the smaller pot. This is the first distillation which occurs between 7 am and 12 pm; the second between 2 pm and 5 pm.

Every 40 litres of cashew juice produces 15 litres of urack, or 20 bottles at 750 ml per bottle. After the first distillation, the resulting drink is about 20 per cent alcohol, or 40 proof. If this is added to soft drinks with a fresh squeeze of lime and you have a delicious, refreshing summer drink. The hearty type, especially those who toil all day in the fields or enjoy a lively Saturday night, drink urack straight without any dilution. During the second distillation, this process is repeated and the product derived is cashew feni, a more highly concentrated form or urack of about 40 per cent alcohol (80 proof). From 40 litres of cashew fruit juice about 11-13 litres of cashew feni can be produced.

Rivona village also boasts its own cashew factory which was built in 1981. The process begins in the months of April and May with the harvesting of the cashew fruits from cashew-tree plantations, work done by the makers of cashew feni. The moist greenish grey nuts are removed from the cashew fruit during this production, collected in buckets and taken to a nearby cashew-nut factory for further refinement. Once sold to the owners of the factory, the nuts are first dried in the sun and then steam-heated for 2-3 hours. The steam-cleaning process is conducted by a metal machine consisting of two chambers. In the first chamber water is boiled and the steam escapes through a pipe into the second chamber in order to heat the cashews. Following the steaming process, the nuts are then cut into halves and cleaned by removing the inside embryo. They are then roasted for one hour inside an oven, cleaned from their light outer shells and packed into boxes for transport.

Among small-scale industries, brick making is another rural occupation in Rivona village. Teams of 3 to 5 people work in one field and they begin work by 8 or 9 in the morning. First, special clay from a nearby river bed is collected and all of the stones and sand are then removed. To the resulting pure clay, water is added until the proper mixture of clay and water is achieved, which becomes a dough mud-like substance. This mixture is then placed in rectangular wooden brick moulds and pressed until the entire mould is filled. The moulds are then turned upside-down and the wet clay brick is left in the sun to dry. Once dried the bricks are collected and baked for several hours in a make-shift oven built on the field itself. In the morning the oven-fired bricks, now red in colour, are loaded onto a pick-up truck and transported to various destinations.

Thus, the village of Rivona provides a vivid portrait of a traditional Goan village. Like its location, Rivona is on the border between a typically Goan Catholic village and a predominantly Hindu one. The attitudes, goals and aims, stresses and daily lifestyles of this village are like those of many others throughout the State of Goa. There are three basic strata emerging in modern day Rivona village. The first is the traditional strata consisting of farmers, artisans, housewives, paunches and other villagers who spend the majority of their day on the premises of the village. The second strata consists of the emerging professional classes who migrate to the cities for higher education and eventually enter professions. The third strata are the traditionally wealthy land-owners and the neveau riche renumerating their Gulf salaries into their Goan villages.

DAVID VERSUS GOLIATH: A CASE STUDY

The Struggle of Agonda Village to Preserve Her Identity

Agonda village is a coastal village situated along the western shore of Canacona taluka, the most Southern taluka in Goa. Her population of roughly 7,000 is divided among Catholics and Hindus, 40 per cent and 60 per cent respectively. There are three government primary schools in the village and two high schools; one belonging to St. Anthony's Church and the second constructed by the government. The nearest town is Chaudi which is almost 10 kilometres from Agonda village and the closest major hospital is in Margao, nearly 45 minutes away by automotive transport. There is one private rural health clinic in Agonda located in Vall Ward and one government clinic. Farming, fishing, toddy tapping and Gulf employment are the main occupations for the villagers of Agonda. Most women either work in the fields (Kunbis, Gaudes), as peons in government offices, or remain at home as housewives performing a number of duties such as child rearing, sewing, crochet and other handicrafts. A few absentee landlords own the majority of the village lands and there are likewise few Brahman or Kshyatria families in the entire village. The majority of members are Shudirs (farmers, toddy-tappers, artisans) and Kolis/Kharvis, Kunbis, Dhangars and Gaudes.

The Catholic Kharvi (fishermen) are found mostly in the coastal areas of Salcete, Tiswadi and Mormugao and members of this group claim to be the descendants of the aboriginal of the Goa territory. They speak Konkani and write in the Roman script, though the percentage of literate community members is low. Generally, boys study until the graduation level and girls finish their studies until the secondary level. Saris and blouses are common among women, otherwise they do not wear other discernible clothing. Men and women tend to smoke bidi, which is a combination of jack fruit leaf and tobacco cigarettes. Owing to their low socio-economic status, some have chosen employment on ships in the Gulf countries as a way to increase their standard of living. Traditionally, this community performed the single occupation of fishing, which was carried out during the season from September until early June. A group of 20-25 men known as a 'band' would have a fishing boat, nets, an on-shore boat shed and would share equally in the day's catch.[18] Of late this number has dropped to 5 or 6 men who own a boat together and among these families the women perform the second part of the occupation which is collecting, drying and selling the fish in the market-place. Marriages between young girls (around 20 years) and young men (25 years) are conducted through social negotiation (proposal) and informal dowry in cash and kind (gifts) in addition to the exchange of rings is typical. Fish-curry-rice and other non-vegetarian dishes describe the food habits of this community and they belong to the Sudir (Sudra) class in the Hindu Varna system. Though they are Catholic, many still attend the annual Temple Zatras (feast days and processions) and maintain the belief in black magic, evil spirits and exorcism. Prior to the onset of the season, many fishing communities will employ the services of an exorcist (ghadi) who breaks a coconut over the boat while performing other rituals in order to drive the evil spirits from the sea. They have a community society known as the Ramponkoranch Ekvoti Ekta whose major concern is the economic activity of the community. Male family members inherit property which is forfeited by female children in exchange for gifts of cash and kind at the time of marriage.

The life of a fisherman, like most traditional occupations in Goa, is determined by the rhythms of nature and involves the entire family. In the daily occupational routine, men first take to the sea in the early morning hours before daybreak in order to set their nets in the water. As the sun rises and the fish begin their daily search for food, the fishermen relax in their boats and wait. By 8 am they pull up their nets and return to the shore with the days catch. After being helped on to the shore by other village fishermen, the nets (made out of clear nylon of late and fine twine in days of yore) are then opened and the fish and crustaceans are removed into baskets with help from the women and younger family members. While the men drag the boats higher onto the shore above the high-tide line, the women carry the catch to the market in a neighbouring town where they bargain with the customers to reach a suitable price. The family also keeps aside enough fish for their own consumption and in some instances may trade it locally with other villagers. In the afternoon, the men return to the sea and again repeat the process of setting the nets and waiting as the sun sets to bring in their nets.

In many villages one boat will be owned by five or six men who work as a team, or one man may own several boats which he then gives out on rent to fishermen for specified rates. A traditional boat is usually 8 to 10 feet in length and made of wood. The bottom is constructed from the trunk of a coconut tree and the sides are made with plywood bought in town. The planks are stitched to the bottom with a heavy twine and the boat is then coated in a thick water-proof black tar which strengthens the wood and increases the lifetime of the boat (which is usually around 25-30 years). A wooden balance is then attached to the body of the boat by thin wooden tree poles in order to provide stability and balance to the boat. While offshore, the boat is anchored by a large stone or cement block tied with twine to the end of the boat. In olden days fishermen fastened their own nets from finely woven twine, but today most are capable of purchasing synthetic nylon nets from the town stores.

As in most of Goa's traditional occupations, the monsoons play a key role in the occupational cycles of fishermen. By mid- to late June, the rough seas and rainy weather prevent fishermen from continuing in their daily routine, thus, substantially decreasing their catch and availability of fish in the market. The majority of Goans, therefore, in the last weeks in May and early weeks of June, purchase considerable amounts of dried salt fish which can last throughout the monsoon season. Among ancient marriage traditions, a newly wed couple in the fishing community would together catch a fish symbolically from a water tub in the centre of the roomas part of the ritual celebrations. Girls marry between the ages of 18 and 20, but may become engaged prior to the actual ceremony. Boys will begin to accept proposals once they reach the age of 21. Most tend to work in menial jobs, selling fish in the market-place, or remain at home to care for the children.

Farming is another timeless, traditional occupation of the Goan people. Goa's staple food, rice, is grown in paddy fields along the low-land coastal areas from Pernem to Canacona. Sorondio (kharif) is the first crop sown during the monsoon and harvested in November and vagana (rabi) is the second crop sown in November and harvested in March-April. In addition to rice and wheat, potatoes, millet, pulses and vegetables are also grown on Goan farms. The work, which involves days of hard labour in the fields, is mostly performed by the Kunbi aboriginal tribes. In the Old Conquests, many of the Kunbis converted to the Catholic religion though they still adhere to most of their ancient customs and beliefs. The Kunbis are sub-divided into 2 groups: the Gaunkars, who are mainly involved in cultivation and the Velips, who are believed to have descended from the original discoverers of the stone Shiva-lingam which is now installed in the Malikarjun temple. Owing to their discovery of the lingam[19] they are able to officiate in the temple pujas for three months in a year[20]. The Kunbis in the southern region of Goa speak Kannada (as in Agonda), but the vast majority speak Konkani in the Devnagiri script. They are known for their characteristic cultural 'simplicity' and strict adherence to age-old customs and usages. Men wear a simple loin-cloth and women wear colourful red and white checked saris tied in a knot below the left shoulder, as in the Gaude style. (The two communities are thought at one time to have been closely related and some historians argue that Kunbis are actually Gaudes renamed as such following conversion to Catholicism.) Married women wear a necklace of 40-50 strings of glass beads and girls marry between the ages of 18 and 20; boys between 25 and 30.[21] Bride-price exists among the Kunbi community and marriages are arranged by proposals followed by negotiation. The formal engagement is held without the presence of the couple to be married and the day prior to the actual wedding turmeric oil is applied to the bride's body. The marriage rituals follow those of the traditional Hindu Samskaras, including the worship of the devak, the Patt ceremony, tying of the Mangalsutra, making five rounds around the sacred fire and the wearing of green bangles as a symbol of marriage.[22] They usually live in small huts of mud walls and roofing made of thatched coconut palm leaves. Usually several families will inhabit the same dwelling and several families will live together in a hamlet. The Budavant/Budavatin is the eldest member of the community and commands much respect in the village as the one who safeguards tradition and addresses conflicts within the community. Women work as housewives and in the fields and their presence at social and religious functions is essential. Following birth, a 21-day, pollution period is observed wherein the woman can neither perform household tasks nor participate in religious functions. On the 21st day the naming ceremony takes place and after the first year of birth the new-born's head is shaven (jaiwal). Following the death of a relative, the body is buried in the east-west direction and an 11-day restriction period is observed for family members of the deceased.[23] On the 11th day the shraddha ceremony occurs followed by a feast on the 12th day for relatives and friends of the recently expired. For the Kunbi community, Shigmo (the Goan version of Holi) is the most important festival during which time the community performs dances, songs and dresses in colourful costumes. Today these dances are staged and used as entertainment and one such dance (Kunbi dance) become incorporated into the 'cultural identity' of Goa in the post-Liberation years. Most members of the Kunbi community are illiterate due to poverty, isolation and the economic necessity of children working in the fields. Their village deities are Vetal, Tulsi, Naga, Shantadurga and Khalnath and their surnames follow from their kul (clan) deities.

Among the Catholic community in Agonda (40 per cent of the village), nearly one member of every family works in the Gulf or aboard international shipping lines and the new housing constructions attest to this wealth from remittances. Though televisions, radios and other modern conveniences are available to the local population in Agonda, they are as yet neatly tucked away in traditional homes. Likewise, some villagers have motorcycles and cars, but these are again relatively few as the community consists of members of the Shudir and tribal communities. However, unlike other modern villages, the effects of Gulf employment and of the tourist industry are relatively minor and the forces of modernity which are revolutionising the urban centres have yet to infiltrate into Agonda. These forces have tried, however, as the subsequent history will attest.[24]

Life in Agonda has not always been as tranquil and romantic as it seems today, particularly after 1980 when a Delhi-based five-star hotel arrived with plans to construct a luxury hotel complete with swimming pool and golf course. For this a piece of land was purchased questionably from an 'absentee' landlord and with grandiose visions of a bustling tourist destination, the company even built its own road to the hotel site which was planned for the beach front of Vall ward of Agonda village. Materials were brought in and the metal scaffolding were constructed for a massive hotel complex.

Their plan might have been executed flawlessly were it not for the members of the Fernandes family, who refused to vacate their lands which divided the hotel's newly acquired property. Two men in particular, John and Carlos Fernandes (then 21 and 29 respectively), decided to help organise resistance to the construction of the hotel which threatened the lands. Initially only the Fernandes family actively launched the protest, but as word spread the whole town united against the tirade. Claiming the contracts fraudulent, the Fernandes family then solicited the help of lawyers and brought the hotel company into the court room. As word spread the Margao-based Toddy Tapper's Association, the Gomank Lokpak Labour Association and other peoples' organisations gave their support to the cause of Agonda village. While the court case was still pending, the hotel company was instructed to cease construction until the validity of the contracts could be verified.

However, the construction continued and what began as non-compliance and verbal protest spread to pilfering of construction materials and physical fights with workers as town youth took matters into their own hands. The hotel company felt compelled to hire a police force to protect their investments, yet from 1981-83 sporadic fighting broke out between local villagers and hired police. Finally, in 1983, with several court cases pending and Agonda fiercely on the defence, construction was halted and the fighting stopped. Mired in expensive lawsuits and attacked from all sides, the hotel company seemed on the brink of collapse. The strength of David, of a small town called Agonda, had seemingly routed Goliath, one of the biggest five-star hotel companies in Asia.

But their celebrations were short-lived as construction began again in 1986 backed by clever lawyers, local and State administrators. By this time some in the community began to support the hotel's construction, arguing that it would bring jobs to Agonda's youth and greater overall wealth to the community. They also argued that a five-star would bring Agonda in touch with the modern world and enable new business enterprises catering to tourists to develop in the village. Activists like John and Carlos Fernandes, however, saw things from a different perspective. They argued that the hotel construction would seriously disrupt the traditional livelihoods of the community's fishermen, toddy-tappers, farmers and animal-herders. Toddy-tappers would not be permitted to collect sap from trees belonging to the hotel property, fisherman would not be able to compete against the rushing motorboats and jet skis and all the animals which roamed freely in the village would detered from interfering with the hotel complex. In addition to the loss of these humble but vital livelihoods, the few positions promised to Agonda's youth were paying a salary too low to maintain their current standard of living. Youth would continue to seek work in Gulf countries and migrant workers would move in to take up these low-paying jobs. The hotel would also produce enormous quantities of waste which would be pumped into the nearby rivers and out into the ocean, polluting their natural environment. Further, many of the tourists' habits such as sunbathing in bathing suits, sexual liberties and public displays of affection were behaviours that the community of Agonda did not want their children to imitate.

As a consequence, the community again united in protest. Knowledgeable courageous youth, John and Carlos Fernandes, the villagers painted red slogans on rocks, flaunted banners, verbally opposed the construction and gathered together in the hundreds around the construction site. Again fighting broke out, but Agonda's community with the strength of David behind them stood unrelenting in their defence. The strength of the protest movement coupled with internal corruption, mismanagement and the expense of lawyers led to the bankruptcy of the hotel company and the cessation of all construction by the end of 1986. Ten years later, only the skeleton of the five-star hotel remains, inhabited by monkeys, reclaimed by the encroaching jungle and guarded continuously by several government-employed watchmen. It looms only a short distance from the coastline, a constant reminder of the victory and of what might have forever changed the identity of Agonda.

Love for the land and sea runs deep through the hearts and minds of Agondans. Harmony with and respect for nature are strong values within a community that lives off the land while simultaneously protecting her. For the beauty and serenity of Agonda are more than tourist attractions, they are the true wealth of a village in a State rapidly being transformed by the rush of tourist hotels and modern conveniences. Here, as the sun rises over quaint fishermen's huts, one awakens to the sounds of tinkling cow bells, chirping birds and gently breaking waves. Before daybreak fishermen launch their boats from a small cove hidden within the rock jetty and can be seen in the distance setting their nets. Toddy-tappers begin their daily rounds, climbing deftly to the tops of coconut trees to collect the delicate sur. Water buffaloes meander across the sand dunes towards the warm ocean lagoon at the southern end of the beach. In the evening as the setting sun glows red on the horizon, women carrying bundles of sticks appear from the nearby forest, returning to their homes in the village. Cows and buffaloes linger by the seashore, resisting the calls of their masters as they soak up the last of the sun's rays. By nightfall the beach is empty, the crickets emerge to fill the cool night air with their music and the vast expanse of sky sparkles with a myriad of stars.

GALJIBAGA: A CASE STUDY

Tradition and Transformation

In Galjibaga, one first feels as if he has entered into a secret enclave, passed over completely by the sands of time. Arriving in an old wooden canoe propelled by an even older sun-withered man, this small village on Goa's southern-most shore seems totally isolated from the influence of modern society. The village is nestled between the Talpona River to the north, the Galjibaga River Inlet to the south, forest and farm lands in the east and an empty beach lined by wispy fir trees to the west. Yet the serene beach, quaint white-washed church, paddy fields and sleepy village belie the modern activities rapidly transforming the identity of this small coastal town.

Located in the far south-west corner of Canacona taluka, virtually on the border with Karnataka, Galjibaga is one of Goa's southernmost settlements. "Bag" in the Konkani language means 'garden' and the lush forests, fertile plains and flowing rivers which surround this coastal hamlet sustain that image. Prior to the Portuguese conquest the region fell under the jurisdiction of King Sonda, who was a feudatory of the southern Hindu Vijayanagara and earlier Kadamba dynasties. The culture of Galjibaga and other southern village settlements was, thus, intricately linked to northern Kanara (Karnataka) in a variety of ways, including the evolution of the Konkani language, the worship of certain deities and the observance of certain folk festivals and traditions.

The Kharvi (fisher folk) and Gabit communities are spread throughout Goa, Karnataka and Maharashtra; and in Goa they are concentrated in Canacona (this case study), Salcette and Pernem talukas owing to their proximity to the sea. They were once employed in the navy of Shivaji and used Konkani at home and Marathi as a literary medium. Today fishing is still the chief occupation and boys begin the trade as early as 10 years old with their fathers. They are non-vegetarian but do not eat beef and pork and they eat fish-curry-rice as their staple diet. Most live as tenants and belonged to the low and low-middle income families. Family deities are Vetal, Lakshmi and Ravalnath and marriage rites are similar to those of other Hindu communities, including proposal, dowry, settlement (sakharpuda), mangalsutra and the seven rounds around the sacred fire[25]. Nuclear families prevail in this community and women have maintained their traditional role as housewives and fisherwomen in the market place. Women are also allowed to participate in religious rituals and they have a voice in matters pertaining to the family. A 7-day post-delivery impurity ritual is followed after which time mother and child undergo a purification bath.[26] The naming ceremony occurs on the 11th day which is the domain of the grandparents and a feast is offered to all well-wishers. Confinement during menstruation is sometimes observed in this community wherein women are isolated and considered impure. Death rituals are parallel to those of other Hindu communities including, cremation, shraddha rituals and the collection and immersion of the ashes of the deceased. They believe in evil spirits, spirits of the dead and sacrifice goats and hens to their family deities at times of great desire or distress.[27] Of late, the youth from the Kharvi and Gabit communities are attending schools, colleges and universities, though economic difficulties hinder their ability to climb the economic ladder and women are still discouraged from receiving higher education.

Catholicism in Galjibaga

Following the transfer of the region of Canacona to the Portuguese administration in 1788, Franciscan missionaries and the Portuguese troops were stationed in the newly annexed territory for religious conversion and protection, respectively. In 1807 a chapel was built in Galjibaga on the beach front as the sea was the centre of village life. The chapel fell under the Karwar diocese, however, (the first city after the Goa-Karnataka border in Karnataka) and initially it remained locked as there were no priests in residence. By 1824, however, St. Anthony's Chapel became St. Anthony's Church and residential quarters were attached to the main pulpit of the church.

Rumours abound as to how the village population eventually became 40 per cent Roman Catholic. In addition to the financial, occupational and social status improvement incentives, the Catholics in Galjibaga believe that some of the Portuguese soldiers threw cooked beef in the well water which the villagers unknowingly drank, thus defiling them and making them outcast in their community. Other rumours abound that the sacred tulsi (basil) plant in front of several houses was touched with cooked beaf resulting in defilement of the household.

A small coastal village of roughly sixty houses, Galjibaga is a relatively isolated village in comparison to others in Goa. Distanced from the National Highway 74 by nearly 15 kilometres, separated on the south by the River of Galjibaga and serviced by only one small single-lane road, this small hamlet falls under the Poinginim district where the Panchayat offices are also located. The nearest market towns are Maxem and Poiginim, the latter which has a rural medical dispensary. As in Agonda, the majority of people living in Galjibaga are sons of the soil belonging to the Sudir and tribal communities. There is one primary school in Galjibaga and one high school until the 10th standard, after which time students must commute to neighbouring towns to continue their studies. Toddy-tapping, fishing and farming have been since time immemorial the primary occupations of villagers, though urban office employment and overseas shipping jobs have significantly detracted from the numbers of youth choosing to enter into the occupations of their fathers.

The largest festival in Galjibaga is the Feast of St. Anthony's on the 19th of January. The feast draws a large crowd from the neighbouring villages when old alliances are renewed, new friendships are formed and often marriage proposals are discussed between the parents of prospective couples. Sweets and souvenir stalls gather outside the church and people attend mass dressed in their Sunday best. Following high mass at noon, many families who have travelled from neighbouring villages have picnics on the beach while their children play along the seashore.

The church of St. Anthony's is the only religious institution in the village as the Hindu community visits the temples of Maxem, Poiginim and other neighbouring villages. The village of Galjibaga does not have its own temple though each house has a small alter decorated with images of favourite local and regional deities. Shivaratri is celebrated at the Mahalaxmi temple complex near Chaudi and Shigmo is likewise celebrated in a regional manner in Canacona. The Shigmo street parade highlights the regional dances and costumes of Goa's southern cultural traditions.

Tradition and Transformation in Galjibaga

Although Galjibaga is situated in a remote part of Goa separated from the main part of the State by the Western Ghats, her residents are hardly untouched by the modern world. Tucked away discreetly (and sometimes not so discreetly!) are a variety of modern household appliances, including an occasional satellite television receptor. In Galjibaga, more so among the Catholic population (roughly 45 per cent), at least one member of every family has worked or is currently working in one of several Gulf countries like Kuwait, Dubai and Saudi Arabia. Advertised both through the local newspapers and returning fathers and brothers, children in Galjibaga grow up with the idea that they too will one day set off for an overseas adventure combined with gainful employment. As a consequence, St. Anthony's school has adopted an English-language medium following Liberation where Portuguese had been the language of instruction. Children, begin learning English at a young age; a skill as valuable to them as mathematics and science. Without mastery of English, future job prospects in the Gulf are slim as knowledge of this language is essential.

Only recently since the 1970's, villagers from Galjibaga have continued this tradition of working abroad, bringing home fortunes relative to the profits made from traditional occupations like fishing and toddy-tapping. Some, like Father Asis Dourado, resident and parish priest of St. Anthony's Church, are concerned about the long-term effects of this quickly acquired wealth. He worried that the wealth gained in haste is often spent lavishly on the latest technologies which serve as trophies of success rather than the satisfaction of real needs. Such lavish spendings also incites jealousy within the community when it could otherwise be invested and saved for future consumption. In his sermons Father Dourado, thus, asked church members to lead simple lives so as to be open to God. He asked them to treat their homes like the church and to raise their children with values consistent with good living. In this way he hoped to curb the negative effects produced by excessive wealth such as insatiable materialism, parental neglect, selfishness and unwarranted feelings of superiority.

Overseas influences, however, are hardly new to the villagers living in Galjibaga. Prior to liberation Galjibaga, like most villages in the New Conquests, experienced the presence of the Portuguese. Though neither colonial administrators nor soldiers had their permanent homes here, the village was frequented by officers from the nearby outposts in Canacona, Maxem and Poiginim. Accounts of this occupation vary among villagers, the Catholics who sing the praises of the Portuguese and the Hindus who found their rule oppressive and stifling. Fortunately today, villagers adhering to both Catholic and Hindu ways of life practise them side-by-side peacefully and with equally whole-hearted devotion. Thus, from toddy-tapping to televisions, from Portuguese to English and from wading through water to waiting tables in Kuwait, the villagers in Galjibaga have successfully mastered transition while keeping the same village atmosphere.

However, all this seems set to change, especially for the Naik family whose house lies directly in the path of the proposed National Highway. In 1982 government officials arrived with such plans and have paid stipends accordingly to those families who will be inconvenienced by the construction. Similarly, just a few hundred meters away, the infrastructure has already been finished for the path of the Konkan Railway, whose path cuts directly through the village. Hardly the image of a romantic, sleepy future for Galjibaga, yet the Naik family at least seems to have accepted the situation in stride and not without a bit of foresight. They hope to benefit from the increasing human traffic and are planning to construct a guest-house and restaurant-bar on nearby land. Other villagers like the Barrettos seem poised to successfully ride the tidal wave of change about to engulf the sleepy village of Galjibaga. They also have constructed a guest-house and hope that an increase in tourism will increase business in Galjibaga so that men returning from several years overseas can also earn money closer to home.

Although residents of Galjibaga welcome a prosperous future, they do so not without considerable caution. In the early 1990's a business-minded local began plans to construct a luxury hotel directly on the beach front. However, the community under the leadership of Father Dourado opposed the construction of this hotel, arguing that it was illegal to construct within 100 metres of the seashore. After writing few letters and fixing appointments with government officials the hotel was stopped, demonstrating that although villagers in Galjibaga are involved in modern society in a variety of ways, tradition, tranquility and timeless occupations remain strong forces in Galjibaga.

The Oldest Man of Galjibaga

Antonio Francisco Dias is the oldest living member of Galjibaga village (still coherent and mobile) born on the 4th of June, 1912. He adheres to the Catholic faith and learned Portuguese in a government school in Margao. At that time the only instruction was either in Portuguese through the Catholic school system or through Marathi via the Hindu system which excluded all but the higher socio-economic castes. He and his wife, who died 8 years ago, had one daughter who has since married and given Mr. Dias two grandsons. Following his schooling in Portuguese he worked in the government military service for nearly 40 years. Galjibaga, he recalls, was not inhabited by the Portuguese except for one or two high-ranking government officials, their families, the church priest and the caretaker. The closest outposts of soldiers were in Canacona, Maxem and Poingimin where at each place between 40 and 50 military men lived in single quarters. Mr. Dias recalls that in the early years the Portuguese were open and friendly with the local converts and he remembers being invited for dinner and casual conversation in the homes of the Portuguese officials residing in Galjibaga. He recalls that the Portuguese men were honest, sincere, decent and well-mannered. If a poor villager was hungry they would provide food for him. However, after a time their character changed and they began to tighten the rules, imposing heavy punishments for small infractions and in some cases accidents. Eventually the villagers were stripped of the rights they once enjoyed.

MAULINGAM VILLAGE: A CASE STUDY

The Far North-East

In the north-east corner of the State of Goa, on the border between Bicholim and Sattari, lies the small hamlet of Maulingam, where most of the traditional ways of the past are alive in the present. Nearly 15 kilometres east of the main taluka centre of Bicholim, the small hamlet known as Maulingam is located just off the main road leading from Bicholim proper to the city of Valpoi in Sattari taluka. Roughly 250 people belonging to the Goan Hindu Dhangar community (who are the traditional buffalo and cows herders) live here in extended families in nearly 50 houses.

The road leading to Maulingam village is made of hardened reddish soil and the entire landscape is covered with this same earthy red hue owing to the type of soil found in the area. Bullock carts still make weekly trips into the village to sell produce such as flour, oil, pulses, vegetables and other goods which are not available from neighbouring communities and must be brought from more distant areas. One or two members of the village work for a transport business and often utilise these small trucks for the transport needs of the entire village, the majority of whom have no transportation of their own except for bicycles.

The land surrounding this village is mostly barren and dry, with a few scattered shrubs and patches of trees. Much of the land belonged to their forefathers, but without proper irrigation facilities it is hardly suitable even for cattle grazing. The village community uses a common water supply drawn from an open well located at the entrance to the village and neither running water nor proper sanitation facilities are part of the village infrastructure. A practice of open-air defecation on the outskirts of the village is still in vogue in many villages both in the coastal and inland rural areas. Electricity has been brought to the village following Liberation, though as in the rest of Goa, frequent black-outs, are a common occurrence.

Maulingam is one of the most traditional villages of the New Conquests and has been virtually untouched by the Catholic influence, resembling more closely the way of life of the neighbouring State of Maharashtra. The community lives in virtual isolation from the Coastal Catholic talukas which give the 'Goan cultural identity' its character. The Konkani dialect influenced heavily by Marathi. Marathi is the language of the community and it is also the only medium of instruction as serious study of English begins only in the 5th standard. Most of this members community as a consequence do not know how to speak English at all, unlike Goa's urban residents where fluency in spoken English is expected among the upper-class residents. The older generation in Maulingam is mostly illiterate and involved in field job and buffalo-tenders, while the younger generation educates itself until the 5th-8th standard before seeking employment in traditional and non-traditional occupations in the transport and public service industries.

Women function as mother, housewife and performing field job. Those who study do so only briefly as they are not expected to work far from the home nor in the large cities of urban Goa. They study until the 4th standard usually, whereupon they help their mother to perform the duties of the household. The marriageable age for girls is usually between 18 and 20 and for boys between the ages of 20 and 22. They try to negotiate marital alliances with similar neighbouring communities so as to diversify the gene pool of the village and prevent birth defects which can result in the offspring of relatives.

As the community living in Maulingam belongs to the labour class, they have few physical recreational activities. Relaxing and discussing matters of local concern on the front verandas of neighbours houses is the most sought after leisure-time activity among both men and women alike. Men and women move in separate social circles and have different locations where they meet to exchange words. The men tend to congregate at the local bar near the entrance of the village or under a large tree, while the women will gather at the side of the well or on the front porch of a neighbours house with their children.

The Dhangars

The Dhangar community is spread throughout Goa and the entire Konkan and in Goa most perform the traditional occupation of buffalo and cow herding. The word Dhangar is derived from 'dhenu' meaning cow and 'dhan' meaning wealth. Most are landless and poor and boys between the ages of 10 and 15 begin the work of cow herding. They follow the Hindu faith and observe important Hindu festivals such as Dassara, Diwali and Holi. During Diwali they decorate their domestic animals with colours. Both men and women smoke bidi and have common surnames identical with their clan dieties such as Choughule, Kokre, Motte, Pavane, Jangale, Humaane, Lambare, Doiphode, Kollekar and Kharat. These deities must be worshipped at the time of birth and marriage ceremonies especially.

Monogamy is currently in vogue and widows can remarry through a ceremony known as Marut which takes place only at night. Mangalsutra and vermillion are marriage symbols for a woman and subsequent to the ceremony she usually takes up residence with her husband's family. Bride price is in vogue among the Dhangar community ranging from (Rs. 1,000-3,000) and cows and buffaloes are preferred as gifts in proposed marriages. In former days girls would get married prior to the onset of puberty, but recent trends indicate that the marriage age for girls is now between 16 and 20; that for boys between 20 and 25.[28] The marriage proposal comes from the boy's father and the wedding date is decided at the girl's residence in the presence of the Budvant (elder community leader), who generally acts as a priest (according to Vedic rites) for their community.

The Dhangar society is traditionally male-dominated and the father becomes the head of the household whose decisions are binding. Women engage in household chores as well as labour (hence the bride price) and collecting fuel and fodder for the cattle is also part of the daily activities. After the birth of a child, Dhangar women are considered impure for 7 days and cannot enter the kitchen nor perform their normal religious duties. As in most Hindu communities, the naming ceremony of the child occurs on the 7th day of birth and the head shaving ceremony (mundan) is performed after one year for both male and female.[30] When a member of the Dhangar community expires the body is buried in their own graveyard and a period of mourning follows for 12 days.

The Zatra of Sirgao: The Social Event of Maulingam

The most anticipated social event and the one best attended by Maulingamis community is the annual Sirgao Zatra, famous for its huge bonfire and the devotees who run across hot coals. The small town of Sirigao in Bicholim taluka, only a few kilometres west of Maulingam, comes alive as thousands of devotees of the Goddess Lairai gather and for the entire day undertakes rituals and pujas culminating in the famous jaunt through hot coals raked from an enormous bonfire. One villager from Maulingam has attended the festival for 38 years and in all nearly 80 of the 250·villagers of Maulingam will attend this Zatra which occurs in the month of May.

This festival originated in the in-land northern region of Goa and is the festival of the Hindu labour class (non-professional). In olden days the zatra would last five or six days and of late the time as been cut down to one full day and night. Beginning in the morning and continuing throughout the day, men and a few women bathe in special water tanks located near the temple. Following this ritual bath, the devotees walk barefoot uphill to the temple as an act of penance, endurance and worship.

In the evening they are joined by more devotees undergoing the same acts of worship and penance, all of whom dress in a particular style of a dhoti in keeping with their traditional dress. This style is akin to that worn by fisherwomen and is wrapped around between the legs allowing greater physical movement and dexterity. They also wear some form of white teeshirt (of late, owing to the inclusion of women), a colourful cape around the shoulders and a scarf-like cloth around the waist for additional decor. They also adorn themselves with necklaces made from jasmine and other tropical flowers. In their right hand devotees carry a 6 feet stick made by twisting vines together and forming a handle, which is used throughout the ceremony. Originally covered with flowers, each stick is made by the devotee who then decorates it with wisps of coloured yarn to symbolise the flowers of past festivals. The more yarn a devotee places on the stick, the more devotion he feels.[29]

At 10 pm, the ritual reaches a climax and those participating in the zatra begin, the celebrated temple dance. Brightly lit for the occasion, inside the temple the devotees gather and form a tight circle in front of the image of Lairai. While chanting and moving in a tight circle to the rhythm of drum beats, the sticks are held in the air and clash against one another in a demonstration of devotion and strength. The beat quickens and the circular dance and chanting reaches a feverish pitch, after which a single drum beat signals the end of the dance. The devotees fall back, drenched in sweat and make room for the new arrivals who have just entered the temple. Those who have already participated in the dance proceed down the hill to bathe once again and repeat the rituals.

Around midnight the dancing ceases and the crowd gathers around the huge pile of wood clearing several hundred metres from the temple grounds. A chosen man emerges from the temple in a frenzy of spiritual possession and racing to the pile with a blazing torch, proceeds to light the massive bonfire and begin the second half of the zatra. Once lit, the bonfire blazes for several hours during which time the ritual participants circumvent the fire, chanting devotions to Lairai and touching the bonfire with their sticks. The closer one circumvents the fire, the more devotion and courage he/she demonstrates. This continues until the early hours of the morning when the fire extinguishes enough to rake its coals.

Once the raking process begins, the devotees converge near the smoking fire in wild expectation, waiting for their turn to walk through the coals. Pressure mounts and finally by 4 am the participants begin the most anticipated ritual which brings people from all over Goa to Sirigao for this special event. One by one and in quick succession, the devotees run through the hot coals carrying their sticks and screaming the name of Lairai. Some perform the ritual only once, while others, not convinced of their bravery and manhood, perform the ceremony several times to the amazement of onlookers. As each participant determines he has ran his last, he throws his flower necklace into the nearby Banyan tree and returns home. As the sun rises the festival draws to a close and those who did not participate, will have to wait until next year to muster their courage to walk through the burning coal.

Maulingam Revisited

Thus, the village of Maulingam on the border of Bicholim and Satari talukas offers insights into the relatively minor impact of the Portuguese influence in the far regions of the New Conquests. The way of life, eating habits, traditional dress, marriage customs, language and occupations of Maulingam have been little altered by the Portuguese and modernization in general. Though following liberation some development occurred in the region such as electrification of the village, which is still seriously lacking in health, sanitation and educational infrastructure. Local disputes are normally settled within the village by the elder male members of the community and the nearest large town is Bicholim which is almost 15 kilometres away. Traditional occupations, religious rituals and even modes of transport are still in vogue among the villagers of Maulingam who have been comparatively unaffected by the influence of the Portuguese. Their culture and ways of life fall completely outside the traditional characteristics of 'Goan cultural identity', yet this community with its cultural traditions has resided in the region of Goa long before the advent of the Portuguese. Maulingam, could be argued embodies the heart of the Goan interior.

GOA VELHA: A CASE STUDY

The Remains of an Ancient Capital

The town of Goa Velha has played an important role in the history of Goa, though today's town is little more than a salt-pan and farming hamlet with an elegant white-washed church and a small market through which the major highway passes. Goa Velha is located in Tiswadi Taluka on the banks of the Zuari River, which at the time of the city's inception was a deep and navigable river, well protected from the monsoons and easily defensible from possible invasions. During the Kadamba dynasty (1008 to 1300 A.D.), the original administrative capital was located at Chandrapur, in modern day Salcette taluka. During the reign of Jayakeshi I (1052 to 1080 A.D.), his power weilded enormous influence and he was able to organise a strong naval fleet at Velakula (part of Gopaka, the future Goa Velha) on the bank of the Zuara River during the first year of his reign. King Mummun of Thana (near modern-day Bassein) was ruling over the neighbouring region when he was defeated by Jayakeshi I who was now the King of the Kadamba dynasty. Jayakeshi I then developed the city of Gopakapattana (Goa Velha today) as the capital of his new kingdom. Many Arab traders and merchants were appointed to high official positions under his rule and in 1081 he was succeeded by Guhalladeva III. This latter ruler was the first Kadamba King to assume the title of 'Gopakapura vardhishva' which translates into 'Lord of Gopaka, the best of the towns.'

In 1106 A.D. during the reign of King Tribhuvanamalla, land and financial grants were offered to 12 Brahman families willing to settle in Gopaka and establish a Brahmapuri (Hindu school for higher learning). The image of the Goddess Saraswati was installed in Gopaka, which has lead historians to conclude that these 12 Brahman families belonged to the community of Saraswat Brahmans. Gopakapattana rose to prominence under the Kadambas and became one of the most important emporiums on the West Coast of India. Located ideally for trade, this port city grew quickly with revenues coming in from the trade of Arabian horses, Chinese silks and spices from the Hindu colonies in South-East Asia. Huge civic projects were completed and massive temples were constructed, a demonstrative opulence which attracted settlers from many regions and caught the attention of Muslim invaders.

Beginning in the 10th century the Muslim armies began raiding the temples of Govapuri and the frequency of damage from these attacks increased throughout the 12th and 13th centuries. Eventually the excessive attacks by the then Sultan of Delhi, Ala ud-din Khilji destroyed the city of Govapuri (modern Goa Velha) and the Kadambas were forced to abandon it and flee to their former capital at Chandrapur. In 1350 the Bahmanis attacked and gained control of the city, lost it in 1378 to the Hindu Vijayanagar Kings and regained it again only in 1470. However, by this time large amounts of silt had accumulated in the harbor of the Zuari River and its prominence as a trading port seriously decreased. The Bahamanis then decided to move their capital to Ela (Old Goa), which in 1490 with the aid of the Sultans of Bijapur became the next city to rise to great heights as the dominant international trading center. When the Portuguese captured Goa in 1510, they kept Ela Goa as their capital.

The Muslim invasions from the north began in 1294 though for a while the city of Gopaka was able to maintain its commercial relationships. In 1312 the city of Gopakapattana was destroyed by invasions from the Muslim Sultans of Delhi. Following this invasion the Kadamba capital was again shifted to Chandrapur. In 1472 Goa was again conquered by the Bahmani Sultans after the local chieftains had forced an earlier retreat and the city of Gopaka surrendered with hardly a fight. Once firmly under their control, the Bahmani rulers decided to move their capital from Gopaka because over the decades the Zuari River had become too shallow for easy navigation. They moved their new capital to Old Goa on the Mandovi river, following which the city of Gopaka fell into decline.

When the Portuguese first arrived in Goa in 1509 they reported that the City of Old Goa (on the Mandovi) was a Muslim city inhabited by Moors, the Hindu upper-class, armed troops and a variety of foreign expatriates. It had superseded Gopaka in both administrative and commercial capacities and had fallen into disuse. It was then known as Vodlem Goem (Konkani for Old Goa) and was renamed by the Portuguese as Goa Velha to distinguish it from Ela Goa, the new administrative capital. During the Portuguese era the town revived slightly owing to the construction of an elegant church, school and the annual Procession of the Saints which draws a large crowd to the now small town during the month of April.

Goa Velha Today

Goa Velha, including the neighbourhood of Batim is divided into 10 divisions: Rumabha, Modsai, Sovosrai Vaddo, Vllem Bhatt, Bondim, Portel Bhatt, Chinel Bhatt, Gaukar Vaddo, Batim Maina and Movla. At the time of Liberation, members of this community were relatively poor; they lived from the produce of agriculture and very few were employed in the Gulf. Even today the community is predominantly an agricultural one; owning several salt pans (among the Mith-Gaudes) and planting rice, sweet potatoes and other vegetables during the rainy season. Local fishermen still launch their boats into the Zuari River in the early morning hours and send their wives to the local market to sell the day's catch. In this way, the village as a whole has not changed drastically in the past 20 years, although there have been new houses built, new shops and the roads are now paved. Many male members now find work in the Gulf, returning to Goa Velha only once or twice per year.

Educators feel that the Catholic 'culture' in Goa Velha has also increased of late among the Mith-Gaudes owing to the instruction given to parish members every Sunday about the life of Jesus, the 10 Commandments, the 7 Sacraments and moral responsibility. During Christmas the church hosts a carol singing competition, a beauty pagent and a dance on the 31st of December. They also sponsor Konkani theatres (tiatr), football games and a few other recreational activities. In addition to St. Andrew's Church located at the entrance to the village, Goa Velha has three chapels; first at Saleria, second near the Zuari River and the third dedicated to St. Anthony.

Education in Goa Velha

Father Miguel DaSilva is the current parish priest of St. Andrew's Church in Goa Velha. Twenty years ago, in 1976, he was the headmaster for 9 years in a school in this same town. The school was started 30 years ago by Father Alvaro Barato Menes and at that time Father DaSilva became the first parish priest. In addition to St. Andrew's co-educational school, there is also the Mary Immaculate Convent School for girls and the All-Male Seminary School in neighbouring Pilar. Prior to Liberation the village of Goa Velha, whose residents were devoted to agriculture, was educationally backward. Few children were attending schools. During the past 37 years, however, both students and parents have begun to realise the importance of education. During the 1960's and 70's, those children who excelled in school would migrate to Bombay and Portugal for higher education. Those who became doctors and other professional people would likewise leave the rural setting of Goa Velha for better prospects in the urban areas. In addition to the increasing weightage given to education, the practise of family planning has been adopted among families in Goa Velha which has decreased the average family size from 4 and 5 children to between 2 and 3.

Mrs. Dias has taught English and History at St. Andrew's School for the past 17 years. She is an immigrant born in Bombay who has returned to Goa after her marriage. Compared to the children and lifestyle of Goans in Bombay, she feels that the children in Goa Velha are not very exposed to the mass media as only 5-10 per cent have access to television sets. She also feels that a greater number of children in Goa Velha have difficulty with the English language once they enter the 5th standard because they have done all of their early schooling (grades 1-4) through Marathi or Konkani medium, whereas Goan students in Bombay are exposed to the English language from the onset of their schooling. In Goa Velha, the uneducated parents do not speak English and the children who come from these families have a more difficult time overall in academics. Among her class of 35, most belong to the Hindu community and the children in general have become fashion conscious owing to their brief interaction with the influence of television. Some of her students come from economically troubled families where both mother and father work, performing odd jobs for daily wages the family's financial suffers because as the father tends to spend the money on alcohol and his friends at the bar. At St. Andrew's, Goan history begins in 1510 with the arrival of the Portuguese and has only been introduced within the past 3 years. There is also a lesson on notable Goan freedom fighters and Goa's integration into the Indian Union, which has helped students from all religious backgrounds to identify with India and think of it as their own country. Prior to that, Goa's history was entirely absent from the syllabus.

After the 8th and 10th standards, students are eligible to receive vocational guidance. If after the 8th standard a student no longer wishes or can afford to continue his education, he may enter a vocational school and learn such trades as plumbing and/ or carpentry. After the 10th standard students have several options. Some continue their formal schooling and earn degrees in the arts, commerce, or specialised vocational training such as computers and other polytechnic vocations. Others earn certificates in hotel and restaurant management, tailoring, brass-making and other arts. Those students who complete the 12th standard are then eligible to continue their training in medicine, engineering, architecture, pharmacology and home science for ladies. The number going to earn these latter degrees is small in Goa Velha, but the numbers have increased slowly over the years and the upward trend should continue.[30]

The Mith-Gaudes in Goa Velha

The Catholic community in Goa Velha are a part of the Hindu Gaude and Mith-Gaude communities which are some of the original settlers in Goa. The Mith-Gaudes are a subdivision of the Gauda community and perform the manual labour required in the manufacture of salt (mith). Some Mith-Gaudes have their own salt pans and employ landless labourers to perform the manual duties. Most inhabit the talukas of Pernem, Bardez and Tiswadi. They have two endogamous subdivisions; one Catholic and the other Hindu and claim a higher social status than their Gauda brethren. The Hindu community is in the majority, but many of the converted Mith-Gaudes in Bardez have blended into the Catholic mainstream and improved their socio-economic position by becoming priests, lawyers and journalists. The Hindus, to which this study now turns, speak Konkani and Marathi and claim their origins in Maharashtra. The traditional dress of men is dhoti and shirt, of women is sari and blouse, though the Catholic Mith-Gaude dress in the modern westernised styles akin to other middle class Catholics. The elder women of this community observe purdah (covering their hair and face) in the presence of men during all social functions. They are non-vegetarian but do not eat pork, beef and buffalo meat while fish-curry-rice is their staple diet. Both men and women chew betel nut and tobacco and alcohol is socially sanctioned among male members. Important clan deities among the Hindu Mith-Gaudes are Nag Gauda, Mauli Devi, Nag Nath, Paik Purush, Alvo, Satpurush and Chumnkar.[31] Marriage is through proposals only and girls usually get married between 18 and 20, boys between 22 and 25. Women are respected and a bride-price as they not only perform the household duties but also assist in the salt-pan agricultural production. The marriage rituals are conducted according to the Vedic rites, with the difference that newly-wed couples circumambulate an earthen pitcher filled with water, coconut juice and a mango twig, in addition to the sacred fire which must be burnt from the wood of the rumada tree.[32] They do not practise pre-natal ceremonies as do other Goan Hindu ceremonies, but they observe an 11-day post-natal restriction period followed by the 12th day naming ceremony as per Vedic Sanskaras. In the area of education, the Hindu Mith-Gaudes have yet to actively encourage their children into further studies and few continue their studies through the college level.

The Procession of the Saints

Now a typical village, Goa Velha, the former prosperous city of the Kadamba dynasty, hosts the renown 'Procession of the Saints' on the first Monday during Easter. This tradition began in the 17th century by the Franciscan order in an attempt to boost the moral values and pious behaviour of the community and inspire them to take into their hearts the teachings of Jesus Christ. The only other place in the world where this procession is held is in Italy and in Goa the procession is designed in conjunction with a narration which illustrates how these Saints gained the 'Glory of God'. By the 18th century, a total of 65 life-size richly decorated statues of saints, martyrs, kings and queens were carried in palanquins on the shoulders of native Christians. In 1835 the event was banned by the Marquis of Pombal and many of the statues were destroyed. The celebration began again only towards the end of the 19th century.

Today no less than 26 statues are paraded through the village of Goa Velha. Today's 'Procession of the Saints' draws hundreds of people from neighbouring villages around Goa Velha. Prior to the sermon, devotees enter the church and express their devotion to particular saints by kissing and touching the statues whilst deep in prayer. An outdoor sermon follows and by sundown the statues, mounted on floats, are brought out in succession from the door of St. Andrews's Church around the square and through the streets of the village. As each of the 26 statues emerges, a priest speaking through a microphone narrates the life-story of each saint in Konkani. As the saints are carried through the crowd, devotees can be seen ducking under the floats to receive the blessing of the saints and to obtain purification for their confessed sins. This ritual is virtually identical to the one practised by the Hindu Gaude community in Rivona's Shirvoi Shigmo festival.

Though a religious occasion, the evening atmosphere is filled with gaiety as the fair (mela) comes to life on the main road outside the church. Typical of any church feast, the roads are lined with stalls selling everything from sweets to wind-up gadgets. It becomes a whole family affair as people come out in formal clothes to hear mass, watch the procession and enjoy the gaiety of the outdoor mela.

KAKRA-OXEL-NAXEM: A CASE STUDY

The Nav-Gaudes of Tiswadi

Kakra, Oxel and Naxem are three small neighbouring communities located on the Western Coast of Tiswadi taluka. Above them on the hill stands the Goa University constructed in 1985 and nearby lies the capital city of Panjim. These villages are primarily inhabited by Shudra and nav-Gaude communities whose members perform the traditional occupations of farming, fishing and toddy-tapping. Though directly below Goa's major centre of learning, the communities of Kakra, Oxel and Naxem are relatively untouched by the modern influences which urban and educational areas tend to encourage.

The majority of residents within these three neighbouring villages converted to Catholicism during the years of Portuguese rule. Prior to conversion, they were a relatively poor and backwards community who had come under the Hindu fold by name only and still practised most of their ancient customs and cultural traditions, including the belief in good and evil spirits, ghosts (*bhuts*) and black magic. However, the Gaudes were never quite able to practise the Christian religion as the Portuguese would have liked and they were often criticised for their maintenance of traditional cultural forms, including their special dress. In 1928, therefore, with the encouragement of a Hindu swami, many members of the Gaude community converted back to the Hindu religion during the first calls for Goan independence.

Following reconversion, however, they were not welcomed back into the Hindu fold as they had hoped. Rather, they were forced to form themselves into a separate endogamous sub-community of Gaudes which were considered lower than the original Hindu Gaudas. Isolated from both communities, the Gaudes suffered financially, culturally and socially following re-conversion and have come to symbolise what happens in Goan society when a community which 'abandoned' the religion of its forefathers then seeks to reintegrate itself into that same community. This study examines three such villages of Nauxem, Oxeland Kakra whose inhabitants live a relatively isolated life, victims of the Portuguese missionary zeal and its aftermath.

Kakra

Kakra is a small fishing hamlet of roughly 75 families in an area not larger than a single square mile. Located on the coastal sea-face of Tiswadi taluka, it is tucked away at the bottom of a hill below the Goa University and is accessed by a single road which passes in front of the village and ends in a dead end on its outskirts. There is a small shack converted into a government primary school for about 15 children in the 1st though 4th standards, whose single teacher Mr. Gurudas Navelkar, teaches through the Marathi medium and provides explanations in Konkani. The government has provided the school with toys, notebooks, puzzles, pens and other learning aids. Mr. Navelkar is the most educated man in the village (probably studied upto the 8th or 10th standard) and enjoys the confidence of the other villagers too. He is responsible for holding onto their saved money, birth and marriage certificates and in giving loans to needy members of the community. Those children who wish to study beyond the 4th standard must then commute by bus to the neighbouring town of Santa Cruz.

The village is without a temple and a church, both of which are in Santa Cruz or neighbouring Oxel. The Sarpanch of the village is also located in Santa Cruz and, thus, disputes are first addressed among the elders of the community. Electricity has been introduced into the village but a common person still uses a common well and practise open air defecation as sanitation facility is absent. The land of Kakra is owned by an absentee Hindu landlord who does not charge the community rent for inhabiting his land. Girls marry around the age of 18 but may become engaged prior to the actual ceremony. Most tend to work in menial jobs or remain at home to take care of home and children. The Goa University, owing to its proximity, employs many individuals from Kakra and other nearby communities to perform the menial and maintenance tasks required by the university. For example, one woman works as a Xerox copy aid and another cleans the floors of the classrooms.

Prabashun Bandekar is one of the 4 brothers living in Gauda-Wada in Kakra. He belongs to the upcoming generation of village boys in Kakra; and the only one to be earning a Bachelor of Arts degree. He studied until the 4th standard in the village primary school, went to a middle school from the 5th to the 10th and recently attended a government school for higher standards education in Miramar. He lives in family of 15 members and belongs to one of the families whose forefathers reconverted to Hinduism between 1928-35. His father, now retired from government service, helps the fishermen to repair their nets and boats on occasion.

Edward da Souza is the head of one of the few Catholic families in the village of Kakra. Though over 50 years of age, he still performs the traditional occupation of toddy tapping and the production of coconut feni. He has two daughters and three sons, of which his second son is employed in the Gulf as the pilot of a ship. Another son drives a water scooter for the Cidade de Goa hotel, while the youngest son has found work as a driver for a Limosine. His eldest daughter is married and living in Taligao and his youngest daughter is living in the house with her parents. The family members living in Kakra attend Sunday mass in the chapel of the neighbouring village of Odxel. The chapel was constructed in 1828 and catered to the three villages prior to their re-conversion to Hinduism. Today, Father Kinley D'Cruz in the nearby living quarters, confirms that of late the chapel is visited mainly by the congregation in Kakra.

TODDY-TAPPING IN GALJIBAGA: A CASE STUDY

The heart of Goa lies in her villages, where even today in this rapidly modernising Indian State the ancient traditional occupations still have a place in society. The Christian and Hindu Goans who performed agricultural and menial labour were grouped into a larger Sudir (Sudra) community which included traditional toddy-tappers, farmers and fishermen. Toddy-tapping, therefore, occupies a special place among the traditional occupations of Goans and they have even established their own Toddy-Tappers' Association with a head office in Margao. The D'Silva family is evidence of this timeless tradition where Eduardo produces feni from traditional methods and machinery in their own backyard. Even today the income derived from toddy-tapping is lucrative owing to the subsequent production of feni, the local drink famous throughout Goa. The toddy-tappers are men of humble origin and even temperament who enjoy rather lase, albeit strenuous life of their profession. They are most concentrated in the coastal talukas where an abundance of coconut plantations are found and every coastal village has at least one toddy-tapper.

A toddy-tapper performs his job thrice a day on each tree nurtured by him every morning, afternoon and evening. In the morning and evening the 'vein' of the tree at its top is opened and the sap slowly drains into the attached clay pot or plastic jug. During the afternoon heat, the toddy-tapper climbs the tree and closes the openings so that the tree has time to recover its lost fluids. He climbs the tree using the foot steps carved in the trunk and supports himself once in the tree tops by the base of the palm leaves.

For three consecutive days, 'sur' (sap) is collected from the coconut trees so as to fill up a large jug. Once enough sur is collected, it is then subjected to a process which results in the production of coconut feni, a distilled drink with a high percentage of alcohol. In this process a large earthenware vessel is heated over a wood fire on the fourth day until the sur boils. Once boiling begins, the vapor which is created rises from the mixture and escapes through a pipe which passes through a large cement 'cooling' water tank. The pipe then emerges at the bottom of the tank and the 'sur', now cooled, recondenses to liquid 'molop' and falls into a smaller clay pot. The remaining contents of the large vessel (gordo) are discarded and the distillation process is repeated, this time heating the molop and an additional amount of sur. The result of this distillation is known as coconut feni and is a popular drink throughout Goa in both villages and urban centres. The entire process lasts from 4-6 days depending on the weather conditions and is arrested by the monsoons.

Though a humble and repetitive occupation, toddy-tapping remains a viable source of income for those who prefer the calm life close to nature. Those who are engaged in this profession demonstrate a remarkable closeness to and respect for nature. Their product, coconut feni, is an acquired taste in Goa whose seasoned drinkers converge on small one-room village bars in order to consume it alone, with water, or with a popular soft drink like Teem or Limca topped with a splash of fresh lime.

Of late, however, owing to increasing education and social mobility in Goa, more and more sons of toddy-tappers are leaving the former traditional occupation of their fathers. Education has given the younger generation of Sudir a sense of dignity and worth, which their community lacked in former times and has provided with the intellectual equipment to take up white-collar jobs, which were once the preserve of the upper castes. They feel a sense of shame regarding these traditional occupations; not because of their new 'western education', as some might argue, but rather because these occupations were caste-bound and relegated to those members of the lower socio-economic communities. It is not 'westernism' and modernism which have caused this occupational change, but rather the desire of youth from among the Sudir community to free themselves of age-old social stigmas and seek greater occupational and social prestige.

ANJUNA: A CASE STUDY

The 'Hippie' Scene Revisited

On the shores of the northern taluka of Bardez, tourism

and the tourist industry have had a significant impact on the local population and landscape of Goan villages. From Calangute through Chapora, virtually the entire coastal length of Bardez has been home to a wide variety of tourists. Whereas Calangute and Baga were developed to cater to the charter tourist scene, the coastal village of Anjuna became the haven for the 'hippies' of the 1960's, 70's and early 80's. Due to cash crunch these travellers would often auction their belongings to other travellers and local people and exchange guitars to jewellery, jeans for money. Thus, began the infamous 'flea' market at Anjuna. Located on the sandy stretch overlooking the waves of the Arabian Sea, what started as an open-air hippie exchange has become one of the most popular attractions for backpackers and tourists alike and though a relatively new phenomena unlike the antiquity of the Mapsa market, the Flea market has a unique style and rhythm all its own.

In today's market, which during the peak season (October-April) covers almost the entire stretch of beach, one finds only a few western residents and long-staying travellers on the selling side of the fence. The majority come to observe and buy, while the hawkers hail from Gujarat, Rajasthan and some belong to the semi-nomadic Lamani tribe in Karnataka. The latter make up the largest majority, selling thick silver jewellery, richly-dyed fabrics and trinkets from all over India. They have a unique style of dress and culture of their own and live on the fringes of Goan society much like the long-staying travellers who reside in Anjuna and frequent the market. The Flea market begins around 9 am and shuts down only with the setting sun. Few traces of Goan life and culture are visible here, however, one can still find traces of the Anjuna 'hippie hide-outs' which has become a legend to these parts.

Following liberation, the backpackers and followers of the 'hippie' culture found their way into Goa during the 1960's and have since settled down in the northern coastal towns of Baga, Calangute, Anjuna and Arambol. Most come from Holland, Great Britain, Germany, Italy, Israel and others from northern European countries. All have cleared the 12th standard and many have attended some form of 2-year or 4-year educational institution. Many rent houses and live in Goa for six months in a year, financed by previous employment in the service industries (restaurants, hotels, secretaries, free-lance) in their home countries. In Goa they do not perform legally sanctioned economic activity and earn salaries only in their native countries to which they return during the monsoon months. The majority exist on the fringe of Goan society and remain in the heavily touristed areas where contact with westerners is frequent. Few speak Konkani, but most have a basic knowledge of English and probably pigeon Hindi. The use of narcotic drugs and alcohol is common among the members of this community, where it is socially acceptable and even encouraged. Women's clothing is similar to styles worn in western countries during the summer months such as shorts, halter and tank teeshirts, sandals and long loose skirts. Men also wear shorts and teeshirts though some also wear long cotton pants and long-sleeve loose shirts. Individualism is a strong value in this society and many of long-staying western residents in Goa come from broken homes or otherwise disrupted social situations. Their cultural patterns and behaviours exceed the normal limits acceptable in a variety of western societies and they do not follow many of the traditional customs and rituals observed in western Christian communities. This community in Goa is well-known owing to their 'deviant' behaviour (relative to the norms of the Goan society) and has also given rise to a new identification of Goa as an international tourist mecca.

In addition to the long-term western community, 'package' tourists, five-star vacationers and several individuals have made Goa a part of their lives. Several western people have married Goans and/or have settled in Goa with business aims. Package tourists arriving mostly from Britain often stay in Goa as long as two months and patronise the tourist enclaves of the northern and southern beaches. Some are able to find common ties with the back-packing crowd, but the majority stay within the heavily tourist areas of Calangute and Baga. This community, (and by community I mean western Europeans with a similar socio-economic status, i.e., the goal orientation and life experience) arrives during the month of December and stays on until the end of January/February. The tourists who prefer the five-star luxury hotels usually stay from several days to a maximum of two weeks in the Cidade de Goa, the Mandovi, or Leela Beach Hotel and foster the tourist industry through large expenditures in short time-spans. They are usually from upper-middle class backgrounds and are looking for a tropical get-away where they have not previously vacationed.

The young western crowd congregating in Anjuna, however, mistook the apparent permissiveness of the locals to mean acceptance of their lifestyle, which led to further public behaviour heavily sanctioned according to the norms of Goan society. Slowly the unemployed low socio-economic strata of Anjuna began to interact with the 'hippies' to earn money through the sale of drugs, specifically marijuana, hash, LSD, heroin and cocaine. Within a few years Anjuna became known for drug peddling, which was the largest possibly in all of south India. Small portable roadside kiosks (gadas) would sell these drugs in addition to normal cigarettes, gum sticks and small snacks. Over time, owing to both invitation and curiosity, those youth involved in the sale of drugs began to use them as well, lured by the temptations they saw the foreigners enjoying and the lack of moral support and guidance from within their own families. Both locals and Europeans alike who became involved in the Anjuna drug peddling business were usually non-religious individuals estranged from their own nuclear families, suffering from depression or other psychological imbalances and rebelling from larger society which they viewed as stifling and manipulating.

Some foreign women who were drug addicts exchanged sex for drugs, a practise which had lasting effects once it spread into the local Goan community which adhered to traditional moral values surrounding the indulgence in pre-marital sex. Boys as young as 10 and 11 who participated in the sale of drugs were encouraged by their elder peers to experiment with sex while all were intoxicated. Following such experiences, these boys often slipped into the scene of their elder peers and became involved not only in the use of drugs but also in the indulgence in sex and a variety of deviant behaviour resulting in conduct personality disorders.

Today, this scene is still alive in Anjuna, though most of the 'hippies' have gone home and the drug and prostitution trafficking has shifted to other areas along the coast of Goa. This village has become more commercial of late and is now frequented by charter tourists. The backpackers are the new 'hippies' who indulge in behaviour considered unacceptable according to the values of Goan society. Disillusioned by the same forces that drove others to the shores of Anjuna, these backpackers are out to see the world, discover some 'mystical' form of spirituality and escape from the conformity and naiveté of their own societies. As they make their way from Delhi to West Bengal, Rajasthan and other States, they eventually converge in Goa for the Christmas season. Here they find a subculture in which the use of drugs are normal aspects of daily life. Like their Anjuna predecessors, some of these backpackers slip into the same vicious cycle which further separates them from their own reality rather than encouraging them to confront the problems that they face at home.

Socio-cultural factors are in large part responsible for such activity. The permissive behaviour of the western 'hippie' culture visible in these tourist beach towns results in a frustrated local youth community who interacts and watches such behaviours but whose own society prevents him from indulging in similar activity. The reputation of a Goan in his/her village is highly valued and to tarnish such a reputation by interacting with individuals considered outcast in the Goan society leaves a black mark on one's character. Sexual prohibitions are such in Goan society that virginity is still a highly valued asset in a woman and one that many villagers strive to protect. Consequently, pre-marital intimate relationships with women and those involving casual sex are few and those that do exist continue behind closed doors. This is in marked contrast, however, to the surrounding cultural environment brought in to the beach towns like Anjuna and Chapora by the tourist industry.

Thus, Anjuna is a beach town whose identity has been forever altered by the arrival of the 'hippies' into Goa. The economy and industry of Anjuna, not to mention its environment and landscapes have been forever altered by the influx of tourists into the region. The cultural identity of Anjuna has been projected as permissive, western, drug-influenced and otherwise related to the 'hippie' culture which once flourished on its shores. Even today in Anjuna some western hippies from the early years have returned to make Anjuna their home, unaware of the locals' underlying attitudes towards them. Even as the drug scene and backpacking crowd shifts to north and south from the village of

Anjuna, it will be a long time, at least decades, before the locals recover from the image that is now the reputation and identity of their village. Anjuna, therefore, is symbolic of the modern-day cultural 'clash' that can result when 'East meets West' on the shores of Goa.

PANJIM: A CASE STUDY

The Modern Capital of Goa

Panjim (Panaji) is the modern-day capital city of the State of Goa. The first records, which mention the village of Panjim, date back to 1107, a time when the Kadamba Hindu dynasty enjoyed administrative control over the region. At that time Panjim was little more than a collection of fishing and farming hamlets inhabited by the indigenous Koli and Kunbi tribals involved in those traditional occupations. During the Middle Ages in Goa when the Bahamani Sultans and successive Muslim rulers controlled the regional trade of Goa, Panjim was still little known. The Bahamani capital had been based first at Goa Velha and then was switched to Old Goa just prior to its conquest by the Portuguese. Panjim, owing to its prime location at the mouth of the Mandovi River, was the location of several hilltop forts which were garrisoned for the protection of Old Goa and its surroundings. Adil Shah had built his summer house in Panjim on the bank of the Mandovi River, a splendid building which still stands erect today.

During the first Portuguese raid in March 1510, Panjim was attacked and it surrendered without a fight, as the majority of troops had been relocated to the hinterlands to fight a separate war. The Portuguese were ousted from the Panjim Forts by the forces of Adil Shah, but they again attacked and seized the Panjim Fort and the city of Old Goa. On November 25, 1510, the Panjim Forts were securely under the control of the Portuguese. Initially, the locus of administration of this new Portuguese regime was based in Old Goa until a devastating outbreak of malaria which killed many European inhabitants of that city in 1759.[33] Following that epidemic which was the result of poor drainage facilities in the area, the Portuguese began relocating their administrative offices to the then small town of Panjim.

Later a Governor by the name of Dom Manual Port e Castro

(1826-35) then initiated a series of land drainage and reclamation projects in the Panjim surrounds in order to reestablish the seat of government in this new locality. Known as the founding Father of Panjim, he further authorised the construction of several administrative buildings, schools, parks and roads.[34] This began the initial impetus resulting in the massive growth of Panjim within a few short years. This new city eventually superceded Old Goa and became the territory's capital in 1843. During this period the old neighbourhoods of Panjim also started functioning, neighbourhoods whose residents soon imitated the culture of the Portuguese gentry and identified with them linguistically, politically and psychologically.

Fontainhas was one such Portuguese-style neighbourhood which arose following the administrative relocation from Old Goa to Panjim. Owing to the rapid and haphazard way in which the land was parcelled out, the houses were constructed first and the streets were squeezed in afterwards, resulting in the winding narrow roads that characterises these neighbourhoods today. The Fountain of Phoenix supplied water to this settlement, hence over time it came to be known as Fontainhas.[35] A small chapel dedicated to St. Sebastian was erected in this residential community in 1818 to cater to the spiritual needs of this Catholic community.

Within Fontainhas both Portuguese and native upper-class Catholics who worked in government service had their dwellings. It was in Fontainhas and similar neighbourhoods in Panjim where the greatest degree of acculturation among the natives occurred, where the most celebrated street dances were held and where the Catholic clubs like Clube Nacional had their beginnings. Today's clubs and street dances are still held in these old neighbourhoods of Panjim, and are patroned by the young educated urban Catholic community. Many long-time older residents likewise still feel very much a part of the Portuguese culture. They are yet to identify with larger India culturally and insist on their own cultural superiority in relation to that of other Goan communities. The double-cheek kiss, elegant western dress, outings to the Clube Nacional and the Portuguese language are very much a part of the culture of this small community which resembles that of the Portuguese gentry during the days of European occupation of Goa. This community was the same one cited by the Portuguese dictator, Dr. Salazar, while making his claim that the natives of Goa were entirely Luso-Indian. Likewise, among these communities the local residents demonstrated their loyalty towards the Portuguese rulers and many even migrated to Portugal following Liberation in 1961. The younger generation are far dogmatic in their adherance to Portuguese culture and ritual. Knowledge of Portugese was passed on in its oral form, but English is most often used.

During the early years of Portuguese rule, when the administration began to enact social changes in Goa, they restructured the caste groupings so as to coincide with groupings similar to their own. The Bamonn (Brahmans) and Chaddhe (Kshatriyas) became the higher and lesser nobles respectively, which then merged into a single upper-class Catholic society similar in both economic and social influence. They also developed Confrarias within the Church, (established special brotherhoods for the upper castes) and concerned themselves with the welfare of the community and the maintenance of festival rituals. Though the urban members of the Catholic communities have adopted many western styles, social behaviours and progressive attitudes, they still have distinctly Indian values regarding family, parents, sexual behaviour and the institution of marriage. Unlike many of the Hindu communities, however, they do not observe various restrictions during menstruation, pregnancy and death.

The Charrdo and Brahmin communities are concentrated in the talukas of Bardez, Salcette and Tiswadi and very few inhabited the inland talukas of Goa. They have surnames such as Dias, Pinto, Menezes and Gomes and have a very high educational level. Most speak Konkani and Hindi, speak and write English and many are fluent in spoken Portuguese or other languages such as French. Many men and women study beyond college to attain higher degrees in medicine, law, engineering, accounting and business and belong to the middle and upper income groups. Catholics found in the high levels of administration normally come from this community. Gulf employments in banks, aboard ships, or in other offices are also common among members of this community as a way to increase the family income. Marriage alliances are usually formed through proposals, though love marriages are on the rise among members within this community owing to their level of education and exposure to western attitudes and ideals. Girls marry between the ages of 22 to 27 and boys between the ages of 27 to 32, depending on career and financial concerns. Informal dowry is given in cash and kind, the latter taking the form of land, furniture, automobiles, gold ornaments, clothing and other movable valuables. Proposals come from the bride's family and the couple usually meet and have the opportunity to interact on several occasions in order to determine their compatibility. Following an accepted proposal, horoscopes are often matched and rings of engagement are formally exchanged. Two weeks before the wedding the bride will wear green bangles (chuda) which symbolise her engagement before the wedding. On the day prior to the wedding, the future bride is given a bath in coconut water by members of her family and a feast is held in her honour. Weddings are held in the village church in the morning or early afternoon hours, followed by an evening reception and dance which lasts until the early morning hours. Bangles of many colours are often worn prior to and during the wedding ceremony. The customary rituals during the reception include the wedding march around the hall led by the newly-wed couple, the cutting of the wedding cake, brief formal speeches given by the best man and a circle dance whereby each unmarried guest gets the opportunity to dance with the bride or groom. Throughout the reception a live band performs English and Konkani songs, the latter having special group dances. At the end of the reception the bride and groom are carried aloft by the remaining guests towards each other at which time they embrace and the reception concludes. Following the wedding the couple lives with the boy's parents for some months until they move into their own house or apartment to begin their married life. A pregnant woman returns to her ancestral house in the last few months of pregnancy and baptism, holy communion, confirmation and other Catholic sacraments infuse religious life into the life-cycles of the child. Upon the death of a family member, a prayer service is held for the soul of the deceased and a coffin is carried in procession to the church graveyard where the priest recites special prayers as the coffin is lowered into the ground. The Catholic community, like the Hindus, practise a death observance annually, including the preparation of a small feast for family and friends. Among Catholics, following the church mass the mourners proceed to the graveyard where the priest again invokes special prayers to insure the safe passage of the departed soul into the realm of heaven. Family planning is in vogue and most young parents are opting for 2 and 3 children instead of the previous 4-6.

Panjim Today

Panjim today is Goa's third largest city following Mapsa (Bardez taluka) and Margao (Salcette taluka). It is the main commercial hub of the Tiswadi taluka and is connected by a series of major roads to all of Goa's main cities and most of her rural centres. Panjim is the seat of government for the State of Goa today, as it was under the Portuguese administration of yore. The palace of Adil Shah houses many government offices and most of Goa's diplomats live on Altinho Hill, directly above the main commercial hub of Panjim. Fontainhas and Sao Tome are now popular tourist destinations even though they are in need of repairs and renovations. Following Liberation a heavy stream of migrants flowed into Panjim from neighbouring villages, the Goan interior and business-minded residents of neighbouring States. As a result, the town of Panjim has since expanded to merge with the surrounding suburbs of Miramar, Santa Ynez, Santa Cruz, Taleigao, Ribandar, Dona Paula and other outlying suburbs. Many new businesses have also entered the city of Panjim and are now catering to Goa's wealthy population seeking of Maruti cars, Benetton clothing, Guess jeans, Reebok sneakers and Internet connection. Panjim and its surroundings also host a variety of cultural programmes, dances and other social events in addition to those sponsored by the Kala Academy in Miramar. Though Panjim has experienced rapid expansion following Liberation, the city still retains much of its old-world charm owing to the tree-lined streets, water-front promenade, well-preserved Portuguese administrative buildings and heavy concentration of Catholics. In this respect the capital city is unlike the towns of Mapsa and Margao which have ammassed large populations and massive cement structures, effectively overshadowing the people and buildings of days gone by.

In Panjim and other large cities situated throughout Goa, commercial establishments and small businesses proliferate along the crowded market streets. The Vaisya/Vani community, third highest in the classical varna system, is a single endogamous group of the Kudali Vanis in Goa. They are traditionally traders and commercial communities, though the Vaisya community in Goa is relatively small in comparison to other States in India. This is probably owing to the Saraswat Brahmans, who have taken to trading and other forms of business which diverge from their traditional occupations. The Vanis are concentrated in urban areas, especially Mapsa, Panjim and Margao and many have moved into the professions of medicine, law, engineering and big business. Following Liberation and the opening of the economy, the prosperity of this community increased in general owing to the new trade links which were soon established between Goa and the rest of the Indian subcontinent. The Vaisyas speak Konkani, speak and write Marathi and some speak and write English fluently as well. They are non-vegetarian though they abstain from eating pork and beef. Marriage rites are akin to those of other Hindu communities, following the Hindu Samskaras, though an increase in love marriages in addition to those negotiated through proposals has been the latest trend in this and other communities in Goa as well. The Vaisya community has a Vaisya Mandal, established in Mapsa in 1908, with the aim to provide scholarships and other aid to needy students as well as to look after the social and cultural improvements within the community. Today among members of this community the religious restrictions and sanctions are less rigid than those of previous generations.

Business communities from Gujarat have also migrated to Goa in recent years; settling all over the region and concentrating in Ponda, Panjim, Margao and Vasco de Gama. They have migrated owing to the prospect of better opportunity and have contributed to the city of Vasco's label as a migrant town. The Gujaratis have opened a variety of businesses in Goa, from restaurants and tour offices to roadside stalls and small-scale industries. They maintain the traditions similar to those in Gujarat and organise dances and cultural programmes in Vasco for members of the community. Marriages are endogamous among the Gujarati community and workers try to visit their native place at least once a year. In addition to migrants from other Indian States, many Goans and non-Goans from the sprawling urban centres have begun to choose Goa as their home. Fed up with pollution, overpopulation and the constant hassles of big-city life, many Goans in Bombay who migrated to that city as young children hope to resettle in Goa during their retirement years. Nomadic tribes from Rajasthan have also discovered that Goa is a lucrative place to sell their wares and can be found in numbers in the tourist towns.

Good Friday and Carnival in Panjim

A small chapel was built in the village of Panjim, following the conquest of Goa by the Portuguese and by 1600 it was enlarged into the Church of Our Lady of the Immaculate Conception. Today's structure is a well-maintained, impressive white-washed church which is the locus of spirituality for the Catholic population in Goa. Likewise, Good Friday is a day of sincere reverence among Goan Catholics. It is the culmination of Lent, an important observance in the lives of devout Catholics. Lent is observed for 40 days from February to March, beginning with Ash Wednesday and ending on Good Friday followed by Easter Sunday. The mass and procession occur in every church in Goa, but the one in Panjim draws the largest crowd.

In Panjim, hundreds of devout Goan Catholics gather in the Panjim Church of the Mary Immaculate Conception to listen to mass and participate in the Way of the Cross. During the afternoon sermon, the priests narrate the sufferings that Jesus Christ took upon himself for the sake of humanity. The mass is in Konkani, Goa's State language, attracts a crowd too large for the church itself and people stand in the doorways and in the premises, dressed in formal clothes with somber countenance. After the mass, the crucifix, which until this time has been kept from view, is now uncovered before the crowd for veneration. A very somber ceremony, the Way of the Cross is a reenactment of the path Jesus took on Mount Calvary before the Crucifixion. In Panjim, which draws the largest crowd, a large wooden cross carried by an image of Jesus is taken from the church, down the steps and through the streets of the town. It is carried by clergymen while the crowd follows in two parallel lines in front of and in back of the statue, some weeping and all with very solemn faces. Those not participating in the actual procession look on from the road sides, both Hindus and Christians alike. Somber music played by a band accompanies the procession which slowly winds its way through the main streets in Panjim before returning to the church.

Carnival is another Catholic festival famous throughout Goa, though hardly resembling the sombre procession of Good Friday. The Goa Carnival, rather, is the celebration which occurs immediately prior to the onset of Lent and is a time where people feel free to indulge in merry-making and boisterous behaviour. The Goa Carnival was likewise imitated by the Portuguese, though the Carnival imported was one envisioned by the common sailor and average man. Thus, while the upper class participated in masked balls within the walls of the Clube Nacional, the procession of floats which slowly moved down the main road in Panjim was marked by revelry and gay abandon. Colour such as that used during Holi celebrations was used and water balloons also came in vogue. In olden days drunkenness was also prevalent, so the church decided to clamp down on the festivities.

Today's Carnival, thus, lacks the merry-making of earlier days, though a colourful, costumed procession is still the attraction of the day. The parade begins around 4 pm and continues into the early evening as spectators line up along the sides of the road to watch the float parade. Youth from within a village gather together in order to design a float and participate in the parade, competing for the prize awarded to the best float. Social themes were encouraged in this year's parade, with the result that AIDS, drug abuse, environmental and traditional occupational concerns were incorporated into the floats in often unique ways. Portuguese dances and music are also played to accompany some floats and English and Konkani music are also popular additions to various floats.

During the evening, street dances reminiscent of the old Portuguese era are held in the open air in one of Goa's old neighbourhoods outside several of the membership social clubs. Participants are asked to dress in red and black or in costume and a live band is hired to cater to the crowd. Konkani, English and occasionally Hindi songs are played and the party continues until the early morning hours. The dance caters mostly to the young crowd in Panjim and neighbouring suburbs and is frequented by tourists and locals alike. In addition to the Carnival parade, a unique New Year's street parade occurs in the adjoining Panjim Suburb of Ribandar. Beginning in the early evening and continuing until the early morning hours, this street parade by and for the people is patroned mostly by the Ribandar youth. Similar to the Carnival parades of North-East Brail, a local band sits atop a large truck, playing popular English, Konkani, Hindi and Portuguese tunes. People congregate behind the moving truck, dancing in groups, alone, or in couples as the band winds its way through the main streets of Ribandar. Ribandar was once a suburb for the wealthy Portuguese residents and this tradition parallel to that existing in modern-day Brauil most likely originated from those early Portuguese inhabitants who wished to add something special to their New Year's celebration.

Shigmo in Panjim

Every year around the month of March, the streets of Panjim come alive in a spectacle which in recent years surpasses even that of the Goa Carnival. From 5-6 p.m. in the evening until the early hours of the next day, streets in Panjim are blocked and for hours crowds of young and old, rich and poor, Hindu and Christian, gather and watch as the Shigmo parade winds through the crowded streets. Held during the full moon period which marks the beginning of spring, this festival is Goa's version of Holi, an ancient Hindu festival.

Long before Christianity made itself a lasting presence on the shores of Goa, Hinduism was the major religion practised by Goa's people and even today two-thirds of Goans adhere to the Hindu faith. Shigmo, besides being a unique form of entertainment, is also a cultural exhibition of Goa's history from time immemorial up to the present day. The procession begins with brass bands reminiscent of the Maratha conquerors, followed by a series of Kunbi folk-dances performed by village tribal women bedecked in gold and brightly-coloured sarees. Regional dances from the northern and southern talukas (counties) of Goa also find expression during Shigmo, as well as various acrobats and 'fire-throwers' from Kerala. Men marching with poles to the beat of drums, others dancing with decorated umbrellas and both sexes parading in elaborate costumes representing various deities;

all can be seen during the Goan Shigmo Parade. The procession culminates in a procession of illuminated floats atop which larger-than-life mechanical figures represent important deities and some even re-enact their heroic deeds.

PONDA: A CASE STUDY

The Taluka of Temples

No discussion on Goan communities would be complete without including the community of Gowda Saraswat Brahmins whose famous, ancient temples are spread throughout the district of Ponda. The history of Ponda both prior to and during the Portuguese rule is a troubled one owing to constant wars and threats from the North, East and West. From Hyder Ali to the Portuguese, the area of Ponda has witnessed many historic battles.[36] During the years of religious persecution and the presence of the Inquisition, most of the sacred images and wealth of the temples in the Old Conquests were carried across the frontier into the Ponda taluka which escaped Portuguese attack. Thus, the city of Ponda and its surroundings are saturated with temples and temple complexes which are the homes of most families and klan deities of the GSBs. Their location is entirely the result of historical events in Goa which resulted in the concentration of temples in the 'safe area' of Ponda taluka. These temples, owing to their unusual architecture, ancient deities and turbulent history, are important pilgrimage sites for many Hindu communities and especially those spread throughout India which belong to the GSB community.

The Manguesh temple, for example, was one such temple whose deity was brought by devotees from Mormugao (Old Conquests) during the high time of the Portuguese Inquisition. Manguesh is a local incarnation of Lord Shiva and the temple is the most prominent, attracting tourist in Goa. Less than one kilometre from Manguesh is the Sri Mahalasa temple near the village of Mardol. Sri Mahalasa is a local incarnation of Vishnu as well as a form of Shakti (power). The temple was built in the 17th century and is known for its exquisite wood carvings of Lord Vishnu. Shri Naguesh temple was built in 1413 and contains ancient stone inscriptions and intricate wood carvings. Naguesh is a local incarnation of Ganesh and is an important temple for many Hindu communities in Goa. Shri Kamakshi is another important religious monument for the Goan Hindu community. The temple was formerly located in Raia, Salcette, but owing to religious persecution by the Portuguese, the temple and Shri Kamakshi were relocated to Shiroda village in Ponda. Shri Shantadurga is worshipped throughout Goa, but her largest and most opulent temple is located among the Saraswat Brahmin community of Kavale. The current temple was built in 1728 during the reign of Shahu Maharaj of Satari, but the deity was originally located in the taluka of Mormugao. Shantadurga is an incarnation of Parvati, the goddess of peace and is known elsewhere throughout Goa as Thamai, Sateri, Bhumka and Adimaya. Shantadurga, Saraswati, Mangueshi and Mahalaxmi are favourite deities of the Saraswat Brahman community in Goa in addition to the kula devtas (family deities) which each exogamous gotra (family group) reveres.

The Saraswat Brahman community in Goa is one of the most progressive and influential communities in Goa. They trace their origin back to the sage Saraswati who lived on the banks of the Saraswati River near Bengal and survived the great famine detailed in the Vedas by living on fish for 12 months. According to this legend, they migrated to the Konkan following Parashuram who gifted to them the fertile province of Gomanchal. They were originally distributed among 96 villages throughout Salcete and Tiswadi talukas.[37] They speak Konkani, which has its roots in the Gaurian languages of north-eastern India and can read and write Marathi fluently. Some also know Sanskrit and Portuguese and most in the younger generation speak English and Hindi fluently. Land is their major economic resource, though business and agriculture are their primary occupations. Saraswat Brahmins are also found in government service, politics and a variety of professions such as law, medicine, science research, architecture and academicians. Those who own land prefer to live in joint families, but urban-dwellers prefer the nuclear family structure. Male elders in the community wear full shirts and dhotis and ladies Wear Sari-blouse and salvar-kameez. They are non-vegetarian but do not eat pork, beef and buffalo meat. Fish-curry-rice is the main staple meal in their diet. They eat 3 meals per day and tend to abstain from alcohol owing to strong religious and social sanctions. Two different sects exist in Goa, those who worship Shiva (Shiavites) and those who revere Vishnu (Vaishnavites). The former sect is divided into 5 subgroups namely the Kavlemath, Chitrapur (Gaud Saraswat), Haldipur, Kudaldeshkar and Pednekar Brahmins and the Vaishnavites are subdivided into two groups, the Partagal almath and the Kashimath.[38] In olden days these groups were strictly endogamous regarding marital alliances, but recent trends indicate that this endogamy has virtually disappeared and marital alliances occur among all the different Saraswat Brahman communities. Marriage is negotiated through proposals, horoscopes are matched between prospective bride and groom and the dowry system exists in cash and gifts. On the eve of marriage the haldi ceremony is performed and the bride then worships the family devak (sacred tree).[39] As in other Hindu communities, the patt, garland, akshata (rice with vermillion on forehead), mangalsutra, green bangles and construction of the mandap in front of the bride's house are marriage rituals followed among this Brahman community. Married women, as in most of the Goan communities both Hindu and Catholic, relinquish their lawful right to the family property in favour of their brothers and instead receive dowry often equal to their property share in gold, clothing, furniture and other movable items of value. Pre-natal, post-mortem and other life-cycle rituals as laid out in the Hindu Samskaras are likewise followed by this Brahman community. During the Barsa or naming ceremony, sweets (often ladoos) are distributed to the guests at the conclusion of the ceremony. During the Jaival ceremony, the Mhalo (village barber) and the Bhatji (officiating priest from within their community) are present for the shaving of the young child's head when he is between one and two years of age.[40] When a young male child reaches between 8 and 10 years of age, the thread ceremony (mundan) is observed and the individual is required to learn several mantras in Sanskrit prior to receiving his first thread. Cremation rituals are observed, including the funeral procession led by the eldest son of the deceased from his place of residence to the funeral pyre, which is then lit by a torch carried by the eldest son. On the 7th day the ashes are collected and later immersed in to a sacred river or sea and on the 12th day following the death rites a feast is given by the family of the deceased.

In addition to the GSB community, the Karhade Brahmins

and Chitpavan Brahmans also maintain several ancient temples in the interior of Goa. The Chitpavan Brahman community is found throughout the talukas of Goa and is primarily a community of Brahman priests. Their mother tongue is Marathi in the Devnagiri script though most also speak Konkani. Older generations of menwear the yellow dhoti to perform puja in the temple and women use the lugde and cholis of different colours. Today's generation follows the modern style of pants and shirt for men and saris for women. They are pure vegetarian with rice and dal as their staple food and few of them also indulge in the consumption of alcohol.[41] Marriages are conducted through proposals from the father of the bride and usually occur between the ages of 18 to 23 for girls and 24 to 29 for boys. They intermarry with other Brahman groups and they follow the custom of matching horoscopes prior to conducting the final engagement ceremony (sakharpuda). Marriage symbols for the woman are mangalsutra, green bangles and vermillion paste in the parting of the hair. Dowry is a part of the marriage arrangement and usually is given in cash and kind. If the marriage is held at the bride's residence a pandal (mandap) is erected in front of the house in which the ceremony is performed in addition to the 7 circles taken around the sacred fire. During the simant poojan the groom is received at the bride's residence, the couple is asked to stand face to face on wooden seats (patt) and they pray to the family deity for a good married life.[42] Puberty rites, pre- and post-delivery rituals are observed and the 'fulam mallap' occurs between the 7th and 9th months of pregnancy during which time the young future mother returns to her ancestral house for a period of care and confinement.

The Karhade Hindu Brahman community is concentrated in the in-land talukas of Ponda, Bicholim, Pernem and Sattari, where their ancestors migrated from the Karnatak region East and South of Goa. Mahalsa of Mardol, Shantadurga of Kavalem, Navdurga of Borim, Vijayadurga of Keri and Mahalakshmi of Bandora are the family deities of this community. They are pure vegetarians though men drink alcohol and both men and women chew betel nut.[43] Marathi is their mother tongue but they know Konkani and use the Devnagiri script. Most of the people, belong to the middle and upper socio-economic, strata, of the community are doctors lawyers, architects and are working in various government departments. Land holdings are their traditional economic resource from which profits are gained from the cultivation of arable lands by local labourers. Intermarriages by negotiation (bride's side proposes) take place within or among the sub-communities of Karhade, Paddhy and Bhatta Brahmins. Girls are married between the ages of 18-20 and boys are married between 24-28. Weddings are conducted in a marriage hall and the family deities are worshipped after turmeric powder is applied to the couple followed by a ceremonial bath. Dowry, simant poojan (reception of bride-groom at entrance), ceremony on the patt, the use of the antarpat curtain, swastik worship, garland exchange, tying of mangalsutra, green bangles, the kanyadan ceremony and the seven circles around the sacred fire are all customs observed during the marriage Samskara.[44] Fullam malap (when the future mother is presented with a green sari and bangles by her female relatives) and confinement are observed prior to the birth of a new-born.[45] On the 11th day of the post-delivery period the house is cleaned and both mother and child take a ritual purification bath. On the 12th day the naming ceremony occurs.

Conclusion

In Goa, therefore, wealth and poverty animal and man, tradition and modernity, past and present exist side by side. Economic activity ranges from traditional occupations of farming, fishing and toddy-tapping to computer engineering and international import-export enterprises. Social liberalism, exclusiveness and female repression can all be found among various communities in Goa and women's education likewise can be from MD's and MBA's down to a basic knowledge of the ABC's. In Goa a wide range of permitted and prohibited social roles for women also exist which vary more *between* socio-economic levels than among the various religions, demonstrating not only the early formation of a class-based society but also the cultural evolutionary trend towards social convergence. In addition, social status measured both in terms of ascribed status and achieved standard of living is still a very significant underlying motivation among the people of Goa. Those who demonstrate a similar standard of living, professional orientation, educational level and social patterning will have much in common though they are from different religions. Yet this religious divide still creates a gulf between the formation of intimate relationships and marriage alliances.

Without doubt it becomes clear that the promoted 'cultural identity' of Goa represents only a segment of the entire population and ignores much of the cultural life of Goa's inhabitants. Whether Hindu Sanskaras, Muslim Prayers, or Catholic Sacraments, the Goan community shares religion as the cultural foundation of society upon which events and outlooks in life are created and refined. Konkani, Marathi, Portuguese and English are all mother tongues of the Goans according to their specific community and of late the use of Hindi has increased in the major urban areas where migrant settlements predominate. Though street parties and parades are part of the upper-class Catholic community in Panjim, the 'fun, frolic and fiesta' atmosphere promoted by the tourist industry is confined mostly to the heavily trafficked tourist areas along the northern coast of Bardez taluka. The Goan society and its consequent 'cultural identity' are, therefore, much more complex, communal and historically evolved than previous descriptions of Luso-Indian culture would have, both locals and outsiders believe. The historical overlays within which the culture(s) of Goa have evolved and have resulted in the formation of distinct societies whose customs and social patterns are often unknown to the members of other communities. Yet these communities do interact continuously and share many of these value-orientations, social experiences and personality traits. Thus, as early experiences of a child remain stored in his memory (often subconsciously) throughout his adult life, likewise Goan society has stored all the experience and wisdom of the ages in its collective consciousness which, having neither beginning nor end, is passed down in a myriad of forms through successive generations. Konkani proverbs are one expression of age-old wisdom.

The communities and cultures of Goa are as wide and diverse as those spread throughout larger India and no one village can possibly represent the multiplicity of village life and culture in Goa. Maulingam is vastly different from Agonda which hardly resembles Anjuna which latter differs from Rivona. Likewise, there is a marked difference between the rural and urban centres in Goa and among the urban areas themselves. Varying shades of difference distinguish one village from another and it is within these shades of difference where the social life and rich layers of cultural traditions flourishing in Goa are found. These variations are the living embodiments of the past as well as the contemporary evolution of the present and attest to the great variety of cultural and historical layers that have found their way into Goa. In the end the question again returns to the nature of culture and cultural identity in an attempt to account for this seemingly endless variety of cultural forms which exist in Goa and give life and character to her people beyond the monotony of their daily routine. Many of these pre-Portuguese cultural forms have their origins in prehistoric times and continue to exist through the continuous processes of creation and evolution. Culture as a way of life and a psychology of the masses, therefore, has been shaped by the Portuguese administration and all those rulers which came before them. Goa, therefore, is a cultural melting pot which has incorporated these various layers that have subsequently found expression through particular migrated and/or evolved communities. At the same time, several communities in Goa have also withstood all of these cultural incursions and continue to adhere to the traditions of their forefathers. Thus, in Goa, as in larger India, tradition is juxtaposed with modernity in a remarkable array of cultures and communities.

REFERENCES

1. Singh, K.S., *People of India: Goa.*, New Delhi, Anthropological Survey of India, 1993, (Introduction).
2. Albeit brown-outs are frequent and during the monsoons some villages are without electricity for days at a time. The urban centres are not often without electric energy, however.
3. Singh, K.S., *op. cit.* p. 2.
4. *As I perceived them during visitations to various villages.
5. Though Panjim is one of Goa's major cities and not a village, it has been included in this study to contrast the lifestyle and communities within Goa.
6. *See Social History of Goa.
7. Singh, K.S. People of India: Goa, p. 103.
8. *Ibid.*, p. 105.
9. *This case study was conducted at the Rivona Dispensary in March of 1997.

10. *I participated in this Zatra in 1997 and witnessed the temple celebration.
11. *See case study of Panjim.
12. *For a better description of Catholic rituals and customs in Goa, see the Chapter on *Social History in Goa.*
13. *The subsequent information was gathered during an interview with Mr. Pednekar.
14. Singh, K.S., *op. cit.*, p. 134.
15. *Ibid.*, p. 135.
16. *Ibid.*, p. 54.
17. *Ibid.*, p. 57.
18. *Ibid.*, p. 30.
19. They found a large smooth black stone in the shape of a phallus which is believed to be a representation of Lord Shiva.
20. *Ibid.*, p. 203.
21. *Ibid.*, p. 25.
22. *Ibid.*, p. 27.
23. *Ibid.*, p. 28.
24. *This author visited Agonda village on three separate occasions in November, December 1996 and April of 1997.
25. Singh, K.S., *op. cit.*, p. 114.
26. *Ibid.*, p. 115.
27. *Ibid.*, p. 116.
28. Gomes, Olivinho J.F., *Village Goa*,. New Delhi: S. Chand & Company Ltd., 1996.
29. *And the more business for the yarn sellers.
30. *These trends are similar elsewhere in Goan villages located within the three coastal talukas of Tiswadi, Bardez and Salcette.
31. *Ibid.*, p. 163.
32. *Ibid.*, p. 165.
33. Abram, David, *Goa: The Rough Guide*, London: The Rough Guides, 1995, pp. 55-56.
34. *Ibid.*, p. 56.
35. Directorate of Tourism, Hello Goa! Panjim: Government of Goa.
36. *See chapter the History of the Konkan Territory known as Goa for a detailed explanation of this history.
37. Singh, K.S. *op. cit.*, p. 185.
38. *Ibid.*, p. 186.
39. *Ibid.*, p. 187.
40. Of note: the Catholic communities also shave the heads of their youngsters

around this same time, however, the reasons are different. Among the Hindu community, the hair of the new-born is considered impure by the Vedic religion; among the Catholic community this practise has been reinterpreted so that it is done with the aim of thickening the hair and making it healthy-looking.

41. *Ibid.*, p. 60.
42. *Ibid.*, p. 62.
43. *Ibid.*, p. 107.
44. *Ibid.*, p. 109.
45. *Ibid.*, p. 110.

PART II

MIGRATION

CHAPTER 6

Migration: Processes and Products

Migration is a process which is integral and natural in the historical evolution of people and places and has gone on even before the earliest recorded history. The history of the world is, in many respects, determined by the migration of one human group from an origin to a new destination owing to a multiple factors which likewise change and evolve over time. Famine, war, persecution, politics, economics and employment are just a few of the causes of regional, national and international migration. Migration results in the flow of finances, ideas, behaviours, languages, technologies and opportunity both to and from the migration destination. In some traditional societies, migration is a way of life and characterises the movement of a community. In industrial societies, migration results from the possibility of better employment or improved climatic conditions. Whereas migration between nations in the current political regimes is strictly regulated, migration within an individual nation is largely free from formal legal hurdles. Migration of communities often determines the course of cultural evolution, which has been the main focus of this study. Migration, therefore, is integral to the understanding of this cultural process and especially important in the study of cultural evolution in Goa.

The first recorded migration of the Aryan population had substantial effects on the population, language and culture of the local aboriginal inhabitants of the Konkan region.

Likewise, the Gouda Saraswat Brahmin migration into the

Konkan has left an indelible mark on the high culture, religion and economy of the Goan region. Following the migration of the Vedic Hindu societies, the Muslim Arab commercial traders also migrated to Goa (by force of conquest) and established their society, administration and economic relations in Goa; developing the natural in-land river ports and building prosperous commercial centres through which international products were transported. Subsequently, the Portuguese community migrated (also by force of conquest) into Goa and established their culture, administration and commercial endeavours. The forceful influx first of the Muslims and later the Portuguese also resulted in the exodus of Hindu and Christian communities during the time of the Inquisition in the late 1500's and early 1600's. These groups migrated in all directions into neighbouring States and have since affected various additional societies, especially in the case of Mangalore, Karwar and Belgaum. In the 1900's Goa further witnessed a remarkable exodus of young native men to the growing urban centre of Bombay, which had significant impacts for both place of origin and their resulting destination. Following Liberation until the present, two major migration trends occurred in Goa; first, the exodus of young Goanese men to work in the Gulf countries or on international shipping lines and second, the influx of families and individuals from neighbouring States within India. The process of migration, therefore, has been an integral part of Goa's cultural evolution throughout recorded history, though the population and nature of the migration trends evolve and change owing to changing needs and circumstances.

This chapter is intended to explore the theoretical framework surrounding migration to enable the reader to place the Goan migrants in their overall socio-economic complex during their various migration trends. Migration theories are first examined from several previous studies in larger India and correlated with the data from my case studies of Bombay and Gulf countries migrants. Personal interviews with non-migrant rural-dwellers, Bombay migrants and overseas migrants in addition to general observations and conversations have enabled me to correlate the current trends in Goa to the theoretical data which seemingly withstand the test of time and space. This introductory chapter also serves to acquaint the reader with the impacts of migration in both rural and urban areas generally and in Goa specifically. Both exodus and influx are discussed, though more emphasis is placed on exodus. Impacts on Goan villages, urban environments, migrants and families left behind in the rural areas are discussed, as are the impact which migration has on the economic status of migrants, educational opportunities, family size and social mobility. Finally, this chapter intends to facilitate deeper insights into the subsequent case studies in Bombay, Bangalore and Mangalore; which examine the ways in which Goan migrants were able to re-establish communities in urban areas thereby maintaining a sense of identity and creating social networks and services.

Theoretical Framework of Migration

Several theories on migration have been postulated by various economists and historians over the decades. Ravenstein's Law of Migration, for example, argues that migrants move from areas of low opportunity to areas of high opportunity, often manifesting as a rural-urban migration flow.[1] His argument further states that each stream of rural-urban migration produces a related flow of urban-rural migration, though the characteristics of each flow are different and the former usually surpasses the latter in number and frequency. The destination chosen is partly influenced by its distance and the availability of public transportation to and from the place of origin and the migration destination. In the case of Goa, topography reveals that Bombay was the closest growing urban centre at the onset of the migration trend and consequently received the most migrants. The city of Bombay is also connected to Goa by ship and road and can be reached in an overnight trip by bus. Even today there are direct buses from Bombay to Goa which divides the city from the old Goan neighbourhood of Dhobi Talao. Cochin, New Delhi, Calcutta and Madras, by contrast, are relatively far away and the expense of migration increases, thus decreasing the frequency with which migrants can return to Goa. Bombay, therefore, was the ideal location demographically as well as economically, the latter because this city in the early 1900's was just beginning its long growth spurt which would render it the most densely populated city in India according to the 1991 census. Cochin was another possible area of migration owing to the Portuguese presence and its reputation as an international city. Cochin, however, was difficult to reach during the early 1900's owing to the presence of the marshy backwaters along the Keralan coast-line.

The L-F-R Model (Lewis, Ranis and Feri) focuses on the labour aspect of migration and argues that the process of migration is an equilibrium factor whereby people from areas of a greater labour surplus migrate to areas of a lesser labour surplus or even labour deficit.[2] In this theory, youth from areas of high unemployment such as the rural subsistence agricultural sector are compelled into the modern industrial sector where money has been channelled into industrial expansion, thus, increasing the demand for labour. In the example of Goa, migrants into Bombay most often came from large rural families where unemployment was rife. Having had a formal education and perceiving few available opportunities on the land, the youth from the Goan villages, especially among the Catholic community, saw Bombay as their only option. Their labour surplus was, thus, absorbed by the fast-growing city of Bombay where industrialisation had taken hold.

'Lee's Theory of Migration' builds upon that of Ravenstein and argues that there are 'positive' and 'negative' outcomes which are weighed prior to an individual making the decision to migrate.[3] These are often governed by personal factors such as one's attachment to family and friends in the place of origin, language difficulties and economic incentives. In addition to positive and negative, 'zeroes' are also considered, which are positive and negative forces cancelling each other out in the final equation. In the example of Bombay Goans, a young migrant may be reluctant to leave the comfort of home and family, yet in the Goan neighbourhood of Dhobi Talao he may have several friends who currently reside there. Similarly, a youth who is debating whether or not to migrate may be lured by the promise of adventure, excitement and an escape from the boredom of the village, while at the same time he fears the strange environment and new faces with which he will come into contact. These are called balanced forces.

In the final analysis that an individual makes, these positive and negative weighted factors will either facilitate or retard the decision to migrate.

Along similar lines, Sjaastad's Human Investment Theory argues that migrants weigh 'returns' and 'costs' both material and non-material, prior to making the decision to migrate.[4] Returns could be financial, such as an increase in salary from a rural Goan village to an urban office job, or they could be non-material, such as the adventure, exposure to new ideas and development of identity which follows migration to an urban area. Costs are those aspects of the current life situation which will have to be given up following migration, such as the fresh air and greenery of a village setting and the proximity of family and good friends. There are also material costs, such as the cost of transportation, moving from one location to another and the purchase of new required property. In the case of Goan migration to Gulf countries, the material returns far outweigh the material costs in terms of the salary earned from Gulf employment and the standard of living of overseas employees in more developed nations.

Todaro's Model of Rural-Urban Migration is the most complete theory, thus, far which argues that the decision to migrate is based on the 'expected' income and benefits and the probability of getting a job.[5] In Todaro's model, migration is the result of rational economic considerations which weigh both material and psychological costs and benefits.

These costs and benefits are dependent on the perceived future wages and gainful employment, such as the Goan ship-workers (a.k.a. 'shippies') who have gained high salaries proportionate to their low levels of education and socio-economic status.

The probability of getting a job, however, is dependent on the urban unemployment rate and the rate of rural-urban migration to a particular destination in relation to the number of available jobs.

According to Todaro, rural-urban migration (which characterises Goan migration) occurs in two separate but overlapping phases. During the initial Phase I, the migrant arrives at his desired destination but is yet to find employment in his desired occupation. Depending on his financial status, he may take up a job in a traditional occupation while continuing to search for employment in the modern sector. The three most important factors which determine success rate of employment are: (1) Individual Qualifications—does the migrant have the needed skills for the job that he seeks? (2) Knowledge of the urban labour market: does the migrant know which jobs are available, what the current salaries for such positions are and where openings are available? and (3) Access to jobs: does the migrant suffer from racial or ethnic discrimination which may prevent him from being offered jobs for which he is technically qualified? During Phase II of migration, the individual has found employment, resettled into his urban environment and is earning a salary which is large enough to offset the initial moving expenses which occurred during the former Phase.[6]

Yet while these theories are able to determine general migration characteristics across borders and nations, a more detailed explanation of Goan migration is necessary in order to understand better not only the migrated communities themselves but also the subsequent development in rural Goa which has come about owing to the migration of village youth into the national and international urban centres and occupations.

This chapter uses examples mostly from the rural-urban Bombay migrant study as well as the current Gulf-employment migration trends, both of which are dated to the present century and have been studied through the first-hand experience of this author.

Causes of Migration

In Goa at the turn of the century, several elements were responsible for the heavy exodus of labour from Goa to Bombay and later Goa to the Gulf. In rural Goa, large families were encouraged and children were considered financial assets who added immensely to the farm labour. However, over centuries the Goan community saw as the development of large families resulted in those with little land, economic resources and opportunity. The Indo-Portuguese Army was primarily the domain of the mestizoes and the mulattoes and the clergy and native administrative posts were likewise dominated by economically well-off upper caste Catholics. The Sudir community and the middle-class Kshyatrias were stuck in their traditional professions which even as small landowners did not earn enough to advance the economic situation of the family. Those who were tenants or share-croppers of large landowners received an unequal amount of the produce relative to their labour, often in the form of non-wage incomes.

Rural incomes, moreover, were highly susceptible to the constraints imposed on them by the prevailing feudal land system under the Portuguese administration. As a result, the income inequalities increased and the problem of landlessness was further exacerbated. (Previously, under the Hindu system, the land was owned collectively by the village and managed by the headmen or gauncars. This system existed throughout the Portuguese rule but was eventually replaced by the European feudal system.) As the number of landless people and the income disparities increased, the traditional village and social relationships broke down and people decided to migrate to areas of greater perceived economic opportunity. Youth became demoralised to work in traditional occupations in which the salary, hours, working conditions and social status were not in correlation with their self-image and education.

The construction of Catholic schools in rural villages also spurred the exodus of rural inhabitants into urban areas. Youth gained skills and improved their education which had little use in traditional village society, resulting in a dissatisfaction with rural life. The attraction of the 'big city lights', adventure and the perceived ability to find a job which matches their skills lured young able men from the rural to the urban centres. This is especially true for Goan youth among the lower and middle-income communities who were further spurred to migrate from the stories told to them from migrants who returned to Goa during their vacations and holidays. Educational opportunities beyond those available in Goa also appealed to many Goan migrants who envisioned a better education for their children. During the early 1900's there were few opportunities in Goa for further studies beyond secondary education if one was not fluent in Portuguese nor intended to enter into the clergy. Many migrated to urban areas in larger India such as Bangalore, Mangalore and Bombay where educational institutions founded during the British regime were available. However, the first migration waves brought migrants to Bombay as Bangalore was still a relatively small city with little industry and Mangalore was primarily an agrarian port.

In addition to the available opportunities in urban centres beyond the Goan borders, the presence of friends and relatives in specific urban areas facilitated Phase I of migration and often provided initial shelter, food and financial security while the newly migrated individuals went in search of jobs. The Goan migrants in Bombay were significantly helped in this regard via the 'Village Clubs' and individual relatives. Often during my interviews with Goans in Bombay they mentioned their forefathers, some of whom lived (6-7 persons) together in a small one-room apartment while new arrivals went in search of jobs and eventually found their own accommodations. The Village Clubs were crucial for the continued migration of young men from rural Goa, who lived together in the clubs quite cheaply. (For more details, see Bombay case-study). Word spread in the villages from visiting migrants that it was not too difficult to get a job in Bombay and that the village clubs were a safe and community-oriented place to put up during the job search.

Why individuals from rural areas tended to migrate to urban centres? Another reason was their desire to break away from the traditional constraints existing in the rural social structure of a Goan village. In traditional Goan society many such restraints curbed the activities of youth who decided to migrate when they perceived greater freedom in Bombay. An individual's caste, family reputation and socio-economic status contributed to the heavy constraints placed on individuals in rural Goan society. An individual from the Sudir community, for example, had little hope of advancement in the traditional village structure where his entire family history was known to the other village members and he was treated accordingly. Deference was paid to the higher castes regardless of the latter behaviour and members of the Sudir community during the early 1900's were barred from attaining positions of respect in society as doctors, businessmen, eminent scholars, etc. Family reputation also created heavy burdens on members in the society in that the behaviour of one's ancestors and family members reflected on younger generations. Thus, if an elder brother was wayward, the younger one was not expected to be better and if a girl was promiscuous then her sister was considered the same. Tradition was well guarded and any changes introduced by youth often met with criticism and disapproval, further driving the creative rural energy into the urban milieu.

Government policies also contributed to an individual or community's decision to migrate. Among the Hindu population of Goa, repressive and prejudicial policies of the Portuguese administration barred their advancement at every step along the way. This compelled many (who were financially able) to migrate to urban areas in the British regime where they enjoyed religious freedom. The Gouda Saraswat Brahmins were one such community whose education level surpassed most and who saw better opportunities under the British rule. The Catholics from the lower communities were also frustrated by biased government policies which enabled only the upper caste Catholics to enter the clergy and high administrative posts. In addition to these policies, the Portuguese administration did not concern itself with the development of industry and infrastructure in Goa. At the time of Liberation, for example, only four villages were electrified and few had adequate sanitary and water systems. Trade was focused on the import and export of international commodities and local agrarian produce and, thus, Goa was not considered for progressive development. All of these incapacitating policies combined to encourage the movement of Goans into the larger, more progressive urban centre of Bombay.

Selectivity of Migration

In developing countries, most migration studies indicate that the majority of migrants are between the ages of 15 and 29 with an average level of education higher than their rural counterparts.[7] Those migrating are mostly single men who marry or bring their families to their migrant destinations after they have entered into Phase II of the migration process. The marriage structure based on proposed negotiation facilitated such marriages whereby the future couple would meet and after a few interviews decide if they wanted to make a life together. Those who migrate at the low age-end of this scale do so for better and higher education which is not available in their place of origin. In Goa this was also the case as the existing universities which enrolled mostly Portuguese and Mestico students and a very few of native upper-class Catholics. Education was in the Portuguese or Marathi medium and those who preferred an English education but could not afford the few private schools went to urban cities in Bombay for such purposes.

In general, the majority of rural-urban or rural-international migration occurs due to an expected better financial income and socio-economic status following migration.[8] A rural labour surplus, high unemployment rate and political discrimination are also responsible for rural-urban migration. Education, a job transfer and lost land are other less statistically significant reasons why migrants leave their rural homes for the big city lights.[9]

However, the question remains as to the relative improvement in the quality of life which follows from rural to urban migration. For while Goans in Bombay could avail themselves of modern amenities and educational opportunities, their natural surroundings and rural settings were replaced by concrete construction and treeless neighbourhoods.

Thus, while migration improves the economic status of individuals and their subsequent families, it also distances individuals from loved ones and family.

Migrants, therefore, do not usually represent a crosssection of a particular community from where they originate. Rather, some individuals from specific communities take the decision to migrate.[10] In the case of Goan migration, many lower-middle class Goan Catholics chose to migrate as they realised that few opportunities for advancement existed under the Portuguese administration and that they would not be permitted to enter into the upper echelons of society through political or administrative positions. Both the Portuguese administration and the rigid caste system in rural Goa blocked such advancement and thwarted one of the basic biological needs for striving which fosters a sense of identity, accomplishment and pride. Owing to the Catholic primary schools which accepted students from all socio-economic strata, these youth began to desire a better life and felt capable of achieving a better socio-economic position. Barred from entering educational institutions, powerful positions in the clergy and any administrative posts, young Goans from the lower-middle and middle class communities were educated enough to realise that the current Portuguese policies on top of the village social structure were the culprits which prohibited their economic and social advancement. Their youthful ambition drove them to succeed but Portuguese policy and rural stratification prevented them from doing so. As a consequence, young adult males from Goa made the choice to risk the comfort and security of home to try and improve their lot and make something of themselves in the nearest growing urban centre of Bombay.

It is interesting to observe from a cultural perspective that once these communities established themselves in Bombay, they expressed their culture by imitating the Portuguese and upper-class Goans through dances and formal parties, yet they behaved in ways conducive to their own class culture; hence it paved the way for the boisterous gatherings, late-night street dances and rowdy fun characteristic of the common man.

Another major community which selectively migrated from Goa were the Gouda Saraswat Brahmans (GSBs), who belonged to one of the top classes, both culturally and educationally, within the Hindu community. Under the Portuguese administration, this community was likewise prevented from achieving its fullest potential and saw migration to Bombay as a way to escape from the heavy prejudicial policies of the Portuguese administration. In addition to Bombay, this community migrated to Mangalore, Bangalore and various cities in Kerala, but they also came to Bombay during the early 1900's. Under the British regime, the GSB community could enter educational institutions for which they were qualified, practice their religion freely and enter into professional occupations. Thus, owing to political constraints the GSB community migrated to Bombay, where their talents were utilised and community members were able to achieve to their fullest potential.

Generally, 95 per cent of the out-migrants of the first generations are males between the ages of 12 and 24.[11] This was the case in Goa as well, though later migrants were often women or children who migrated following marriage proposals which were negotiated between the families of the women and the migrants. Most migrants in this age group are looking for gainful employment for the first time. In Goa a typical pattern emerges from the rural areas which is followed by the ambitious youngsters from rural areas:

Most from rural villages migrate between 16 and 19 years of age and are predominantly unmarried men. They are characteristically younger than the immigrants who return to the rural areas after years of urban living and who intend to set up families or retire accordingly. Eighty-five per cent of migrants receive some form of formal education with roughly 50 per cent finishing the 10th standard.[12] Goan migrants also follow this pattern; those looking for jobs on the ships would get the bare minimum of education necessary to secure jobs, often completing only up to the 4th or 5th standards in a formal setting before deciding to migrate. Middle class and above, such as the Saraswat Brahmins, would complete the education that was available to them in Goa, with the intention of furthering their education in Bombay institutions. Over 60 per cent of those migrants going out are single, whereas over 60 per cent of those coming to rural areas are married and have families.[13]

Unemployed rural family members tend to migrate more than do already employed individuals.[14] Those seeking wage-employment have an increased tendency to migrate to urban areas where the wages are higher. Those who are self-employed have a greater tendency to remain in the rural areas, though in Goa this was not always the case.

The Daidayana Brahmins migrated to Bombay, for example, and created additional gold shops which catered mostly to the dowries of Goan communities. Other individual Catholic Goans migrated to Bombay with special trades and began tailor shops. Resourceful Goans began restaurants and guest-houses to cater to the needs of incoming young single migrants who needed a place to clean up and eat food which reminded them of home.

The very low social and economically backward communities in Goa, such as the Gaude, Chamar and Dhangar communities, however, did not characteristically migrate from Goa. The majority of the Kunbi tribals also did not migrate to urban centres nor encourage formal education as their traditional occupation has been the tilling of the soil and reaping of the harvest. They survived on a subsistence level and did not have the financial savings which are required to change one's place of residence. Most were also labour-bound to wealthy landowners and were caught in dependent relationships with them. Second, these communities were often tradition bound and received little formal education which would enable them to have foresight and ambition. Fear was also a big impediment in the process of migration, as low caste communities were treated poorly and were not welcomed by any society urban or otherwise. Finally, these communities did not have access to communication and hence information networks to know about the job opportunities which might be available to them. Though most such communities remained stuck in their socio-economic status, a few did migrate to Bombay where they took up their traditional occupations before entering into the modern sector in available menial jobs.

They often took up jobs as part-time cooks, cobblers, cleaners and other insecure jobs in the informal sector. Their lack of education enabled other communities to exploit their labour and only a few were able to escape this vicious cycle.

Migration Phases I and II

In the rural areas, those intending to migrate are 95 per cent male, of those 75 per cent are between the ages of 15 and 29.[15] Many Goans migrating to urban areas within India and most going abroad to the Gulf countries. They do not plan to take their families with them at first, though several hoped their families would join them once they were settled.

Women rarely migrated on their own, though migration following marriage proposals was a common occurrence in rural-urban migration of Goan women. Prior to leaving, most prospective migrants have an expected destination, temporary residence and employment plan. In the case of Goa, Bombay was the place to migrate during the early and mid 1900's, but has since been replaced by the Gulf countries, following trends in that direction. Migration to the Gulf is temporary and dependent on a work visa, as settling in these countries is not permitted by Indian nationals. Bangalore, the United States, the United Kingdom and Canada are also popular destinations for Goan migrants in recent years.

Of those rural-urban immigrants, the majority find work within 6 months of arrival and most within 2 months assuming they do not already have a job waiting for them. Sixty per cent go in search of employment on their own whereas normally only 30 per cent are able to get jobs through relatives, friends and other urban contacts.[16] Only a small percentage engage the help of a government agency in order to secure employment. In Goa, those migrants from rural villages who arrived in the all-Goan neighbourhoods received a lot of help from relatives and friends. Formal and informal associations for community members, such as the Goan Hindu Association and the Goan Association in Dabul, also help new migrants to resettle in their urban environments. Many Goans took temporary employment (as cooks, hotel staff, cleaners, etc.) while waiting for a job on a ship, but never secured the latter and ended up as permanent employees in the former occupations. However, migrants relocating to urban areas within their own country do not have exact information regarding job opportunities whereas those migrating to foreign countries already have jobs and know what their prospects are.

Following the initial job hunt, physical resettlement and psychological adjustment, migrants began the second phase of migration during which time they learn new patterns of behaviour possibly including language, food habits, work hours and leisure activities.[17] Many perfected an old or learned a new trade in the city and went on to open up their own business harnessing their skills for gainful employment. Those individuals who opened tailor shops and the Brahmin goldsmiths are only two examples of such activity. Migrants who opened their own businesses or were otherwise self-employed had larger recorded incomes than the wage-earners. Roughly 75 per cent of the migrants were able to increase their incomes as they entered into phase II of migration, though 25 per cent of individuals suffered a decrease or no change in their income following the stabilised phase II.[18] Life stories collected reveal Goans as both army generals and selling sugarcane juice in the streets of Bombay, though both extremes are few. Migrants who settled with family spent a greater portion of their incomes on land, property and business enterprises in the urban areas as compared to those single migrants who left their families in the rural villages of Goa. Earnings, in general, tend to rise the longer the migrant stays in the city at a particular job, though wage-employees earn less than the self-employed migrants. Phase II of migration, being a stable time and one of economic security, also results in the adoption of new attitudes, behaviours, speech patterns and preferences owing to immersion into a cosmopolitan urban environment.

Impact of Migration on Rural Areas

Migration between rural and urban communities produces three flows: human resource, income and information.[19] The high rate of unemployment in the rural sector creates a large surplus labour force which can be harnessed in the industrial sector resulting in an increase in urban development. Bombay during the 1900's was a city with a very high growth rate and one that could easily absorb this excess population during its formative years. Industry, international trade and infrastructure were needed and thus a lot of labour was absorbed in these new enterprises. Likewise, as the excess labour force is removed from the land, new farming and agricultural techniques may be adopted leading to the mechanisation of farms. This has not happened to a large extent in Goa, however, owing to the continuation of large families (6-9 children), who did not create a labour-deficit in the rural areas. Rather, migration has prevented the adoption of mechanised farming techniques except for the use of chemical fertilisers and high yielding seed varieties. The labour of the Gaude and Kunbi tribals is still used in agrarian production and when their demands for wages reach unacceptable levels, migrant workers from Karnataka and Maharashtra are there to accept the wages which the large landowners offer. Similarly, an increase in urban activity increases the demand for rural agrarian produce because the urban dwellers who are not engaged in agricultural production still consume food products from the rural areas. This demand increases the price of food products and helps to support the agrarian system in the rural areas by increasing the demand and thus relative wages of labourers. Exodus generally increases wages in the rural areas owing to a low unemployment level which favours employees. Remittances from urban migrants also have marked effects in rural areas, (a topic to be taken up in later paragraphs).

Migrants who return to their rural Goan villages periodically bring with them new ideas and a demand for urban consumer goods and conveniences which infiltrates into their homes and eventually diffuses into the village as more and more migrants who returned to their land, share these same adopted attitudes and preferences. Each migrant acts as a microcosmic agent of cultural diffusion and helps to develop the rural areas by encouraging different attitudes and behaviours within village communities. Similarly, each Goan migrant effectively acts via media for rural-urban and rural-Gulf migration when he returns home.

Exodus of young adult males also alters the age and gender of rural Goan villages. The majority of the village inhabitants are young married women, children, elderly parents and those few male adults who have remained in the village to continue in their fathers' traditional occupations and look after the ancestral property. Family size may also decrease owing to the exodus of males and those villagers who are productive and capable are away from the villages. Thus, the traditional village is kept largely intact and does not evolve greatly as many of those who would normally enact change have migrated out. Goa's 'proposal' marriage system alleviates the normal problems associated with massive exodus of male members from the rural areas. Under this system, a future couple need to meet only a few times before wedding arrangements are made. They choose their partners by village sentiment and through bio-data which is furnished upon request. Through this system a Goan woman from one rural village can agree to get engaged to a Goan male migrant in Bombay from another village, having known each other only briefly. However, for those who marry migrants and continue to reside in the rural villages, there are consequences.

Husband and wife are often separated throughout their marriage owing to the migrant's absence from his home and family for nearly seventy-five per cent of the year, thus, leaving the young wife alone to raise their children.

Effect of Remittances

Ninety-five per cent of husbands and fifty per cent of unmarried males send remittances back to their place of origin.[20] Individuals from low socio-economic households, interestingly, have a greater tendency to remit and remit a greater percentage of their earned income in comparison to those households in the upper income strata.

Likewise, the uneducated migrants remit almost twice the percentage of their income as do highly educated migrants.[21] This is owing to the poverty which such families confront in rural areas and the migrants' desires to alleviate such poverty even if he must sacrifice his own accumulation of wealth. These remittances can at times account for the entire family income if the migrant is the only family member gainfully employed. This is also the case in large rural families in Goa where the mother is a housewife and the children are involved in formal education, leaving the male as the only wage-earner. Migrants from higher socio-economic status will remit similar amounts in absolute terms but a lesser percentage of their overall income. In other words, remittances as a percentage of household income decrease as higher socio-economic levels are taken into consideration. Remittances are received by most socio-economic classes and in general, the absolute amount of remittances increase as a migrant's salary increases. Seventy-five per cent of remittances are used for food and clothing, twenty-five per cent is consumed by household items including TV's, refrigerators, radios and kitchen appliances and ten per cent is used for ceremonies, weddings and individual dowry. Only five per cent of households spend remittances on anything other than consumption, revealing the lower-income wage-earning status of many households in this category.[22] In addition to basic food, clothing and household consumption, remittances can also be used to increase the property of the family and dowry for the unmarried female members. Though dowry is often seen as an unproductive investment, from the perspective of a villager in Goa, dowry is an excellent investment. It not only secures a better husband (financially and character-wise) for a woman, but also frees her husbands earnings for more productive investments.

Remittances in Goa may be used to improve housing, education and generally decrease the income gap between rich and poor in the rural areas. This is particularly true in the rural Goa of the 1990's, where 'shippies', 'Gulfies' and other migrants from the middle and lower-middle classes have earned incomes abroad which easily distinguish their families from others in the village. The major portion of remittances are used in everyday household needs, including food, clothing, household repairs, appliances and other home technologies. A smaller portion is used for education and only in the families where its value is recognised. Very few households invest these remittances in agriculture and agricultural technologies, which holds true in the case of Goa where very traditional time-honoured techniques are still in vogue and mechanisation has not developed on the farms.

Exodus is often thought to close the gap between rich and poor in the rural areas.[23] In Goa, exodus and the subsequent remittances to rural areas create a sizeable middle class whose wealth is distinguishable from those in the non-migrant lower classes but which does not quite add up to the wealthiest community. Each migrant group effectively bumps up its socio-economic status owing to remittances.

Migrant families from the Goa's Sudir community move into the middle economic class (from the low-middle class) and those from the Kshyatria community move into the upper-middle and upper classes. In addition, those families who utilised their remittances for education and housing demonstrate a remarkable improvement in their standard of living and children's choice of careers. Beyond raising the rural income of families in Goan villages, remittances from migrants also help to diversify the non-agricultural activities in the rural areas such as the opening of new businesses based on the imported technologies (computer classes, printing shops, E-mail facilities, etc.).

Both size and frequency of remittances are key factors which determine their impact on the rural areas. Rural migrants are more likely to remit than urban migrants and while over 80 per cent of single migrants remit, only roughly 10 per cent of the migrants who settle with families remit to the rural areas. The greater the distance of migration, the more likely an individual will remit finances to his place of origin.[24] Generally, the percentage of remittances increases over time, which is true in the case of Goan Gulf migrants as well. During the first two years subsequent to migration, much of the money is spent on the consumption of consumer goods and services as migrants become established and accustomed to their new environment. They also have to reach a certain standard of living above the subsistence level before they can start sending remittances. It takes from two to three years before the majority of those migrants, going out to re-establish themselves and send home regular remittances.[25] The largest remittances usually come from recently married men who support their new families which are left behind in the rural villages of Goa. Though living abroad or in migrant cities, the newly-married Goans of this type is attached to Goa and views his home as in Goa.

As immigrants become permanent residences in their migration destination, remittances begin to fall.[26] This is true for Bombay-Goans, where all-Goan neighbourhoods began developing churches, schools and recreational facilities in their neighbourhoods with extra funds collected from residents. The current residents in Bombay hardly remit at all to their Goan villages, except when they have ancestral homes which need renovation and maintenance. Thus, though remittances initially increase over the years, the longer a migrant lives permanently in a particular city, the more his ties to his place of origin weaken and eventually may even break. When this happens, such as in 2nd and 3rd generation Bombay-born Goans, they demonstrate the same perceptions and stereotypical responses of the larger Indian population towards Goa and have little additional knowledge or experience regarding their ancestral origins.

Remittances in Goa have had a marked effect in the creation of a sizeable middle class population with newly constructed houses, modern technologies, fashionable clothing and surplus savings. Though the poorest communities in Goa do not substantially benefit from the exodus, many from the Sudir and Kshyatria communities have benefited significantly, moving into the middle and upper-middle classes, respectively. Members of the middle-class Sudir community in Goa have consequently left their land-based traditional occupations except for some small farmers who have their own fields. Over 60 per cent of the youth from the artisan, toddy-tapping and small-scale fishing occupations have, thus, left these professions to seek further education and urban employment. If they have purchased the land following their occupational switch, they did not invest in the development of agricultural techniques other than the use of chemical fertiliser and irrigation canals.

It, thus, follows that as land holdings increase, family labour decreases while hired labour increases. Thus, many of the middle Sudir and upper middle class Kshyatria communities required more labour as individual family members ceased work on the farm for more gainful employment in other venues. What we do not find occurring in Goa, consequently, is the shift in agricultural techniques towards less labour-intensive crops or labour-saving capital equipment. The lower socio-economic communities, therefore, were able to continue in their traditional labour-intensive agrarian production and were not compelled by technological advances to expand their employment nor advance their opportunities. Kunbis, Gaudes and other land-less labouring communities now account for the majority of labourers involved in agricultural production.

Impact of Migration on Urban Areas

As the rural areas are affected by migration and remittances, so the rural destinations of migrants are likewise affected by the incoming stream of migrants. An inflow of migrants into cities puts pressure on the existing infrastructure and social services such as schools and health care clinics. In the case of Goan migrants in Bombay, this industrious community decided to rely on themselves rather than the government, creating Goan high schools, health clinics, recreational organisations, churches, primary schools and scholarship funds. They were aided by the clergy in this endeavour, but it was the work of the entire community which created the classic 'Goan' neighbourhoods in Bombay known as Dabul and Dhobi Talao. The formation of such communities also encouraged migrants to settle permanently in Bombay.

Temporary migrants will invest little in their place of employment, but as the Goan migrants demonstrate, they were responsible for the creation of two of Bombay's oldest neighbourhoods. An influx of migrants also raises the value of land and the demand for rented apartments. This is also the case in the aforementioned neighbourhoods in Bombay, where cramped one-room apartments cost as much as spacious three-room apartments in areas more distant from the city centre.[27]

An increase of migrants in the urban areas in general tends to increase the specialisation of labour, thereby encouraging the development of large-scale industries.[28] Migration of young, productive members of society will improve the chosen area of destination by increasing the labour pool and bringing in needed skills to the urban area. Rural outgoing migrants are often a resourceful portion of the population and, therefore, increase the resource base in their new destinations. An increase in migration also promotes the use of labour-intensive industries rather than mechanised production, thereby decreasing the unemployment rate. The ability of migrants to move upwards on the socio-economic scale will determine the size of the income gap between the native urban-dwellers and the new migrants.

In the example of Goa, the migrants arriving to Bombay in the early years came from two major classes of people; skilled or educated Hindu Brahmins and semi-skilled Catholics from lower middle and middle income families, both of whom perceived little opportunity under the Portuguese administration. The first group, whether goldsmiths or Saraswat Brahmins, arrived in Bombay highly skilled and availed of educational opportunities and later professional and administrative employment.

The majority of the middle and lower-middle class Catholics, however, came through the 'Village Clubs' during the early to mid-1900's. They intended first to find jobs within Bombay, but as the shipping jobs on international and British-owned vessels became available, many Goan youth opted for this type of employment. As a result, Bombay and the existing 'Village Clubs' became transit points rather than places of residence, stop-overs between off-shore employment and their place of origin. In this respect, therefore, the 'shippies' as they came to be known contributed little to the economic development of Bombay.

However, taking non-material 'returns' into consideration, the Goan Catholic 'shippies' were integral to the development and maintenance of the Goan communities in Bombay. Upon arriving in Bombay they brought news from home and detailed descriptions of the latest happenings. On their journey from the boat to Goa they could relay messages from migrants to urban-dwellers, thus, keeping both communities closely linked through a steady stream of human communication. Similarly, they not only helped to maintain the 'Goan identity' for the migrated communities in Bombay but also were the main motivation behind in cultural and technological innovation and evolution within Goan society. From experience abroad the Goan 'shippies' brought with them new ideas, attitudes and technologies and introduced them into their families.

Accommodation in urban areas is also affected by migration. As the migrant population increases, the land and apartment rental rates rise. As the time a migrant lives in the city increases, so do the chances that he will purchase an urban dwelling, usually in the form of a small one-room apartment. Natives tend to have larger apartments than migrants, however, this holds true for 1st generation Goa-Bombay migrants who crowded entire families into one-room apartments and 'shippies' who slept in the same 'village club'. On the negative side, however, migration into urban areas tends to decrease the quality of life, at least for the first generation of rural-urban migrants. Shanty towns and squatter settlements proliferate during Phase I of migration and even the Goan migrants crowded entire families into small one-room apartments. Those who are desperately in need of employment will often work for much less than would a settled native, thus depressing the average wages for menial jobs and arousing animosity within the native population. In many cases, rural-urban migration produces uneven economic development between the urban and rural areas; concentrating wealth in the former and depressing development in the latter.[29] Those who can migrate to urban areas owing to the strength of their economic base often will and the result is a concentration of the lower socio-economic communities in the rural areas. However, remittances can counter this effect by adding to the family income, thereby improving standards of living and educational opportunities.

Impact of Urban Migration on Migrants

Early immigrants tend to have larger family sizes than do native urban dwellers, but smaller than those of their rural counterparts. Migration among the first generation often increases the marriageable age and subsequently increases the age when parents have their first child owing to resettlement costs and psychological adjustments.[30] Because their desired family size is patterned from their original culture, early immigrants will desire larger families than their urban neighbours, thus initially increasing the urban population. With time, however, as the second and third generation migrants become enculturated into their urban environments, the desired number of children corresponds with that of the urban culture. Goan migration to Bombay exemplifies this theory when the family size of rural, immigrants and second generation urban-dwellers are compared.

Rural Goan families normally had between six to nine children, a practice which continued up until Liberation and the adoption of family planning practises in Goa. Thus, when the first Goan migrants started their families in all-Goan neighbourhoods in Bombay, this cultural practice was reinforced and families having five to seven children crammed into one-room apartments. Though they desired large families, spatial and economic constraints limited their ability to have as many children as they would have, had they stayed in rural farm areas. Likewise, whereas children in rural farm areas are an asset, children in urban areas were encouraged to get educated rather than enter the labour force. They also are more expensive as they are not part of the urban labour force.

The children of those urban migrant families, however, were enculturated into the norms of urban life and, thus, demonstrated a desire for fewer children. Thus, in the mid-1900's we find that most families had decreased family size from five to seven or five to two children. Those parents born in urban areas during the 60's and 70's usually have between one to three children and those married in the 80's and 90's will have only two or three. By the first generation, the majority of the Bombay-born Goans had adjusted their family size to that of the urban life, thereby decreasing the family size of migrants faster than the families in rural areas. The same areas in rural

Goa continued to have between 6 to 9 children until Liberation in 1961, following which time family size dropped to between 3 to 4 children. Today's Goan youth anticipate a family size between 3 to 4 children tending towards three whereas urban families are contended with two children.

In addition to family size, migration followed by an increase in income affects preferences and norms which determine the use of that income. A new worldview often results owing to immersion in urban society and occupational opportunities which weakens the influences that promote large families.[31] The desire for material goods and luxuries increases, thus, decreasing the desire for large families. As the desire for material goods related to children increases, the size of the family decreases.

The increasing participation of women in the workforce also affects their education, income, preferences and subsequent desired family size.[32] Women's participation in the labour force tends to alter women's perceptions of their role and enables them to derive satisfaction, identity and pride from activities other than childrearing, which decreases their desire to have many children. This further reduces the desired number of children by increasing the activity available to women. Women's economic independence also increases their ability to limit fertility and voice their desires regarding family size and use of contraception. The more education a woman has, the stronger is her desire for fewer children. The education available in the urban areas likewise shapes values surrounding family size and planning and fosters communication between husband and wife which may enable her to express her desires for a smaller family. Likewise, the adoption of modern hospitalisation techniques for child birth and health care decreases the infant mortality in urban areas and increases the chances of survival for each new-born child. Parents also begin to set aside funds for their old age (social security) which reduces their dependence on children to take care of them during their 'golden years'. Migration also often results in the separation of nuclear families from extended ones left behind in the rural areas. When this occurs, goods and services formerly provided by the extended family now have to be purchased, further increasing the costs of child care and reducing their economic necessity.[33]

Educational Impact

Education, surprisingly, consumes only a small percentage of household remittances, though in Goa this is a growing percentage owing to the increasing importance placed on education and the increasing number of students (especially female) wishing to continue their education beyond the 10th standard. The growing importance of education in rural Goan culture is the result of two simultaneous processes: First, the introduction of Catholic primary schools in rural villages imparted education to all those who could attend classes, thus, inculcating its value in children. When this formal primary education reached the lower socio-economic communities, as it did during the late 1800's and early 1900's in Goa, a psychological revolution occurred within these communities who had been formerly barred from receiving formal education, the domain of the upper castes. With education began the stirrings for equality and the realisation of oppression, followed by concrete steps in the direction of its alleviation.

Migrants realised not only the importance of finances but also that of education, which then sparked the second trend. There is a strong correlation between first-generation migrants and the high value of education imparted to their children.

This is owing to the struggles and 'ceilings' which Bombay and Gulf migrants discovered during their attempts to climb the socio-economic ladder which were thwarted owing to their lack of education and qualifications. Also, the urban migrant worker is thrown into a world of competition where he has few contacts and, therefore, must rely on his own knowledge, skills and understanding of others. Urban migrants are also exposed to higher role models and standards of living which they are too old to achieve but which their children have the opportunity to realise. Thus, second generation migrants/first generation urban residents are often instilled with additional values that emphasise education, ambition and accomplishment. Among those educated migrants we find such notable personalities as General Sumith Rodricks, the Indian Army General and General Ribeiro, a Bombay-Goan Inspector General. Among medical specialists, Bombay-Goans boast of India's foremost Cardiologist Dr. Luisito and eminent gynaecologist Dr. Shirodkar, the latter who developed a world-famous gyne-surgical stitch known by his surname. The parents of these and other notable Goans in Bombay struggled to 'come up' and desired their children to avail of their new opportunity to better themselves. Parents learned during those early years, that if an individual is educated then the sky was the limit.

In general, however, rural-urban migrants do not normally do as well as their urban-urban migrant counterparts and move up the socio-economic scale at a slower pace.[34] Rural migrants usually have less education than their urban brethren because the educational facilities in rural areas are not always adequate in comparison to urban educational facilities. Migrants from such educational backgrounds often have difficulty in securing better employment and in rising up the socio-economic ladder. Educated migrants experienced much greater upward mobility and were not stuck in menial low-wage jobs. The ability to secure employment in the formal, wage-earning sector increases with education and years of residence in the particular urban environment. Migrants that are graduates show a much higher rate of employment than do non-graduates, though recent immigrants will have a high rate of employment regardless of their educational status owing to their necessity to take any job offered to them.[35] Earnings of those with no formal education are roughly less than half of those of graduates and above.[36] Generally, migrants from the rural areas tend to have lower incomes than those migrants from the urban areas owing to both education and related cultural factors such as social motivation, value-orientations, etc. Interestingly, these income differences do not diminish with a corresponding increase in the duration of stay in the urban centre. As their level of education increases during subsequent generations, however, these income disparities even out and offspring of settled migrants are able to move up the socio-economic ladder.

Similarly, the skills acquired in rural areas are often less relevant in urban environments and, thus, have less relative value. As a consequence of these two factors, rural-urban migrants are often initially concentrated in employment surrounding industrial production process, as assembly-line workers, truck-drivers and other semi-skilled jobs. Migrants, therefore, tend to have a lower average income than native urban residents and rural migrants have the lowest average income.[37] In addition to formal educational benefits available to the migrant, immersion into urban environments tend to weaken traditional attitudes, beliefs and aversion to new things.

Constant interaction with a wide variety of people from many religious and ethnic backgrounds results in a greater understanding of human variety and a greater tolerance for different religious and cultural beliefs. Bombay in the 1900's was also a religiously liberal city under the British regime whose administrators guaranteed religious freedom to all of Bombay's residents.

Current Trends in Goan Migration

In Goan communities today, both influx and exodus has reached steady levels following liberation when there was a heavy influx of individuals from neighbouring Indian States. Now, however, trends show a constant stream of influx from neighbouring Indian States and a constant stream of exodus to Bombay, Bangalore, the Gulf, the UK, USA and Canada. The massive migration of Goans into Bombay tapered off following first Indian and then Goan Liberation, with a corresponding deterioration of the all-Goan neighbourhoods as people sold their properties and moved into more spacious suburban apartments. Migration within India has also been replaced by migration to the Gulf countries following the Gulf oil boom of the 1960's and 1970's. Goans were preferred as cheap employees on the oil rigs owing to the prejudice held against the Hindu community following the disastrous massacre on the border between India and Pakistan in 1947-48. The Gulf jobs, thus, created a fresh stream of migrants who used the clubs in Bombay as transit points while they applied for such jobs and awaited the necessary clearance certificates. This oil boom lasted until the late 1970's early 1980's wherein Gulf jobs began to dry up. The Gulf War in 1987 caused many Indians living abroad on Work permits to flee these countries for fear of their safety. They resettled in Goa, bought houses and invested in farm lands, small businesses, or other productive enterprises. Owing to the political crises in Kuwait, the increase in job competition and decrease in job availability in the Gulf; the State of Goa also began to develop infrastructure and economic planning following its incorporation into the Indian Union as a State in 1987. The construction of communications, the electrification of the State and the construction of the Goa University in 1985 all effectively reduced several reasons which led to migration in former years. Migration into Goa between 1961 and 1987 was also a major source of concern as well as productive investment. Thus, while many Goans themselves had left their native place to seek more fruitful economic opportunities elsewhere, the migrant population in Goa increased substantially owing to a heavy influx of people from neighbouring States. Following Statehood, this migration wave diminished significantly and Goa has since maintained a relatively stable influx and exodus of individuals primarily owing to economic incentives.

Migration of Goans, therefore, is not a phenomenon which affected only those migrants who made the decision to migrate over the years. Their rural villages, mostly those located in the coastal talukas of Salcette, Bardez and Tiswadi, have benefited economically, educationally and some might add culturally owing to the existence of a large migrant community. Remittances have had a positive affect on the standard of living and educational levels of families in the rural areas and children have been siphoned off of the lands and towards the development of their intellect. Migration is, thus, a two-way street, affecting both the areas of origin and the areas of migrant destination, especially in the case of Mangalore and Bombay.

The case studies which follow are only few examples of Goan migration and the resulting communities which have arisen in migrant cities. The case study of Bombay, which is where the vast majority of migrant Goans settled, illustrates the effects of migration on the individuals as well as their reformed communities. Though the case-studies stress the communities and destinations into which the migrants entered, the effects on the rural villages of Goa were likewise substantial and certainly important in explaining some of the cultural evolution and adaptive identifications which are taking place in today's State of Goa.

REFERENCES

1. A.S. Oberai & H.K. Manmohan Singh, *Causes and Consequences of Internal Migration: A Study in the Indian Punjab.* Jaipur: Rawat Publications, 1992, p. 25.
2. *Ibid.*, p. 26.
3. *Ibid.*
4. *Ibid.*, p. 27.
5. *Ibid.*, p. 28.
6. *Ibid.*, p. 29, This footnote covers the preceding paragraph.
7. *Ibid.*, Chap. 3.
8. *Ibid.*
9. *Ibid.*
10. *Ibid.*
11. *Ibid.*
12. *Ibid.*
13. *Ibid.*
14. *Ibid.*
15. *Ibid.*
16. *Ibid.*, p. 185.
17. *Ibid.*, Ch. 1.
18. *Ibid.*, p. 87.
19. *Ibid.*, p. 112.
20. *Ibid.*, p. 323.
21. *Ibid.*, p. 317.
22. *Ibid.*, p. 323.
23. *Ibid.*, p. 325.
24. *Ibid.*, Ch. 11.
25. *Ibid.*
26. *Ibid.*
27. See the Bombay Case-Study of the proceeding chapter for more details.
28. A.S. Oberai, *op. cit.*, Ch. 8.
29. *Ibid.*
30. *Ibid.*, Ch. 13.
31. *Ibid.*
32. *Ibid.*
33. *Ibid.*, Ch. 13.
34. A.S. Oberai, *op. cit*, Ch. 11, p. 331.
35. *Ibid.*, Ch. 11.
36. *Ibid.*
37. *Ibid.*

Chapter 7

Migrants in Bombay

Overview

The history and cultural identity of Goa would be incomplete without mention of the Goans who have migrated to and settled down in Bombay. Starting in the late 1800's Goans began flocking to Bombay in search of well-paid jobs and within a few years Goan village "Clubs" sprang up to provide room and boardings at cheaper rates for newly arrived young men in the community. Within decades, the entire neighbourhood arose inhabited only by Goans and during Christmas, New Year and the Goa Carnival the streets came alive with late night dances and parties. Schools and churches sponsored by these Catholic communities were constructed and Goan 'cultural identity' became synonymous with Catholicism, drinking and merry-making, dances and western living. But while these fun-loving people were busy expressing their cultural forms and confirming to the 'Goan' identity, other communities also from Goa were silently arriving and blending in to the Bombay crowd. Also arriving in the late 1800's and early 1900's were the Goan Hindu communities like the Gowda Saraswat Brahmins and the Daiwdnya Brahmins. Though less conspicuous among Bombay society, these communities also had adjustments to make, success stories to tell and neighbourhoods to create.

Yet no community migrates into a vacuum and all the communities in Goa had to adapt to Bombay's urban environment; an existing and ever-changing milieu of cultures and communities. For the Catholic Goans, they came face to face with two different communities of a similar religion originating from the same foreign influence, the East Indians and the Mangaloreans. How they interacted and which places on the social ladder they came to occupy is largely a result of both pre-and post-conversion culture and economy. For the Gowda Saraswat Brahmins who arrived with education and ambition, Bombay was an open world where they could utilise their talents in gainful employment. For the Daiwdyna Brahmins, their main aim was to gain a strong foothold in the gold market, which they did as evidenced by the success of the Chira Bazaar.

This chapter examines the history of Bombay, its evolution as the recipient of so many cultures and communities and the State of the city before the arrival of people from Goa. The neighbourhoods of Dabul, Dhobi Talao, Bandra and Malad are also included as case studies of Goan migrants in Bombay. East Indians and their interactions with Goans are two topics considered, along with their relationships with Mangaloreans. This chapter, therefore, looks specifically at the aforementioned migrated communities; how they re-established community in Bombay, what aspects of their cultural identity have been preserved/lost over time, as well as the current socio-economic status of each group under study.[1]

Origin of Bombay

Bombay (now Mumbai), India's concrete jungle with over 14 million inhabitants, was at one time a sparsely inhabited stretch of fertile off-shore island. From the 6th to the 12th centuries, the Sassanian and Satraps ruled over the North Konkan and after them the Shilaharas ruled over the area for 500 years from their capital on Elephanta Island.[2] Credit for the foundation of Bombay, however, goes to a Chalukya prince of the house of the Solankis (Gujarat), known as Bhimadeva, who brought the first settlers to the island and laid the foundation for the city of Mahim. He was a powerful prince who reigned from 1022 A.D. to 1064 A.D. and his followers were called Prabhus after their venerated incarnation of Shiva, God Somanatha of Prabhasa.[3] During Bhima's reign, his country was a great maritime power. Local tradition states that Bhima marched into the northern Konkan and conquered it from the Nayak chiefs, establishing his domain over the territories under discussion. On his arrival he found the area covered with babul trees (arecanut) and a few scattered houses belonging to *Kolis*, (fishermen). Only two temples existed; one dedicated to Sri Walkesvar and the other to Sri Mumbadevi to which Bombay (Mumbai) owes its name.[4]

The Kolis were Dravidian in origin and consisted of several tribes whose religion at that time can best be summed up as animism.[5] They worshipped demons and spirits and whenever a feast was held, a fowl was sacrificed to the spirits of the dead. It is interesting to note that their religious practices could not be suppressed, even by the Aryan invaders arriving in 350 B.C. Eventually, many of their Kuladevas were gradually incorporated into the Aryan Brahmanical Pantheon. The temple of Mumbadevi was the second most ancient temples of these aborigines. It was left untouched by all proceeding conquerors and the residing goddess, Mumba, is claimed by the Kolis as theirs from time immemorial.[6]

In addition to the pre-existing Kolis, Bhima brought with him four communities (castes) of settlers: (Patane) Prabhus, Palshis, Pachkalshis and Bhandaris. The Prabhus were the principal followers of Bhima and legend holds that they were degraded from the position of royalty by the sage Brighu to that of scribes. They also have legends connecting them with the kings of the Solar race and their occupations were said to be administrative in nature. The Palshis were the priests of the Prabhus who performed religious rites and practised medicine and astrology. The Pachkalshis who came along with Bhima were carpenters, gardeners and jack-of-all trades in general. The fourth community, the Bhandaris were toddy-tappers and distillers of feni and arack. Bhima also encouraged other communities of Brahmins and traders to settle and engage themselves in the cultivation of coconut trees. Consequently, he divided his territory first into 15 Mahals (districts) and then he divided each Mahal again into twelve pakhadis, attaching a manor to each pakhadi. His development scheme worked and many Brahmins and traders arrived and built houses and temples in the area.[7]

While this community slowly grew in size and wealth, the Muslim army was preparing to invade these same territories. In 1204 A.D. they attacked Devagiri (then known as Devgir) and in 1312 the north Konkan was invaded. By 1318 both Mahim and

Salsette (a neighbouring village) were occupied by Muslim troops and until 1403 the village of Bombay paid tributary to the Pathan kings. In 1492 the area of the north Konkan came under the control of Malik-u-Tujar, the General of Sultan Ahmaid Bahmani.[8]

Portuguese in Bombay

In December 1534, while Portuguese power was on a steady incline, Bassein and the islands of Bombay and Chaul were conquered from the Muslim ruler Bahadur Shah. After the conquest of Daman by General Don Constantino de Braganca in 1560, the entire coast of the north Konkan from Daman to Karanja came under the dominion of the Portuguese. The Portuguese soldiers, during their explorations along the north Konkan coast, had chanced upon the Bombay island and nicknamed it "The Island of the Good Life" due to the relaxed, pleasant atmosphere and lifestyle which they encountered.[9] Upon acquisition, the lands of Bombay and neighbouring islands were divided among the Portuguese officers for paltry amount and often entire villages were included in these estates. To create more land, the Portuguese decided to drain the swamps, thus, joining several islets together, forming the location of modern Mumbai.[10]

In this way, between 1534 and 1548 the island of Mumbai, known then as Monbaym, was granted to Mestre Diogo. The next occupant of the island was Garcia da Orta, the famed physician who was granted the land during the Vicer-royalty of Don Pedro Mascarenhas (1554-55).[11] The island was granted as the Portuguese were approaching the peak of their power and Monbaym was given to him for life on the condition that he undertake improvements on the island. Garcia da Orta collected rent from his farmers and lived in a large manor surrounded by lush gardens. His house was situated nearby a small garrisoned fort which offered protection to the small island.

The Portuguese made records for habituating in the areas over which they now ruled. The Curumbins (Kunbis) were tillers of the soil and planted rice and pulses. The Prabhus were the clerks, accountants and great merchants who collected revenue from the village inhabitants for the Portuguese administration. The Coaris (Parsis), Baneanes (who observe the precepts of Pythagoras), the piaes (peons), the lavradores (farmers), Gentiles (caste Hindus), Moors and Naitias (Hindu-Muslim mixed race) were also residing in these Portuguese territories.[12]

As with most newly-formed Portuguese colonies in India, the process of conversion began among the native inhabitants of these islands. The language spoken by the original fishermen and cultivator communities was at first considered a dialect of Marathi. Later, when a Portuguese missionary recorded the grammar of this dialect, he titled his work "*Grammatica da Lingua Concani no dialecto do Norte* Grammar of the Konkani language in the northern dialect).[13] When the Portuguese arrived, this was the only language spoken in Bombay and was adopted by the Portuguese missionaries for their religious instruction.[14]

Prior to 1546 A.D., all the efforts put towards conversions were undertaken by individual priests and zealous missionaries. However, on March 8th in 1546, Vaz arrived from Portugal with a royal decree, establishing conversion as Portuguese policy. The missionaries gave large sums of money and granted favours to new converts and spent lavishly on the construction of churches and religious buildings. The excessive zeal with which the missionaries carried out their activities eventually provoked Mr. Simon Botelho, (collector of treasury, 1547 A.D.), to complain to the then King of Portugal, Don Joao III, that their attempts toward converting the local population had resulted in a steady migration of people *away* from the Portuguese colonies.[15] The workmen involved in the construction were treated like slaves and many were the result of forced labour. New converts received many special privileges, while those who were adament not abandon their former religious beliefs, were treated with contempt by the missionaries. Disregarding caste, social standing and occupation, the Portuguese would often grab any native walking along the street and force him to do menial tasks and hard labour.[16] Even the Prabhus, who held high-ranking administrative posts under the Portuguese, apparently under the pain of forceful conversion, had to perform their religious worship in secret. Unlike other Hindu communities, however, the Saraswat Brahmins (Prabhus, Kamats, etc.; were employed by the Portuguese and residing within the Fort during the Portuguese administration. The Pagoda of Venkatesha (epithet of Vishnu) was built in 1689 at the northern end of the Fort by a Ramaji Kamat and belonged "to the Saraswat Brahmins who formerly used to reside within the Fort."[17]

By the end of the 1500's, Bombay had four churches; the first , Our Lady of Dolours across from the Espalande at Marine Lines, the second located at Parel, the third in upper Mahim and the fourth in Dadar (Lower Mahim).[18] In order to impart the true Christian doctrine to the natives, several missionaries founded the village of Trindade on the island of Salsette, set apart from the rest of Bombay society. New converts were complaining of taunts from Hindu Brahmins and the former were finding it difficult to give up their previous religious practices. It was the first entirely Christian village, modelled after a utopian society and flourished until 1697.[19] However, it was abandoned due to the Marattas who invaded and captured nearby Bassein in 1739.

During the Portuguese era, Mahim was the main town servicing the group of islands which included Bombay. Bombay island itself had merely a Fort (Government House), the House of the 'Senhora da Ilha' and small scattered fishing communities.[20] The reason that the island of Bombay received little attention by the Portuguese was owing to the proximity of Bassein, the main aristocratic and international trading centre of the Portuguese Indian empire. Located less than 100 km from Bassein, Bombay was used more as location where the wealthy dwellers of Bassein made their homes and did not rise to prominence until the British took the island in later years.

In the years between 1498 and 1612, Portuguese supremacy of the seas was duly recognised. But the Portuguese defeat off the coast of Surat in November 1612 at the hands of the British, marked a turning-point which laid the first foundation for the British empire in the east. In 1618 a devastating hurricane hit the islands in and around Bombay, razing buildings, uprooting trees and severely damaging 35 Portuguese churches.[21] In the year 1625 A.D., the Dutch and English plotted a successful seizure of the Portuguese Fort at Bombay and with 400 soldiers landed and burnt down the city. On October 15, 1626 A.D., Bombay changed hands to a joint occupation by the British and Dutch.

Bombay under the British Empire

On the eve of the transfer of Bombay to the British, the only 'industries' existent in Bombay were those of fishing and cultivation of cash crops like coconut, arecanut and rice paddy.[22] Due to its location between the major international trading centres of Chaul and Bassein, Bombay during the period of Portuguese rule had little chance of rising to such prominence as those of its neighbours. The little importance it received was due to its lying between these two cities and, thus, made a convenient stop-over for travellers bound for either place. Bassein, at that time, was the "seat of the flower of Portuguese aristocracy in the East" and a place described by opulence and leisure.[23] When the island of Bombay was ceded to the British, it contained 5 Portuguese churches, 6 affiliated chapels, a fort, warehouse and a population of 25, 480.[24] A bureaucratic system of government had been put in place by their Portuguese predecessors and it is these pre-existing systems which some scholars argue laid the foundation for the rise of Bombay. Gerson da Cunha writes, "it is to Portugal that England is indebted for the facilities she found here, on her taking possession of Bombay, introducing western methods of life and modes of thought."[25] Writing in 1900, he further writes that "Thousands of Indian families had been converted by the Portuguese to Christianity and hundreds of them still continue to speak the language (Portuguese) which their ancestors had adopted as their own throughout the province of Bassein."[26] Yet, though the Portuguese may have laid the foundation, Bombay owes its rise and prosperity to its transference from the Portuguese to the British, the former a nation on its decline and the latter a nation with rising international prestige and climbing towards its zenith.

The British era in Bombay begins with the signing of the treaty of marriage on the 23rd of June, 1661, between the King of England, Charles II and the Infanta of Portugal, Dona Catharina.[27] Prior to this agreement the British and the Dutch had entered into a joint-occupation of the island. More diplomatic than matrimonial, the alliance was created to reestablish the old alliance between the English and the Portuguese. The English fleet arrived on September 18th, 1662 (some historians mention the 29th as the actual date of arrival) to demand the cession of the island and harbour of Bombay as well as that of Salcette.

Though desirous of Salcette, the Portuguese had no intention of giving up one of their last strongholds at Bassein and eventually a Mr Humphrey Cooke took possession only of the island of Bombay on February 18th, 1665.[28] Apparently this new Governor of the island caused problems for the 11 Portuguese families still inhabiting the island and who had been allowed to remain on island in possession of their lands. At the time of succession, the Island of Bombay belonged to Dona Ignez de Castro, a widow of the late D. Rodrigo de Moncanto. Cook obliged the Roman Catholics to take a vow whereby they denied the jurisdiction of the Supreme Pontiff and Head of the Roman Catholic Church.[29]

In addition to his prejudicial treatment of the Portuguese inhabitants, Governor Cook also invited native merchants to settle in Bombay, arousing the jealousy of the Moghal Government in Surat, the then most prominent and wealthy trading post held by the British. Though the Dutch and English had been allies during the seizure of the island, rivalry between them resumed and trouble off the coast of Surat was reported. While Henry Gray was the Governor in 1667, the relations between Surat and Bombay became antagonistic, so much so that when the East India Company offered to take over Bombay, the King of England, Charles II, readily agreed so as to avoid any further fights between the two cities. Consequently, on March 27th, 1668, the ownership of the Island of Bombay was transferred to the East India Company. From the latter records, the population was estimated at 10,000 people; and from those most were considered the 'dredges' of society. The English government in Bombay was apparently quite liberal, allowing everyone "to live as he liked, but did not permit the Holy Office to carry on their work as they saw fit."[30] Thus, within a span of 100 years, the Island of Bombay changed hands thrice. In 1534 from the Mahomedan Kings of Gujarat to the Portuguese, in 1661-65 from the Portuguese to the British Crown and in 1668 to the East India Company based in Great Britain.

Following the transfer of the island to the EIC, it was governed first by deputies from the English factory at Surat. However, the quarrels between civil and military branches which the transfer was intended to end only intensified and by 1671 chaos prevailed. To put an end to the bickering and to fortify the

Bombay Fort against possible Dutch attacks, the president of the EIC, Gerald Aungier, relocated his base from Surat to Bombay in 1672. Owing to Aungier's fortifications, Bombay was able to successfully defend itself from a Dutch attack in 1673.[31]

The famous French physician, M. Dellon, describes Bombay as he found it in 1673. "The English have built there a very fine Fort, where the President of the East India Company commonly keeps residence. They have also laid the foundation of a City, where they grant liberty to all, strangers of what religion or nation soever to settle themselves and exempt from all manner of taxes for the first 20 years."[32] This renewed the impetus for large-scale immigration into Bombay. Some were attracted by the religious freedom promised by the EIC, others by the light tax burden and still others by the mildness of the Government compared to the Muslims and the Portuguese religious fanatics. Consequently, between 1668 and 1673, the population in Bombay increased from 10,000 to 60,000.[33]

Upon Mr. Aungier's arrival in Bombay, he set about the task of 'nationalising' the tiny island of Bombay and from that point on Bombay began a period of steady growth. First, he argued to keep the residency of the EIC's President in Bombay, a decision which was formally ratified only on May 2nd, 1687. In addition, the proceedings of the upper courts formerly conducted in Portuguese were to be carried out in English and only English standards of measurement were to be used in commerce and construction. Children born of English Protestants and native Roman Catholics were to be raised as Protestants and in order to propagate a British colony in Bombay, English women were sent to India. In order to improve the revenues of the island, Aungier established a mint from which gold and silver coins could be produced. He also promoted the construction of the government dockyard in the Fort whose foundations were laid in 1671. Further, Aungier invited the Banias of Gujarat, an industrious merchant community, to settle in Bombay with promises of protection and religious freedom. Two additional merchant classes also helped to propel Bombay towards greatness; the Armenians and the Parsis. General Aungier is remembered as the founder of the prosperity of

Bombay due to his tireless efforts and sound judgement in the development of Bombay as a mercantile city.[34]

As a consequence of the transferral of the seat of the Company's presidency from Surat to Bombay, the latter now became the 'Key of India' for the British and plans were devised to strengthen her position. In 1695, Sir John Gayer was nominated as the Governor of Bombay and he set himself to the task of making Bombay the hub of English trade in western India.[35] Bombay was, at that point, the only British possession in western India other than the factories they had built on leased land in Surat.

However, two years earlier, a rival joint-stock company, the English East India Company, was granted a charter by the Queen of England and set their sights on Bombay. Prolonged rivalries between the two British Companies ensued and consequently, scant attention was paid to the city's development and sanitation needs.[36] Even after their formal union into one company was completed in 1702, internal squabbles between different interest groups continued to occupy the main stage and impede the Company's overall development. As a consequence, the living conditions on the island deteriorated over time and widespread epidemics ensued due to poor hygenic conditions and neglect by the Governors of the island. By the last quarter of the 18th century, Bombay became known not as the 'Island of the Good Life', but rather as the 'Cemetery of the Europeans'.[37] Epidemics prevailed in this island and from 500 new arrivals, only 100 would still be alive after 6 months. According to one traveller visiting Bombay at this time: "All kinds of vice were in the superlative degree and the most detestable sins were indulged in to an almost unlimited extent."[38] The city acquired an evil reputation and it would take another 20 years before she began again to flourish under the British rule.

By 1802 the fortified Fort of Bombay was nearly a mile long and a quarter of a mile wide.[39] Many warehouses, imported timber for building ships, a dry dock and a large dockyard all contributed to make Bombay a well-known naval base property of the Company. Road construction and land drainage were also underway to promote Bombay as a commercial centre. In 1838 the causeway joining Bombay and Colaba (formerly "Old Woman's Island) was built, which increased the commercial activity in the area. The population of the British territories likewise increased owing to the liberal and attractive policies offered by the East India Company. By 1720 the population within the Bombay Fort had reached its limit; increasing from 16,000 in 1718 to 70,000 by 1755. By 1780 the population of the city of Bombay (not including Mahim) reached 100,000, increasing more than 10 times within a century. Additional population figures note the following: In 1814, population reached 1,80,000; in 1830 it broke 2,29,000; in 1836, 2,36,000 inhabitants were recorded, in 1872 not less than 6,44,405; and by 1881, already 7,73,196 people lived in the now city of Bombay. In the 1890's, during the decade that the first pioneer Goans began arriving in Bombay, the population of Bombay had increased to 8,21,764.[40]

The Britishers were Protestants and although Catholics and Protestants at that time were fighting over issues of a Christian religious nature, Britain nevertheless allowed the Roman Catholics to practice their religion freely as they allowed all other communities. Between 1715 and 1717, in fact, a friendly relationship was established between Portugal and Britain, two formal rivals on the Western Coast of India. However, the Britain insisted upon the cessation of conversion activities in Bombay and by 1760 the Order of the Jesuits was caused to be extinct.[41] In addition to the Portuguese Catholics, the English Protestants, Dutch Presbyterians and American Methodists also established churches in Bombay during the mid to late 1800's. Added these groups to the already present Hindu, Muslim, Jewish, Roman Catholic and Parsi communities and Bombay by the late 1800's was a true cosmopolitan city in the realm of religion. Under the Britishers, all were encouraged to practice their own religions and respect the rights of others to practice theirs. It is interesting to note that under the British an environment of tolerance quite unlike that of the Portuguese missionary fanatics, Muslim invaders and Maratha conquerors developed in Bombay. Owing to such an ambience, Bombay was able to prosper and evolve as a major city for international trade by the 19th century. Though cultures, languages and faiths divided these communities, one thing certainly united them; the desire to reap profits from trade and make Bombay a great commercial port-city.

Bombay, along with larger India, achieved Independence in 1947. Independence resulted in another wave of influx into Bombay owing to the rural poverty which had been created by the policies of the British empire combined with the urban power vacuum left after the British vacated the city. However, as the British left and the World Wars came to an end, the seemingly endless flow of available jobs in Bombay soon dried up. The result was an influx of migrants in excess of available jobs, resulting in the proliferation of shanty-towns, the increasing congestion and pollution and the massive concrete jungle which describes the Bombay of today.

Possibly more than any other city in India, Bombay does not leave the visitor untouched. It's current population of 14.5 million gives only the bare skeleton of the true picture of life in Bombay. If employed under a typical nine-to-six schedule, an average Bombayite faces the 'mad train rush' in the 2nd class compartment or the overcrowded buses and vehicular traffic congestion. Though men and women travel in separate compartments, the phrase 'lady-like' is a gross misrepresentation of the behaviour in those crunched compartments, where incidents of pushing, shoving and screaming are amundane examples. During the rush hours on the trains, which are the most widely used form of transportation to reach near and distant suburbs, it is a 'kill or be killed' attitude which enables one to get in and out of the train at the desired locations. There is no place in Bombay for the 'sussegarde' attitude previously characteristic of Goans; 'you snooze, you loose' is the order of the day. Quick response, a sharp intellect, a guarded face and a hard heart are the qualities necessary to survive the streets of Bombay. Apathy towards the poor is a must when faced with an onslaught of beggars in the course of a typical day. The term 'concrete jungle' does justice to the environmental conditions in Bombay in the 1990's. Sympathy is rewarded with ingratitude, laziness with condescension and cheating with financial reward free of social reprisal. Whether you are a newcomer or a seasoned Bombayite, this city offers an ample number of challenges on which to sharpen your wit or get played in the first round after the shuffle. Those who fail to soon master Bombay find themselves, instead, controlled and mastered.

Goan Migrants in Bombay

Thus, arose the cosmopolitan, religiously liberal, fast-urbanising and quickly expanding commercial centre in which the first Goans dared to venture in order to increase their earnings. In addition to dreams of financial success, adventure and freedom from village confinement, Goans brought with them their religious beliefs, culture, language and social behaviour. This chapter examines this historical migration which resulted in numerous changes in the lives of these men and their descendants now permanent residents of Bombay. From Village Boys' Clubs to Konkani-speaking neighbourhoods, the Goans who migrated to Bombay became a well-known community in that massive metropolitan city and solidified the 'Goan identity' which became the hallmark of Goans throughout India. The history of Goans in Bombay is interesting from the perspective of social science because it shows not only how a migrant community creates and maintains itself but also how it slowly lapses into decline and eventual disappearance once various forces have been removed. This chapter also details (from their beginnings) the communities and organisations established by and for Goans, their impetus, rise and decline. It also examines Goan cultural identity as a collection of elements, many of which have undergone significant change in the past 50 years.

Why then, would anyone want to live in this sprawling concrete jungle? For some it is the desire to earn higher wages and Bombay in the early years offered ample opportunity for employment more lucrative than that available in Goa. The Portuguese in Goa, besides being partial in favour of Roman Catholics, were also partial to upper-caste Roman Catholics, who received the majority of jobs reserved for Goans in government and/or administration. Those individuals from the Sudir (Sudra) community who wished to come up in life and found Goa then own land which was at that time mainly an international trading centre, offered few job possibilities. In addition to higher wages, the education in Goa was either in Portuguese or Marathi and those who had foresight but could not afford private English classes in Goa chose to send their children out in order to obtain an English education of superior quality. For many young men, Bombay also offered freedom from the restrictions of village life, a chance to meet new people and satisfaction for their ambition and spirit of adventure. These young men were lured by the charm of Bombay itself, employment being rated as important as the 'experience'. Thus, although Bombay is tough and trying, it is also full of adventure, new experiences, a variety of people and a lifestyle altogether different from that of a village in Goa.

Goan Village Clubs in Bombay

Old wooden staircases, ancient buildings, Catholic altars and the smell of fish-curry-rice are what first strikes a newcomer to the Goan Village Clubs in Bombay. The initial impetus for the clubs began as young men from the villages came to Bombay after the 10th standard, looking for work and a better lifestyle during the first half of the 20th century. Like the California gold rush, young Catholic men from Goa arrived in droves and often several from a particular village would arrive and rent a flat together. The area nearby Marine Lines was, at that time, relatively distant from the city centre and apartment rates were cheap. These flats soon became informal 'clubs', which usually housed those Goans who took up jobs as cooks, waiters and other jobs in the service sector.[42]

Many of the boys came with the hopes of escaping the confines of rural life. Consequently, in the early days of the clubs, there were few rules and the inhabitants enjoyed a certain amount of freedom. On special holidays and sometimes for no justifiable reason, they organised dances and parties as were held in Goa which would last late into the night. Noisy parties, excessive drinking and other revelries proliferated during these early years, the result of which gave the clubs a reputation among their more sober neighbours. Eventually this reputation reached Goa and the community and clergy decided to raise funds to employ a caretaker, manager and cook for the clubs. Supported by worried parents and anxious priests, the church then took an active role in curbing the activities of the youngsters which jeopardised the name of the Roman Catholic community in Bombay and that of Goa in general.

One of the largest Goan clubs is St. John's Club of Benaulim, located in Dhobi Talao, Bombay. Forty men in the 20-60 age bracket are currently residing there.[43] Some were long-staying residents, some only came in passing from the ships to Goa and one man present had been an active club resident since its inception in 1955. Those currently residing there are either waiting for visas to work on ships in the Gulf countries, employed in the city itself as temporary cooks or as office workers, or looking for jobs in other places. Several rectangular wooden trunks were lined up along the walls and on the floor, each one containing the personal possessions of someone either living in the club or away working on a ship. The price of accommodation, including meals for club members was about Rs. 10 per month and if any man from Benaulim village wished to come to Bombay as a 'tourist', he could stay in the club for Rs. 10 per day. While the men hunted for jobs, money coming from home sustained them for the duration of their stay or until employment was procured. 'Influence', usually of someone already working on a ship, was cited by the young men as the most important factor in securing a job.

In order to become a member of the Benaulim club, or any village Goan club for that matter, a young man must first belong to that particular village, in this case the village of Benaulim in Salcette, Goa.[44] He either must have a family member belonging to the club or must be nominated by one of the existing members. The application process takes approximately six months, after which follows a one-year probationary period. After both are successfully completed, the man becomes a member for life whether he stays in the club or eventually returns to Goa.

St. Anne's of Ponda is another such club located near Marine Lines. Established in 1939, its members elected a manager to oversee the club after several boys from that village had been renting the place. Most secure overseas employment on ships and can only become members after meeting the manager, Mr. Henry Fernandez, an original member of the Ponda Club. Mr. Fernandez arrived in 1950 and for 12 years he lived in the club while becoming a master cutter in a tailor's shop. He now has his own small shop next to the club and is settled in Bandra with his wife and children.[45]

The Rivona Club was started on October 15th of 1933, an event marked by the signing of the rules and regulations posted on the wall of the clubhouse.[46] Out of a total membership of 250, only 30 members were in residence of this one-room second-storey corner flat tucked away in an old congested neighbourhood near Marine Lines.

Near Marine Lines in two parallel dilapidated buildings known as Dincha and Jar Mahals, there are no less than 11 of these Goan village clubs. They all share a mess hall in which a plate of fish-curry-rice costs Rs. 12. The clubs of Bastora, Raia, Nuvem, Assorna, Guirim, Majorda and Corlim figure on the list of clubs located in this building couplet. St. Anthony's of Vagator in Dincha Mahal, Marine Lines, had a total of 44 members, only 6 of whom were currently in residence. After preliminary interviews and background investigations, a young man from Vagator can join the club after paying an entrance fee of Rs.150 and Rs. 5 per month while away on the ship. After 5 years of membership a man becomes able to help formulate the club rules.

In this same building, like Goan Clubs, the Club of St. Lawrence, Mangalore, was started by those. young men from that city in Dakshina Kannada who came to Bombay together seeking employment. St.Lawrence of Karkala is the patron saint of this club, which also offers a sense of community and cheap living rates for those Mangaloreans hoping to find employment in Bombay. With a total of 210 members and a reputation as one of the oldest clubs, the Mangalorean club's first registered name dates back to 1932. Long-time residents remember that by 1943 over 150 young men were piled into a two-room club, sleeping on floor mats, on top of trunks and anywhere they could find space. During those early years, those men who arrived from Mangalore were usually the lesser educated youth or poor villagers who took up jobs as bakers, tailors, house servants and hotel staff.[47] Later on during the 1950's they sought employment on British ships and began working overseas, leaving only their trunks in the club. Today the number of those residing there are around 20, with the oldest man in the club over 65. The men's educational levels have changed along with their numbers. Those staying in the club today come with an education and are now working as clerks, secretaries and even some lawyers. They have a 10 pm curfew and a daily Catholic mass at 7 pm in front of the small altar.

An examination of trends over the past 70 years reveals that those who first came to Bombay with an education found Bombay to be ripe with opportunity and potential for socio-economic advancement. Those who were uneducated, however, dealt first with the language barrier before finding low-paid jobs as cooks, tailors and house servants. Most were from the lower-middle to middle class and have improved their economic status somewhat since then.

As for the fate of the clubs, many of them have closed their doors of late owing to a variety of factors. The bad reputation that they acquired during their early years has since left an indelible mark and many of the young men currently in residence are ashamed to admit that they do in fact live in the clubs. Even though the notorious impression these clubs had created has quieted down substantially their reputation as a haven for rowdy, low-class 'village boys' remains. Also, many rural Goans have relatives, friends, or other contacts now settled in Bombay and can stay with them while they search for employment. Following Liberation, infrastructure and institutions for higher education have arrived in Goa, thus, decreasing the necessity to migrate to major urban cities. Bombay has also become congested and the job competition fierce, the result of which discourages potential migrants from choosing Bombay as their target destination. Finally, the quality of life in urban Bombay is now recognised as less than that available in rural Goa, owing to the congestion, pollution, crime and long distance travels which Goans in Bombay must face on a daily basis.

Dhobi Talao

The neighbourhood of Dhobi Talao, owing to its large number of clubs and consequent Goan establishments, became known as a mini-Goa during the 1940's, 50's and early 60's. Many men who had migrated there now brought their families to settle in the area, attracted by the strong sense of community and cultural identity. Goan restaurants run by Goans sprang up, as well as shops selling Goan newspapers, trinkets, postcards and religious items. Christmas dances were organised in halls and New Year's balls attracted large crowds and people decorated buildings and hung huge paper mache stars between the buildings. The Goa Carnival was celebrated with gay abandon, music and coloured water in the streets, drawing crowds from neighbouring localities. Our Lady of Dolours,[48] built during the Portuguese era in Bombay, was the unofficial community church and Konkani the lingua franca on the streets. The name Dhobi Talao became irrevocably associated with Goa and the identity of Goans became further associated with Catholicism, Christmas, Carnival and fish-curry.

Though this identity remains, the reality of Dhobi Talao has changed substantially. First, it is now located in a central part of the city which has become a heavily-trafficked commercial district. Prices for basic one-room flats have soared and as a result many families have moved out to the suburbs to 3 and 4 room flats worth the same amount. Today only 4,000 families, roughly 2 per cent of the population of Dhobi Talao, are of Goan ancestry. The rest are newcomers from Gujarat and other neighbouring States who have purchased flats for commercial purposes. Konkani, the former lingua franca of the area, is rarely spoken in this new cosmopolitan neighbourhood and only on Fridays can Konkani prayers be heard in Our Lady of Dolours. Carnival and Christmas dances have all but disappeared owing to lack of interest and organisation and only on September 4th, the church Feast Day, do old community members return regularly to Dhobi Talao.

Case Studies: Residents of Dhobi Talao

Several case studies were conducted on Goans living in Dhobi Talao in the year 1997. From priests to shop-owners, all were asked some basic questions which attempted to examine their sense of self in relation to Goan identity and culture. What the studies reveal is that in today's climate, people have reacted with mixed feelings to the separation from their original cultural heritage. The following paragraphs examine cases of extreme disassociation, extreme association and for the majority, a kind of nostalgia for the days gone by tempered by an acceptance of the prevailing situation.

The first, a 30-year-old bachelor, gives an example of cultural disassociation resulting from his social environment. One of the four brothers and the part-owner of a Goan bakery in Dhobi Talao, characterises himself as 'cosmopolitan' and identifies with the international culture of Bombay. Viewing economic status as more important than caste, he has come up in life and equates 'Goan' with a common 'shippie'[49] who stays in a virtually rent-free, rowdy village club. Born and brought up in Bombay, he began an export business which enabled him to spend several years in many countries, including seven years in the USA. He demonstrates some contempt for the Konkani-speaking Goans in the neighbourhood and confesses that he himself knows little of the language. Though his grandparents originated in Mapsa, he himself does not have any attachment to Goa nor does he have any Goan friends. His Goan roots, owing most probably to the reputation of the shippies in Dhobi Talao, have become for him a source of shame. Consequently, he de-emphasises caste and communal elements of his identity and instead emphasises those which he himself has created through personal achievement.

The second case is that of a woman from Panjim settled 15 years in Dhobi Talao. After her marriage she shifted to Bombay with her husband and now runs a 'Goa-store' which carries such items as Konkani musical tapes, Roman Catholic religious icons and Goan newspapers like the *The Goa Post* and the *Navinhind Times*. Her husband is a mechanic and they have 2 children, the eldest who is nine-year-old. Though Our Lady of Dolours School is closest to their flat, she sends her children to St. Anne's where the student body is predominantly Catholic. She enjoys speaking Konkani and laments that Goans are 'feeling shy, i.e., embarrassed, to speak their mother tongue in the streets of Bombay. She readily admits of her strong attachment to Goa and would like to live there. As she sits all day in a small one-room store surrounded by things typically 'Goan', she admits with nostalgia that her heart is still there.

Another long-time Goan resident of Dhobi Talao is a 30-year-old woman running a Konkan grocery store opposite the Church of Our Lady of Dolours. Born and raised in Dhobi Talao, she often takes in paying guests from Goa who have come to Bombay for a variety of reasons. She feels both distinctly Goan and yet cosmopolitan at the same time. Goa, to her, is "our country" and a place that Goans can call home and feel safe. She, like others interviewed, expresses concern with regard to the status of Roman Catholics in India. She feels like a tourist in

Goa, but recalls that Goans in Dhobi Talao resemble tourists as well when they first arrive. She has maintained the typical Goan dress of skirts and blouses rather than saris and feels very much a part of her cultural heritage. Regarding Goans here and in their native place, she feels that Goans in Goa are more friendly and will approach you rather than waiting for you to approach them as is the case in Bombay.

One particular interview with the Dias family lasted for several hours and revealed a well-documented family history beginning with the first Goan migrant in Bombay. It details the circumstances which caused their migration to Bombay as well as the obstacles overcome and the achievements accomplished. The great-grandfather of the Dias family owned a shipping vessel which transported salt to Mangalore and tiles from Mangalore back to Goa. After having ten children he died at the young age of 45, leaving his mother to care for them all. Their great-grandmother then moved to Bombay and opened a hotel on the ground floor of a building in Dhobi Talao which offered home-cooked Goan food to shippies and a place to shower and freshen up. The 7th son, their grandfather, got a job as a baby-sitter for his uncle's daughter and could only afford to study until the 3rd standard. He then became a tailor's apprentice, mastered the trade and opened his own tailoring business with two of his other brothers. At that point of time (1920's and 30's), Dhobi Talao was similar to a small Goan village with Konkani widely spoken in the streets. Mr. Dias was living in a one-room tenement in Dhobi Talao[50]. In 1938 their grandfather purchased and named the 'Dias building', in 1944 he purchased a second building and in 1947 bought a third building known as the 'A.S. Dias jubilee'. They lived under a joint-family system and had five sons and three daughters. Joe Dias, the Father, was the second son. He studied in Mt. Abu (Cambridge School), followed by two years at St. Xavier's College in Bombay. He married in 1965 and now has 2 sons and 1 daughter. The latter were not interested in continuing in the family tailoring business, so the shop closed down in 1992 once the Father retired. The eldest son works in the Gulf on a ship, the second son is studying the fine arts and lives with him in Dhobi Talao and their daughter is studying fashion design in Bombay as well.

The Dias family comments that Goans are still coming to Bombay either through marriage alliances[51], friends and relatives, or through the village clubs. In 1938 Dhobi Talao was sparsely populated and not very convenient from the city centre. The clubs were full and rules and regulations were enforced. During World War II many Goans were needed to work on warships and this coincided with the highest rate of Goan migration into Bombay. During the 60's and 70's the Gulf boom began and many Goans were made to work on oil rigs and passenger cruises. Now the job openings have decreased and there is more competition from other communities. Of late, most Goans have moved out of Dhobi Talao and those who arrive are mostly in transit from ship to Goa. They stay in the clubs or with family for a night or two and take the next bus out of town. Thus, the clubs still functional are not well-maintained and many have been closed down or sold off.[52]

Regarding the current state of affairs of the Goans in Bombay, the youngest son takes a critical outlook. He considers himself Goan '1st, 2nd and 3rd,' and that the Catholics of Goa are a special breed. While most countries have a negative perception of Indians, saying you are 'Goan' makes you more successful in getting a job abroad. In India, however, he feels an underlying pervasive attitude that 'if you are an Indian, you must be a Hindu,' and occasional bouts of discrimination. While 80 per cent of the schools in Bombay were founded and administered by Catholics, the majority of the students are from other communities due to the recent quota system adopted by the city. He feels that the importance of an education is not stressed in Goa, the result of which is that other, more ambitious communities have come in to do business and are currently in control in areas of finance. They feel that 450 years of Portuguese rule had a huge impact on the character development of the Goan Roman Catholic people which influenced individuals beyond a mere change in religion.

Our last case study concerns the Rodrigues family living in Dhobi Talao. Mr Rodrigues was born and raised in this neighbourhood and came from a very poor family. He received his education at Our Lady of Dolours School (attached to the church) and was taken in by the Parish of Our Lady of Dolours to work as a school clerk. He has occupied various clerical positions within the church ever since for the past 37 years. Under a proposed marriage, his wife migrated from Mapsa, Goa to Dhobi Talao, Bombay. They initially rented a one-room flat for Rs. 100 per month and he now receives a pension of Rs. 2,000 per month. Now over 60, he still works for the church and registers approximately 20 birth certificates per week for Goan Catholics. In today's parish, he has seen the numbers dwindle considerably over the years and currently only 40 per cent of the parishioners are Goan-Catholics, the remaining 60 per cent come from Mangalore and Kerala.

What then seems to be the fate of Dhobi Talao? As village clubs forever close their doors, Goans move out to the suburbs and new communities of Muslims and Gujaratis arrive, the identity of Dhobi Talao as a mini-Goa seems to be rapidly deteriorating. Owing to a variety of factors such as fewer ship jobs, poor conditions of clubs, family located in and continuing to relocate to the suburbs, industrial development of Goa, the saturation and congestion in Bombay and migration trends to foreign countries, this trend does not seem ready to change. Within fifty years, the identity of Dhobi-Talao, as 'Goan', might remain only in the history books and in the minds of a few of the younger generation who remember the nostalgic tales of their ancestors.

BANDRA: THE SECOND WAVE

Origin and Early Church History

The Island of Salsette was the largest of the original group of 25 islands surrounding Bombay. Its name is derived from the Sanskrit Shatshashti, or sixty-six, owing to the number of villages on the island. When the Portuguese took possession of Bombay island and surrounds, they also gained control of Salsette. Separated from Bombay Island by the Mahim Creek, Bandra has become known as the 'Cradle of Christianity' on this, the South West corner of Salsette Island. In 1548 an entirely Christian village called Trinidade was founded on Salsette island. Records of a Fr. Goncalo Rodrigues state that: "In a few years there was a population of 3,000, all neophytes and poor, who lived by their labour, without there being a single idle person among them."[53]

In totality their possessions numbered 100 bullocks and ploughs, a variety of field tools, besides each having a house on land purchased by the Church. The new converts were taught the tenets of the Roman Catholic faith at daily scheduled meetings, learned religious songs and even taught their elders the doctrines of Christianity. As documented in the Oriente Conquistado, "Everything was in innocence and simplicity of manners; no greedy traffic, no insolent wealth."[54] Their style of living was modelled upon visions of a utopian society, free from the degradation of common society. The community constructed a church, an orphanage and the priests would purchase orphaned children and bring them to the village before they were sold into slavery to the Muslims. Until 1697 the village was flourishing, but when the Marathas invaded Salsette in 1739, the village was abandoned.[55]

In 1566 a mall chapel was built and two Jesuit priests began the unrelenting process of Christian conversions characterised by missionary zeal, the hallmark of that era. In 1568 the villages of Bandra (Wanara) and Kurla (Colorem) where transferred to the Jesuit Fathers and between 1568 and 1570 the first shrine was erected on the island.[56] In 1570 the Church of Bandora was founded and shortly after 1577 St. Anne's church and attached school were constructed. In 1578 two villages with a total population of 10,000 came under the Christian fold and in that same year the Church of St. Joao Baptista of Condotim was built followed by St. Andrew's Church in 1583.[57] By the end of that same year nearly all the inhabitants of Bandra, mostly fishing and agricultural communities, came under the Catholic fold. In 1640 the famous Castella de Aguada (Fort of the Waterpoint) was constructed and in that same year a chapel was built to serve the spiritual needs of the Portuguese garrison then manning the fort. In 1678 that same chapel was again enlarged and was renamed "Nossa Senhora de Monte" (Our Lady of the Mount).[58] However, in 1739, owing to an invasion by the Marathas, the Portuguese destroyed both the shrines of Our Lady and St. Anne's church because of their strategic positions. The icon of Our Lady was rescued, ferried across the river and installed in St. Michael's Church at Mahim. (On the English side, there it remained until 1761, during this time the Marathas were defeated).[59]

After the defeat of the Marathas by the British in 1761, both the island of Salsette and the Bassein fort were ceded to the British. The island, after only 22 years of Maratha domination, was again owned by a Christian power. Salsette and specifically the area known as Bandra, then became the residential area for the wealthy upper-class British. They built stately two-storey homes complete with outdoor staircases and covered porches in the typical British fashion, interspersed with winding narrow lanes and open courtyards. A bandstand was erected on the beach side sponsoring entertainment for the British on the weekends. Three communities, thus, made their homes here; the old Portuguese residents, the converted East Indian communities and the British aristocracy. The former church of Our Lady, having been raised to the ground during the bombardments, was then rebuilt and has since earned the rank of a Minor Basilica.[60]

The East Indians of Bombay

In Bombay today, there are three Catholic communities; Goans, the Mangaloreans and the East Indians. The first two have been discussed at length in other sections of this book. The latter is interesting subject matter for the social scientist interested in cultural evolution, but an exhaustive study of this community goes beyond the scope of this study other than for its relation to the Goan community. However, from the historical background outlined regarding the migrants and settlers into Bombay, it becomes obvious that *those Catholics known as East Indians are in fact the ancient converts from the Portuguese era in Bombay*. Yet most people, including parish priests, do not even know of this ancient history. *The Portuguese era has been virtually erased from the collective memory in light of the most recent British rulers who built Bombay from a tiny village into a great international trading port in less than 100 years*. Though ancient Portuguese churches are scattered throughout Bombay from Dhobi Talao near Marine lines to Malwani village on the outskirts of the Malad suburb, this part of history has been seemingly erased from memory.

Based upon Da Cunha's work, *The Origin of Bombay*, records state that the Portuguese missionaries, in their zealous efforts to bring the 'heathens' under the Christian folds, converted entire fishing communities (who were previously animists then converted to Hinduism) to the Roman Catholic Faith.[61] Unlike Goa, however, which experienced a full 450 years of Portuguese cultural influence, the island of Bombay was taken by the Portuguese in 1534, only to be handed over to the British in 1661, a little more than one hundred years later. Thus, before the Portuguese could really get a 'cultural foothold' on the fishing communities, they were dispossessed of their lands in Bombay. And though these missionaries were allowed to practice their religion and construct additional churches, they were forbidden from attempting conversions and cultural changes in the lives of their parishioners following the occupation of the island by the British.[62] By 1760 the Order of the Jesuits was forcibly made extinct and little by little the conversions ceased.

Thus, while the Portuguese went on to change the language, style of dress, codes of behaviour and allowed roles for women among the natives in Goa, they had little such opportunities in Bombay. Consequently, when their power and influence declined and that of the British increased, the native Roman Catholic coverts in Bombay returned to their original customs, language, outlook and dress (excepting religion as they remained Catholic). Though the original fishing communities spoke a northern Konkani dialect, once new migrants began settling in large numbers Marathi became the language in vogue among the local population. It is still the mother tongue of the East Indians today, many of whom also speak English and Hindi.

Case Studies: Bandra

By the time India gained Independence in the post-World War II era of 1947, most of Bandra's British residents had already returned to England. Many Goans, especially those who had intimate contact with the British or served in her navy, knew about the locality of Bandra when it was occupied by the British and rushed to buy land there once Independence was achieved. Consequently, Goans from Dhobi Talao and Dabul who had saved their earnings during the 30's and 40's now bought land, houses and flats in Bandra during the 1950's and 60's. Further, the cost of land and rent in Dhobi Talao and Dabul had skyrocketed, its streets were congested and polluted and the population of all communities in Bombay had increased the previous decade owing to the easy jobs secured on British war vessels. Less than an hour away and linked directly to Bombay via causeway and railway, Bandra offered a greener environment with less congestion and more natural surroundings. After the first wave of Goan migrants into Bandra, the prices of land increased substantially and only those with significant salaries could continue to occupy flats in that suburb.

Our first case study is that of the Sequeira family currently living in Bandra. The grandparents of Mrs. Sequeira migrated from the Goan village of Siolim to Bombay in search of employment. Her father was born in Byculla, found work as a barber and spoke English in the house even though they were fluent in Konkani. They moved to Dadar Bombay, where Mrs. Sequeira was born. She worked as a secretary and took voluntary retirement after serving for 25 years. She now helps out at the Diocese. She describes her husband as a "pakka"[63] Goan who, although born in Pune, considers his home the village of Saligao. His grandfather worked for the Hyderabad Maharaja and was a big businessman. Theirs was a proposal-turned-love marriage and after marriage the couple moved to Bandra. He works at the National Bank. They have 2 children, one daughter currently working for JET airways and another son in the United States working as an officer for Mobil Shipping.

The Sequeiras are life members of the Saligao Association in Bombay, which holds an annual social on the last Saturday in November. The event opens with a Catholic mass conducted by a priest flown in from Saligao, followed by games, competitions, scholarship awards and an evening dance. Mandos, Dulpods and other arts which make up the traditional 'Goan identity' are also performed. Throughout the year the group receives a newsletter mailed to individual homes which keeps members informed of happenings in Sirigao as well as upcoming events of the organisation in Bombay. Though Mr and Mrs Sequeira remain attached to Goa and visit their native place every year, she admits that after 10 days she gets fed up of the 'sussegad' lifestyle and yearns for the hectic pace of Bombay.

Our second case study is that of the Fernandes family living in a 4-room flat near St. Anne's Church, Bandra. The father of Mr. Fernandes migrated to Bombay through the St. Joseph's Club of Shiroda and found work on a passenger ship.

While his wife stayed behind in Goa, their two sons were also brought to Bombay in order to provide them with higher education in English. They had been born in Goa and had studied in a Portuguese medium until the age of ten. They stayed with their uncle on Grant Road who worked for Air India and after two years Mr. Fernandes went on to a boarding school while his father returned to his job on the ship. Only on school holidays did Mr. Fernandes return to Goa to visit his mother and during his eleventh year he remained there after having difficulty in adjusting to Bombay. After Goa was liberated in 1961, he returned to Bombay and completed two years of higher secondary education. He then completed a radio course, studied electronics and joined an Indian shipping company. In 1973 he became a full-fledged radio officer after studying radio electronics in London. In 1979 while attending a dance function, he met and fell in love with a pretty girl later who became his wife. In 1978 bought this flat in Bandra immediately prior to their marriage. The price at that time was 2 lakhs, it is now valued at over 50 lakhs. From 1979 to 1981 the couple travelled on the ship together.

Mrs. Fernandes (wife of the aforementioned), whose native village is Baga, was born in Dadar, Bombay in 1954. Her grandfather was the captain of a ship who went to Bombay though a village club and was eventually posted in Gujarat. Her father worked for the railways in Canacona. She earned a degree from Sophia College in Bombay and then found employment as a stenographer for Siemen's, a German engineering company. After marriage she travelled with her husband to Thailand, Singapore, France, the USA, Canada, Italy and Kuwait. They have one 16-year-old daughter who is studying in school. When they first moved into Bandra in 1978, it was a quiet, peaceful suburb much like a 'mini-Goa'. It has since become crowded and the view of the sea disrupted by many neighbouring high-rise apartment complexes. Ultimately they hope to settle in Goa on land which they have purchased.

Our third case study, Father Ferrao, is a first generation Bombayite. His father came from Tivim to Bombay at the age of 15 to study at Cavel, close to St. Sebastian's School. He lived in Dhobi Talao with his sister, obtained a government job as a clerk. Originally from a 'low-caste' Catholic family, he married a girl who had also migrated to Bombay from Goa. His mother, currently in Andheri, encouraged English in the house, though she and her husband spoke Konkani to one another. Father Ferrao was born in Dhobi Talao and learned to speak Konkani with his school friends who were from the same area. He joined the seminary school after finishing his studies and was posted first in Andheri, then Bycullah and is currently at St. Peter's Church in Bandra. Among his friends, his best friend is a Goan and most of his good friends are Goans from his childhood building in Dhobi Talao. Regarding the young generation of Bombay-born Goans, Father Ferrao mentions that he can not discriminate a Goan child from another Christian child and that of the 100 Christians who join the parish every year, 25-30 per cent of them are Goans.[64] On Goan identity, he believes that according to the typical stereotype, Goans are 'expected' to be affable, loving, carefree and music-oriented. On his own Goan heritage, Father Ferrao does not even eat fish nor does he have the stereotypical Goan qualities, yet he feels good about having a personal history connected to Goa.

Our fourth and final case study in Bandra is that of Father Pereira, a Goan priest working in the Diocese Centre opposite from the Minor Basilica of Our Lady of the Mount. Born in Navelim, Goa, he studied in the Portuguese medium until the 11th standard when the medium of instruction became English (1961). Portuguese was the language spoken at home and he admits that his parents "would swear by Portuguese culture." They were both fully raised and educated in the Portuguese culture and were angry regarding independence. Father Pereira himself does not feel so attached to the Portuguese culture as he was only five when Goa achieved independence. After completing his education in Goa, Fr. Pereira studied in the seminary at Goregao for seven years. Though he continued to stay in Bombay, every three or four years he is transferred to a new Parish. He does return to Goa approximately three times per year in order to visit family and friends. Regarding his own cultural identity, Fr. Pereira classifies himself optimistically as a 'misfit' and rather rootless for several reasons. Regarding languages, he speaks Portuguese with a Goan accent, English with an Indian accent and muffled Konkani with the servants. His religion makes him feel as an outsider in Bombay and in

Goa, also, he feels like an outsider owing to his lack of fluency in Konkani and the absence of the calm, happy-go-lucky attitude 'typical' of the Goan nature. But with a smile he takes it all in stride as would a typical Goan.

MALAD: CASE STUDY OF A 'POCKET' OF GOAN CATHOLICS

Historical Overview

The suburb of Malad originally consisted of the four villages of Marve, Malwani, Karore and Ratori. They were inhabited by *Kolis* (fisherman), who earned their livelihood from the nearby river. Colonised by the Portuguese upon their conquest of Bombay and various areas along the Konkan coast, many of these early inhabitants converted from Hinduism to the Roman Catholic religion and became known as East Indians. St. Anthony's Church, situated at the entrance to Malwani village, was built more than 400 years ago and still contains gravestones of several priests written in Portuguese. Over a period of time these villages were connected to each other and to other suburbs via paved roads and have now been absorbed into the larger suburb known as Malad.

Until 20 years ago, these villages remained as such with few people wanting to live in such a poor area with no access to public transportation. The only migrants into Malad were people moving in from slum areas and setting up 'challs' (illegal one-room tenements) for rent. As land prices soared in Bandra and Santa Cruz, new migrants and lower-middle class families found those rates too expensive. Instead, they bought flats at lower prices in Malad and held on to them, speculating that soon public transportation, including buses and train lines would be made available. Close to the train stations and surrounding the Church of St. Anne's, Orlem became a neighbourhood dominated by Roman Catholics of Mangalorean, Goan and East Indian descent. Dominique Colony in particular became one of these 'pockets' of Roman Catholics in Orlem. Currently, about 45 per cent of residents of Malad are a combined force of Goan, Mangalorean and East Indian Catholics.

In the past seven years, the number of parishioners coming to St. Anthony's Church, Malwani, has increased from 5,000 to

10,000. Land rates in neighbouring Orlem have skyrocketed due to their proximity to the train line, causing many to settle in Malwani which is almost a half an hour from the train station by bus. Though both Goans and Mangaloreans are coming in to Malad, the highest rate of migration is among the Mangaloreans, who have a majority among the Catholics in Malad. Both St. Anthony's and St. Anne's hold Konkani mass on Sundays which is attended mostly by Mangalorean Catholics. The Goans and East Indians prefer to attend mass in English. In St. Anne's parish, four of the priests are from Goa and the parish cook is a Goan. The remaining administrative personnel are from Mangalore.

According to Father Fonseca in St. Anne's Church at Orlem, Goans migrated to Bombay under the impression that the 'grass is always green on the other side.' Also, those who worked abroad on ships, in the African colonies, or who have relatives living abroad were challenged to succeed and 'come up' in life. During the Portuguese era the migration wave directed Goans to the African colonies, where Goans could settle and become the new aristocracy. The second wave resulted from the job opportunities opening up in the then growing city of Bombay followed by those on British and Indian warships during the First and Second World Wars. The third wave came during the 60's and 70's following the Gulf boom, when thousands of Goans secured employment in Gulf countries or on international shipping lines. The most current trend in the last 3-4 years for Goans in Bombay is to migrate back to their native place. Those who came to Bombay in earlier are fed up with the hectic, congested life in the concrete jungle and feel that the quality of life is better in Goa. Those who have heritage homes in Goa are concerned that caretakers may try to usurp their properties, many are apprehensive about the current social attitude which seems to promote discrimination against Catholics and others are beginning to feel that Goans are indeed a 'special' breed.

But for those middle-income families who are intent on making their fortunes in this massive urban centre, they choose Malad because they can obtain superior housing at lower cost and still maintain a bank balance. When they initially arrive they seek out a 'Catholic' identity, ask to register the head of their household and have their new flat blessed by the neighbourhood priest. A new 'Goan' arrival in Bombay will definitely stand out. His rounded paunch, flamboyance, casual smile and relaxed mannerisms reveal his background. But as time goes by he finds himself joining in the rat race, adopting customs peculiar to 'Bombayites', altering his manner of speaking and most probably loosing a bit of his paunch during the scramble to get in a rush-hour train. Unless they quickly develop street smarts and a distrust of casual relationships, Goans tend to be 'taken for a ride' by others in Bombay.[65]

The social role allowed for women is also slightly different from that in Goa. In Bombay, many Goan women feel suppressed owing to the apparent 'blind obedience' characteristic of women from other communities. Goan women are raised to think for themselves and many are educated and hold important positions. *On the whole, Catholic women and especially Goans often have an identity beyond their connection to their husband and children, an identity which is not yet fully accepted by other communities in Bombay.* Regarding their reputation, other communities feel that Goan women are 'cheap' and 'easy targets' if/when they say hello to menfolk as was Portuguese custom, owing to the disapproval these communities feel towards the social interaction between the two sexes.

Konkani: A Second Class Language in Bombay

When a Goan family settles down to family life in Bombay, they usually speak only English at home to their children. Their native language Konkani, useless in Bombay, is not encouraged by parents who believe that English will enable their sons and daughters to get better jobs and salaries. Konkani is considered a second-class language; an attitude fostered by the Portuguese colonists and continued by those who, having learnt English, were able to get high-paying jobs abroad owing to knowledge of this international language. Consequently, the first generation Goan children in Bombay can follow Konkani but are not as fluent in the language as native Goans. They grow up speaking English fluently, but in turn have difficulty in understanding both Marathi and Hindi. This is because their parents do not encourage the learning of these latter languages and consider them inferior when compared to the usefulness of English. These same children are tough to tell apart from other Christians, though the way they speak English, certain expressions and surnames peculiar to Goa can sometimes offer clues to their cultural backgrounds. However, others are of the opinion that 'Goan culture' can be discerned in children born of Goan parents. They are more 'God-fearing', attend church more regularly, are usually well-mannered and honest children and more easily managed in school. However, the negative aspects are that Goan children are not always good at their studies, with Hindi and Marathi being serious trouble spots.

Self-Expression of Goan Identity

Of late, pressure to "be an Indian first" and not "a foreigner in one's own country" has caused many Goans to deemphasise their cultural heritage. Feelings of shame connected with their personal history have infiltrated into the Goan psyche owing to the current social climate permeating Bombay. Consequently, new attempts are being made among Goans to identify with the larger Indian community by naming their children with Hindu names and dressing or behaving in a manner similar to larger society. Other long-term Goan migrants in Bombay feel that as a result of these attitudes, Goa is their real home and, thus, the inability to identify with the larger society is further exacerbated. These cultural differences begin as early as grade school, where children tend to pick on each others gods. In one instance, a young Hindu boy purposely tore the picture of St. Anthony belonging to another young Catholic boy. The latter went home and told his mother, whereby she prepared him a special lunch to take to school. The following day at lunch time, the Catholic boy stood in front of the Hindu one enjoying his meal of beef masala whereupon he said, "See, you tore my God, so I'm eating yours."

In general, however, most intercommunity relationships between children are cordial and instances like these are few. Most Goans are adjustable and within months adapt to their new social environment. Economics plays the centre role in Bombay life, politics second and religion trailing close behind. So much so, that intercommunity 'love' marriages owing to similar socio-economic stations occur on a regular basis.[66]

Case Studies: Orlem and Malwani

Orlem

The first case study considers the migratory history of Father Fonseca currently working at St. Anne's Church in Orlem. His grandparents migrated from Assagao and started a bakery in Bombay. Though running a business in Bombay, they continued to maintain their residence in Goa and made frequent trips between the two places. His son, Fr. Fonseca's father, studied in Bombay and Karachi before becoming the managing director of a government office for 43 years. The family members spent their lives in Bombay and Fr. Fonseca himself is city-bred. He believes that people in Bombay have to become tough in order to survive. He has a basic working knowledge of Konkani and went to Goa for the first time in 1949. At that time Goa was without electricity and proper sanitation and he had a bad impression of his native place. Even during his second visit in 1960-61 he saw Goa as mostly a collection of 'backward' villages. Only in 1981, when he returned to Goa for a holiday, did he begin to truly appreciate the natural beauty of his native place. Regarding his cultural identity, he feels his home is in Bombay albeit his heritage is in Goa.

The second case study was conducted on Father Braganza who is also a parish priest and school principal at St. Anne's in Orlem. His grandparents migrated to Bombay where his grandfather found work in the postal department. They returned to Goa for all of their holidays. His son, Fr. Braganza's father, was a permanent way inspector (PWI) under the British-Indian Rail Group (renamed Great Indian Peninsular Railway after Independence). The family moved around considerably owing to his job and in 1947 when Fr. Braganza was 6-year-old, he was sent to a Catholic boarding school to get a continuous education. In 1956 the family was transferred to Bombay where the children finished school and then college. Afterwards Fr. Fonseca joined seminary school and eventually became a priest. He was ordained in the Holy Name Cathedral in Colaba and every 3 or 4 years has been transferred to Bandra, then Santa Cruz, the Fort Area, Byculla and now Malad. On Goa, he mentions that as a child he did not like going to Goa. Born and bread in the city, he found the lack of basic amenities annoying and the place 'primitive'. Only later while visiting Goa with friends did he come to appreciate the natural beauty and charm of Goa. After establishing a personal history connected to Goa, he says: "I can't deny my origins but I don't *feel* like a Goan." Though he has a love for his native place and would defend it, he feels that certain qualities like open friendliness, casualness and the 'happy-go-lucky' attitude are lost among the Bombay-born Goans. For those born in Bombay, Fr. Fonseca believes they are an adjustable people who try to mix around and avoid forming into cliques.

Our third case study is conducted on Mrs. Pauline Dias who is the cook at St. Anne's Church in Orlem. She was born in Assagao, Goa (near Anjuna) and moved to Bombay with her parents when she was 8-year-old. She came from a poor family and her father died at a young age, leaving behind 7 children. As a consequence, Mrs. Dias did not receive a formal education and made her living by working as a housekeeper and cook for Goan families in exchange for room, board and a small living stipend. While working for these upper-class families she learned the English language and developed a sense of shame surrounding her native tongue, used only by servants. She worked in homes in Mahim, Dadar, Bandra and Andheri and married a boy from Goa when she was 22-year-old. In 1971 the family went to Kuwait, but when the younger of her two daughters was diagnosed with meningitis she was forced to return to India. As a result of the illness her daughter, now 21, suffers from mental retardation and cannot take care of herself. In 1973 owing to financial difficulties she secured employment as a cook for the Parish priests in Goa where she currently works.

Our fourth case study examines the life history of Mrs. Lalwani, the daughter of Mrs. Dias. Mrs. Lalwani was born in Bombay and met a youngman who later became her husband while working at a printing press. He had already left home and was living in a separate flat and after falling in love they received a court marriage in 1986. That time he was a 27-year-old Hindu and she was a 20-year-old Catholic, both parents did not approve of the marriage, though time has tempered their attitudes. Mr Lalwani works as a set inspector/ contractor in the film industry and they have two children; Harsh and Yoshita. On religion, they have decided to celebrate both religions and festivals with their children and claim they are 'not bothered with caste'. He is very religious-and goes often to the temple, they both attend church on occasion and both altars are kept in the house. On customs, the family does not eat beef or pork and she cooks all types of Indian food. They live in Saibaba Park which is a more cosmopolitan complex compared to the all-Catholic Dominique Colony where they would not be fully accepted. On having a personal history connected to Goa, Mrs. Lalwani is proud to be a Goan and approves of the current development efforts of the Goan State government.

Our fifth and final case study is the Fernandes family living in Dominique Colony in Orlem, Malad. Born in Ribandar Goa, the young Mr. Fernandes met his future wife while making frequent trips to Bombay to visit a friend. He studied until the 10th standard and went on to become professional football players. Though he speaks some English, Konkani is the language he knows best. She is a Bombay-born Roman Catholic belonging to the east Indian community and their love marriage took place in October 1991. Fluent in both English and Marathi, Mrs. Fernandes studied until the 16th standard in Bombay and has a job as a hotel receptionist in Dadar. They have a 4-year-old daughter who studies in a nearby private Catholic school and Mrs. Fernandes would like her child to receive the best education possible. During a typical work day, she leaves the house at 6 am reaches office after an hour and returns home only after 8 pm sometimes not until 11 pm Mr. Fernandes plays football (soccer) for Metro and practices on most mornings. He comes home to drop their daughter off at school, relaxes at home and then picks her up at 3 pm. Of late, owing to his wife's new and hectic job schedule, Mr. Fernandes looks after their daughter. He himself is a recent migrant to Bombay, coming there only after his marriage. Though not forced to take up a hectic job with long hours owing to his excellence in the sport of football, still he suffers some adjustment problem in moving from his heritage home on the Mandovi river front to a 4th floor flat in the middle of a concrete neighbourhood. Regarding culinary differences, Mrs. Fernandes makes both typically Goan cuisine as well as East Indian food, which differs slightly in the preparation of curries, meat and the use of rotis. Regarding cultural differences, she places a higher value on the importance of an education and seems to be happy in the hectic Bombay life. Mr Fernandes, however, seems never short of sleep and enjoys his frequent naps. Their daughter is taught English at home, muffled, though her parents often speak Konkani with each other in front of her. They go home regularly to his native place in Goa, especially during the holidays and at Christmas.

Malwani

Malwani is a village within the larger suburb of Malad which houses low to low-middle income families. Tucked away in the winding narrow lanes of the old quarters are Roman Catholic crosses as well as Hindu icons. Most of the people who live there belong to the fishing community, though in recent years many have traded in their fishing boats for formal education and office employment. While the village centre has itself undergone little improvements and remains much like it appeared hundreds years earlier, the city of Bombay has grown and eventually engulfed this previously isolated village.

Our first case study in the village of Malwani is Mrs. Salian, the headmistress-cum-librarian for the primary school of St. Anthony's. Born an only child in Guirim, she came with her parents to Bombay when she was young. Her father worked for Kodak in Worli and they bought a flat in Orlem. While studying at the college level she met and fell in love with her future husband, a textile designer whose roots were in Mangalore. Mr. Salian had been educated in a Christian school and had taken to the teachings of Christ. Soon after her father passed away he converted to Catholicism and they married, with the approval of his father. They now have two children, a son who is a mechanical engineer and a daughter studying in the 12th standard. For the last year her husband has gone to Goa to look after the heritage home and has become "Goan". He lives with her parents who have taken him as a son. He is taking care of the financial issues dealing with the property and wears in his Mangalorean lungi and shorts when in the house. According to Mrs Salian, her husband loves living in Goa and has taken on a 'Goan identity'. On the flip side, her husband does not go much to visit 'his people' in Mangalore.

The second case study involves a low-income family, the

Lobos. Born in Bicholim, Goa, Mr. Lobo migrated to Bombay and found employment in a Mahindra assembly plant. He married an East-Indian girl from Vile Parle. After ten years and a total of eight miscarriages, she gave birth to an only son, Dominique. From very young age Mr. Lobo has suffered from polio. After spending his earnings on alcohol and his friends, few resources are left for his family or maintenance of the house. On the death of Mr. Lobo's father, land disputes arose among his two sons. The eldest has gone down to live with his widowed mother and take care of her and the ancestral home, but not before dividing the property in Orlem in order to build new flats. As a consequence, Mrs. Lobo was evicted by her husband's brother and given only one lakh as monetary compensation. They were forced to leave Orlem where land prices were two high in order to purchase a rickety 2nd floor, one room flat next to the garbage dump in the old quarters of Malwani village.[67]

The third case study of 'Sybil' is a continuation of the previous case study, as she is Mrs. Lobo's eldest brother's daughter and lives in the apartment next to that of Mrs Lobo. Her father worked in Dubai for Commercial Chemical Bank and was able to buy an apartment in Vile Parle. Sybil was the second of three sisters to take care of the house. She studied until the 10th standard after which she took her first job as a clerk in an STD booth at the age of 14. She received her first monthly salary of Rs. 1,000 and through subsequent jobs she added to the family income and helped to put her sisters through school. While working as a receptionist in a hotel she met and fell in love with her future husband, the only son of a Hindu family. They entered into civil marriage last year which infuriated her mother-in-law. Eventually things cooled down and since then she has come to see her son and 6-month-old grandson, Raju. On religious differences, Sybil says that though they both attend church services, only he goes to the temple to perform pujas. Raju, it seems, will be raised in the Hindu religion. Sybil complains that society looks down on their marriage, but firmly believes that they "have no problem" regarding religious differences.

Recent Trends in the Cultural Identification of 'Goans'

What has happened in recent years, however, is an

increasing linguistic 'confusion' and dislocation which accompanies living in Bombay as a Roman Catholic originally from Goa. Father Pereira throws some light on some of the historical reasons for the confused 'cultural identity' of the Goan people as a whole. Prior to the arrival of the Portuguese, the Konkani language was primarily an oral one. No distinct philosophy, literary works, or grammar texts were available to give the language credence and attention. It had no script of its own and, thus, it was easier for the foreign rulers to suppress it. The first grammar texts in the Konkani language were written by the Portuguese missionaries in order to teach their religious doctrines to the natives and they wrote the language in the Roman script to facilitate their personal understanding of the language. Konkani was put into the Devnagiri script among the Hindu communities following Liberation, when it became recognised as a language distinct from Marathi. Even regarding Konkani as the language of Goa, in areas beyond the State's borders such as Karwar, Hubli and Belgaum, Konkani is the regional language. The language itself is amazingly resilient though it has suffered over the ages from neglect and repression. Further, it is not wholly valued by even those people who speak it and the language preferred in today's society is English. Prior to that, it was surpassed by Portuguese among Roman Catholics and Marathi among the Hindu community. As a result, 2nd generation Catholic migrants tend to loose their ability to speak Konkani.

Yet except in select cases, the majority of Goans find their own balance and by the second generation Bombay-born Goans feel at home in this large urban metropolis and less concerned about their Goan heritage and identity. They find community within the larger Catholic circles and maintain close relationships with Mangaloreans and east Indians alike. They also easily fraternise with the Hindu segments of society who form a part of their professional circle or socio-economic bracket.

Gowda Saraswat and Daiwadyna Brahmin Migration

'Goan' cultural identity, as it is known in the international community and among many people living in Goa, still means Indo-Portuguese, Roman Catholic and reminds one of fish-curry-rice. But if one is searching for a greater truth, or for that which seeks to examine several sides of an issue through new perspectives, the inclusion of migrated communities who claim they are 'from Goa' though not 'Goans', creates a more rounded portrayal of Goan communities. While they do not fall under the current and most widely accepted identification as "Goan", to ignore these groups in this study would result in a serious misrepresentation of the people of Goa and their historical migration. With a slight alteration in semantics but a wide cultural and religious divide, these communities are more popularly known as "Konkanies", who identify themselves as "*from* Goa."

Among Hindu-Indian circles, the Gowda Saraswat Brahmins are a well-known community whose beautiful, unique temples are well known in Goa. Each member of the GSB community possesses knowledge of his original roots and of the location of his Kuladevtas (family deities) in Goa. Pilgrimages to Goa are common and certain religious functions can only be performed in those temples. The GSBs form Goa have made a name for themselves in *every* city where many have migrated; from Cochin to Bombay. Whether because of the magnificent temples they have built, the banks and institutions they have founded, the research they have conducted or the cultural pride they have demonstrated, the Saraswat Brahmins have evolved a distinct cultural identity of their own which, while having its locus in Goa, still retains very close links with the Hindu-Indian community. Another community briefly mentioned below is the Gowd Daiwadnya Brahmin Samaj. They also migrated to Bombay and lived near both Saraswat and Catholic Goan communities; catering to their desire for gold. A consideration of these communities is not, therefore, out of the scope of this study, for the main impetus for this research was to resolve the question surrounding the identity paradox and come to terms with the Goan reality which is manifested in both Goa and Bombay.

This study is by no means exhaustive, however, I have taken the liberty to assume that some influences such as urbanisation and modernisation, which affect all communities in Bombay, will also affect the Goan Hindu Brahmins to some extent. In addition, they also followed similar migration patterns to Bombay during the same aforementioned periods and were affected by Portuguese policies, national Independence, World

War I & II and Goa's Independence. In addition to employment, an English education beyond the 10th standard enabled many to become successful in Bombay. Like Catholic Goans, the Goan Hindu Brahmins reformed separate communities in Bombay, first at Charni Road and most recently near the Shitra Devi temple in Mahim. These communities were likewise self-contained, exclusive communities which fostered the culture and identity of Gowda Saraswat Brahmins and established support services for individual community members. While they did not go through village clubs, several new migrants would move in with relatives already set up in Bombay. In those days five or six people would be living in a one-room flat until they first finished their education in English and then found work and saved enough money to buy their own flats. Residential dependence of new migrants on members of their own community is, thus, characteristic of many communities of early migrants from Goa.

One major difference, however, is that most of the Saraswat Brahmins who migrated were already educated and well-off, thus, they were able to quickly move up the economic ladder. That, combined with their schooling in Portuguese and familiarity with the Christian culture, enabled them to secure high posts within the British government as managers and administrators. In addition to education, another major difference between the Goan and Brahmin communities was that the Brahmins commanded much respect among the other communities, both Hindus and Christians alike. They blended well into the Bombay society in terms of their religion, culture and customs, while their high level of education endeared them to the British who were seeking educated locals to help manage their affairs. Though educated, 'enlightened' and fluent in many languages, the Hindu Brahmins always ensured the survival of their native tongue, whether Konkani or Marathi. In similar manner, though financially well-off, these Brahmins adhered to the customs and traditions of their forefathers, especially regarding marriage alliances, the pursuit of advanced degrees and cultural observances which begin prior to birth and continue even after one's demise.

Walking in the streets it might be difficult to differentiate between a Goan Hindu Brahman from any other highly educated member of the Hindu society in Bombay. Unlike Catholic Goans who had a different dress and different form of cultural expression owing to Portuguese influence, the Saraswat Brahmins blended smoothly into Bombay society while at the same time maintaining distinct communal ties and forming separate communities. Educated and highly skilled, this community has climbed its way to the top of the economic ladder and today's members surface as doctors and researchers in Tata Memorial Hospital; as goldsmiths in Chira Bazaar and as lawyers, chartered accountants, managers and engineers in most highly paid jobs in Bombay. The following brief outline documents the organisations founded by and for their communities as well as several case studies of individual migrants.

Community Organisation of the Saraswats

Founded in 1902 and registered as a public organisation in 1914, the Saraswat Vidyarthi Sahayak Mandali is one of several organisations founded during the first migration wave of Saraswats into Bombay. The founder of this organisation, a Marathi-speaking Saraswat by the name of Yashwan. H. Sukthankar, was a social worker who devoted his life and finances to the organisation. It was founded with the aim of providing educational scholarships to children whose parents were not financially sound. These are conditions based on merit and a student must have 50 per cent marks in order to be considered for one of the 350 awarded scholarships. As advertised in their newsletter, a student must make an application to the foundation and two of the current life members must certify that the financial records stated by the application are true to the best of their knowledge. Parents of a student do not have to belong to the organisation, but they must belong to the community of Saraswat Brahmins. The organisation enables three types of members: life members, fellows and patrons. A life member contributes Rs. 250, a fellow Rs. 500 and a patron Rs. 1,000 to the scholarship fund. Every year between 30 and 40 Saraswats become members of the association and all committee members work voluntarily. They are elected each year in September by the existing members and meet on approximately sixteen different occasions throughout the year in addition to an annual general body meetings.

Approximately 75 years ago, another organisation was established to cater to the needs of the growing Goan Hindu community in Bombay. Dr Amandokar, President of the *Goan Hindu Association,* comments on the impetus and evolution of this association: "Hindu Goans arriving in Bombay had one of two options. If they had friends and relatives willing to provide them with a place to stay, then four or five people would crowd into a one-room tenement. If not, then they put up 'challs', or illegal housing constructions and shacks, in which to find shelter. In either case, those early migrants who grew up remembering the adversity they faced upon first arrival decided to pool their money and purchase a building where other migrants could go for help and temporary shelter when they first arrived in Bombay. During the 1930's and 40's this building was utilised for this purpose. After the liberation of Goa in 1961, the migration rate substantially decreased as schools, industry and infrastructure were established in Goa under the new State government. Though the Goan Hindu Association still offers help to those few new migrants in need, the primary role of the institution has changed. It now functions primarily as a cultural institution known as the *Kalavi Bagh* which is designed to promote the talented young Goan Hindu actresses and actors in the performing arts and as an organisation which provides educational scholarships to needy students. Today's members number 1,500 and together they provide 2 lakh worth of educational financial aid to 150 deserving students from Goa and Bombay".

Another Saraswat social organisation in Bombay is the *Saraswat Brahman Samaj Marriage Bureau* located above the Saraswat Bank in Kotachi Wadi, Bombay. Open from 6:30 p.m. to 8 p.m. from Monday to Friday and 4:30 p.m. to 6 p.m. on Saturday, this organisation is run by volunteer members of the community who help match prospective bachelors and spinsters with members of their community dispersed around Bombay. In that same building, the *Saraswat Deen Vatsal Sangh* is an organisation devoted to helping widows with financial and social concerns. Other social organisations set up for Gowda Saraswat Brahmins are the Saraswat Hitvardhak Mandali in Matunga/ Mahim, Bombay and the G.S.B Seva Mandal in Prabhadevi.

Case Studies: Saraswat Brahmins in Bombay

In addition to several formal organisations, the Saraswat Brahmins created their own 'colonies' where only GSBs could live. The locations of these colonies have increased and changed over time; starting with Charni Road, then Goregao and most recently near the Shitradevi Temple on Jamshetji Road in Mahim. In the last one, about fifteen different apartment buildings are home to Gowda Saraswat Brahmins only and the following case studies are collected from members of the Goan Saraswat Brahmin who live in these and similar communities spread throughout Bombay.

Our first case study is that of Puja and her family, a 30-year-old, unmarried Gowda Saraswat Brahmin girl whose grandfather was the first family member to migrate to Bombay. Before coming to Bombay, he finished the 12th standard in Goa through the Portuguese medium in one of the Catholic schools. He was also able to become well-versed in English and, thus, secured a job in a British oil company (known through post-independence parlance as the Indian Oil Corporation). He settled first at Charni Road, which was at that time a large community composed entirely of Saraswat Brahmins. He married a girl from the GSB community and settled there, where his son was born. This son eventually married a Saraswat Brahmin from Maharashtra, whose ancestors had migrated north from Goa during the height of Portuguese missionary fanaticism. They settled along the north Konkan coast where they found a similar community already in existence whose native tongue was Marathi and formed a sub-set of the Saraswat Brahmins in Ratnagiri, Rajapur and Sawantwadi. Marathi, therefore, was the language spoken at home in Puja's family. After her father's marriage the family moved to Dadar and from there to Vile Parle. Both husband and wife worked in government offices and were given a flat and enough money to eventually buy their own. Today, this man of 68 says he is a Bombayite first and then a Maharashtrian, but he won't deny his ancestral roots in Goa. He is very proud of his identity as a Gowda Saraswat Brahmin and has passed on the knowledge of his cultural traditions to his descendants.

As for Puja, she completed the 12th standard at Vila Parle

College and then went on to receive a degree first in hotel management at Dadar College followed by a master's in mathematics and statistics from the University of Bombay. Desiring international exposure, she relocated to the United Kingdom and conducted research in economics from a British university. She remained there for three years as an employee of the University (in research) before continuing on to the USA for another three years. As a consequence of her international experiences, she feels like an 'atypical' Saraswat and a bit of a 'black sheep'. She feels that compared to other GSB women, she is more independent and has as a result many western friends who appreciate her broadened perspective.

Our second case study is a Mrs. Redkar whose family history in Bombay begins with her grandfather who was transferred there because of his job with Hindu Petroleum. They eventually settled in Goregao where her parents were born and raised. Mrs. Redkar and her two siblings were also born and raised in Goregao, Bombay and their kuladevtas are Mangueshi and Shantadurga in Goa. She received a B.A. in arts from Bhavans College in Andheri and then at age 25 married a Bombay-born GSB from Goa. Currently she is working for a research department of the Tata Memorial Hospital. She returns to Goa once every two or three years to perform religious rituals at the aforementioned temples and had she given birth to a son he would have undergone his thread ceremony at Mangueshi temple. She has two daughters. The temple she regularly visits in Bombay is Mahalakshmi and she currently lives in Chimburgh. Though her grandparents knew Konkani, her native tongue is Marathi and she is also fluent in English. Regarding culture, she is not a pure vegetarian and eats fish, chicken, mutton and eggs. Most Gowda Saraswat Brahmins that she knows are highly educated and have taken up a variety of professional occupations in chartered accounting, medicine, surgery and research.

Our third case study is of Dr. Gude who is actively involved in Cancer Research at the Tata Memorial Hospital in Bombay. His parents were born and raised in the village of Shiroda near Ponda and they maintain an ancestral home there as well. After the untimely death of both parents, Dr. Gude moved to Margao where he was raised by his relatives. There he studied in the Portuguese schools, became fluent in that language and was exposed to Portuguese culture and the Roman Catholic religion. Due to financial constraints he was compelled to finish his entire matriculation in Goa where he was also able to learn the English language to a relatively proficient level. After working in Margao for some years he migrated to Bombay in 1951. He settled first in Barnangar (near Girgao) and secured a job as a clerk with a British company. He married soon after in 1952 to a girl from the same GSB community from Aquem (near Margao) through a proposed marriage. She then migrated to Bombay and they rented a flat in Matunga in a neighbourhood heavily populated with GSB's. When their son Rajiv was born in 1954 Dr. Gude's wife returned to Goa as was customary during the birth of their first child. Later they shifted to Kar near the seashore, a place with fewer Saraswats but an attractive sea breeze. In 1964 the family shifted to Parel where they currently reside. Regarding his current profession, Dr. Gude graduated from St. Xavier's College in microbiology after which he received an MSc. from Seth G.S. Medical College and K.M. Hospital in Parel. For the last 17 years Dr. Gude has been involved in Cancer Research.

Regarding cultural trends among Saraswat Brahmins, he feels that those who were born in Goa and brought up in Bombay still follow the cultural traditions of their forefathers; but those who are fully Bombay-bred have begun to take such traditions all very casually. He knows Konkani well and remembers that Marathi was deemed a 'foreign' language in the 1960's and 70's during a call for separate statehood. During that time a hatred for Marathi was developed and people used to say 'speak English or Konkani'. Regarding education he commented that even before the 1950's , the GSB community educated their girls. Regarding Catholicism in Goa, Dr. Gude remarked that he was educated in Portuguese schools and likes the teachings of Catholicism. He sometimes visits the Navina church in Mahim on Wednesdays when people from all different faiths gather to hear the weekly sermon. He does not have any Catholic friends, because Catholics and Hindus live their lives in different social circles. On Goan character, Dr. Gude comments that a Goan of whatever religion is usually very God-fearing and very religious. They are good and honest than some other communities. Those educated and from good families are well-mannered and respectful of others.

The Daiwadyna Brahmins

In addition to the arrival of Gowda Saraswat Brahmins, other communities of Hindu Goans also migrated to Bombay during those early years. The Daiwadyna Brahmins, commonly known as the goldsmiths in Chira Bazaar, came to Bombay in order to set up gold shops and increase their business. Chira Bazaar, one of the oldest neighbourhoods in Bombay, is still home to many Daivadnya Brahmins who live in the inside lanes behind the central J.S. Road. Of late it has, like the other old neighbourhoods of Dhobi Talao and Dabul, become over-crowded, polluted and severely congested. The apartments buildings are very near to each other and the flats are very small and cramped.

When they first arrived, there were no institutions in place to help them and, thus, they relied on relatives and friends to take them in until they could find work and move out. During the first years the young boys came after completing an SSC in Goa around the ages of 17 and 18. They knew that the area in Chira Bazaar was home to many Saraswat Brahmins as well as Catholic Goans, thus, they followed similar lines and moved into the same area. As was custom, they continued in the business of their fathers, setting up their own shops in the near vicinity. During the early years education was not stressed and as gold is a prominent dowry gift of both Goan Hindu and Catholic communities, they prospered and established an entire street lined with gold shops. In addition to the gold trade, Bharat Petroleum offered many jobs to these Brahmins who were often managed by the Gowda Saraswats. However, after Indian Independence in 1950, the importance of education was recognised among members of the Daiwadnya Brahmin community. Subsequently, they began earning advanced degrees as engineers, accountants and lawyers; whereas in the olden days all the sons would follow in their father's profession. Now only one son will usually continue his father's trade. The Daivadnya Brahmins have surnames such as Verlekar, Anaokar, Bandodkar, Raikar, Chodankar, Lotlikar, Kalgutkar and Chonkar.

The Daiwadnya Brahmins, in the year 1920, began a social organisation aimed at the socio-economic improvement of the poorer sections of their community. The resulting Gomantak Daivadnya Brahman Samaj, offers scholarships to students demonstrating financial need and who have achieved at least 45 per cent marks. The student must be assessed by two committee members who can vouch for the financial situation of the family. The money from the scholarships comes from the interest on investment money donated by the community. In 1996 the organisation of 1,500 members celebrated its 75th anniversary at which time they honoured important and prominent men of the community. Membership in the association is around 15,000 and there are three types available depending on the amount donated by each family. The booklets and newsletters of the association are written in Marathi, which was the only written language in the educated Hindu community during the Portuguese era.

Mr. Lotliker is a member of the Daiwadyna community whose parents were goldsmiths in Margao, Goa. His uncle was one of the founding fathers of the aforementioned association and his family belongs to the highest class of membership. In order to expand their business they came to Bombay in 1930 and became part of the D.B. community located behind Chira Bazaar. When they arrived the Saraswats and Goan Catholics had already formed communities in the nearby vicinity. Mr. Lotliker's father and uncle started a gold business in Chira Bazaar and has since expanded to three shops in the current generation. With the money earned from their businesses they purchased properties in Bombay, kept their house in Goa and rented out their Bombay flats. Regarding languages, Konkani was spoken in the house but Marathi and English were also well known. Mr. Lotliker was born in 1927 and studied through an English medium until the 10th standard in the nearby St. Sebastian's Goan High School of Dabul. He took over his father's business, at that time the only option and had an arranged marriage. From that marriage he had three sons, two of which are now living in Australia after completing advanced degrees and the third who has remained in Bombay to continue the family business. This young Mr. Lotliker has his own shop next door to his father's and has recently married a girl from the same Daiwadnya community. Previously, they had a gold factory and employed workers from Goa to craft gold, but of late they are hiring Bengali employees (cheaper labour) who work within their own homes.

Regarding their cultural identity, the G.D. Brahmins are part of the larger Hindu social system and have undertaken various life-cycle rituals required of Brahmins such as the thread ceremony. Their special temple is Ramnathi in Ponda, which was in existence in Goa prior to Portuguese rule. During the Zatra in April many families in Bombay will go and watch as the temple deity is carried in procession around the temple complex in an ornate palki. In 1950 Mr. Lotliker went to Goa to perform his thread ceremony, when he gifted a Rs. 80,000 crown bedecked in jewels to be worn by the God during this April event. Though the temple can be visited by any community, only the GDB's are allowed to stay within the temple complex.

Thus, the Goan Hindu Brahmans also migrated to Bombay during the early 1900's and have since made substantial contributions to the socio-economic development of Bombay. Other Goan communities such as the Nabhiks (Saloon owners), the Korlis (fishermen) and the Dhangars (herdsmen) also came to Bombay, though tracking them is difficult owing to their dispersion throughout Bombay and their less-prominence among communities in Bombay. Also, the Goan Hindu Brahmins do not identify themselves as 'Goans' at first, though they readily admit that they are 'from Goa' and have cultural traditions connected to their motherland. This is owing to the promotion of a particular representation of 'Goan cultural identity' and especially to the 'Goan' Catholic communities in Bombay which identified themselves as 'Goans' first and foremost. The word 'Goan' became synonymous with the culture and identity as determined by the Catholic community, to the cultural exclusion of the Goan Hindus who distinguished themselves from their Catholic brethren and, thus, retained the term 'Konkanies'. Thus, even in Bombay, the term 'Goan' referred to only one particular community in Goa and not to the multicultured society which existed in the land of Gomantak.

Dabul: An Original Goan Neighbourhood

Dabul, near Grant Road and Chira Bazaar, is another neighbourhood which became synonymous with the word 'Goan' during the late 1800's and early 1900's. Like Dhobi Talao, this neighbourhood also had its share of street dances, Christmas carols, Carnival revelry and community spirit. Ninety-five per cent of the residents were Goan Catholics and each building sponsored a Christmas party. Those still around to create nostalgia for past times remember the strong sense of community that Goans expressed and call Dabul an 'urbanised Goa'. Some buildings were reserved only for Goans, who crowded 6-8 people into one-room flats. The Rele building was one such building, as was the Goan Society Building and the Michael House is located a few streets away. All the children grew up together and came from similar middle to lower-middle income families. Though most have moved out to the suburbs to more spacious flats, they still keep in touch and the old families return on the Feast day of December 3rd. At Christmas time the families which have moved out often return to Dabul to visit old friends and neighbours. Though the street parties have gone, those Goans who remained still lit up Christmas lights and 3-foot wide stars of Bethlehem in the streets.

As Goans flocked to Bombay in search of employment, they began to settle in this neighbourhood and devise plans for the construction of a church which would satisfy the spiritual needs of the community. Dedicated to St. Xavier, the patron saint of Goa and one popular with those in the tailoring profession, the foundation stone was laid on December 4, 1870. The original Dabul church, dedicated first to Our Lady of Happy Voyage, was consecrated on May 12th, 1872. It was renamed to honour St. Francis Xavier in 1886. However, only about 300 parishioners could congregate in this small church, so adjacent land was purchased with the aim of expanding the existing structure. The two properties were divided by a small lane, which the municipality refused to sell, leading to the erection of an entirely separate church no less than a meter away. The foundation stone was laid on June 21st, 1891 and it was consecrated on June 7th, 1896. Eventually in 1934, the 3-foot stretch of land was purchased and it was decided to join the two churches. On the feast day of December 3rd, 1937, this new, combined church was blessed and on November 28th, 1964 it was consecrated.

In addition to St. Xavier's Church, a school dedicated to St. Sebastian was built by and for the Goan community. From the 1st to the 10th standard, Goans could receive their education within blocks from their homes under the guidance of Goan priests. The Goan Institute on St. Francis Xavier street is a still-operating members-only social organisation established by the community. Located on the 2nd floor, this spacious room functions as a library/reading room, game room and social/ dance hall which can be rented by members upon request. During the early years it attracted large crowds, but of late those frequenting the club are the remaining Goan residents of Dabul. It is well kept up and during the early evening a few Goans can be found reading newspapers and playing carom. The Michael House is another building reserved primarily for Goans. Situated a few blocks distance from St. Xavier's, Dabul, the building even today has a majority of Goans in addition to the Aldona Village Club for Men.

Case Studies: Dabul

The members of Martis family was one of the original residential families of Rele building. Their father arrived in Bombay in 1930 with his family, when he was just 17. Two of his children still live there today in a one-room and kitchen flat on the 2nd floor. His daughter, born in Bombay, works as a school teacher close by in St. Sebastian's. His son married a Goan girl from Dhobi Talao and they have one daughter. After studying Economics at St. Xavier's College, he then worked in Dubai for five years in an office. He returned to Bombay in 1984 to join a pharmaceutical firm owned by a Goan and is currently employed by him.

The members of Pereira family of the Michael House are 1st generation Bombayites whose grandparents were from Siolim, North Goa. On the husband's side, his father was born in Goa and received his education in a Portuguese medium, but then came to Bombay in search of employment. He spoke fluent Portuguese and was able to find work in the Bombay Yacht Club. He had five sons, the youngest of whom, Francis, is the object of our investigations. He lived in Siolim with his mother and helped to increase the family income. The youngest of five brothers, he was 35 when he got married. After his marriage they moved to Bombay and rented the flat in which they still live today. When they first moved in, all the residents of Michael House were Goans, including the owner. His wife, Maria, was born in Mapusa and came to Bombay with her husband when she was 21 years of age. She found a sense of community in the Michael House and remembers how the other Goan women befriended her because she was new to the area. At that time three Goan clubs were in the building and the men from the families would fraternise freely with them (the women did not as was the social custom). Maria has Goan friends and readily admits that it is Goa where her heart is. They have 3 sons and 2 daughters, so when school closes in April/May they spend vacation in their homeland. At home she still prepares fish-curry-rice and enjoys the fresh produce easily available in Goa.

Among their two sons and two daughters, all were educated at St. Sebastian's in Dabul. One son has married a Goan girl from Siolim who has come to live with his parents in Bombay while he worked as a customs officer in Saudi Arabia. The eldest son is recently married and works as a hotel manager in Kuta. He and his wife are also staying with his parents in the one-room flat while they await the purchase of a separate apartment. Their eldest daughter graduated from Sophia College (an all-women's college near Grant Road) and currently works as a secretary. Their youngest daughter has an SSC from St. Anne's.

When asked about the types of activities still organised by the community, Maria says that the youth sometimes organise Christmas and New Year's dances in a rented hall. Regarding Carnival, she said that Goans born in Bombay do not know what Carnival is all about and, thus, they do not have motivation to organise anything. Members of St. Xavier's Church, Dabul, said that the Feast Day draws a large crowd and many Goans come, some appearing for the first time after many years.

Kotachi Wadi

In addition to Dabul and Dhobi Talao, Kotachi Wadi (Girgaum) also hosted a small Goan community during the early and mid-1900's. Only a block away on a now busy street corner of Girgaum, lies St. Theresa's Church, better known as the Portuguese church owing to its origins which date back to that period. Declared a world heritage site (and, therefore, a no-development zone), the small neighbourhood of Kotachi Wadi, with its narrow, winding lanes and ancient houses seems completely out of place amidst a major commercial district of Bombay. Yet tucked away down a narrow lane, the noise and commotion of the city which has grown up around Kotachi Wadi disappears steadily and for a moment one imagines he is in Goa. Judging from the nearby presence of a ancient Portuguese church and the large east Indian population, this neighbourhood was one of the most ancient ones in Bombay and has, since the Portuguese era in 1534, been inhabited by Christian communities.

The history of this community during the 1900's closely resembles that of other Goan neighbourhoods in Bombay with a few minor differences. Like other Goan neighbourhoods during that era, children would sing Christmas carols door to door, houses would be decorated, street parties would run late into the nights and the Catholic Club would sponsor a dance. However, both east Indians and Catholics lived side-by-side here during the 1960's and 70's, a time when friendly childhood teasing gave Goans the nickname "Pao-walas" and east Indians 'milkman'. A Catholic social club was also created in the late 1800's and during the evenings young men would gather for billiards, song and merry making. Most of the Goans have migrated to the suburbs now, however, the club largely remains closed.

One house on this small, winding lane is the oldest house in the neighbourhood and dates back more than 350 years to the Portuguese era. A typical early Goan house, this yellow mud walled, tiled-roof abode is a living memory of the times when Bombay was merely a small fishing hamlet full of coconut trees. Today the house has sunken almost a foot into the ground and the walls are buckling after centuries of support.

The first case study traces the history of the Ferrao family, Goan migrants in Bombay, who have lived in this ancient house for generations. Their grandfather was born in Chandor and came to Bombay through the village club of Chandor looking for better employment. He became a tailor and according to family legend he was a Goan from the old school who 'enjoyed his wine, women and song'. He bought this house, settled in

Bombay with his wife and they had seven children. Due to the family economy, they were not able to maintain a heritage home in Goa and, thus, in subsequent generations the family frequented their native place less and less. Among the current generation of three, two brothers are living in the house of their ancestors and were available for interviews. The eldest son married a Hindu girl which was approved only after several years elapsed. He works as a clerk in a Bombay office and their two children are being raised under the Catholic religion, even though his wife has decided to continue in the practice of her own faith. The youngest son is unmarried and is currently trying to secure a job overseas on a ship. Previously he worked in the Taj Mahal hotel with several other 'Catholic boys', all of whom would go to Goa for a holiday. His knowledge of Konkani has deteriorated because English was the language spoken at home and it is through this that they were educated. They also know Marathi because many of his childhood friends spoke their native tongue. Only when he was 17/18 he was forced to learn the Konkani language. When asked about his affinity for Goa, he said that because he was born and brought up only in Bombay, his nature is cosmopolitan and urbanised. Though he enjoys vacationing in Goa, after two weeks he feels ready to return to the active, hectic Bombay lifestyle rather than remain in Goa. When asked about the Goan culture, he offers the typical 'outsider' stereotype of Goans as 'calm, happy-go-lucky, sociable and prone to drinking'.

Our second case study is that of a young Mr. Fernandes whose grandparents migrated from Goa to Kotachi Wadi. They bought this same property where Mr. Fernande's father and then he himself, were born and raised. Though his father was a Bombay customs' officer, he always wanted to work on board a ship and consequently in 1990 he began work on a Mobil Oil Rig. Prior to that, he studied in St. Mary's School till the 10th standard and St. Xavier's College for an additional two years before securing employment. Mr Fernandes who is still unmarried and lives with his father who is in ill health and suffers from memory loss. He does not visit Goa often and his relatives are spread around in various parts of India. When questioned about Goan culture, Mr Fernandes believes that 'Catholic life is somehow different' and India tends to be more conservative. He feels the Western media and television have had the greatest influences on youth culture in India because what they watch on T.V. is what they want to emulate.

Our third case study regards the family which owns and operates the Anatashram Restaurant across the lane from the Ferrao house. The father migrated to Bombay from Camorlim in the 1920's and first opened a printing press in that same building. In 1932 he started a restaurant where all five of his sons worked in the family business. Serving typical Goan Hindu cuisine, the restaurant prospered under the main chef from Ratnagiri who has been working in Anatashram for over 40 years. The restaurant features food from the southern Konkan coast but does not have any Portuguese dishes such as sorpotel and vindaloo. Of the five brothers, one has moved out to start his own transport business. The others, none of whom received an education beyond the 8th standard, continue to run the family business with no plans for expansion. Business is prosperous, long cues are typical on Wednesdays and Fridays and tourists come from afar to taste their unique cuisine. Though labelled as 'Goan' cuisine, the curries and fish preparations differ from those available in Goa and can be said to originate along the Konkan coast, including the district of Sawantwadi.

Conclusion

In this chapter, the history and life stories of Goan migrants in Bombay were studied to determine the effects of urbanisation, physical separation, community reformation and Bombay's social environment on the cultural evolution and identity of Goans. When Goans first began arriving during the early 1900's, they came looking for better employment from that which was available in Goa. The initial impetus for the clubs began as young men from the village arrived together and rented a communal flat. The area where they settled in Dhobi Talao was, at that time, distant from the city centre and flat rates were cheap. Those arriving were usually the lesser-educated Goans who took up jobs as cooks, waiters and other service jobs. At first there were few rules in the clubs and the men enjoyed freedom from the constraints placed on them by village society. At this time, the British were still ruling India and the Christian religion was a strong source of pride for Goans in Bombay. They could identify with the ruling class and had adopted similar dress codes as well. Consequently, Dhobi Talao evolved into a mini-Goa were Christian culture was lavishly celebrated with dances and street parties. Men who had migrated to Bombay now settled down with their families and Konkani became the lingua franca on the neighbourhood streets. Goan restaurants run by Goans sprang up, as well as shops selling Goan newspapers and trinkets. Our Lady of Dolours, built during the time of the Portuguese era in Goa, was the church of this community and Goan identity became further associated with Catholic, Christmas, Carnival and Curry. This was a clear example of community reformation and strong identification with and pride in Goan cultural identity. This was in large part owing to the culture of Bombay, which under the British occupation accepted and even supported the Christian communities, preferring them as employees and as companions. The British would frequent their cultural celebrations which were welcomed in such a distant land. In fact many Anglo-Indians were products of these close alliances with Goans which often ended in marriage.

In addition to Dhobi Talao, other Goan communities in Bombay also arose during these early years. One such community, Kotachi Wadi (Girgaum), has a history which follows the same pattern. Built in the near proximity of a Catholic Church of the Portuguese era, both east Indians and Goan Catholics lived side by side here during the 1960's and 70's. A Catholic club was created and during the evenings young men would gather for billiards, song and merry making. Now most of the Goans have left, taking with them their Christmas parties and community character. Today the few blocks known as Kotachi Wadi have been declared a World Heritage Site and are a popular tourist destination in Bombay.

Dabul, the area in the vicinity of St. Xavier's Church, was also home to a large Goan community which arose during the 1920's and 30's. Strong communal ties existed here as well, to such an extent that a new church was constructed and a separate St. Sebastian's Goan High School was established by and for members of the Goan community. In 1930 the Rele building was established adjacent to the church and was home to Goans only. The Martis family were the first residents and recounted how each building would host a Christmas party and on Christmas eve a street party was held following midnight mass which brought together Goans from all the surrounding buildings such as the Goan Society Building and the Michael House. Though the Michael House has retained its "Goans only" identity, the other buildings have witnessed a gradual exodus of these families from their tiny one-room flats to more spacious accommodations in the suburbs.

For those who moved out during the 1960's and 70's, Bandra was the premier place for the Goans to settle down. Land prices were very cheap, the Portuguese had previously established several churches there, the British had had their residential homes there and green parks were in abundance. Those who bought their flats were able to continue living there once prices soared, but those who were not as financially sound or farsighted had to move farther from the centre of town into more remote suburbs. Orlem, Malad, is one such community were Goans have tended to migrate. The result of this migration are 'pockets' of Catholic communities scattered throughout the Bombay suburbs, arising wherever churches are located. These communities, however, are much smaller and more interwoven with Catholics from other backgrounds. Mangaloreans, east Indians and Goans tend to settle in the same areas of town, merging into a larger, more loosely defined culture based on religion and economics. Nowhere in Bombay has another Dhobi Talao or Dabul emerged, and most Goan migrants from previous generations are content to join the rat-race that describes the middle-class Bombay lifestyle. They are still proud to be Goan, but the daily routine of activity in order to make ends meet has taken priority over what are for some, ancient roots.

In addition to those communities known commonly as 'Goan', several other communities with a personal history connected to Goa have migrated to Bombay. Though left out of Goan 'cultural identity' as such, the Gowda Saraswat and Daiwadnya (goldsmith) Brahmins have also resettled and re-established communities in Bombay. Whereas the middle and low-middle income Catholic Goans arrived with few skills, the GSBs arrived with prior education and the Daiwadnya Brahmins arrived as skilled craftsmen. Both groups demonstrate successful community reformation and integration within urban India and have risen through the socio-economic rank in Bombay to emerge as highly educated and skilled members of Bombay society.

The ability of those early migrants to succeed in Bombay was owing to several factors. Returning to a case study, at one point during his career Father Pereira acted as the priest in Our Lady of Dolours in Dhobi Talao. Having interacted with and counselled various families, he points to education and individual mentality as the key factors which determined whether or not a Goan became successful in Bombay. Those who experienced difficulty were usually uneducated Catholics who spoke only Konkani and did not mix around with other people. While for those who were educated, the 'sky was the limit' in Bombay, those without proper education found it difficult to climb up the socio-economic ladder. Those who have to live in the clubs were considered 2nd class citizens and held an inferiority complex because they could not afford 'proper' housing. Some became 'stuck' in Dhobi Talao as cooks and servants while the ladies took up boot-legging liquor.[68]

Of all the influences pervading the Bombay society, four have had the greatest impact on Goan culture is urbanisation, modernisation, the presence of other Christian communities and the current state of political affairs. As regards urbanization, the city of Bombay has grown tremendously and Goan communities became congested and overpriced. Children of migrants were born and raised in an urban environment and began to identify with urban life. Some of the effects of urbanisation are an increase in competitiveness, greater interaction and knowledge of other cultures and communities, a sense of anonymity, stress owing to the fast pace of city life, materialism and consumerism, perception of success determined by financial status and an identity increasingly defined by cosmopolitan, urban and modern cultural forms. As a consequence, the sense of community feeling has left these neighbourhoods and people have internalised these urban forces which are stronger and pervading their everyday environment.

For many second generation Goans in Bombay, a feeling of rootlessness, of belonging neither here nor there, has arisen. Their culture is still connected with that of their Goan-born parents, yet they themselves have been raised in a huge urban metropolis. As a consequence, they often feel 'foreign' in Goa when they are influenced by a language which they cannot speak fluently. In addition, the rhythm of life and social relations in a large city like Bombay are quite different from those of a small village. In Bombay, a person is just one of the masses vying for a seat on the crowded trains. A sense of anonymity and certain social freedom has become second-nature to a Bombay-born Goan, who may find the semantics, gossip and politics of a small village unhealthy interference on private matters. Likewise, the rhythm of life is slower in Goa compared to Bombay. After a few weeks boredom sets in and they long for the faster pace available in a big city.

An offshoot of urbanisation is the growing influence of modernisation. Finding its greatest receptivity among the working middle-class and the youth culture, it is effecting all communities, Hindus and Christians alike. Through television, radio, movies and advertisements that accost the viewer everywhere, global media forms based on predominantly western culture and values have penetrated into many corners of urban society. The desire to be modern and materialistic have been internalised by many and the race for portable phones, modern electronics and spacious apartments is on. Urbanisation has also contributed to the breaking down of some caste and communal barriers (except in the avenue of marriage). Rather, what is beginning to develop is a 'caste of economy' whereby success in life and sources of pride stem from education, occupation and consequently financial position. Among the younger generation in Bombay there are also new avenues opening for social interaction copied from western social spaces like bars, discos and eateries. These spaces are currently open mostly to the elite, internationally travelled class, but the trend is strong and similar places will most likely open to attract an educated, self-made crowd who also want to participate in this 'modern' social culture. This influence has also broken down religious barriers among youth as they all absorb the same ideas, fashions and behaviours from media images. The fluency in a similar language (English) as well as similarities in dress, musical tastes and social functions may also help in breaking down communal barriers and developing greater understanding between a variety of communities.

Regarding the third major influence, when Goan migrants arrived in Bombay they soon learned that another community of Roman Catholics, (the east Indians), already resided in Bombay. Coming primarily from poorer fishing communities, they were considered low caste among Bombay society and, thus, evoked a sense of shame Goans. Whereas initially the Goan community made great efforts to distinguish itself as different and superior to East Indians, in today's society they share the same churches and attend many of the same religious functions. Whereas before uniquely Goan neighbourhoods existed, now in the suburbs one finds 'pockets' of Catholics who are from a mixed background, depending on financial resources. The addition of the Mangaloreans added another community and soon a much debated hierarchy was established among them.

The fourth most important societal influence which has shaped the expression of Goan cultural identity and contributed to its decline is the pro-Hindu attitude adopted by the government following Independence. Once the British left India, Goans no longer identified themselves with the party in power and successive governments have been increasingly nationalistic regarding the minority communities. Similarly, the "be an Indian first" attitude coupled with the pervasive attitude among the 'mass' mentality that minority communities are foreign to Indian soil, has given rise to a new sense of shame regarding a personal history connected to Goa. As a consequence, some Goans have given their children Hindu names in an attempt to identify with the larger Indian community. Some have chosen to wear saris and churidas in addition to and in place of traditional Goan-style dresses. In extreme situations, some Goans choose to basically deny their roots altogether, claiming themselves true Bombayite and cosmopolitan in character.

REFERENCES

1. *From a legal standpoint, in order for a Goan living in Mumbai to be considered a "Goan", a birth certificate must be brought to Goa and the child registered there to ensure property rights. This holds true not only for Goans in Bombay but for Goans migrated to foreign countries. Under the current laws put in place during the Portuguese era, both men and women have equal property rights.

   The information from the case studies was collected in January of 1997 as part of my Fulbright Thesis.

2. Da Cunha, J. Gerson, *Origin of Bombay*, New Delhi: Asian Educational Services, 1992, 1st Pub. 1900, (Ch. 1).
3. *Ibid.*, p. 34.
4. *Ibid.*, p. 35, footnote includes the preceding historical references.
5. *Ibid.*, p. 37. The Kolis were later integrated into the Vedic system.
6. *Ibid.*, p. 37.
7. *Ibid.*, pp. 38-40. Includes the preceding paragraph.
8. *Ibid.*, pp. 68-90. Includes the preceding paragraph.
9. *Ibid.*, pp. 95-100.
10. *Ibid.*, p. 130.
11. *Ibid.*, p. 131.
12. *Ibid.*, pp. 155-57. Includes preceding paragraph.
13. From my research study I would like to add that this same dialect appears to be the one spoken in Bassein and Daman, the latter among the tribals which language is today known as Konkana (See p. 1 of Daman case-study).
14. Da Cunha, *op. cit.*, p. 163.
15. *Ibid.*, p. 135. Includes preceding paragraph.
16. *Ibid.*, p. 137.
17. *Ibid.*, p. 61. *This quotation is in contrast to other records which indicate that the Portuguese treated the Saraswat Brahmins poorly. Research reveals, to the contrary, that the Saraswat Brahmins in all of the Portuguese colonies enjoyed respectable positions in society and found employment in the Portuguese administration. (See Bassein and Cochin case studies.)
18. *Ibid.*, pp. 140-50.
19. *Ibid.*, pp. 150-55. Includes preceding paragraph.
20. *Ibid.*, pp. 155-60.
21. *Ibid.*, p. 185.
22. *Ibid.*
23. *Ibid.*, p. 184.
24. *Ibid.*, p. 186.
25. *Ibid.*, p. 235.
26. *Ibid.*, p. 260.
27. *Ibid.*, p. 186.
28. *Ibid.*, p. 268.
29. *Ibid.*, p. 269.
30. *Ibid.*, pp. 270-75. Includes preceding paragraph.
31. *Ibid.*, pp. 273-75. Includes preceding paragraph.
32. *Ibid.*, p. 278.
33. *Ibid.*, pp. 280-85. Includes preceding sentences.
34. *Ibid.*, pp. 280-90. Includes preceding paragraph.
35. *Ibid.*, p. 323.

36. Da Cunha, *op. cit.*, pp. 324-26.
37. *Ibid.*, pp. 315-20. Includes subsequent sentences.
38. *Ibid.*, p. 320.
39. *Ibid.*, p. 324.
40. *Ibid.*, pp. 330-50. Preceding paragraph included in the notation.
41. *Ibid.*, p. 280.
42. *As long as their signs were kept to a certain size, they did not even have to register as clubs and thus, avoided all the red tape and formalities which such organisations would usually require.
43. *Information for this and subsequent case studies in Bombay was collected in January of 1997.
44. *Few women migrated from Goa in the early days and thus the club was designed for men only, or for men with their families under special circumstances. In the latter case the family occupied a special room set apart from the main hall and only the largest clubs had such facilities.
45. *Mr. Fernandez remembers that at the time of Goan liberation , the Catholic Goans were either apathetic or concerned while the Hindu community was happy.
46. *Outside the club in the narrow flanking lane hung a tattered white paper-mache star of Bethlehem with Merry Christmas and Happy New Year messages written across its front. Otherwise this club is virtually indistinguishable from the surrounding buildings as it was a single room located on the 2nd floor.
47. *The majority of Mangaloreans tended to migrate to Bangalore during the late 1800's and early 1900's. Bombay was a two-day journey by bus or other vehicle whereas the early city of Bangalore was within a half-day's journey from their place of origin.
48. *This church is over 450-year-old and was probably instrumental in attracting the first migrant to the neighbourhood of Dhobi Talao. It was built by the Portuguese in the washermen's ward where the Portuguese had exerted effort towards the conversion of the low-caste communities.
49. "Shippie" was a derogatory term used to describe an uneducated young man making money by working for foreign shipping companies.
50. *His shop gained a good reputation and in 1930 Mr. Dias stitched a suit for the Governor of Goa without even taking measurements. It fit exquisitely and he was given a gold medal and certificate of appreciation.
51. *In the case of women.
52. *Information collected in an informal interview with 3 members of the Dias family.
53. Da Cunha, Gerson J. *op. cit.*, pp. 135-40. Includes preceding paragraph.
54. *Ibid.*, pp. 135-40.
55. *Ibid.*, p. 141.
56. Jungblut, Fr. Leon J., *Our Lady of the Mount*, Bombay: Institute on Indian Culture., p. 2.
57. Jungblut, Fr. Leon J., *op. cit.*, p. 3.

58. *Ibid.*, p. 5.
59. *Ibid.*, p. 7.
60. *Ibid.*, p. 15.
61. Da Cunha, *op. cit.*, p. 135.
62. *This occupation also gave rise to the term 'east Indian' to describe the Catholic Indians living in Bombay. It has become generalised of late to apply to all of the communities in Bombay and outlying surrounds (Bassein, Thana, Gorai etc.) which follow the Catholic faith.
63. *'Pakka' here is used to mean complete, full, etc.
64. *Percentage determined through the church registrar.
65. *From a legal standpoint, in order for a Goan living in Mumbai to be considered a "Goan", a birth certificate must be brought to Goa and the child registered there to ensure property rights. This holds true not only for Goans in Bombay but for Goans migrated to foreign countries. Under the current laws put in place during the Portuguese era, both men and women have equal property rights.
66. *In these cases, marriages between Catholic boys and Hindu girls are usually quite successful. The girls are happy with greater freedom and the boys are content with the increase attention they are given. However, in the opposite case, when a Catholic girl marries a Hindu boy, 80 per cent of these marriages fail. The girls often become outcaste in the Catholic community and are considered to be either 'uneducated', 'backwards', 'very poor', or 'married to the first man that loves them'. But unfortunately in many cases the couple cannot adjust to the culture and expectations of the other and the boys leave. The girls take up work as cooks, servants, or labourers.
67. The authenticity of this history is a bit sketchy concerning the property matters.
68. The children of these families suffered and the boys often end up as wayward youth. Fr. Pereira also comments that it takes about two to three generations for a poor, illiterate family to become educated. Trends in Dhobi Talao demonstrated that if a mother was totally illiterate than her daughter generally studied up until the 4th standard. The latter's daughter will study until the 8th standard and so on. This is owing to the mothers neither understanding nor instilling the value of education in their children.

Chapter 8

Goan Migration to South: A New Mangalorean Identity and Southern Migration of the Konkanies: GSB's and Kunbis in Bangalore

During the previous chapter we discovered that in Bombay the Goan Catholic migrants and Hindu Brahmans successfully recreated several self-contained, culturally-conscious communities. While such patterns of migration were characteristic of most Saraswat Brahmin communities spread throughout India, such neighbourhoods were the exception and not the rule for the Catholic Goan migrants. Not all of the communities which migrated away from Goa have retained their cultural identity. For instance, while the GSBs have been able to maintain links with their ancient origins, linguistic developments and migration patterns, the Goan Catholic communities have not fostered as extensive an involvement from members of their own community. For example, for those Goans who migrated to Mangalore, the Catholic community existing there today hardly even recognises their roots in Goa. Accordingly, when asked where they are from, 'Mangalore' is the unanimous response. It would seem, therefore, that at some point in time this former Goan community underwent the process of reidentification as 'Mangalorean', with the result that their original roots in Goa have been wiped out from the collective memory of this community.

A migrant's distance from his place of origin following migration is often responsible for the weakened bonds and lessened ties between a migrant's traditional culture and identity and that which evolves following migration to a new location. However, Mangalore is less than nine hours by bus from the centre of Goa and a journey facilitated by a continuous stream of traffic between the two regions. Likewise, the Gowda Saraswat Brahmins in Mangalore have their family deities located in Goa and make frequent trips to and from the area. Thus, the distance is not the reason why the Goan Catholic identity of Mangaloreans has disappeared without a trace.

Fear of persecution in Goa might also have been the reason why Goan migrants changed their identity, but the Inquisition reached all the outposts along the Western Coast and attacked especially the Syrian Catholics in Kerala. Migrants also continued to practise the Catholic religion, which is seemingly odd if they were running from the Inquisition in Goa. Thus, the persecution and Portuguese policies do not explain why the Goan Catholic migrants altered their identity to take on the self-label of Mangalore.

Had politics of later years during the agitation for Indian independence helped to contribute to the reidentification of former Goan Catholics now migrated and settled in Mangalore? Might they have wished to distinguish themselves from their Goan neighbours still under the sway of the Portuguese rule and also to participate in the wave of national sentiment prevailing over the people in Mangalore? Yet in such a fever, they probably would have become concerned with the plight of Goans still under the Portuguese rule if they had held a recent identification with them, as did the Bombay-Goans. Thus, a recent switch from identification with Goa to one with Mangalore would still remain in the collective consciousness of the community and their origins in Goa would still be traceable if the re-identification process had occurred within the 20th century.

Mangaloreans, however, have been living in and identifying with Mangalore for several centuries and have lost their historical contact and knowledge of their Goan ancestry. As far as most Mangaloreans understand their forefathers have always lived in Mangalore. Thus, the Goan Catholic migration to Mangalore must have been ancient, voluntary and permanent. Once again, as in the previous case studies, this research now turns to the past in order to explain the current cultural identity of the Catholic 'Mangaloreans'.

In the following case-study, the example of Goan migration to Mangalore is explored in an attempt to understand the process though which cultural identity is maintained and that through which it becomes lost. Migration of Goans to Mangalore is an interesting study because in this one of the two major communities originating in Goa has since erased its association with Goa and somehow wiped that portion of history from the collective memory of the community. Today their perception of a separate identity from that of Goans is very strong and their pride in being 'Mangalorean' dominates their concept of cultural identity. This chapter examines the historical events leading to the migration of these ancient Goans to Mangalore and the resulting conditions within which their culture evolved into an identity which they profess is separate from that of Goa, their ancient home.

Mangalore: A Brief Historical Outline

Karnataka, for most of its history, was not a single integrated State politically nor geographically. Geographically the State is divided by the Western Ghats which result in dry upland areas on the eastern side and a humid, tropical climate on the Western Coast. The Kaveri, Tungabhadra and Krishna rivers flow form the Ghats across the Karnatakan plateau to the Arabian Sea. Agriculture from time, immemorial has been the chief source of income for the regions inhabitants. Fifty per cent of the State is cultivated and a majority of the people are employed in agriculture.[1] Karnataka has 320 kilometres of coastline, bordered on the north with Goa, the east with Andhrah Pradesh and the south and south-west with Kerala and Tamil Nadu. Kannada is the primary language of the people, though Konkani is spoken by many on the coast and especially in Mangalore and its surroundings. Three per cent of Karnataka's current population is Christian.

Today's capital of Karnataka is Bangalore and Mangalore

is one of her largest port cities. Modern Mangalore is a well known coastal port-city of Karnataka with a rich history. Situated on the mouth of the Netravati River, Mangalore is an ideal port because it not only is suitable for water transport to more inland areas, but also the flow of the river creates very fertile land between Banataval and Mangalore. The city is visited by both south-west and south-east monsoons and shielded by the Ghats rising in the east; all of which provide Mangalore with a constant source of rain and consequently forest wealth and fertile land.

The Monds were the earliest known rulers of the Karnataka region, followed by the Maurya's in 300 B.C. Ashoka, the Gangas (200-1000 A.D.) and the Vijayanagar Empire (1300's -1500's) were a series of Hindu dynasties which ruled over the region of Karnataka.[2] In 1763, Hyder Ali followed by his son Tippu Sultan conquered the Karnataka region, but were eventually defeated by the British in 1799. Finally, following a series of Satyagrahis and the awakening of the people, Karnataka gained independence in 1947 along with the rest of India. In 1956 the linguistic areas were brought together into a single State named Mysore and on November 1, 1973 the State was renamed as Karnataka.

As early as 600 A.D. the economic life of Mangalore's people revolved around income gained from agricultural products and their sale both locally and overseas.[3] Land was owned by both royalty and private citizens and most communities participated in the cultivation of agriculture. The right of cultivating royal lands was held by those officials serving the King and rulers often donated lands to religious institutions, learned Brahmins and persons who rendered valuable service to the State. Both high and low cast Hindus were involved in the cultivation of rice paddy, grains, areca nut, coconut and pepper; the former as land-owners and the latter as labourers. These crops were, thus, main sources of revenue for the kingdom. Land in the villages belonged to the State and was managed by agricultural groups within the locality. Joint ownership of land known as 'Genikara' was held by associations or communities and was the prevailing system of land tenure in which tenants had part ownership of the lands and some basic rights.[4] Tenants of private landlords laboured on the land in exchange for the right of temporary residence and cultivation much like the traditional share-croppers of western Europe. The majority of their produce was given to the landlord and the rest was allotted to the family for their provisions.

In 1000 A.D., Mangalore was a prominent sea port and trading centre monopolised by the Arab Muslims who had a monopoly of the entire sea trade on the Western Coast.

During the mid-1300's the Vijayanagar rule commenced in the region of western Karnataka and eventually the whole of the Karnatakan coastal region, including the southern half of Goa fell under their administration. The Vijayanagar governors of 'Mangaluru' (modern-day Mangalore) encouraged the Brahmin communities to settle in their domains by offering them villages and lands.[5] Eventually they became the rightful owners of the lands given to them in such grants and a large land-owning class evolved in Mangalore and its surroundings. During these same years, the taxation policy of Vijayanagar rulers further enabled the Brahmans, Jains and high-caste Sudras (Gowdas, Nayaks, and Bunts) to become powerful landed gentry.[6] The revenue administration was also managed by Brahmins and through some manipulations they acquired additional land rights.

Most of the agrarian commodities produced within Mangalore were sold at the ports or carried overland to distant kingdoms by caravan with the aim to increase State revenue. Agrarian products were transported overland to sea ports during the 1500's and 1600's by bullock-carts. Inland rivers also facilitated transport of agricultural products by ships and small rafts. In 1512 pepper and sugar were in great demand from Portugal and in 1516 a foreign traveller, Barboso, wrote about the 'very great town of Mangalore where many ships and cargoes of black rice were to be sold in Malabar.'[7] In 1522 roads from Goa to Mangalore were constructed and were made accessible to the bullock-carts by bullock-carts.

In 1554 the Nayaks of Keladi (Sadasiva) became governors of the region, including the present day Mangalore. They continued to expand their empire and by the mid-1700's their empire had extended as far south Cannanore. During 1598-1763, the taxation policy of the Keladi Nayakas enabled the Gowda Saraswat Brahmins, the Goan Christians and the Vira-Saivas to emerge as land-owning castes in the coastal regions.[8] Moreover, the religious institutions of the GSBs (Gowda Saraswats Brahmins) received gifts of land virtually tax-free, which facilitated the consolidation of their lands. During this administration the GSBs also served as court merchants. Their 'marketing' strategy coupled with the Portuguese dependency on rice and pepper imported from Mangalore widened the market for this produce and further enhanced the revenue of the State. Similarly, the Nayakas of Keladi took full advantage of the Portuguese dependency on rice imports, charging the latter high prices for their products. Portuguese records from 1560 to 1580 often mention agrarian convoys from Mangalore to Goa and Malabar and many ships owned by wealthy Hindus also participated in this trade route. In 1594 Mangalore was exporting pepper, sugar cane and coconut to Arabia, Ormuz, East Africa and Europe.[9]

During the reign of Keladi Nayakas, Brahmans acquired land to such an extent that even their rulers were compelled to purchase land from them. Thus, these land gifts to the Brahmins (Brahmaswom)[10] began during the Vijayanagar rule and continued under the Nayakas of Keladi. The lands were granted with the expectation that increased fertility and the cultivation of revenue crops such as coconut and paddy. Other land grants were called Devaswom and lands were given directly to the temple and later divided among the trustees of that particular religious institution.[11] The temple during that era functioned as the central institution which organised the surrounding community for agricultural production.[12]

It was by the means of these grants that from the mid 1500's the religious institutions of the Gowda Saraswat Brahmins acquired landed property in many areas, including Mangalore. However, rather than tilling the land themselves, when they migrated from Goa they brought with them many Kunbi agricultural labour families who cultivated the temple lands.[13] This enduring alliance with the Kunbis and the Brahmins resulted in a fusion of Brahmanic culture with the folk traditions of the Kunbis in such a way as the local deities of the Kunbis were incorporated into the Hindu pantheon and the Kunbis began to observe some Vedic rituals.[14]

During the 1550's, skilled agrarian Christians from Goa

were invited by the Nayakas of Keladi to settle in the coastal lands surrounding Mangalore.[15] They were said to be specially skilled in the cultivation of coconut due to the introduction of superior agrarian methods by the Portuguese. When they migrated, priests and missionaries arrived as well in order to establish the Catholic religious institutions in Mangalore. The church was recognised as a religious institution and, thus, was awarded land grants under the 'Devaswom' system. 'By 1623 the Catholic church in Mangalore owned landed property and was receiving rent from its native Catholic tenants'.[16] These properties were managed by a committee of elders and vicars who supervised the production of coconut.

From 1550 to 1763 the Christian population in Mangalore gradually increased as more and more migrated from Goa to cultivate lands in Mangalore and surrounds. In the mid-1600's, in large part due to the Christians' methods of cultivation, large tracts of barren and otherwise unproductive land were converted into coconut and areca nut plantations in and around Mangalore.[17] These skilled Christians also converted many hilly areas around Mangalore into coconut plantations and paddy fields using the extended shift system of cultivation (Kuman), characteristic of Kudubis (Kunbi) tribal cultivation patterns.[18] In addition, the Goan Catholics introduced the cultivation of cashew nut, tobacco, pineapple, papaya, pepper and cardamom into Mangalore. Over the years the Christians became large landowners of these coconut plantations and were living prosperous lives until the arrival of Tippu Sultan in 1792 A.D. From 1763 to 1799, the Sultans of Mysore gained control over the entire coast of western Karnataka and seemed destined to control the whole of India down to Travancore. When Tippu Sultan gained effective control over Coastal Karnataka, he invited merchants from different parts of India to commence trade in Mangalore. He altered the agrarian policy to raise the status of the Muslims, which adversely affected the agrarian Christians and Gowda Saraswat Brahmans.[19]

In 1792, fearing that the native Catholics would ally themselves with his enemy the British, Tippu captured many Catholics and held them captive at his capital in Srirangapatanam for seven years.[20] The lands of the Catholics were reduced to ruins and only in 1799 were the Catholics permitted to leave

Mysore. Upon their return, many discovered that their lands were inhabited by other agrarian communities and had been under different ownership for many years. As a consequence they were forced to relocate to less fertile lands and even barren lands, diminishing the wealth and social esteem which they previously enjoyed. This political decision damaged the agrarian interests in Mangalore which had since fallen under the control of both the GSBs and the Muslims[21], but the trade continued to be lucrative despite the Sultan's destructive policies.

In 1799, in a historic battle against the British, Tippu Sultan was defeated and his kingdom of Mysore restored to its former rulers, the Wodeyar dynasty. The coastal region was detached from the Mysore kingdom and given over to the Madras presidency of the British and, thus, began the reign of the British empire in coastal Karnataka. Under the British administration, Mangalore continued as an agricultural community and centre of trade until the early 1920's, at which time the Nationalist Movement was beginning to flourish in the minds of the people.

After Mahatma Ghandhi's visits to the city in 1920, 1927 and 1934, public morale was raised to considerable heights and Mangalore became one of the centres of the Independence movement.[22] Mangalorean citizens participated in the Salt Satyagraha in April 1930 as well as the Quit India Movement of August 9, 1942. Many Saraswat Brahmins were active in the Mangalore Freedom Movement, including M. Madhava Rao, Ramaro Mallya, Shesh Bhatt, V.S. Kudva, K.Shankar Bhatt, K.K. Shetty and several others.[23] Students and Catholics were also involved in the Independence movement in Mangalore and it was an experience that momentarily broke down the communal bonds which normally divided social life in Mangalore. Independence was achieved in 1947 and since then Mangalore has continued in the earlier tradition of agriculture and port-trading.

However, beginning in 1976 with the opening of the all-weather New Mangalore Port, the city has begun to move from a primarily agricultural economy to an industrial one as well. This new and highly sophisticated port has facilitated the establishment of today's seven large industries, much to the chagrin of environmentalists who argue that Mangalore's identity has been destroyed in this mad rush to commercialise and industrialise. Formerly known as a 'garden-beautiful city'[24] the result of these policies has been the unfettered urbanisation of Mangalore and the destruction of her natural beauty.

The previous section described the historical migration of the Konkani-speaking people into Mangalore and the reasons, all economical in nature, which resulted in this migration pattern. Thus, in Mangalore today, the largest communities of Konkani-speaking people are the migrated Catholics, the Gowda Saraswat Brahmans and the Kudumbi (Kunbi) tribals who arrived in conjunction with the Saraswats and worked the fields which were granted as Devaswom lands. Under the empire of Vijayanagar (1336-1565), lands were offered to Brahmans who settled in the town of Mangalore. The Brahman migration continued under the subsequent administration of the Keladi Nayaks who, in addition, enticed the Goan Catholic agriculturists skilled in the cultivation of coconut to settle in Mangalore by offering them land grants.

The Formation of a New Catholic Mangalorean Cultural Identity

Possibly as a consequence of the wealth and privilege which these Catholic agricultural communities now enjoyed, they began to feel superior from their landless brethren in Goa. The majority came from the lower economic strata and had been left out of government and administrative jobs under the Portuguese. In Mangalore, however, they had come up in life and are now in positions of economic prosperity and land ownership. As they had achieved the status of landed gentry, they no longer felt identified to their caste-based community in their homeland. Moreover, the late settlers of these generations probably felt a sense of shame stemming from their ancestors' low socio-economic status in Goa and, thus, a process of communal white-washing began. By erasing their former caste allegiances, they could free themselves from those negative stereotypes and self-perceptions which caused disharmony within their social environments. This also provides insight into how 'Mangaloreans' who identified themselves as such could claim to have eliminated the caste system among their community. Like the evolution of Catholic Daman Indo-Portuguese identity, the Catholic community in Mangalore created a new identity for itself which was in accordance with their new psychology, socio-economic status and regional location.

The Mangalorean Catholics have since promoted their 'Mangalorean' identity with a remarkable amount of pride and esteem. From Bombay to Bangalore, the Mangalorean is well known among Catholics who acknowledge this special identity which claims a socio-economic and cultural status higher than that of Goans. Even in Dubai, where 70,000 ex-patriot Mangaloreans now reside, there exists an informal association called the Mangalorean Konkans.[25] While people from other pockets of Karnataka have a back stage role, this community gives live performances during such events as the Dubai Shopping Festival. "The Mangaloreans add glitter with their contemporary western styles that are in vogue" and the May Ball is an event organised by the Mangalorean Konkans which draws a large crowd and witnesses the crowning of the year's 'May Queen'.[26] The level of affluence among these Mangaloreans is high and they are involved in a variety of skilled occupations, the women as well as the men. The jobs in the Gulf have brought renewed wealth to the Mangalorean Catholic community which suffered persecution and major financial loss under the regime of Tippu Sultan. As in Dubai, the term 'Mangalorean' means well-off, educated, Konkani speaking, Catholic and progressive while simultaneously adhering to tradition and to an Indian identification.

'Mangalorean' cultural identity, like the term 'Goan' described in earlier chapters, is an identity that has likewise come to be dominated and represented by the Catholic community of that city. And like the identity of 'Goans', only the Catholic portion of Mangalore's inhabitants will identify themselves as Mangalorean, though all will admit to being 'from Mangalore'. As a consequence, the remainder of the city's inhabitants are often left wondering both quizzically and at times cynically what is so great about proclaiming oneself a Mangalorean.

Krishna Murthy, a writer from Mangalore and a native himself, questions the very idea of a Mangalorean identity in his "The Soul of Mangalore". He refutes Mangalore's reputation as the article, "city beautiful", alluding to the fact that the green gardens have transformed into concrete blocks and the city centre itself bears a striking resemblance to Bombay with little of its prior old-world charm.[27] He says that although Mangaloreans are proud of their culture (i.e. Yakshagana) few city-dwellers take the time to watch one. He alludes to the pride people feel in authors like Dr. Shivarama Karnath, Sediyapu and Kadangodlu, but most have not even examined a copy of their literary works.[28] Mangaloreans as a community enjoy white collar jobs in banks and in the Gulf; nurturing the 'good life' with little hard labour.

Thus, there exits within Mangalore's non-Catholic inhabitants some confusion regarding the cultural identity of Mangaloreans. This indicates that the 'Mangalorean' identity known as far as Dubai is only applicable to a portion of the population in Mangalore and does not apply to non-Catholics. While other communities struggle to understand what is so wonderful about Mangalore, the issue becomes transparent when the history of the Catholic Goan migrants into Mangalore is accounted for. In attempts to reveal their former origins, the Catholics who have since become owners of landed property have created a new identity which reflects this status and wealth and instils in them a sense of pride. In order to accomplish this however, they had to first deny their origins in Goa and sever all ties with old alliances who might try and force them into a former social State.[29]

Consequently the pervading feeling among the Catholic Mangaloreans for whom this Mangalorean identity reigns most supreme is a strong sense of pride in their heritage. First, Mangalorean Catholics are characteristically industrious unlike their stereotypically 'sussegad' Goan rivals, another glimpse to the days when they migrated and were able to improve their socio-economic status. Mangalorean Konkani is a different dialect; it incorporates words borrowed from Kannada and other languages found in southern Kanara, whereas Goan Konkani incorporates the Portuguese words. Mangalorean culture is also more traditional and 'Indian' in comparison with Goan society because they migrated in the 1,500's removing themselves from the Goan environment.[30] Though the Portuguese traded quite frequently in Mangalore and many of the priests who came down with the Christian labourers were Portuguese, there did not develop as an elite native Catholic community identified with Portugal. Few, gained extensive knowledge of the Portuguese language. Different customs are observed during the wedding celebrations in Mangalore. Before the wedding day, the family of the bride sponsors a 'Roast' on a feast when the bride's family sings Boyos in Konkani, songs about the bride leaving the house. Also, Mangalorean Christian women get married in a white sari and mid-way through the wedding ceremony she goes and changes into one that is a red and gold.

More than the differences, the similarities between the cultural traditions of caste Mangaloreans and Goans are striking. The food habits of Goans and Mangaloreans are likewise similar and include the consumption of beef, chicken and pork. However, Mangaloreans claim that their pork preparation is slightly different from the Goan Sorpotel.[31] Mangaloreans even make sannas, a steamed rice-paddy accompaniment to a meal thought to exist only in Goan cuisine. In addition, whereas Goans are noted for their dances and gay abandon, Mangaloreans also enjoy their own Christmas dances and lively social functions. One Mangalorean woman interviewed was married to a Goan man and she commented that she has hardly noticed any cultural differences between the two, other than a different method for addressing one's elders and a slight dialect in the language. Mangaloreans, she explained, also tend to be more clannish than Goans.

Yet Mangalorean Catholics have actively propagated within their community and to others the notion of Mangalorean identity as distinct and unique compared to other communities within India. Even in Bombay where Catholics of many types share the same houses of worship, it is commonly understood that there are three types of Roman Catholics: Mangaloreans, Goans and east Indians. They have effectively created their own community (a modern caste) which prefers to intermarry and engage in social functions separate even from Goans, their ancient yet unrecognised ancestors.

With all the similarities between Goans and Mangaloreans, the reason for the separate and distinct identity from that of their Goan ancestors seems owing to communal sources of pride and shame. Starting as landless labourers on foreign soil, these Catholics, armed with drive and a knack for cultivating coconuts became landowners and prominent members of society prior to 1763 (Tippu's invasion). Though much of that former glory was lost following his persecution, the British employment on ships, massive migration to urban centres and most recently employment in the Gulf has enabled this community to once again gain a foothold as contributors to society. But if you ask them about their history, very few will know how it is that they came to speak Konkani since they neither recognise a personal nor ancestral history connected to Goa.[32]

Migration of the Gowda Saraswat Brahmins to Mangalore

The Gowda Saraswat Brahmins (GSBs) migrated to Mangalore in two waves: the first was owing to the invitation of the Vijayanagar rulers and the second was at the request of the Kalaydi Nayaks, both of whom offered reduced taxes, educational funds and 'Devaswom' property to incoming Brahman communities. They, unlike the Mangalorean Christians, have kept in touch with their roots and are able to trace them as far back as their origin near the Saraswati River in West Bengal. Their birth, marriage and daily customs are virtually identical to those of other GSB communities in Goa and close ties are retained with people living there. They are a middle and upper-middle income community whose members eat fish as do the GSBs in Goa. Many still make pilgrimages to their favourite *Kula devtas* (family gods) which are located in Goa. The GSBs in Mangalore generally earn elevated degrees at the doctorate and post-doctorate levels and pride themselves on having gained all that they have through ambition, achievement and honest hard work. Today, the GSBs control much of the business and commercial community in Mangalore, including several banks and construction companies.

The communal lands which were previously owned by the GSB temple went to the Kunbis who had cultivated them for centuries, following the Land Tenancy Act.

Though the traditions, cultural identity and value-orientations of the GSBs in Mangalore closely resemble those of other GSB communities in India, there are some traditions peculiar to the

GSBs in Mangalore. Unique to the GSBs of Mangalore is the annual 'Rathotsave' or Car Festival of the Venkatramana Temple; a 6-day temple festival held in the Hindu month of Magha. (late January or early February). The temple's origin dates back to 1736, when it was only a small shrine whose grounds served as the meeting point for members of the community. The presiding deity, Veera Venkatsha, was installed in 1804 and legend holds that a Sanyasin brought the image to the city and became disturbed by all the people who converged day and night to have the darshan of the splendid image. The prominent Baba Pai family is then said to have procured the image from the Sanyasin and gifted it to the spiritual leader of the GSBs in Mangalore, Srimad Vibhudendra Thirtha Swamiji of the Sri Kashi Mutt. With his approval the image was installed at the Venkatramana Temple.

The Car Festival begins on the Tratiya or third day of the bright moon and ends on the seventh, followed by Holi. For 6 days the temple is illuminated, decorated and surrounded by make shift stalls selling an assortment of food and items. The festival opens on the first day with the Dwajarohan, the raising of the flag bearing the picture of Garuda. During subsequent days, GSBs perform 'poojas', 'homas' or 'yagas' and in the evenings the deity is taken for utsava around the sanctum sanctorum in well decorated silver palanquin. Every evening the 'Jevana' or mass meal is served on the temple grounds and every member of the community must eat here with his fellow brethren on at least one of the six days to demonstrate their spiritual unity and social equality. Throughout the festival, the GSB community also hosts a variety of cultural programmes from Indian classical music to Konkani dramas and folk dances. On the 5th and final day, the 'Great Chariot', a massive wooden chariot adorned with red and white flags and flowers, is drawn through the crowds carrying the temple deity, Veera Venkatesh. Holi begins on the concluding day of the Car Festival, a day when normally reserved members of the GSB community can let loose their inhibitions and make merry in the streets and play with colours.

The Car Festival for the GSBs is more than a religious festival, it is a social occasion as well, a time to renew old friendships and foster new relationships. It is a special time set aside every year in the life of a GSB to experience and promote the brotherhood and cultural identity of their community. Business meetings are planned, marriage proposals are conducted and communal bonds are strengthened. It strengthens tradition and reminds GSBs not to forget their spirituality and the community even as modernisation seeps into peoples' lives. It is a time for the GSBs in Mangalore to assert their cultural identity for themselves and for the lakhs of people who come to watch from various communities in Mangalore.

Life-Cycle Rituals of the Gowda Saraswat Brahmins

Like most Hindu communities, the Gowda Saraswat Brahmins have special rituals which occur throughout the life-cycle. During a woman's 8th month of pregnancy, she moves into her mother's house, especially during the delivery of her first child. In this way, her nearest kin and relatives can provide her with the emotional and physical support which she needs. The expecting mother also performs Ganpati pujas for a successful delivery and a healthy child. Where in olden times deliveries would be performed with the aid of a mid-wife in her mother's house, today most deliveries occur in hospitals. On the 6th day a book, pen and lighted lamp are kept near the child's head symbolic of a wish for an intelligent child. On the 12th day the cradle naming ceremony is performed, when the grandmother from the father's side whispers the child's name into its ear and a horoscope is cast. During the 8th year the thread ceremony is performed. This year is chosen because the child's mind is considered clear and undisturbed; where anything taught to the child will remain stable. On this occasion the boy child must recite the full Gaitri mantra, which he has been developing prior to the ceremony until he can chant it fully thrice a day. The Gaitri mantra is chanted in Sanskrit and is suppose to continue throughout his life. As the Aryans consider themselves descendants from a Solar Race, they offer prayer to the sun for health, happiness, success in life and scholarly concentration. Marriage is always within the GSB community but exogenous among the gotras, or families. The youth of today are getting married only after they have completed their degrees, usually around 22-23 for girls and 24-25 for boys. Sixty per cent in the Mangalorean community opt for advanced degrees in medicine, law and engineering and the women also obtain MBA degrees, dental, engineering and doctoral degrees.

Conclusion

This section examines three communities originating from Goa who migrated from south to Mangalore in the 1500 and 1600's. The first community under study, the newly converted Catholic agriculturists, were invited along with Portuguese priests to cultivate the lands surrounding the city of Mangalore owing to their expertise in the cultivation of coconut. Though relocated in southern Kanara where the Kannada and also Malayalam languages predominate, the Catholics have kept their mother tongue Konkani and imbibed some Christian habits such as the consumption of beef and pork. However, over the years as their language developed differently owing to the Kannada rather than Portuguese influence and their surrounding society was Indian rather than western, Catholics in Mangalore began to perceive Mangalore as their native place and no longer considered Goa their place of origin. These new self-perceptions in addition to the property and wealth which these former landless labourers now held as their own caused them to break ties with their Goan heritage and develop into a separate community which befitted their new socio-economic status.

The other community studied in this chapter are the Gowda Saraswat Brahmins of Mangalore. They also migrated from Goa, though the first wave did not come as was originally supposed. Invited by local rulers to settle and cultivate lands, these GSBs brought down Kunbi agrarian tribes who worked the land that they managed. The GSBs then entered into more managerial and commercial occupations and on the eve of the Portuguese they along with the Muslims were in control of the trade in the port of Mangalore. Academics being integral in the lives of GSBs; this community has become a prominent force in Mangalore; owning banks and other commercial enterprises, their own Venkateshwara temple and hosting the famous Car Festival in late January. While hailing from Mangalore is important, their cultural identity as Gowda Saraswat Brahmins remains their dominant self-concept and accordingly their heritage dating back from time immemorial is well-documented and known to all community members. They are very proud of their cultural identity as Gowda Saraswat Brahmins and residing in Mangalore is at the most only second in importance to their older roots.

The third community, the Kunbis, began the folklore now considered a part of Mangalorean cultural identity and are thought to be the original agrarian tribes living along the Konkan coast prior to the Aryan migrations from the north. They migrated to Mangalore in order to cultivate the lands of the Gowda Saraswat Brahmins in return for a percentage of the produce and land on which to live. Their community originated the folk dances which were sung during the reaping of the harvest. Subsequent to the Land Tenure Act drafted in the last quarter of our century, the Kunbis now own the lands once owned by the GSBs for whom they laboured. However, due to their lack of prominence in the trade and commercial centre and their absent voice in the propagation of Mangalorean identity, they are relatively marginalised in the conception of Mangalorean identity. In their efforts to include this community whose cultural traditions are as ancient as their people, the dances have been absorbed as part of the aggregate cultural identity of Mangaloreans and are performed as such in places as far away as Dubai. But, for a community which at one time were virtual slaves from that State, the Kunbis in Mangalore have improved their lot to a considerable extent. Though it will be a long time before their voice will be heard in a city dominated by Roman Catholics and Gowda Saraswat Brahmins, they were instrumental in the early success of the GSBs and in the agricultural prosperity of Mangalore.

GOAN, MANGALOREAN AND GOWDA SARASWAT BRAHMIN MIGRANTS IN BANGALORE

Communities in the Fastest Growing City of India

As both Mangalore and Goa offered limited opportunities for those who sought higher education and lucrative employment, many felt compelled to leave their homelands and migrate to urban centres. For Goans, Bombay was the ideal destination in the late 1800's and early 1900's, owing to the desire of the British administration to make Bombay an international trading centre. Through liberal economic and religious policies they promoted Bombay as a desirable place to seek lucrative employment, resulting in the mass migration of thousands of individuals and communities into this rapidly expanding commercial centre. In addition to the scores of Goans who arrived in Bombay, Mangaloreans also migrated to this expanding urban conglomerate in order to improve their economic welfare. They even established a Mangalorean club modelled after the Goan village clubs, the result of which brought more Mangaloreans to this city.[33]

However, Bombay was not the only city upon which Goans and Mangaloreans set their sights. During these years Bangalore was the seat of the British administration in the south of India and a town likewise destined to expand. Bangalore, albeit a longer journey from Goa, was less than a day's journey from Mangalore and located within the same State. Many Mangaloreans chose to migrate here seeking employment and education and, thus, 400 years after separation, both the Goans and Mangaloreans found themselves inhabiting the same geographical space once again. The second half of this case study, thus, explores the meeting of these two closely related communities in Bangalore and the interrelations which evolved between them. It also explores the Saraswat Brahmin migration into Bangalore as further examples of how GSBs today are establishing integrated societies and support systems for incoming migrants belonging to their community.

Historical Overview

Bangalore city was founded by Kempe Paji Gavouden in 1685 after he abandoned the city of Kodookkoopally seven miles to the west.[34] Gavouden (Gowda) named this pioneer village Biliakkipally and constructed three pavillions to mark the village limits. Around 1763 the whole of the region was conquered by Ranadulla Khan and was occupied by the forces of Adil Shah. Shahji became the Governor of this conquered territory and established his headquarters at Petta (modern-day Bangalore). During the 1700's Petta's city centre was bordered on the north and south by suburbs of wide streets interspersed with gardens and parks.

In 1799 during the battle of Srirangapatanam (350 km from Bangalore), the British forces defeated and killed Tippu Sultan. As victors, the British restored the Wodeyar rulers to the Mysore throne.[35] In 1809 the British first stationed a garrison in the city and from 1831-81 Bangalore was the seat of the British administrative headquarters, replacing the Wodeyar dynasty. Wealthy residents of British-occupied Bangalore resided in majestic colonial bungalows, enjoyed such entertainment as golf and two seasons of horse-racing. In 1865 the Maharajah's Palace was built for an English merchant by the name of Garret, who ceded it to the Maharajah of Mysore in 1881. Until Independence in 1947, the city of Bangalore remained an important hub for the transport of military equipment and personnel.

Today, in an area of 120 square miles, 41,08,013 people speaking Kannada, Telugu, Tamil and English carry on the activities of their daily lives. Forty per cent of this population follow the Christian faith and of that 40 per cent, 20 per cent are Roman Catholics. Of those 20 per cent, 10 per cent speak the Konkani language. Of those 10 per cent; 75 per cent trace their roots to Mangalore and 25 per cent claim a Goan heritage. The Roman Catholic communities studied under this research consist of the latter 10 per cent of Mangaloreans and Goans.[36]

MANGALOREANS IN BANGALORE

Establishment of St. Mary's Church in Blackpally, (Bangalore)

The origin of Christianity in Karnataka can be traced back to the first Dominican and Franciscan preachers in the 15th century, but the true founders of the Mysore Mission were the Italian Jesuits of Malabar during the early 17th century.[37] In 1685, those who had come from Ginji with Kempe Gowda to settle in modern-day Bangalore hailed from both Hindu and Christian faiths. In this first village two temples and a small thatch-roofed church were constructed, the latter of the two was called Kanikaimatha Kovil. However, when the Society of Jesus was suppressed in 1763 following the invasion of Hyder Ali, the French Fathers of the Foreign Mission Society took charge in 1776, followed by the Carnatic Missions from Madura.[38]

In 1792, when Tippu Sultan was attempting to expand his empire to cover the south of India, many Christians from Mangalore and its surroundings were forcibly captured and held at Srirangapatanam, accused of helping the British forces against him.[39] In 1799, after the seize of Srirangapatanam and the simultaneous murder of Tippu Sultan at the hands of the British, Abbe Dubois, arrived in Bangalore and began his famed contributions to the Catholic community in Bangalore and Mysore State. In 1811 he built a small chapel in Blackpally with a residence for priests, who prior to the construction of this edifice had rarely visited the small thatched roof chapel in Bangalore.[40]

The present structure of St. Mary's was completed and consecrated by 1882. On the 26th of January, 1974, St. Mary's Church was raised to the status of a Minor Basilica, a great honour for a parish church.[41] St. Mary's is, thus, a sacred place whose ancient history has resulted in its status as a pilgrimage site and place of reverence for both Catholics and non-Christians alike.

By the early 1800's Mangaloreans were entering into the priesthood in ever greater numbers and had stopped requesting priests from Goa for many years. This further improved upon the socio-economic status of Goan migrants in Mangalore by enabling them to enter into professions formerly restricted to the upper-castes of Goa. This also spurred the decision to sever communal links with Goa and form a separate identity based upon their new wealth and prestige. As a consequence of this new social mobility, many Mangaloreans entered into the clergy and were later stationed in Bangalore to cater to the needs of the growing Catholic community in that city.

In this way from 1813 to 1821, Father D'Souza from Mangalore was placed in charge of St. Mary's in Blackpally and in 1853 another Father from Mangalore, Fr. F.B. Coelho, was put in charge of St. Mary's Parish. From then onwards, no less than 22 priests in charge of St. Mary's originated in Mangalore. J. Noronha (1868), M. Correia (1883) and A.J. Pinto, assistant, (1970) were Mangaloreans and from 1908 until 1939 those priests in charge of St. Mary's Church were all from Mangalore, with one or two exceptions hailing from Goa.[42] The list does not end there, however, with Mangalorean priests figuring prominently through the years either as chief administrators or assistant administrators in the church of St. Mary's, Blackpally.

By 1882 the population of Christians belonging to St. Mary's Parish had risen to 4,000 and by 1940 roughly 6,000 residents of Bangalore were parishioners of St. Mary's. Ten years later in 1950, 6,622 Catholics were members and the population by 1974, when it was raised to the status of Minor Basilica, that figure reached 10,000.[43] At St. Mary's Konkani mass is held once a week owing to the dominant presence of Mangalorean and Goan Catholics both as parishioners and as members of the clergy. From this ancient parish of St. Mary's Blackpally, three churches have arisen to cater to the spiritual needs of the growing Christian community: St. Francis Xavier's Cathedral (1851), St. Joseph's Church (Bangalore City, 1867) and the Sacred Heart Church (Asoknagarl, 1874). Five chapels are also attached to St. Mary's: St. Sebastians (Pioneers Cherry, 1888), St. Anne's (Dospet, 1894), St. Anthony's (Blackpally); St. Anne's (Queen Road) and a Visitation Chapel in Chuppercherry.

St. Joseph's Church in Bangalore Proper

St. Joseph's Parish is another church in Bangalore which has catered to the spiritual needs of the Mangalorean Catholic migrant influx. Out of approximately 11,000 Roman Catholics, about 10 per cent speak the Konkani language and trace their roots to Mangalore. A smaller percentage claim a 'Goan' heritage. The church was built in 1867 under the British and like most parishes in Bangalore, the clergy is dominated by Mangalorean Konkanies. In the whole of Karnataka, 6 out of every 7 bishops hails from Mangalore and they form a majority in almost every parish in Bangalore. Owing to the large numbers of Mangalorean migrants who are members of St. Joseph's Church, Konkani mass is held once a month.

The clergy members interviewed for this study in May, 1997 recall only one Goan priest about 25 years ago by the name of Father Salinas. In addition, there are two Goan families who migrated 10 years back and are now settled and engaged in business. Most of the Catholics in Bangalore today have been settled for several decades, have sons and daughters born here and are no longer considered 'migrants' in the true sense of the word. Whereas Goan migrants are a relatively new addition to Bangalore with a small population and integrating community, Mangaloreans have a long established history in Bangalore dating from 1853. Earlier they established themselves within the Roman Catholic community, especially in official church positions as priests and administrators. The clergy belonging to St. Joseph's also freely admits that the opinions of Mangalorean Konkanies dominate in most church-related matters.

The 'Cultural Identity' of Mangaloreans in Bangalore

In addition to their long tradition of migration into Bangalore, Mangaloreans in their new urban environment still adhere to the traditions and cultural identity of their forefathers and promote it as distinct and separate from that of Goan culture. Though similar in religion, food habits, folk-dances and language, Mangaloreans insist that the similarities should stop there. First and foremost, they consider themselves more Indian than Goans and higher in relative social status. In matters of economy, Mangaloreans as a whole tend to have retained their ancestral property in Mangalore and make frequent trips to their heritage homes and on important feast days. Regarding language, Mangaloreans in Bangalore argue that their Konkani language is different from that of Goan Konkani owing to the influence of Kannada, Telugu and Malayalam in south Kanara. They also demonstrate a desire to pass on their native language to their children, though in personal interviews with several families all admitted that their children are not fluent in Konkani. Most can understand it, but few are fluent in their native language. Regarding the historical experience of the community, the Mangaloreans do not perceive themselves as having been influenced by Portuguese or western culture unlike some Goans and feel that their culture and ways of life are much more Indian than European. Many also took part in the freedom movement while Goa was still under the yoke of the Portuguese administration and few Mangaloreans opposed the Independence movement.

Regarding marriage alliances, most Mangaloreans like to marry within their own community and caste distinctions figure prominently during the formation of these alliances. In the case of a traditional proposed wedding, Mangaloreans are keen to know the surname of the proposed suitor and attach certain social qualities accordingly. Of late, however, intercommunity marriages with Goans of similar socio-economic status are frequent and financial status plays an increasing role during the formation of these alliances.

Within the 'upper-caste' Mangalorean community, the latest trend has been to revert back to pre-Catholic surnames such as Kamat, Shennoy and Pai. These surnames are common among the individuals that belong to the community of Gowda Saraswat Brahmins settled in Mangalore, a group which traces their ancient roots to Goa. Many of the Mangaloreans who have migrated to Bangalore claim Brahmin status and identify themselves as 'Brahmins that left Goa'. Yet this claim is questionable at most, as the only record of Catholic migration from Goa to Mangalore between the years 1500 to 1800 was that of the cultivating class who were given lands in exchange for turning barren lands into fertile agrarian plains.[44] Further, most Catholic Brahmins already owned landed property in Goa and enjoyed exalted positions within the Portuguese administration. They also did not tilt the land but rather leased it to cultivators in exchange for a percentage of the produce. Thus, few incentives were available to induce a community of Catholic Brahmins to resettle in the foreign land. The only native Catholic Brahmins who migrated to Mangalore were the original Goan priests which came with the community. These had taken vows of celibacy and were shifted after every three years to a new post. Finally, the Brahmin groups migrated from Goa would most likely have kept extensive records of their Brahmin heritage owing to the importance of such a social status in Indian society. Lack of these records indicates that these people were more probably illiterate, further supporting the existing evidence that the Mangaloreans of today are descendants of the migrated coconut cultivators who settled there in the mid-1500's. As these cultivators became landowners and subsequently educated people in positions of power, some felt they should deny their Goan roots as they were of a lower origin and a source of shame for the new community. They preferred to distinguish themselves as a separate community distinct from their roots in Goa rather than trace their ancient links.[45]

Mangaloreans in Bangalore

Several interviews with Mangaloreans settled in Bangalore have been conducted in an attempt to discern the current life histories and understanding of the Mangaloreans as regards their cultural identity.[46] The Menezes family is an interesting case from a Goan-Mangalorean cultural comparative standpoint. It is an example of an intercommunity marriage where she is a Mangalorean and he is a Goan. Mr. Menezes, like the father of Mrs. Menezes, is in the Merchant Navy and from the time of their marriage they built a house and settled in Bangalore. They now have three children, two daughters aged 14 and 17 and one son aged 20. Their children do not speak Konkani and even Mrs. Menezes admits that her scope with her mother tongue is limited. She can understand and speak a little, though her husband is fluent in the language. As English was spoken at home, none of her children are fluent in their ancestral tongue. They have an ancestral home in Mangalore looked after by the spinster aunt of Mrs. Menezes and go to Mangalore once a year and on special occasions. In relation to Goan-Mangalorean cultural differences, Mrs. Menezes admits that she has not noticed too many cultural differences among Goans and Mangaloreans. The Mangaloreans demonstrate different dialect and have a different method of addressing elders, some marriage customs are different and the preparation of curry and pork sorpotel vary slightly. Mrs. Menezes knows of her roots in Goa and believes that her ancestors 'felt they wanted to settle in a new place and so wandered down to Mangalore.' Few psychological differences appear between this married couple and the relationships and expectations between men and women appear to be relatively similar.

In the Coelho family, both husband and wife were born in Mangalore. However, his job in the army required that they live in cities before finally settling down in the Bangalore army station in 1977. They trace their roots only to Mangalore and are members of the Mangalorean Kendra Catholic Club, which sponsors programmes such as picnics, Christmas dances and bands from Mangalore, once every 2-3 months. Though Mrs. Coelho is fluent in Konkani, her children, one son and two daughters, do not speak the language. Mangaloreans are very proud of their culture, though she feels intermarriages between Goans and Mangaloreans are common. Her aunt, in fact, married a Goan.

The Fernandes family settled in Bangalore 20 years ago, migrating directly from Mangalore. Most of their relatives are still there and they visit their native place once a year and on other special occasions. In Bangalore Mrs. Fernandes still prepares Mangalorean food, though the quality of the ingredients have deteriorated and some are not readily available in the market. Mr. Fernandes has a private business in building/developing and they have two children. They want their children to grow up with knowledge of their native tongue and they feel that Mangalorean culture is 'quite different' from that of Goan in the sense that Goan culture has a stronger 'western' influence. They are the members of the Mangalorean Kendra Catholic Club and regularly attend dances and other functions sponsored by the organisation. Both her husband's aunt and cousin have Goan husbands.

Like the Coelho family, the D'Souza family has a history of constant migration within India. The parents of Mrs. D'Souza were born in Mangalore, but her father's employment in the Imperial Bank of India necessitated the family's constant relocation to a variety of places. Though they sold their property in Mangalore and her father retired in Calcutta, they grew up feeling 'very much Mangalorean'. Both she and her husband speak fluent Konkani, though Mr. D'Souza, an army officer, has passed away long ago. Their children do not speak Konkani as English was spoken at home to prepare them for the future. When comparing Goan culture to that of Mangalore, the Konkani dialects, certain food preparations and the lack of Portuguese cultural influence are what Mrs. D'Souza feels separates the two cultures. Several persons in her extended family have married Goans, all of which were approved love marriages.

In the Gomes family, the parents are from Mangalore and migrated to Bangalore about 20 years ago in search of better employment opportunities. Their grandparents are still holding property and living in Mangalore and the family makes annual trips to see their relatives in their native place. The parents have three sons, the youngest of which was born in Bangalore. The children barely know Konkani, but are fluent in both Kannada and English. They do not have any Goan relatives nor claim any heritage in Goa and all of the brothers have remained in Bangalore.

Goan Migration in Bangalore

Many of the pioneer immigrants from Goa got jobs in Bangalore under the British administrations. Many IAS (Indian Administrative Service) officers in Karnataka were Goans and many others received employment as cooks in private homes and public establishments. Even the cook of the Maharaja of Mysore, Mr. Carvalho, was a Goan.[47] Their desire to learn English as well as their familiarity with European culture further enabled them to secure positions as cooks in British homes and in administrative institutions. In addition to culinary jobs, Goans in the 1920's and 30's came as teachers, nurses and doctors; especially those who were able to get an English education. Priests and nuns hailing from Goa were also transferred to Bangalore.[48] In addition to jobs in Bangalore itself, many Goans now settled in Bangalore arrived from the British and Portuguese colonies in Africa where they held high-ranking positions under the former colonists.

In financial matters, most Goans settled in Bangalore today belong to the middle and upper-middle class socio-economic strata. The Goan community boasts of giving scope to Bangalore's top lawyers and many migrants of the first generation belonged to the medical profession. David Lobo, known for creating the second largest poultry farm in Asia, also claims a Goan heritage. Within a booklet prepared to commemorate the raising of St Mary's Church to a Minor Basilica in 1974, some Goan and Mangalorean businesses figure prominently. Among the sponsors listing Portuguese surnames can be found to be wine merchants, painting and interior decoration, private educational/vocational training institutions, auto garages, printing presses and manufactures and designers of tools and sheet metals.

But not all Goans in Bangalore are successful. However, the Goan Association has been actively involved in helping these families in financial matters to gain ground and become self-supporting. In one of these families, the father was a miserly sailor who died leaving his children under financial strain and without proper education to get ahead in Bangalore. Though the sons tried their best to support the family, once they died their spinster sisters were evicted from their residence by the landlord. Having few financial resources at their disposal, the Goan

Association tried to sustain them for sometime and still helping them in times of crisis. Today, one of the sisters can be found selling sugarcane from a street vendor.

Social Institutions of Goans and Mangaloreans in Bangalore

In the early years the Mangalorean and Goan communities were united by their similar cultural heritage. The first impetus to form an association for the promotion of Konkani culture and financial aid for community members in need resulted in the informal formation of the Konkan Association in 1967, thirty years ago. It was a combined organisation consisting of both Goans and Mangaloreans and in 1973 it became an official organisation. They united behind their similar 'cultural identities' which included Catholicism, the Konkani language, the Kunbi folk dance and special food habits such as the consumption of pork sorpotel and fish-curry-rice.

In 1975, however, due to perceived cultural and socio-economic differences, the rift between the two communities widened to such an extent that the organisation split into two groups: the Mangaloreans and the Goans. Economic conditions also played a significant role in the decision to divide into two groups. The Mangaloreans from Mangalore arrived in Bangalore with more financial resources at their disposal from home and large tracts of land utilised for coffee, coconut, areca nut and rice plantations. Those migrating to Bangalore, therefore, perceived themselves as superior, more industrious and of higher social standing in comparison to individuals among the Goan community. As a result of the first rift and the issues raised during that first division, the Mangaloreans have since divided themselves into five sub-groups based on socio-economic and geographical lines.[49] The Mangaloreans do not have an office of their own at this time, though plans are underway to purchase land and construct such a social club for the community.

However, the Goan Association (GA), created after the first split, did not again divide and today's membership reaches 700 out of an approximate 1,000 Goans residing in Bangalore. In addition to those 700, seven associate members belonging to the Anglo-Indian community also take part in dances, cultural programmes and other activities sponsored by the association. To become a GA member, normally a new migrant family goes through their newly chosen Parish Church, such as St. Mary's of Blackpally or St Joseph's of Bangalore City proper, which directs them to the Catholic 'family' Club in Bangalore. People from all denominations and socio-economic backgrounds can become members of this organisation and it sponsors youth groups, social dances and Christmas cultural events. From there they can meet other Goan families in the area and opt to join the GA. Membership costs Rs 50 per year and Rs 500 to become a lifetime member.

Mr. Santa Maria, the current President of the GA, has a personal history connected to both Goa and Bangalore. He arrived from Goa as a child in Bangalore during the 1930's with his uncle in order to receive English education. While studying at St. Patrick's, his five brothers and four sisters were all brought to Bangalore to get an education. Mr Santa Maria's uncle, a brass and copper merchant, had started a business in Bangalore while his father remained in Goa as a dentist. During these years Bangalore was an administrative capital of the British Raj and Mr Santa Maria's uncle dropped his former surname and adopted Roberts (his first name) instead, to sound more British and thus increase the family's social standing. After getting an education in Bangalore, Mr Santa Maria (now aged 54), went to Saudi Arabia for employment. He returned to Bangalore only in 1981, when he started his current business of Altech Opticals. Like him, all of his brothers and sisters have remained in Bangalore except one sister whose husband resides in Saudi Arabia.

Mr. Santa Maria, who registers new members into the GA, states that approximately 15 families per year joins the association. He also observes that migration trends in the past few years are slowly shifting from Bombay to Bangalore, as networks and associations become more established and stories of life in Bangalore slowly reach home to Goa. Exodus is another common occurrence among Goan families in Bangalore, whose sons and daughters, after receiving jobs in Canada and the USA choose to remain in these and other foreign countries. Four families were lost due to such exodus last year alone. Because of this trend, elderly parents unable or unwilling to receive foreign citizenship remain in Bangalore, some unable to care for themselves and their ailing spouses. The GA hopes to alleviate some of the issues arising because of this trend in their community through the purchase of land on which to construct a home for the aged. The GA also has a scholarship fund available, but no one claims it because, as Mr Santa Maria admits, "Goans are a proud people" and don't like to accept money.

According to Mr Santa Maria, whose 'heart is in Goa' and who is in the forefront of the association promoting Goan culture and identity, the outlook of the GA seems 'bleak' judging from recent years. Only five years back, the GA had 300 youth members, many of whom were nurses and other young professionals. Those from his generation (he is 54) have their hearts in Goa, but those born and brought up only in Bangalore have their hearts here and find Goa a bit backward and sluggish in comparison to a big city like Bangalore. Whether due to the "generation gap", near total integration and identification with the urban culture of Bangalore, or just plain apathy towards celebrating the seemingly obsolete cultural traditions of their forefathers, he does not know for sure. But the results demonstrate that the youth do not fully patronise the social gatherings initiated by the GA and girls complain that they cannot find suitable boys among the Goan community. They prefer to choose their own prospective husbands from different backgrounds and communities, resulting in many marriage alliances with Mangaloreans and Anglo-Indians. One event, i.e., a get together sponsored in the month of May, attract does get a large crowd and is popular among the Goan youth.

Generally, though Mr Santa Maria feels the community has become diluted among the younger generation who mix freely with their peers and pay less attention to their own community and cultural heritage resulting from immersion into urban Bangalorean society. With the Bangalore pub culture and its patrons growing, this scene has become the meeting place for friends and a place for young couples and singles to interact with one another. However, even here young adults come in their respective groups and little mixing between groups occurs unless they are already known to each other. Beyond the pub culture, daily life in Bangalore offers ample opportunity for youth to meet and mix with one another, from college and universities to outside social activities and gatherings of friends. Consequently, youths take little interest in attending social events sponsored by the GA which they feel is more for their parents than for themselves.

Yet for most 'Goans'[50] of the younger generation in Bangalore, the Catholic religion and family life still establish the foundations of their culture. Consequently, most have at least a vague knowledge of the history and traditions of their forefathers such as the Kunbi folk dance, the Portuguese legacy, culinary specialities like pork sorpotel and the Konkani language. For others it is their social nature and ability to mix and mingle with a wide variety of people from different walks of life that they would characterise as 'uniquely Goan'. Some consider the greater degree of freedom[51] given to women regarding the choice of a life partner and the ability to participate in a social life apart from home and family as integral to the Goan cultural identity of recent years.

Among migrated Goans, their mother tongue Konkani has fallen out of use amongst the younger generation, especially in an urban environment like Bangalore where English is the language of employment and Kannada and Tamil the languages of the common man. As a consequence, many migrated Goan youths have only a very basic working knowledge of the language and some demonstrate no knowledge at all. In the families where Konkani is not known, English was spoken at home in an attempt to create fluency in that international language from childhood.

The obvious language shift amongst the youth negatively affects the activities proposed by the GA. For example, one year a Konkani theatre group was brought from Goa to Bangalore, but the programmes 'flopped' because the people did not understand Konkani well enough to fully grasp the jokes. Last year the society tried to host a Carnival Parade down the main Mahatma Ghandi Road,[52] but they could not find enough sponsors to cover the costs of such a cultural festival. Every year, however, a successful "Mangoshaz" is held in Bangalore. In this joint effort between the Goan and Mangalorean Associations, groups participate in folk dances and mandos, with prizes given out for the most outstanding group performances.

Though both Mangaloreans and Goans assert their superiority over one another resulting in a constant 'friendly' rivalry, when faced with an outside adversary the Goans and Mangaloreans unite as Catholic Konkanies. Whether issues within the church regarding mass in Konkani or issues outside regarding the current social climate regarding non-Hindu communities, the Goans and Mangaloreans will forget their petty differences and join hands if their well-being is threatened. And in spite of this friendly rivalry, many Mangaloreans and Goans have intimate friendships with each other and those developed while overseas in the Gulf countries tend to last for a lifetime.

The influence of migration into Bangalore has had further effects similar to those which stem from the general process of rural-urban migration and need not be reiterated here. A unique and visible difference among Goan migrants in Bangalore was the tendency to change family surnames to resemble those of the British administration in order to more fully identify with them and receive social and economic benefits accordingly. The 'sussegard' attitude formerly characterising Goans finds few adherents in an urban environment like Bangalore where intelligence, ambition and education (in addition to personal contacts) make a man successful.

The Saraswat Brahmins in Bangalore

The Saraswat Brahmins in Bangalore today number approximately 12,000 families from an original 25 that migrated during the 1950's. At that time most were arriving from Mangalore in Dakshina Kannada and received employment in the Kanara Bank, whose founder was also a Saraswat Brahmin from Mangalore. As the Kanara Bank opened several additional branches in Bangalore during the 1960's, more GSBs from Mangalore were brought in to fill the vacant positions. By 1965 community members involved in business began arriving and such chains like Kamat hotels and Lori transport appeared in Bangalore city. The main businesses of the GSBs in Bangalore are restaurants/hotels, finance (banking, accountants), real estate/ construction and small-scale industry. Others can be found in managerial professions in the Kanara and Syndicate Banks and as doctors, engineers and accountants. Economically, therefore, the GSBs fit within the limits of the middle and upper-middle classes of Indian society. Surprisingly, with such numbers and highly skilled professions, the GSBs are relatively unknown in Bangalore. As they are recent migrants into Bangalore, they are yet to establish themselves into a unified residential community and likewise have not yet constructed their own temple as is the case in Cochin, Mangalore and other places where they have migrated. They have also made it a point to steer clear of politics 'in an attempt to maintain their honesty and integrity as a community'.

On March 3, 1955, the Gowda Saraswat Samaj was registered and recognised as a formal organisation. As of 1996, 2,541 GSB's have joined the association (an annual increase of 120) and the numbers have neared 3,000 in 1997. The foci of the organisation are several: which provide scholarships for needy GSB families, conduct religious functions particular to their community, sponsor cultural programmes and create a community housing development for middle-income GSB families. Three types of membership in the Samaj are available depending on the amount of money donated to the organisation per annum. To become an Aajeeva Sadasya, a donation of Rs 100 is necessary, for membership as a Poshaka Sadasya, Rs 500 is required and a gift of Rs 4,500 earns the recognition as a Mahaposaka member. As of July 31st, 1996, 48 Mahaposhaka members were registered with the Samaj. Elections to the Managing and Building Committees take place annually and nomination forms are included in the annual reports sent out to Samaj members.

The main office of the GSB Samaj is located in Basavangudi, Bangalore. Though the committee is at work to build a temple of their own, they currently have one small room converted into a shrine, the Sree Venkatesha Bhajana Mandali, which houses an opulent image of Ganesh placed in a silver throne. Important annual religious festivals in the lives of GSBs are held here such as Sri. Ramothsava, Samoohika Upanayanam and Sri Ganeshothsava. The committee also sponsors cultural programmes such as a series of Bhajans (devotional songs), classical Indian music and Sitar concerts, Bharata Natyam (classical south-Indian dance) and Yakshagana (a theatrical form unique to Karnataka, especially Mangalore). Dramas in Konkani used to be sponsored by the Mandali, but have been dropped since 1987 due to lack of patronage. A free monthly publication called "Soirika" invites marriage invitations from members of the GSB community. Social functions for the purpose of forming matrimonial alliances are also sponsored by the GSB Samaj, to which horoscopes and bio-data of eligible young adults are brought by parents. Such activities and meetings are advertised in the annual report of the Gowda Saraswat Samaj and sent to all participating members.

Education aid is another main priority of the GSB Samaj, as they consider it a part of their culture and religious tradition to continue with higher studies and earn advanced degrees.[53] In their annual report of 1990-91, a sum of Rs 9,400 was donated to 87 Samaj students demonstrating financial need and Rs 6,000 went to help two engineering and one medical student earn their degrees.[54] In their 1995-96 report that figure jumped to a total of Rs 59,000. Most of the children wish to finish their degrees prior to marriage, and, thus, boys usually marry after the age of 25-27 and girls after 21-22.

The most large-scale project of the GSB community, sponsored by the GSB Welfare Society, is the creation of a self-contained, exclusive Gowda Saraswat Brahmin neighbourhood from land purchased at Shree Ananthanagar on Hosur Road, 19 kilometres from downtown Bangalore. The project, still in process, will upon its completion have a total of 750 housing sites, a Suvidya School and College from nursery to higher secondary, a private temple, water supply from an overhead tank, underground drainage, asphalt roadways, planted avenues and private buses. The cost of land per square foot is Rs 40 and once finished, the housing development may resemble that of Cochin which has its own temple, schools and surrounding neighbourhood.

In matters surrounding cultural identity, the Gowda Saraswat Brahmins adhere strictly to the traditions of their forefathers.[55] Most GSBs in Bangalore have migrated from Mangalore and Cochin and speak Konkani with a Mangalorean dialect. They are determined to perpetuate the knowledge of Konkani among members of their community, even though most speak English fluently as well as Kannada, Hindi, Tamil and Malayalam. Members of the Gowda Saraswat Samaj belong to the Sri Samsthan Gokarna Parthagali Jeevotham Mutt and follow the teachings of Srimad Vidyadhiraja Tirtha Sripada Wader Swamiji. They eat fish like their forefathers, but are otherwise strictly vegetarian and abstain from alcohol and by-products.[56] Marriages are arranged strictly within their own community and those seeking outside marital alliances meet with disapproval from parents and community members. The Kuladevtas of GSB migrants in Bangalore are located in Goa, except for those recently transferred to Cochin. The Gowda Saraswat Brahmins are composed of three mutts, the first mentioned above and the other two are the Kashi Mutt (directly from Varanasi) and the Kailvali Mutt in Goa.

Conclusion

In Bangalore, as in Bombay, three communities from the Konkan territory: Goans, Mangaloreans and Gowda Saraswat Brahmins, have migrated to the same urban centres and started a new life in modern urban India. Unlike their fellow Bombay-born Goans, those in Bangalore did not create the all-Goan neighbourhoods such as those which evolved in Bombay. Rather, Goans and Mangaloreans in Bangalore have tended to demonstrate similar residential patterns which are now occurring in Bombay, wherein they choose to live in communities with a preponderance of Catholics and in accordance with their economic means. Thus, Mangaloreans and Goans resettling in Bangalore will prefer to live within the same neighbourhood rather than among different communities. In a more extreme form, the Gowda Saraswat Brahmins are currently constructing a self-contained residential neighboured modelled after that in Cochin which is meant exclusively for their community.

Yet, while their ancestors occupied the same geographical space, members of each community still speak the same mother tongue of Konkani and most members of the community are relatively well-educated, there are wide cultural and social divides which separate the Catholic communities from those who adhere to the Hindu faith. Though 'Goan' and 'Mangalorean' Catholics intermarry and share similar social circles, the GSB community maintains its own social circle and interacts with other Hindu communities within the same socio-economic bracket.

Konkani, spoken by each community is slightly different as well. While the GSBs from the Gokarna Mutt have incorporated many words of Sanskrit, Kannada and Telugu into their Konkani, the GSBs of the Kashi Mutt have added Marathi and Hindi into theirs and the Cochin GSBs have included Tamil and Malayalam words and intonations into their Konkani. Likewise, the Catholics from Goa have adopted Portuguese and English words, whereas the Mangaloreans have inserted Kannada, English and a few words of Malayalam into their vocabulary. Marriage alliances between Hindu and Catholic Konkanies are rarely heard of and never encouraged and their cultures differ in many ways especially regarding relationships within the family, the social lives of women, food habits and religious beliefs. Therefore, though both groups are fairly well educated, interaction other than on a professional level is strictly limited. Though the educated youths are interacting with different communities more than ever before, the older generations still maintain their traditional perspectives and do not encourage strong friendships among different religious communities. Perhaps with time, further education and greater understanding, additional interaction between Catholic and Hindu Konkanies will occur in large cities like Bangalore. However, this does not seem to be the latest trend. In Bangalore's urban environment, Catholic and Hindu Konkanies maintain their separate lifestyles and have only vague understanding of one other. The Catholic community does not encourage their members to attend Hindu festivals and neither do the majority of GSBs attend Catholic mass.

Though independent of one another, both Hindu and Catholic Konkani-speaking migrants deal with similar issues which result from rural-urban migration into a rapidly expanding city like Bangalore.[57] For example, the preservation of their cultural identity is one of the major issues which both communities are addressing simultaneously, albeit through different organisations. These organisations, besides sponsoring programmes considered part of cultural identity, also help those community members in financially through scholarships and occasionally through financial gifts. The promotion of the Konkani language in an environment where it has little practical utility is again an issue of concern in both Hindu and Catholic communities. The GSBs have been able to deal with this issue most effectively, resulting in fluency in several languages, including both English and Konkani; whereas among the Catholics knowledge of their mother tongue is rapidly deteriorating among successive generations. Both communities fit into the middle and upper-middle class socio-economic status and, thus, issues of financing education, finding suitable employment and arranging marriage are issues of concern which cuts across religious and cultural divides.

Today, Bangalore is Asia's fastest growing city and one of India's major industrial centres.[58] As a consequence of this rapid industrial expansion and human migration, another issue facing both communities is that of personal safety in an urban environment labelled as the 'New Crime City' by Outlook magazine. Gangs and other 'underworld' groups have also surfaced in Bangalore in recent years turning Bangalore's reputation as that of a 'garden' into that of a 'gang city.' With all the alarm bells being sounded concerning safety in Bangalore, the future migration trends of these communities is uncertain. As industries and job opportunities pick up in both Mangalore and Goa, fewer people may find it necessary to risk their lives and sever their home ties in order to migrate to big cities like Bangalore. Further, youngsters from both communities are seeking employment and residential opportunities abroad in the USA and Canada, thus, opting for foreign rather than domestic employment. Wherever the future may lie for these migrated communities, one thing is certain: whether in banks or churches, Hindu or Catholic, Marathi or English, these communities from the Konkan coast have made their mark in Bangalore and continue to do well miles away from their native place.

REFERENCES

1. *Coffee, sandalwood and timber are her chief agrarian products in addition to aircraft, electronic equipment, watches and gold. Karnataka's rocks are rich in minerals like chromite, copper, iron ore, gold and manganese. Karnataka produces most of the world's sandalwood and in the western forests the land also produces teak and bamboo gum.
2. See History of the Konkan territory for more details regarding these dynasties.
3. Madhava, Dr. K.G. Vasantha, Agrarian Relations of Western Karnataka; A.D. 1500-1800, New Delhi: Naurang, 1991, p. 17.
4. Ibid., p. 19.* This land system is related to that prevailing in Goa both lignuistically (Gaunkar) and in definition. (See Social History of Pre-Portuguese Goa, *Economy and Administration).*
5. *Ibid.*, p. 47.
6. *Ibid.*, p. 50.
7. *Ibid.*, p. 14.
8. *Ibid.*, p. 48.
9. *Ibid.*, p. 145.
10. *Ibid.*, p. 89.
11. *Ibid.*
12. *The GSBs in Mangalore, Cochin and Bangalore maintain this system whereby the temple trustees manage the lands belonging to the collective community.
13. *Ibid.*, p. 49.
14. *Ibid.*, p. 50.
15. *Ibid.*, p. 52.
16. *Ibid.*
17. *Ibid.*, p. 54.
18. *Ibid.*, p. 126.
19. *Ibid.*, p. 125.
20. *Ibid.*, p. 53.
21. *Ibid.*, p. 54.
22. *Mangalore Today*, "The Turbulent History of a Vibrant City," April 1997, p. 24.
23. *Ibid.*
24. *Mangalore Today*, "Industries: A Real Threat to the Environment", March 1997, p. 6.
25. Rao, Navin Kumar, "A Dubai Round Up", *Mangalore Today*, April 1997, p. 15.
26. *Ibid.*
27. Murthy, Krishna V. 'The Soul of Mangalore'., *Mangalore Today*, April 1997, p. 25.
28. *Ibid.*, p. 26.

29. *It is important to keep in mind that in a traditional village in rural Goa, social mobility was extremely limited and the ideals of equality implanted into the young minds of Catholics confronted the existing caste-based system.
30. *Though the Portuguese did have control over Mangalorean trade for a few years.
31. *In Mangalore they first fry the onions and masala and then add fresh pork to the mixture, whereas in Goa the pork is fried before it is placed in the curry and the dish is slightly sweeter owing to the addition of sugar in Goan recipes.
32. *Possibly the question of identity came up around the time of Goan independence in 1961. When the issue of Konkani as a recognised language was making news and people realized how out of touch they were with their ancient heritage, they began to make active steps towards the establishment of their own identity, which after 451 years of both physical and emotional separation seems like a likely thing to do.
33. For more details, see the Bombay case study.
34. Karunan, Victor J.R., History of St. Mary's Basilica, Bangalore: Self-published Souvenir, 1974, p. 1.

    *Kempe Panji Gavouden , aka. Kempe Gowda, the Chikka Deva Raja of the Wodeyar family.
35. Prior to being renamed Karnataka, the region was known as Mysore and included the towns of Bangalore, Mysore and Srirangapatanam.
36. *The information was collected from first-hand interviews (personal and by phone) of laymen, priests, presidents of associations; as well as historical records, church accounts and community newsletters etc
37. Karunan, Victor J.R., *op. cit.*, p. 1.
38. *During this early phase Bangalore was under the Pondicherry diocese. On March 16, 1845 this mission was divided to create a separate Mysore Mission which included Bangalore.
39. *In 1775 an unusual alliance developed between Hyder Ali and a Christian priest from Kanakou (near Pondicherry). Having been baptized in 1765 and suffered persecution from family and friends as a consequence, Devasagayam Pillai and his wife Mary Ammal were sent to Srirangapatanam upon recommendation. They were greeted warmly by Hyder Ali and appointed as the commandant of his troops, many of whom were Roman Catholics captured from Mangalore by Hyder Ali and taken to Srirangapatanam in 1763. Pillai did much to assist the small Christian community in Mysore State under the famous Abbe Dubois.
40. *When the administration was handed over to Father Andreas, a native Roman Catholic, he constructed a more permanent Chapel in the shape of a cross; Right wing for Europeans, Left wing for Caste people and the nave in the East for the 'depressed' communities. Thus, even during the early years of the Roman Catholic diocese in Bangalore, caste distinctions were formally recognised and upheld.
41. *Even before the birth of Christ there were Basilicas existing in Rome, the only city to have four Major Basilicas. All others outside of Rome are

deemed Minor ones and in India five exist. The Basilica of St. Mary's has since assumed the title of "Annai Arokiamarie" (Our Lady of Health).

42. Kinatukara, Paul Fr. St. Mary's Basilica. Bangalore; Souvenier self-publication, 1974, pp. 6-7 of article.
43. *Ibid.*, p. 4 of article.
44. Madhava, Dr. K.G. Vasantha, *op. cit.* p. 126.
45. *The previous paragraph is an educated guess as to the historical origins of the Catholic Konkani speaking Goans who migrated to Mangalore. If someone want more substantial information regarding this matter, please feel free to contact my publisher as I would be most interested.
46. These interviews were conducted by person and over the phone in May 1997.
47. *The reasons for this high-rate of Goan immigrants employed in the culinary field are several. First, Catholics in Goa under the Portuguese administration had been for several hundred years preparing beef and pork using condiments and spices from the native soil and, thus, had developed many such dishes which were appealing to the western palate. Hindu people would not cook beef, nor Muslims pork and they could not be expected to go against their religious observances in matters such as these. Mangaloreans, having much less exposure to the Portuguese customs and culture, may not have been so adept at preparing food according to western tastes and, thus, in the end Goans were preferred as cooks. Also, many Mangaloreans owing to their improved socio-economic status considered such menial tasks beneath them and, thus, rejected such job offers. Many Goans, in contrast had been working on British ships, during which time they most likely learnt how to prepare various dishes from the west and returned from these posts with such knowledge.
48. *At this time it was standard practice in every Goan family of three children or more to offer one to the service of the church.
49. *The educated and the Brahmins preferred to remain aloof from their lesser educated brethren.
50. 'Goans' in this sense of the word is taken as its traditional definition which is used to describe a Catholic Indian living in Goa who identifies himself as such.
51. Relative to traditional India. In Goa the majority of women still get married through the proposal system and their social activities are fairly restricted. Only among the upper class Catholics are traces of western influence visible in such forms as love marriages, the use of western clothing and an un-chaperoned social life.
52. *For Mangaloreans, the Goa Carnival is not a celebrated part of their cultural identity and, thus, sponsorship from that community was lacking.
53. The Goddess Saraswati in the Hindu pantheon is the Goddess of wisdom and learning.
54. Gowda Saraswat Samaj., 36th Annual Report, Bangalore; Self-published, 1991, p. 13.
55. See Communities in Goa Today.

56. *At least in theory.
57. *Though Mangalore today has begun to industrialise, during the late 1800's until the mid-1900's there were few available avenues for expansion.
58. *Like most major cities in India, Bangalore has a mixed economy, including federal, State and privately owned industries. The federal government controls industries like aircraft and railway carriage factories, the State controls those factories which supply electronics, porcelain, telephones and soap and the private sector dominates in the production of agricultural tools, glass, medicines, paper, textiles, watches and leather products, etc. Besides its reputation as a growing industrial centre, Bangalore is also India's major silk market and export centre, producing 80 per cent of the nation's silk. In the field of agriculture, farmers in the outlying areas produce coffee, millet, oil seeds and herd sheep and cattle. Since 1970, Bangalore is the centre of some of India's most advanced telecommunications industries.

PART III

PORTUGUESE INFLUENCE

CHAPTER 9

Fort Cochin

Attempts at Trade Domination and Acculturation

The sleepy, ancient and slowly deteriorating town of Fort Cochin today bears little resemblance to the opulent, heavily trafficked Portuguese trading port and site of vicious battles that at one time brought its name to the four corners of the globe. The history of Cochin is inextricably linked to that of the Portuguese and were it not for the foothold they gained on this island in the early years of their arrival in India, the history of the Western Coast of India might have taken a vastly different turn. This chapter traces the early history of Cochin, including its foreign trade relations with the Portuguese, culture of Syrian Christianity and migration of the Saraswat (Konkani) Brahmins. It examines the social relationships among these various communities as well as the ancient society of Latin (Roman) Catholics in Kerala. It further documents the rise and fall of Fort Cochin under the Portuguese, its transference to the Dutch and then British and the effects which these political events had on the Saraswat Brahmins and converted Roman Catholics. The final section examines the state of Fort Cochin today, the current socio-cultural status of both Latin and Syrian Catholics, the settlement of the Gowda Saraswat Brahmins and the resulting attempts of a few Goans to make Cochin their home.

Ancient Commercial History of Kerala

Kerala's history and her economic development have been influenced by a continuous stream of foreign trade relations from a variety of regions around the globe. Since time immemorial, the coast of Kerala has conducted trade relations with foreign countries. From 3,000 B.C. there are mentions of Kerala in the annuls of international trade between India and the Indus Valley and the Red Sea. A pictograph discovered at Mohenjo Daro in the Indus Valley reads: "Karmugil Malayalam Nadu" i.e. the land of Malabar having rain clouds.[1] Another historian of Rawlinson, records that: "Logs of Indian teak have been discovered in the temple of the moon at Mugheir and in the palace of Nebuchandenezer, 3,000 B.C."[2] The Book of Kings also mentions Kerala under descriptions of the fabulous wealth of Solomon in gold, silver, ivory and peacocks (970-930 B.C.); gold which the historians state was at that time mined from Wynaad and the Nilambur of Kerala.[3] The Queen of Sheba presented spices to Solomon, which at that time were considered more precious than gold. Heradotus believes that the products sold to the Hebrews in Aden were brought by Arab traders from Kerala and that after the Romans conquered Egypt they went in search of the source of the spice cultivation (484-413 B.C.).[4]

The Roman historian Pliny of 77 B.C. states that the discovery of the Hippalos (the direction of the south-west monsoon and the short-cut from the Red Sea to Kerala) gave early navigators from Arabia and Persia the courage to sail to Muziris, (a now defunct port known as Kodungalloor) in Kerala.[5] The Roman Empire had continuous commercial connections with Malabar, demonstrated by coins recovered from Kodungalloor and other places of Kerala dating back to 57 B.C. to 58 A.D., from the rule of Augustus Caesar to that of Nero.[6] This trade was conducted by the Cheramans of Kerala who gladly obliged the Roman market's heavy demand for spices. Under the Cheramans, pepper, pearls, ivory, muslin, silks, diamonds, perfume and jacinth were exported while topaz, plain cloth, coral, white glass, copper, brass, tin, wine, musical instruments and beautiful young women for concubinage were imported to Kerala. Marco Polo, on his return from China to Venice in 1293 A.D., stopped at Quilon (Kerala) and remarks on the heavy trade between Kerala and the merchants of China and Arabia.[7] In the 1300's, when the port city of Calicut was dominated by the Arab moors, it was engaged in a prosperous international trade and both it and Quilon were visited regularly by Chinese and Arab traders.[8] In 1410 Nicolo Conti and Italian, went to Calicut from Cochin (then a small kingdom) and records that "Calicut is a noble emporium for all India, abounding in pepper, lac, ginger and a larger king of cinnamon."[9]

It was this wealth and incredible trade potential which the Portuguese crown sought when it sent Vasco da Gama around the Cape in search of this spice route which could then circumvent the Arab traders who at that time had a complete monopoly on the spice trade with India. Thus, in 1498 when Vasco da Gama landed in Calicut, he mentioned a vast number of ships loading and unloading in the harbour, all belonging to the Arabs and Moors who were residents of Calicut. Owing to this monopoly and the wealth accumulated in the port of Calicut, the Moors colluded with the Samorin ruling Calicut to prevent the Portuguese from gaining a foothold in the market. Furious, the Portuguese sailed south to Cochin, where they found the Raja of Cochin keenly interested in obtaining some of the spice trade for his own kingdom. Thus, began the longest war in recorded history, the 250-year war, which resulted in the rise of Cochin as an international trading centre and the inception of Roman Catholicism and western culture in the land of Kerala.

Arrival of the Portuguese

When the Portuguese first rounded the Cape of Good Hope, they did so with the intention of finding a direct sea route to India through which to establish trade relations. They had been sent by the Portuguese Crown because at that time the spice trade was under the monopoly of the Arab Moors, who exacted exorbitant prices for these products. The discovery of the Cape Route effected momentous changes in the mercantile affairs of Europe. Previously, only two trade routes existed between Europe and India, i.e. India-Arabian Gulf-Bassora-Damascus-Port of Beirut (Syria)- Europe via Venetian/Genoese merchants; and India-Red Sea-Cairo -Alexandria-Europe.[10] With the opening of a direct sea route, the Europeans were no longer dependent upon the Arabs for produce from India and Portugal specifically could reap the financial benefits which such trade brought to the Crown.

Thus, when Vasco da Gama and his fleet anchored off the coast of Calicut on the 20th of May, 1498, they did so with the purpose of establishing direct trade relations with the Samorin and returning to Portugal laden with pepper and other spices for the Portuguese Crown. While en route to gain audience with the Samorin, they were stopped outside the Pagoda. 'Believing it to be a Christian Church and their idols to be crude representations of the Virgin Mary and other Saints, they allowed themselves to be sprinkled with 'holy water' by the Brahmins and prostrated themselves before the images.'[11] Owing to this 'mistake' they received a friendly reception by the government, established a treaty of perpetual friendship with the Samorin and secured permission to carry on their trade relations. The Moorish traders, however, fearing the loss of their trade monopoly, contrived with some chief officers of the Samorin and instigated an enmity between the latter and the Portuguese traders. Eventually some spices were loaded, however, they set sail for Portugal, reaching Belem in September of 1499.

The second voyage began on March 5th, 1500 conducted by Captain Pedro Alvarez Cabral. He left Portugal with 10 ships, 2 caravels, 1,500 men and 5 Friars of the Franciscan order and arrived in Calicut on September 13th, 1500 with just 6 vessels.[12] Though they were permitted to establish a factory (trading outpost) in Calicut, the Muslims were still a serious impediment. For two months he waited for his ships to be loaded, but only the Arab merchants received the spices. Outraged, Cabral attacked and seized a Muslim ship which was loading in the harbour on December 17th, 1500. In retaliation, the Moors seized the on-shore Portuguese factory and slaughtered 50 men, another 20 of whom escaped by swimming to boats anchored off-shore.[13] Cabral sought vengeance and seized 10 of the Samorin's vessels and bombarded the town of Calicut, killing 600 inhabitants before sailing to Cochin.

Cochin at that time was situated on a long, low sandy island covered with coconut trees and divided by a deep river from the neighbouring island of Vypeen.[14] The town itself was small and located close to this river near the Raja's palace (modern Mattancherri). Except for the palace and temples, no construction of stone or brick was permitted in the town. On December 20th, 1500, Cabral's fleet arrived off the coast of Cochin. A Syrian Christian by the name of Michael Jogue, who had been taken on board the vessel and offered a passage to Rome and then Palestine, was dispatched on shore with a Portuguese sailor to gain audience with the Raja Trimumpara of Cochin.[15] The Portuguese were given a friendly reception and signed a treaty of perpetual friendship in which they agreed to exchange spices for money and merchandise. In return for permission to erect a factory the Portuguese promised to gain Calicut for the Raja of Cochin. Fearing retaliatory attacks by the Muslims, the Portuguese were given asylum and allowed to sleep within the protected walls of the Raja's palace.[16] Their trade aspirations did not proceed as planned, however, owing to the pre-existing Arab traders who convinced the local merchants not to trade with the Portuguese.[17]

Meanwhile, upon learning the news of the Portuguese treatment in Calicut, the King of Portugal dispatched Vasco da Gama on March 3rd, 1502 in command of an 'avenging squadron' of 15 ships. After rounding the Cape of Good Hope en route to Calicut, da Gama attacked a Moorish ship, seizing its merchandise. He then burned the men on board alive, hung the natives and sent their hands and feet to the Samorin.[18] He then sailed south Cochin where a new trade agreement was executed with the Raja so that the construction of a factory would be permitted and pepper sold at fixed rates.[19] Once Vasco da Gama left, the Samorin of Calicut prepared for war against the Raja of Cochin, whom he felt was sympathetic to the Portuguese and defiant of the Samorins entreaties.[20] On the 31st of March, 1503, the Samorin marched into Cochin and burnt down the town. The Raja was forced to flee to the neighbouring Vypeen Island, but owing to the monsoons and the timely arrival of a fresh Portuguese fleet under Francisco de Albuquerque, the Samorin's progress was checked and he was compelled to retire to Cranganore.[21]

Creation of the Cochin Fort

When Albuquerque arrived in Cochin, he requested permission to erect a Fort at Cochin in order to protect the Portuguese factory and the town from further attacks by the Samorin's troops. On Sept. 26th, 1503, the foundation was laid for the construction of the Fort,[22] which was built in the form of a 180 ft square long with bastions at each corner and walls composed of coconut tree trunks bounded together with iron hoops and nails. It was surrounded on all sides by a moat and Christened "Manuel" on the first of October, 1503.[23] The people marched around in procession preceded by the squadron bands whilst the Fort Vicar carried the crucifix. The Fort was then blessed and consecrated with the celebration of mass in a small wooden church within the Fort dedicated to St. Bartholomew.[24]

The celebrations were short-lived and war resumed against the Samorin who along with the Arabs had been the active agent in preventing the Portuguese from acquiring spices the previous years.[25] At Cochin a blockade was established and no one could leave nor enter without a Portuguese pass and permission. Muslims who had been residing in Cochin were also prohibited from leaving and all trespassers were stopped and examined. Incursions into neighbouring territories continued, resulting in much plunder and slaughter in the name of glory. The Samorin instigated another war against Pacheco (the general in charge of the Portuguese Fort in Cochin) in March of 1504, but the Portuguese troops easily routed the former's troops and the Samorin subsequently retired into religious seclusion.[26]

Subsequently, many of the Samorin's former allies made haste to establish peaceful relationships with the Portuguese and many of the Arabs came to Cochin after seeing their trade destroyed in Calicut. In December of that same year the Portuguese fleet left Cochin to 'guard the coast of India' against piracy and Moorish invasions, who by now had completely abandoned Calicut.[27] As a result, the Portuguese had fulfilled their promise to the Cochin Raja to give him Calicut, as all of the major trade previously conducted in that city was now transferred to Cochin.

In the end of 1505, Don Francisco de Almeida arrived in Cochin as "Viceroy of all the Indies" and built a Fort at Anjediva.[28] In 1508 the Sultan of Egypt sent a fleet to engage the Portuguese in battle off the coast of Chaul. The Portuguese suffered a major loss and Lorenzo de Almeida was mortally wounded. In 1509 Francisco de Almeida attacked and routed the Sultan's fleet off the coast of Diu, restoring for the time being the Portuguese supremacy of the seas. On the 2nd of January in the year 1510, Albuquerque with 3,000 troops made an abortive attempt to destroy Calicut.[29] Subsequently, he established an alliance with the infamous pirate Timoja who showed them an easily accessible island-port on which to establish their trading post. After two failed attempts, in November of 1510 the Portuguese took possession of the city of Old Goa without using force.[30] The Samorin subsequently entered into an alliance with the Portuguese in 1512 and allowed them to construct a Fort in Calicut. Several other 'petty' princes and minor chiefs readily formed alliances with Albuquerque and his name reached the far corners of the globe.

Yet the presence of the Portuguese in the Cochin territory did not go uncontested by both natives and the Arab merchants. In 1515 Soarez replaced Albuquerque as the Viceroy of the Indies and during his administration relations between the Portuguese and the local Rajas deteriorated owing to the 'surly character' of Soarez.[31] In 1518, however, Diego Lopez de Sequeira became the next Viceroy and was able to restore honour to the Portuguese name in Cochin. In 1521 Sequeira sent Alexius de Menezes to Cochin to run the government and while there he successfully defeated another attack on Cochin by the Samorin's troops. In 1524 when Don Vasco da Gama returned as Viceroy with 13 ships and 3,000 men, he found Cochin threatened by the Samorin.[32] He met with an untimely death in December of 1524, when Don Enrique de Menezes, then residing in Goa, left for Cochin to succeed him. Again the Portuguese were attacked at Calicut by the Samorins' troops and again reinforcements arrived from Cochin to successfully quell the invasion. Menezes then decided to destroy the Fort at Calicut because it was no longer worth the trouble and expense. In 1529 Nunho da Cunha landed at Goa as Viceroy and after learning that Sampayo had been keeping the Raja of Cochin a virtual prisoner in his own palace, da Cunha quickly proceeded to Cochin an attempted to establish cordial relations once again.[33] He succeeded and for the time being trade and prosperity was restored to Portuguese India. In 1538 Don Garcia de Noronha became Viceroy and in 1539 he concluded a peace treaty with the Samorin of Calicut.

In 1542, however, cordial relations between the Raja of Cochin and the Portuguese traders suffered when the former confiscated the property of any of his subjects who became

Roman Catholics. He was joined by some petty Hindu princes/chiefs, who persecuted the Christian converts and made them martyrs.[34] In 1550 Fort Cochin was again attacked by the Samorin, this time with the help of the Raja of Pimenta. Supported by only 600 Portuguese troops under Captain Francisco de Silva, a vicious battle ensued during which D'Silva and Pimento lost their lives. Governor Cabral arrived with reinforcements of 6,000 Portuguese troops and 40,000 Nairs and just as he was about to attack he received orders to retreat from Don Alphonso de Noronha who had arrived from Portugal to assume control of the administration. The Fort was successfully defended, but later that same year a town near Cochin was again attacked by 8,000 Nairs and pirates of the seas once again began harassing Portuguese vessels.[35] Thus, the Portuguese presence in Cochin, like that of Goa, was contested and often bitterly resented, though while they were a strong naval force they could keep their enemies at bay.

In 1557 an ordinance was proclaimed whereby anyone who married and settled in Cochin would receive an office or employment according to his trade.[36] If married, they paid no duty on sugar or silk, but a 4 per cent duty on all other products which went to the Raja of Cochin. Bachelors migrating to Cochin paid an 8 per cent duty on everything to the King of Portugal.[37] By 1580, the word had spread regarding the atrocities of the Portuguese and the natives formed a league to 'expatriate' the Portuguese from India.

During the 1600's Cochin was a 'gay' city where travellers came to spend money they had made elsewhere. Like Goa during its hey-day, the style of living in Cochin surpassed the incoming finances and people reluctant to give up their luxurious life became involved in corruption. Owing to the Spanish conquest and the subsequent neglect of the Portuguese colonies in the east, many inhabitants were suspicious of the Portuguese government and as a consequence the councils were divided. The whole nation became dominated by Priests and even the administration cow-toed to the religious authorities. Beyond the internal factors which were slowly consuming the Portuguese power in Cochin, they were increasingly disliked by their old allies. Owing to some disputes, the Portuguese in Cochin had dethroned the Raja and dubbed his aunt as the reigning Ranee. As a consequence, the native Kings formed an alliance to oust the Portuguese from Cochin.

The Dutch in Fort Cochin (1663-1795)

In 1595 two Dutch vessels rounded the Cape of Good Hope on their way to India. They came owing to Philip of Spain, who while in control of Portugal had prevented Holland from trading with Lisbon for spices. In 1597 Vasco da Gama's grandson became Viceroy and in 1598 eight more vessels arrived from Holland. Between the years 1619 to 1622 Cochin remained quiet though visited by sporadic attacks from the Dutch, the British and the natives at Ormuz. In 1639 the Dutch destroyed the Portuguese vessels off the coast of Goa while the latter were pre-occupied in throwing off the yoke of the Spanish in their motherland. The Dutch then extended their tirade against the Spanish to war against Portugal. Though the Portuguese were once again masters of their own territory by 1640, their supremacy on the seas had been seriously contested and their empire in the east began its rapid decline.

It is of little surprise then, that in 1661 the Dutch were able to enter into a treaty with the Paliat of Achen, the hereditary Chief Minister to the Cochin Raja.[38] In it the Dutch would agree to remove the Portuguese by force and subsequently occupy the area once controlled by the latter. The Raja would gain possession of his territories from the Ranee, but would accede to the Dutch in all matters of importance. Consequently, the Dutch entered Cochin via Vypeen island, seized a Roman Catholic church for use as an outpost and attacked the Ranee's palace at Mattancherri. They attacked the Port and Cochin Fort though the garrison was successfully defended. However, this victory was short-lived and in 1662 the Fort of Cranganore fell to the Dutch, who then attacked Cochin in October of that same year. A combined force of natives and Portuguese officers successfully defended this second attack, but on January 8th, 1663, the Portuguese commander Pierre de Pou surrendered after the third attack which lasted eight days and nights.[39] A combined force of the Dutch, the Raja of Cochin and the Paliat of Achen were the victors as assistance was unable to reach the Fort from Goa in time and their native allies had forsaken them to join the new

Dutch power. Thus, the Dutch came to be masters of Fort Cochin and the Portuguese power in India suffered serious setbacks.[40]

In 1663 following the transfer of the Cochin Fort to the Protestant Dutch, all the European Catholic missionaries were compelled to leave the area or face severe punishment. The Syrians had been able to partly remove their allegiance to Rome and the violence of the Jesuits had left the latter hated and feared by the community in Cochin. Further, the Roman church itself was a divided force between the Portuguese and Italians who harboured animosities towards one another. "The Dutch power being now firmly established in Cochin, they turned their attention to removing everything they considered obstructive to their rule."[41] The Roman Catholics, who had hitherto enjoyed their elevated status under the Portuguese, now watched as their churches were destroyed and their security wiped out. The only church left was the Cathedral of Santa Cruz, which was used as a warehouse for incoming shipments of sugar, spices and other commodities. Those Catholics who wished to go to Goa were allowed to do so, but the remainder were forced to give an oath of allegiance to the Dutch. Within the Fortress, Roman Catholics were forbidden to practise their religion and their priests were banished. All those employed by their former Portuguese rulers were expelled from their official positions unless they renounced their religious beliefs and embraced Dutch Protestantism.[42] Some converted again to Protestantism, while others left Cochin and received asylum in the territories of the Cochin Raja. The resulting outflow of natives alarmed the Dutch Government, resulting in a compromise whereby the former Catholics could practise their religion outside the walls of the Fort. A new church was erected for this purpose and all of the icons and statues belonging to the former church were installed in this new edifice. They further attempted to halt the exodus by proclaiming the lands of Dutch descendants, native Catholics and the Konkanies as rent-free.

In subsequent years the Dutch continued to seize Portuguese Forts along the Malabar Coast and enter into alliances with the Raja of Travancore and petty chiefs to secure trade relations in their domains. The year 1742 ushered in a time of anxiety for the Dutch Governors owing to the constant succession of landlords of the smaller States.[43] By 1757 the power of the Dutch began to deteriorate and in that same year they lost many of their alliances with petty chiefs to the Samorin of Calicut. The Dutch then appealed to the Samorin who responded with insults and the seizure of the Dutch Forts at Paparetty and Ayroor.[44]

A war might have ensued between the two as reinforcements arrived from Batavia, but in 1758 a major threat in the north by the name of Hyder Ali caused the Samorin to sue for peace with the Dutch.[45] Again in 1776 the capture of Fort Cochin by Sirdar Khan's troops seemed eminent, owing to its dilapidated structure and meagre garrison of only 200 effective soldiers.[46] The Mysoreans, as Hyder Ali's troops were known, numbered in the thousands and the Travancore Raja declined to assist the Dutch fearing retaliation from Hyder's troops. Just as they seemed destined for victory, Dutch reinforcements arrived by sea and the Mysoreans retreated. The retreat was only temporary, however, in 1783 Tippu Sultan took control over his father's (Hyder's) army. In 1787 he conquered Calicut, destroyed a Danish factory and began preparations for the invasion of the whole of Malabar.

Meanwhile, the power of the Raja of Cochin had increased over the years and he was again in a position of authority and in their influence over the Dutch. His biggest complaint arose owing to the inland Roman Catholics (Latin converts) who were caught killing cows, a crime calls for death penalty.[47] The Raja further accused the Roman Catholic priests of baptising many Hindu 'vagabonds' who had agreed to convert in order to escape the punishments which their crimes required under the laws of the Cochin State. In addition, the converts of Portuguese Catholicism were given 'peculiar' privileges under their Dutch overlords, though according to the Dutch the Raja and his Ministers were constantly oppressing the inland Catholics. In 1785 Van Angleback entered into a new alliance with the Cochin Raja with the results that the native Catholics would pay their taxes to the Raja but would report to the Dutch regarding civil and judicial concerns.[48]

Meanwhile, Cochin was a prosperous international trading centre. Forbes, during his visit to Cochin in 1775, remarked that the city "was a great place for trade and presented a striking contrast to Goa; a harbour filled with ships, streets crowded with merchants and warehouses stored with goods from every part of Asia and Europe."[49] The city of Cochin, thus, remained a major international trading port throughout its change of hands and prosperity was the rule, not the exception.

The British in Fort Cochin (1795-1947)

On the 8th of January, 1795, the French Republican Army invaded the Dutch territory in Europe. Subsequently, in March of that same year England issued a degree to seize all Dutch possessions in the east to keep them out of French hands. The British requested entry into the Dutch Fort in Cochin but were refused by the Dutch governors overseeing them. After several futile attempts of negotiation, the British fired warning shots into the Cochin Fort. Subsequently the Dutch Governor opened negotiations once he calculated that his chances of successfully defending an attack by the British were slim.[50] On the 19th of October, 1795, the Dutch signed over the Fort to the British East India Company and the troops became prisoners of war.

After the British occupation of Fort Cochin, the freedom of religious worship was granted to all religious communities. Article 12 stated that: "The convent at Verapoly and all other Roman churches as also heathen Temples will receive the (same) protection, that they have hitherto enjoyed, under the Dutch Company."[51] Article 13 confirmed that "All Topazes (half-castes or mesticos) and inland Christians, who are subjects and vassals of the Dutch company, will retain their property and also all privileges and protections, which they have always enjoyed of the said (Dutch) company..."[52] The Christians of the aforementioned Articles belonged to two communities of native Roman Catholics: The Moondoocars, as the first group was known, wore white clothes and turbans to distinguish themselves and the Topazes who dressed in hats and pants and were either descendants of the Portuguese, freed slaves of the Portuguese, or offspring of native women and Portuguese fathers.

In 1768 the English engaged in war against Hyder Ali and by the end of 1791 all of Malabar country had become British 'possessions'. In 1799 in the battle of Srirangapatanam , Tippu Sultan was defeated and killed by the British, putting an end to his army and their territorial expansion. In 1803 the Cochin Fort was destroyed by the British after 300 years as a military stronghold, reducing Cochin to a 'mere' mercantile port.[53]

However, from 1800 to 1811 under the British Governor, Colonel Collins Macaulay, the seeds of dissention were sown which would eventually lead to the struggle culminating in Indian Independence in 1947. Sporadic uprisings occurred owing to Macaulay's dictatorship-attitude and preference given towards the Christians in Kerala, resulting in bitterness against the latter.[54] On December 28th, 1808, Paliath Achen and Padmanabha Pillay with 1,000 Nair troops attacked the Residency located in the Cochin Fort.[55] For the next 20 days the Nairs massacred any British or native Christian that they found, especially the Latin Catholics. Only on the 21st of January, 1809, after reinforcements arrived from the British outpost in Cannanore, were the Nair troops defeated. During the early 1900's the native protests against British rule in Cochin paralleled that of other Indian territories and in 1947 Cochin became Independent along with the rest of India.

Catholic, Syrian, Konkani and Goan Communities in Cochin:

Early Communities

When the British took control over Fort Cochin, they documented the existing society and its interrelationships, modes of dress, customs and castes. There were four castes; the three twice born and the Nairs. All others were considered outcast in ancient Keralan society. The Namboorie Brahmins were the highest order and very caste-conscious, following all rituals regarding untouchability, pollution and food habits. The Nairs totalled one-fifth of the total population of the Cochin State and they were Shudras of the highest order.[56] Owing to the scarcity of Ksyatrias and Vaishas in Malabar, the Nairs were considered nobility and were in those days the effective military for the Raja of Cochin. They are from an aboriginal race and offered gory sacrifices to the God of Kati. They regularly consumed venison, chicken, pork, goat and fish, etc. The Chogans were one of the aboriginal tribes and were the former slaves of the Brahmans, Nairs and Syrian Christians. Some other castes existing in ancient Keralan society were the weavers (Tarrogans), the potters (Cojawuns), the cobblers (Chucklers), carpenters

(Arjarees), moojarrees (Brass-founders), the schoolmasters (Cunya Cooroopoos) and many others.[57]

The Jewish people were also a part of the Cochin society and date their origins as far back as 1,500 B.C. They carried on trade between the Coast of Malabar and Palestine for hundreds of years and in 72 A.D. owing to persecution in Palestine, 10,000 fled to Malabar.[58] Their history fascinating subject, goes beyond the scope of this study except in brief mention regarding their relationships with the Portuguese and native Syrian Christians. They were welcomed by the Rajas and petty chiefs of various regions and were given asylum by Kesava Rama Varma, (Cochin Raja), nearby his palace in Mattancherri. On the eve of the Portuguese arrival to Cochin, Jewish communities were prospering in Kochangadi and Cranganore. However, in 1524, their settlement in Cranganore was attacked by the Arab Moors who accused them of interfering in their spice trade.[59] All were massacred, their houses were burnt and the synagogues were demolished. They fled to Saude, a village one mile south of the Cochin Fort and were given asylum there for fifty years. In 1567 they relocated to their current site at 'Jew Town', within walking distance of the Mattancherri palace and the Fort. They lived there peacefully until 1662 when they were attacked by the Portuguese in punishment for keeping quiet regarding the retreat of the Dutch forces.[60]

The Syrians

While the Roman merchants enjoyed a steady, prosperous trade relationship with Kerala, St. Thomas the Apostle landed in Kodungalloor (the now defunct port of Muziris) around 52 A.D. Legend records that after landing and travelling inland to Palayur, he met with some Hindu Brahmins bathing in a shallow pool. As was common in Harappan and Persian cultures, they worshipped the sun by throwing water upwards from the closed palms of their hands. The water, after thrown, would fall back into the pool were the Brahmins were bathing. St. Thomas challenged them remarking: "Your God is not accepting your offering, or else the water would not come down." He then made a deal that he would throw water up to his God and if it remained, the Brahmins would embrace Christianity. This 'miracle' he performed and, thus, baptised the first converts of

St. Thomas, the 'Peishcara Brahmans'.[61] Some of the families left rather than convert to Christianity and from those remaining, St. Thomas ordained one son from every family into the priesthood. In order to retain their caste and social position, the Brahmins agreed to gain additional converts but only those from the highest castes. These converts were later joined by more of St. Thomas's followers from Syria who traced their paternity to St. Paul and owned the supremacy of the Patriarch of Babylon. Under the rule of Cheramal Permaul, both Jewish and Syrian Christians (as St.Thomas' converts were called) enjoyed extensive privileges by 378 A.D.[62]

In 572 A.D., several Christian churches had arisen in Malabar and Ceylon whose bishops were sent from Persia and followed the doctrines of the Bishop of Nestorius.[63] After 600 A.D. the Moplahs began seriously oppressing the Syrians in the Northern parts of Malabar, causing them to migrate south into the territory of Cochin.[64] During the late 700's a missionary by the name of Thomas Cana arrived in Malabar and obtained enormous power and influence over the Syrian Christian community. Under his influence and protection, the community left their inland forested areas in Malabar to settle along the coast. Upon their arrival, the Princes of Malabar treated their new subjects well and gave them equal and at times superior ranking in relation to the Nairs who wielded considerable power within the community.[65]

These Christians were held in high reverence along the Malabar Coast and it was said that 'the more Christians a native Prince had in his domain, the more he was feared by his enemies as they (Syrians) were said to be faithful and trustworthy.'[66] They carried weapons and were educated for over 15 years in the martial arts. They united together when their rights were infringed upon and protected the silversmiths, brass sculptors and carpenters. A low caste man who wounded a Syrian either received the punishment of death or else had to offer a gold or silver hand to the Church in repentance. As was customary of Brahmins, they became polluted if they touched a Sudra and even a Nair and were the only community besides that of Hindu Brahmans and Jews who could construct covered porches outside their homes, ride on elephants, or sit in the King's presence.[67]

And, on the eve of the Portuguese arrival, the Syrian Christians were under the governance of the Raja of Cochin.

While the Portuguese gained a foothold in the Cochin territory and began plans to expand their trading activities, the missionaries were busy determining the belief system of the Syrian Christians which they encountered. Regarding the clergy, the head of the Syrian church was known as a Metropolitan and the inferior clergy were called Catanars. It was discovered that their Bible and prayers were in the Syriac language (unknown to the Portuguese), they practised Hindu rites of purification, attended the latter's feasts and used charms, consulted fortune tellers and submitted to ordeals.[68] Moreover, they held prayers to the Saints and the dead, erected monasteries and had heard neither of Rome nor her liturgies. A priest could marry and his spouse wore a golden cross around her neck as a sign of recognition. In the matter of religious beliefs, there were several important differences between the Syrian Christians and the Portuguese Roman Catholics. Some Syrians denied the divinity of Jesus Christ, though they 'showed unanimous reverence for the Holy Cross'.[69] They believed that the souls of the recently expired remained in 'Eden' prior to their final judgement and admittance into the presence of God. They practised only three sacraments: baptism, the last supper and the consecration of Priests.[70] Palm wine (arack), in the manner of the Nestorians, was their 'consecrated wine' and the 'host' was a preparation of wheaten flour mixed with salt and oil. Holy water was a preparation of river water mixed with some earth brought from the grave of St. Thomas in Mallipuram.[71] Mass was not obligatory on Sundays and on those same evenings everyone ate the flesh of animals. A Syrian festivals would last nearly 24 hours, beginning in the evening and ending the evening of the following day.[72]

These differences though seemingly small in relation to other religious divides, nonetheless alarmed the Portuguese missionaries who came to India. When the Inquisition arrived in Goa in 1552, its activities spread down to Cochin. Menezes (the then Archbishop of Goa), began the process of bringing the Syrian church under the rules of the Roman Catholic Pontiff. Based on the aforementioned differences in ritual and belief, the Roman

Catholic Inquisitors concluded that the Syrians were heretical in their beliefs. They tried to change their faith in accordance with the Roman Catholic rites, but were unsuccessful as both Mar Abraham and Mar Joseph continued to teach the Syrian doctrine even after 'swearing' allegiance to the Pope in Rome.[73] They also refused to worship in the style of the Roman Catholics and many of the devout lost their lives at the hands of these fanatics. Following several complaints, the Cochin Raja prohibited conversions to the Roman Catholic faith, but in 1560 he again allowed the practice of religious freedom and voluntary conversions.

The Pope in 1594 commanded the Portuguese "to reduce the infidels of the country to the Faith by force of arms", a decree which in addition to spurring religious intolerance, also authorised the pillage of Hindu temples.[74] Consequently, from June 20th to June 26th, 1599, the Synod of Diamper was conducted during which the Archdeacon of the Syrians and the high priests finally acceded to the demands of Menezes and agreed to abjure the Nestorian doctrine and uphold primacy of one Christian law. All books considered heretical would be burnt and only a bishop sent by the Pope would be duly recognised. In addition, the practice of 'untouchability' was allowed only outside the church when in the company of high caste Hindus.[75] Married priests who refused to leave their wives were ex-communicated, the Roman sacraments were enforced and the entire community fell under the Sea of Goa. Names of churches were changed and Francisco Rotz (a Jesuit) became the first Latin prelate to rule over Malabar.

Latin Christians in Malabar

As the Portuguese power increased along the Western Coast of India, their missionaries devoted their conversion attempts to the impoverished fishing communities along the coastal and backwater areas. In 1577 the Cochin Jesuits published the Roman Catholic religious doctrine in Tamil through which to instruct the fishing communities.[76] Their attempts were successful and villages converted en masse to this new religion. Owing to Roman Catholicism these communities improved their social status and became a separate caste altogether in the Cochin territory. Consequently, both high and low caste communities were brought under the Christian fold and the high caste Syrians became anxious that under this new system their social status would decline. Eventually what evolved was a social stratification whereby Syrian Christians retained their high social status in the aftermath of the Inquisition and the Latin Roman Catholics came to occupy an inferior position in the social hierarchy.[77]

Social stratification based on caste was always a part of the Christian religion in Malabar. Separate churches were constructed for people of high and low birth and within the walls of one church separate sections were reserved for Europeans, high-caste Hindus and those belonging to the lower castes. The Syrian Brahmins refused to give up wearing the sacred thread and following a meeting of the Catholic clergy in 1619 at Goa, it was decided that the Christian Brahmans could continue to wear the sacred thread as a sign of nobility. Consequently, four Roman Catholic castes evolved and were present beyond the seizure of the Fort by the British. The first, the Arawutnar Leecars, were the converted Brahmins and Nairs. The second caste were the Moonootecars, the communities converted by the Portuguese missionaries (Latins) and the Topazes (domestic slaves of the Portuguese). The third group were known as the Unutecars and were the converted fishermen and other low caste communities. The fourth were known as Erunoortecars and were the descendants of soil slaves.[78]

Thus, while Syrian Christians enjoyed high rank, the Europeans and Latin Christian converts occupied low positions in the social hierarchy, a stratification determined by their pre-Portuguese caste rankings. They were prohibited from using the same roads as the Brahmins and Nairs and according to Brahmanic culture were defiled and impure owing to a variety of European habits unacceptable by Brahman standards. First, Europeans held no sanctions against the consumption of beef, which was an abominable crime according to the moral code of Hindu Brahmans at that time. Second, the Europeans in Cochin employed the Pariahs as their servants, a community from the lowest castes whose very presence caused pollution for a Brahmin. Thirdly, the Europeans drank alcohol and appeared in public places under its influence, a practice considered debased and unsophisticated according to their culture. Fourth, European women were allowed to participate in social activities, including dancing, behaviour considered unbecoming for ladies of high rank. Finally, the mode of dress of Europeans shocked members of the Hindu community as well as some of their peculiar habits. Those Christians who converted to Christianity under the Europeans were attributed these same characteristics, thus, solidifying their community as inferior to Syrians who retained the culture of their forefathers.

Among all Christian communities, certain spiritual beliefs remained even after conversion to Christianity and the atrocities of the Inquisition. Both Hindu and Christian communities held certain superstitious beliefs surrounding the 'evil eye'. In rank, a Brahman priest and an exorcist were about equal. These groups employed certain charms to avert evil eye such as tiger's claws set in silver, a round black mark placed on the cheek of a child and the skull of an animal perched on a stick amidst a paddy field.[79] The use of charms superseded that of medicinal drugs, owing to the cause of disease attributed to the influence of demons. (evil eye). During epidemics of cholera, malaria and smallpox, evil spirits are believed to be roaming around after dark through towns and villages. Thus, with the onset of dusk they would lock their windows and doors to prevent the entrance of these spirits. The Christians in particular also held fasts to St. Sebastian, asking for the cessation of the plague.[80] The sacrifice of a cock to the Goddess Kali was believed to be more effective in the prevention of small pox than a vaccination. Though the native Christians would trust a European doctor regarding surgical operations, they would rely on home remedies for any of the numerous common afflictions.

The native Christians also employed a certain dress which distinguished them from their Hindu brethren. The men did not wear turbans or caste marks on their foreheads and arms[81] and women donned white close-fitting jackets whose backside tapered into what is commonly known as a 'Cochin Tail'. Prior to entering the church, they wore a white scarf over their heads. Women of the Eurasian class would sometimes wear magnificent lace veils when walking the streets, the elegance of which depended on the financial situation of the family. The Moondoocars wore white clothing and consisted of the Latin Christian fishermen (Mucuas), the Dhobiwalas and other castes of 'low' occupation. The 'Topecars' or 'Portuguese' distinguished themselves by the use of hats and pants, though they could have come from any racial stock and needed only to mimic European culture.[82] The Christian men would wear a strip of muslin over their shoulders or carry a pocket handkerchief.

All Roman Catholic and Romo-Syrian girls without dowries were given financial assistance by the parish to which they belonged, a practice which still continues today, though in a low-key form. Female orphans belonging to each parish could also receive dowries raised by the wealthy community members and the Church was obliged to provide them with husbands. Prior to the marriage ceremony as was the custom in Kerala, holes in the women's ear lobes were enlarged in order to support two golden eggs which were worn on the day of the wedding.[83] In addition to the two eggs, women wore a crown made from pasteboard and wrapped with chains of gold, silver and precious stones. During the wedding procession the bride and groom marched under a decorated parasol as a mark of honour and a large feast would follow the marriage ceremony for which a pig was slaughtered. After the birth of the first child the native Christians would often remove the bangles worn at the time of marriage.

Regarding their food habits, both native Christians and Nairs considered the pig a luxury consumption and the animal was raised in the homes of Latin Christians and low caste Hindus.[84] As was customary among both Hindu and Christian communities, large amounts of hot ginger water were consumed along with food, the latter of which was formed into tiny balls and quickly thrown into the mouth with the forefingers. Among the lower castes all types of rodents, cats (probably the influence of the Chines centuries back) and reptiles were eaten and the consumption of arack (palm wine) and toddy was high.[85]

The history of the Syrian Christians and Latin Catholics in Cochin, thus, explains their present status today. The Syrians were an ancient Brahman community in Kerala and took great pains to prevent the spread of the St. Thomas religion into the lower socio-economic strata of Keralan society. Rather than opt for mass conversion attempts, the Syrian Brahmans charged exorbitant prices for the services of baptism which enabled them to remain an exclusive wealthy community while at the same time professing the Christian ideals of equality and brotherhood. Likewise, the Brahmins retained their traditional Indian notions of purity and ritual forms of worship. Even today in Syrian churches men and women remove their shoes before to entering the church, sit on opposite sides of the church hall and worship while sitting cross legged on the floor. The Latin Catholic converts similarly retained their pre-Portuguese habits, customs and lifestyles characteristic of fishing and other agricultural occupational groups. They did not recognise the importance of education until relatively recently and likewise remained a economically disadvantaged community. As a result of these wide differences between the two converted Christian communities, a caste-system developed in accordance with the traditional society in Kerala.

Konkanies (Saraswat Brahmins) in Cochin

Prior to the arrival of the Portuguese, the Gowda Saraswat Brahmins from the Konkan coast had already established themselves in Cochin during the 13th century. "The traditions that exist regarding the first immigration of the Konkanies into Cochin State maintain that owing to certain religious disputes they were obliged to leave their native country Konkan, with their idols in 1294 A.D. After travelling southward they came to the territory of His Highness the Raja of Cochin and having obtained grants of land and assured promise of protection from His Highness, they settled in Cochin and formed themselves into a community which they named, 'the Konkani Mahajanams'.[86] The 'Mackenzie Manuscripts' also record that the Konkanies emigrated to Malabar owing to 'some trouble and prevailed upon the Raja of Cochin to permit them to settle and build temples in his dominions".[87] This trouble led to the destruction of Hindu temples in Goa by Allaudin Khilji in 1294 A.D., coinciding with the mass migration southwards of the Konkanies. Again in 1470 history points out that Muhmad Shah III took his turn to destroy Goa. Based on subsequent historical records, this is the most accurate account of the original Konkani migration which occurred prior to the Portuguese conquest of Goa.

Other accounts arguing that the Gowda Saraswat Brahmins came down to Cochin in the 1500's to escape the Inquisition established in Goa are also a bit controversial. First, we know from historical records that the Inquisition also permeated down to Cochin, reaching its height in the late 1500's and that Cochin was a Portuguese stronghold. Why a community fleeing from the Portuguese would then resettle only a kilometre from Cochin Fort is paradoxical to say the least. Other records indicate, to the contrary, that the Saraswat Brahmins were heavily involved in trade with the Portuguese as was the case in Bassein, Mangalore and other places where the Portuguese had outposts. An enemy to the Portuguese, Sri K.M. Panikkar, himself writes that the Konkanie Brahmins were the 'trade agents' of the Portuguese and Prof. A. Das Gupta in his work remarks that a certain Chalaga Prabhu (GSB) of Cochin was the most prominent merchant for a time.[88]

Furthermore, the community which flourished in Cochin is situated directly outside the Fort within walking distance of the Raja's palace in Mattancherri.[89] This land was given to them rent-free, it seems by the Cochin Raja Kesava Rama Varma in order to build their Tirumala Devaswom Temple in 1599. Moreover, the Gowda Saraswat (Konkanie) Brahmins, were apparently under the protection of both the Portuguese and later the Dutch as can be inferred from a clause in the 1663 Treaty between the two whereby the Konkanies and the Latin Christians would enjoy the same rights and protection as they previously enjoyed under the Portuguese rulers.[90] They became answerable to Dutch laws and taxes for the next 100 years, though they suffered persecution culminating in several murders by Saktan Thampuran, the Cochin Raja during the Dutch period.[91]

History notes that the Konkanies were noted traders and very clever in their business dealings. On the capture of the Cochin Fort by the Dutch, the Konkanies (Canarese) "were up to everything, had ingratiated themselves so with the high officials about the Raja, were ready to barter anything for money, that much required information could be obtained from them."[92] They were divided into four groups. The first were the Tuttans (goldsmiths), the second were the Wunnears (oil merchants), the third were the Chetties (shroffs and general merchants) and the fourth were the Cudumis,[93] who pound rice and perform inferior offices. Unlike other communities, their sons were not obliged to take up the same profession as their forefathers, which Moens remarks that: "the Banians were originally identical with the Wunnears and though they dabbled in all trades, were masters of none. Many of the hawkers were Konkani Brahmans and often had large shops selling clothing and virtually anything necessary for house maintenance."[94]

In 1772 after the Dutch had been in possession of the Cochin Fort for some time, strained relationships developed between them and the Cochin Raja resulting in the transfer of authority to the Konkanies through a document from the former to the latter. The Cochin Government was given the right to collect taxes from the province of Mattancherri and to "conduct the affairs of Mattancherri, Chellye and of the Konkanies and their temple", with the understanding that the Raja would "impose no new demands upon the Konkanies and they shall have full liberty to the Dutch governor if aggrieved and that the Raja shall not interfere in any matters of the temple without the knowledge and consent of the Dutch East India Company."[95] This agreement was the result of a contested ordinance in 1791 in which the Raja gave the Konkanies new official positions which were contested by the existing Cochin Council.

The Konkani Brahmins maintain the history regarding their 'Chief Bhimmum' or idol.[96]

Uptill 1589 A.D., they (the Saraswats) possessed in Cochin a small metal idol and in that year their High Priest, Coombaconum Madum Swamiyar visited the place, bringing with him a Bhimmum, before which he performed his private devotions. Having remained about six months, he prepared to depart, but at every attempt to leave he became seriously ill. Alarmed at this, the soothsayers were consulted and they discovered, that his little God had taken such a fancy to Cochin, that he declined to leave the place. The Swamiyar then offered to give up the Ghimmum, provided he were given as many Venetian gold sequins, as would cover the image, when placed in a large salver. This was acceded to, but as fast as they heaped up the money, the higher grew the idol's head, until all the sequins in Cochin were expended. Again soothsayers were consulted and they discovered, that although the Bhimmum wished to reside in Cochin, he had an aversion to lose sight of his former master and his family. So a contract was drawn up, in which the Pagoda worshippers stipulated, that they would always obey the Swamiyar, or one of his family as High Priest and that his descendants should have the right to perform three days' devotion yearly, in the Pagoda.

Another Legend

The Thirumala Devar (Bhimmum) originally belonged to one of the Vijayanagar rulers, Saluva Narasimha Raya, who usurped the throne of Vijayanagar in 1472 A.D. He was a great devotee of Lord Venkateswara of Thirumalai Hills and used to go to Thirumalai often. When he became physically incapable of visiting the Seven Hills to worship at Seshachala, it is said one day, in his dream a resplendent figure appeared and assured him that he need not make further visits to Thirumalai as the God of Seshachala himself had decided to come over to this capital city. The king was told that an 'Image Maker' would come over there asking whether he should carve any image for the King for which he (the King) had to give all the materials required by him and that the image he would make would be none other than God of Thirumalai Himself. The king was also asked to worship that image.

An image-maker appeared before the King the next day and getting all materials required for the carving out of the image, went to a room and closed all the doors and windows. As he did not come out of the room even after waiting for a long time, the King ordered his men to break the doors and the king was surprised to found a lone resplendent image of the God of the Seven Hills standing in the room. The Image Maker was none other than Viswakarma himself. The King then decided to build a temple for the installation of the image. It was said that after the passing away of the King there occurred a wild fire in the Temple when the image of Sri Venkateswara was thrown into a nearby well by the priest.[97]

In 1719, however, the Bhimmum disappeared during the rennovation of the temple and was found in the house of the Dutch Governor.[98] It was returned to the Temple until 1791 when the Raja of Cochin demanded that the Temple trustees give a large amount of sugarcane jaggery towards a feast at Tripoonterah. They refused, and a skirmish known as the Dagwars Kinni war ensued, during which time Dagwars Kinni was slain for refusing the orders of the King and the Canarese (Konkani) Bazaar was raided.[99] The Konkanies gained asylum inside the Dutch Fort, but secretly carried their Bhimum to Allepey where it stayed until the British gained control of the Fort. In 1853 a Konkanie Brahman from Cochin stole the idol from the temple in Allepey, (the latter whom had refused to give it back upon request) and reinstailed it in the Cochin Temple. After several attempts to gain back the idol the matter went to the government in Madras where it was decided to keep the Bhimmum in Cochin as that was its original residence.[100]

Gowda Saraswat Brahmins (GSBs) in Cochin Today

Owing to the history of prosperous business relations between the Gowda Saraswat Brahmins and successive Cochin administrations, the GSB community has been prosperous. Today in Mattancherri, located less than two kms from the Cochin Fort area, lies this homogeneous colony of the Gowda Saraswat Brahmins of the Kashi Mutt.[101] Approximately 2,000 families live in this compound, in whose centre is located the famous Tirumala Devaswom Temple. They are divided into 12-15 gotras, so named according to their family deities (*Kuladevtas*). Members of their community are employed as bankers, doctors, lawyers, accountants and many other business professions. The community boasts a 100 per cent literacy rate and fluency in five languages: Malayalam, Hindi, English, Konkanies and for many, Sanskrit. They have created many of their own social organisations within the compound itself and entertain marriage alliances strictly within the community. Their food is of the Keralan variety owing to available local produce and they claim 80 per cent are pure vegetarians. Their community is close knit, self-supporting and very involved in the social and educational welfare of its younger members. They are exemplary of successful community reorganisation and cultural evolution.

Institutions of the Gowda Saraswat Brahmins in Cochin

Within their compound, GSBs lived on the outskirts of the Devaswom (temple lands). In the center of the complex is the Thirumala Temple, its adjoining temples and a lake within which an additional Mandapam was constructed.[102] On the periphery of the temple are located the various GSB institutions outlined below. It is a self-contained community wherein the children become educated until the 10th standard. Currently a secondary school is being planned wherein GSB students can receive their education privately until the 12th standard. The presiding deity is Lord Venkateshwara, who is an incarnation of Vishnu. Other deities also revered by the GSBs in Cochin are Shantadurga, Manguesh, Naguesh and Mahalaxmi.[103] These are family deities which are connected to one of the 15 gotras, or family names.

Cochin Thirumala Devaswom Temple in Mattancherri is the main socio-religious institution of the GSB Community in Kerala. According to their records, the current temple was built in 1599 under the rule of Kesava Rama Varma. They were then given special rights and privileges by Vira Kerala Varma (1624-37) as outlined by the Thitooram inscribed on copper plates. The temple was renovated in 1719 and again in 1881. The installation of the image of Lord Venkateshwara in 1719 was presided over by H.H. Srimad Devendra Tirtha Swami of the Kashi Mutt (whose origins are in Varanasi). It is a home to the largest temple bell in India it and contains splendid wood carvings depicting scenes from Kerala. The property of the temple also includes an elephant worth 9 lakhs and a Palanquin layered with 9 kilos of gold. In addition to the main temple, whose architecture is that of the 'Nagara' style, there are four minor temples in honour of Hanuman, Garuda, Ganesh and Mahalaxmi. The Udyaneswara Temple, the Vrindavan Temple and the Karnakodam Temple are all subordinate to the Thirumala Temple, the first two being situated within the walls of the compound. The statues of Hanuman and Garuda are roughly six feet tall and the northern Gopuram of the temple is of a 'Pagoda type resembling a Tibeto-Indian architecture. The roof is copper plated and 2-storyied. Within an artificially constructed lake lies the Lake Mandapam, commonly known as 'Papańasam', located on the north-eastern side of the eastern Gopuram. A small statue of Saluva Narasimha Raya and that of the Swamiji who had the vision of Lord Venkateswara are carved on either side of the walls of the Mandapam. The temple also maintains cattle and sheep in a *Goshala* (cowshed) from the Devasom funds. Other temples under the management of the Cochin Thirumala Devaswom temple are the Sindoora Bhagavathi, the Keraleeswara Siva Temple, the Vittobha Temple, the Dhanvantri Temple, the Dharma Sastha Temple, the Kotwal Temple and the Mullakal Bhagavathi Temple.

Several institutions were established solely for the members of the GSB community in Cochin. They are the All Cochin Saraswath Association, the Gowda Saraswath Association, the Saraswath Youth Association, the Gowda Saraswath Students Organisation and the Gowda Saraswath Mahila Mandali. In addition, the Madhwatatwa Prachar Sabha was founded in 1968 for the study of the teachings of Madhwacharya, (founder of the Dualistic System of Vedanta). The Sabha hosts several lectures and discussions on the Vedas, Upanishads and for three days every year celebrates the day of Madhwacharya.

The Gowda Saraswat Brahmins have also founded several educational institutions. For the maintenance of Vedic and Sanskrit Studies, the T.D. (Thirumala Devaswom) established a Vedic and Sanskrit Pathasala in 1877 which is the oldest in Kerala. In 1963-64 the institution received a grant of Rs 6,000 for the upkeep and maintenance of its library. The T.D. High School (1st-10th standards) was founded in 1962 by Sri R.S. Hari Shenoy and is one of the oldest high schools in Cochin. The T.D. Basic Training School and two primary schools are additional educational institutions founded and maintained by the Thirumala Devaswom Temple.

The Gowda Saraswat Brahmins of Cochin have also established many social and cultural institutions for GSBs and other deserving members of the Cochin Community. The Sree Venkatesha Seva Samithi is one such organisation founded in 1935 and registered in 1942 under the Charitable Endowment Act. The Samithi was created as a Bhajana Mandali to instruct youths in the performance of the bajana of Sree Venktachalapathi, the presiding deity. It's role expanded, and in 1965, with donations from community members, the Samithi constructed a cremation chamber to ensure the proper and sanitary disposal of deceased community members. The Samithi also manages an orphanage and a home for the destitute for GSB members around the country. The Anathashram, as the orphanage is known, houses boys and girls so that they can receive a proper education and aim for advanced degrees. The Athuralaya is their home for the sick, aged and invalids of the GSB community. Those who remain left behind as sons and daughters have gone abroad or are otherwise the 'unwanted' find asylum and support here. This same Samithi also runs a public library and a reading room which has become one of the leading libraries in Kerala. Moreover, it manages an Industrial School where ladies can learn the tailoring profession as well as a Marriage Bureau to help ensure suitable matches among the GSB community. A final activity of the Samithi is the management of a Trust (1966) which utilises member donations to finance the construction of low-income housing.

In addition to the Samithi, several organisations were established which cater to the larger community as well. The Kamath's Music College was established in 1955 with the goal of promoting the study of Classical, Karnatic and Hindustani music. The Yogya Pai Narayana Pai Trust is a Lecture Hall-cum-Kalyana Mantapam which can be rented by the members of the larger Hindu community for marriages, Upanayanams and lectures. This trust was created by the Pai sons in memory of their father, who was a well-known philanthropist. The Konkani Bhasha Prachar Sabha of Cochin was founded in 1966 to promote the study of the Konkani language as a State language in Kerala. It has subsequently been able to introduce Konkani as a minority language until the 4th Standard. The GSBs have, since 1971, completed the construction of a Bhavan (centre) specifically for the study of this language. The Sukrateendra Oriental Research Institute (founded 1972) was created with the aim of promoting the study of Sanskrit and Indology. It also houses a rare collection of books and palm-leaf manuscripts. Two additional libraries were established by members of the GSB community; the Sri N. Govinda Pai Memorial Library and the Sri Venkateswara Seva Samithi Library.

Beyond the various institutions and cultural organisations established by the Saraswat Brahmin Community, several festivals are celebrated throughout the year which are unique to the T.D.T in Cochin. The 'Aratu' festivals in the months of December and April are famous, each lasting a total of eight days.[104] On the first day the ritual raising of the Garuda flag occurs in solemn observance, followed by two processions on the 2nd through 4th day in the morning and then in the evening. During one procession, a symbolic image of Lord Venkateswara is carried on the temple elephant and in the second style the 'Utasva' image of the same Lord is carried in various 'Vahanas' bedecked with jewels and flower garlands. 'On the 5th and 6th day of the Mahotsava, the 'Utsava Image' is taken in 'Palanquin' along the southern and northern streets respectively via elephant where the deity is said to have absolute jurisdiction, temporal and spiritual.' On the evening of the 7th day the 'Ashwa Vahana' (horse vehicle) circumvents the parameters of the temple, symbolic of a wild animal hunt. In the afternoon of the 8th day, Lord Venkateswara is taken to the Lake Mandapan and circumvents the temple 7 times in a richly decorated pontiff before being immersed 'Avabritha Snanam' in the lake by GSB priests. That night the image of the deity is again carried atop the Temple elephant in procession from the main temple, around the Lake and then back to its original abode within the Temple grounds. The 'Arat' festivals are the most famous and draw large crowds, that in April of 1997 occurring from the 15th to the 22nd. Other festivals celebrated by the T.D. T. are Karthika, Pournima, Vaisaka Pournima, Anathachathurdasi, Ashtami Rohini, Deepavali and the Car (temple) Festival on Mahanavami day during the days of Navarathri.

The Kuladevtas (family deities) of the Gowda Saraswat Brahmins have also been established in Cochin, *thus, eliminating the necessity for pilgrimages to Goa.* Consequently, they have virtually no ties with modern Goa, though they believe that they at one time came down from Goa as Konkani is their mother tongue. This may be unlikely, however, as they belong to the Kashi Mutt which is distinguished owing to its direct migration from Varanasi.[105] In addition, the Konkani of these GSBs is significantly different from that of their ancestors. Whereas the Goan Hindu Konkani has become infused with Marathi and Portuguese, in Cochin the Konkani language has evolved over the years in a completely different society. Owing to external influence and the natural evolution of a language, their Konkani is infused with Sanskrit, Malayalam and Tamil words. Thus, it becomes difficult for even a native Goan Konkani speaker to fully grasp what is said in this new hybrid language.

The Gowda Saraswat Brahmin Community has, since their migration to the land of Cochin in the late 1300's, been involved in business and mercantile activities. As in most places where the Saraswats have migrated, in Cochin too they are distinctly absent from the political scene and prefer to earn their living in an honest and socially beneficial manner. Today they are involved in a host of business activities in addition to professional positions in banking, medicine, accounting and law.

Regarding the cultural traditions of the Gowda Saraswat Brahmins, they practice the same traditions as their forefathers and of those GSB's residing throughout India. Pre-birth rituals, the naming and thread ceremonies (Upanayanam), the matching of horoscopes, arranged marriages within the community, use of mangalsutra , pavitra ketha and the wedding ring, reception in marriage halls and cremation rites are practised in a fashion consistent with this larger GSB culture. However, there are some differences unique to the GSB's in Kerala. During processions, the use of a long flute of Tamil origin is one musical difference among the Cochin Saraswats, as is the ownership of a temple elephant. The latter is a typical display of wealth in Keralan society and has been adopted by the temple Trustees of the GSBs.[106]

Their community is remarkable in the sense of maintaining cultural traditions and high standards of excellence and from the interviews I did arrange and I was able to ascertain that the GSB's in Cochin are similar to other GSBs in the areas where I conducted research regarding their strong sense of cultural identity and pride. Likewise, the knowledge of their historical migration, mother tongue and ancient cultural traditions is unmatched among most Indian communities which I encountered.

The Kudumbi Tribals: Other Konkani-Speaking Migrants

In addition to the Brahmins, a Konkani tribal community known as the Kudumbis (Kunbis in Goa) also migrated to Fort Cochin. When the Gowda Saraswat Brahmins migrated to

Cochin, they brought with them a Konkani-speaking tribe known today as Kudumbis. They were the servants and agricultural labourers of the Gowda Saraswat Brahmin community and in former days were given a portion of the agricultural produce as payment for their labour on the lands owned by the Brahmins. Though little is known about this community owing to their illiteracy throughout the majority of history, it can be ascertained that they did in fact migrate with the Brahmins as in Mangalore and other places where the GSB's migrated. Their complexion is darker when compared to the GSBs and were formerly under the control of the Temple trustees. Allowing for a slight evolution in terms, they are most likely the 'Kunbis', the farm labourers found in Goa along the Konkan Coast.

Today, owing to the National Land Tenancy Act, many of them were given the lands of the GSB community on which they had lived for centuries. Whereas in that era few were able to read and write, today approximately 60 per cent are literate and they attend schools in the Malayalam medium which are located throughout Cochin. Only 5-10 per cent are able to speak the English language and they are given scholarships and reserved government jobs owing to their status as OBCs (Other Backward Castes). They have a folk culture altogether different from the sophistication of the Saraswat Brahmins and until 10 years back they celebrated the 'Phutka' festival, including dances, folksongs and melodies.[107]

Goans Migrants in Cochin

Most Goans preferred to go to Bombay during the migration years as there were ample opportunities in this new mercantile city where the British dominated and allowed freedom of worship for all religions. Cochin had a history marred by religious persecution of Latin Catholics, a more conservative society and a business community saturated from various communities, including the Jewish, Muslim and Hindu communities. It was a city whose hay days were in the past, while the story of Bombay was about to be written. Beyond the social and economic conditions of the city of Cochin, the monsoon climate starting in May and lasting through September-October held little appeal for those Goans used only to three months of downpours.

In addition to the presence of other growing cities, the proximity of Cochin to Goa affected the number of Goans choosing to migrate south to that city. Cochin, located in the southern half of coastal Kerala, was a three-day overland journey from Goa during the early 1900's, owing to infrequent and erratic transportation routes in addition to the necessary back-water trip through Keralan lowlands which necessitated hiring a boat. The only other way to reach Cochin from Goa was by ship, but passenger boats travelling between the two regions were infrequent.

Also, the Goan Catholics enjoyed a relatively high social position in Goa, whereas in Cochin the position of Latin Catholics was relatively low. This is the third important factor that resulted in the minimal migration of Goans into Cochin. Most Goan Catholics considered themselves somehow 'superior' to other Indians owing to the Portuguese who had indoctrinated into them feelings of cultural superiority and sophistication. Even those who had little contact with Portuguese culture other than through education believed themselves to be different and somehow better. Consequently, when they arrived in Cochin they confronted two issues, namely, the loss of prestige owing to Latin Catholics in Cochin falling into a 'second-class' category of primarily fishermen and backward castes, as well as a traditional Hindu environment somewhat resentful of Latin Catholics based on the preferential treatment they had been given under earlier European regimes.

Goans in Fort Cochin

Today in Fort Cochin 1000 families live, of which 75 per cent are Catholic and 230 are Anglo-Indian.[108] Only 5 families are of Goan descent. The following case studies of Goans living in Fort Cochin further demonstrate that the climate in Cochin was not conducive to the maintenance of Goan identity. Among the Catholics in Cochin, there are only a few Goan families living in the Fort area and some in Ernakulam city. Those Goans who did migrate to Cochin usually did so on account of work and most of them were the sailors who were docked there for several months. Though the majority of people in Fort Cochin are Christians, they are Syrians and native Latins rather than Goans. The cultural foundations of both of these communities stem from Keralan customs and habits rather than those of Portugal and most do not identify with the 'western' style of living. Native Latin and Syrian Catholics are more 'orthodox' than either Goans or Anglo-Indians and the latter rarely fraternise with them outside Church functions.

The first case study is that of the family of Mr. Noronha who has lived 23 years in Cochin. He claims that Goans do not mingle with the other communities and that Cochin never saw the development of village clubs or Goan neighbourhoods. In the 1920's and 30's some Goans migrated to Cochin to start or expand their own businesses, while others came owing to their employment on British and later Indian ships. Many of the Goans who initially migrated to Cochin have gone back to Goa, others have moved on to Bombay. Mr Norohna himself works for SHS Shipping and met his future wife who was an air hostess. Married in 1974, Mrs Noronha is a Keralan-born Goan whose parents migrated from Anjuna during the 1930's. Though she was born and raised in Kerala, she claims her heart is in Goa and she would like to live there forever. She does not often go out of the house, owing to the culture in which she was raised and her ailing mother. She speaks Malayalam, but Mr Noronha does not know the language. They have one son who is completing the 11th standard. They admit that they know few people from Kerala and Mr Noronha himself lives in Kerala only two months out of an entire year.

Our second case study is that of a Mr Monteiro who came to Kerala as a young boy. His grandfather had minor 'trade links' in Cochin which enabled his son, Mr Monteiro's father, to settle down in Kerala. From a poor family, his father's main aim was to provide his two sons and daughter with an education. One by one he succeeded in bringing his three children down to Cochin where they could enroll in an English-medium educational system. Consequently, Mr Monteiro grew up in the cultural environs of Kerala as a young boy and became fluent in Malayalam. His family proposed to a Keralan girl in a 'proper' marriage and today he is the manager of a prosperous business in Mattancherri. He is proud to be from Goa but feels that there is little point in hanging on to a Goan identity when one is settled in Kerala.

Our third case study is a Mr Fernandez whose grandparents came and settled in Cochin owing to the lack of opportunity in Goa. His parents settled on the island of Verapura, which is a community entirely composed of Latin Christians. At first glance he appears as a typical Keralite, wearing a blue plaid lungi, a white tee-shirt and sandals. He was born in Kerala and raised in the local schools and culture. He has two daughters and a wife who is a native Latin Catholic from Kerala. Though he fluently speaks Konkani, especially with Mr Noronha and the ship people who are on leave, his two daughters neither speak nor understand the language. They study through an English medium and fluently speak Malayalam. His own first language is English through which he completed his Bachelor of Arts; his wife a Bachelor of Commerce. Currently he runs his father's metal shop and arranges food and provisions every three or four days for incoming passenger ships. If asked, Mr Fernandez would identify himself as a Goan and has twice visited Goa where they have purchased property in Calangute.

Conclusion

Without knowing at least a brief overview of the history on the Malabar Coast, it would be difficult to place todays Gowda Saraswat Brahmins, the native Christians and the migrated Goans into their proper perspective. The historical events, political relationships and social interactions among people in the city of Cochin are pivotal in explaining the current situation of the above communities today. Thus, while an outline of Cochin history has been presented above, it is confined to the general history of Cochin highlighting the course of events directly related to the communities under study. Nonetheless, such an historical outline is necessary for a better understanding of the position which describes these communities today and especially their historical and cultural evolution.

The Saraswat Brahmins, owing to their uninterrupted business dealings with and political/economic asylum under a variety of ruling powers especially the Portuguese, Dutch and British, have today one of the most opulent temples in all of Cochin, possibly in the whole of Kerala. They derive a strong sense of communal identity and pride from their Gowda Saraswat Brahmin cultural heritage and many efforts are being made to preserve their ancient cultural heritage and forms of expression. As a result, education in Konkani and Sanskrit language are available within the 'walls' of the compound and most of their members have extensive knowledge of their culture and roots. The GSBs are value-oriented towards education as well as tradition, with the result that this community demonstrates progressive attitudes and behaviours regarding professions and the role of women in the society. By placing a high value on that which causes change as well as that which maintains stability, the Gowda Saraswat Brahmins in Cochin, as in other parts of India, demonstrate a remarkable synthesis and harmony between these two forces. In Cochin, owing to their severed ties with Goa and ancient migration, the GSB community has allowed some traditional aspects of Keralan society to permeate, at least superficially, into the lives of GSBs. Owning a separate temple elephant (as all temples who can, do, as a sign of wealth) and adopting Malayalam and Tamil words into the Konkani language are just two of these more obvious examples.

The Syrian Christians still enjoy a high place in the Keralan society, being both ancient and of noble birth. They have retained their traditional 'Brahmin' status and continue as wealthy landowners and the like, though over the years their power and influence has become diluted. They are important in this study when considering the environment and social hierarchy into which Portugese (Latin) Roman Catholicism entered. Owing to their exalted status in the Keralite society, the Portuguese had greater difficulty in converting individuals over to their religion.

These factors and others caused the Portuguese to concentrate their conversion efforts on the lower strata of society; the fishermen, farmers, washermen and other low caste. As a result very few if any upper-class educated individuals from Kerala converted under the Portuguese regime and those who did convert continued in many of their former ways. Though an elaborate description of such behaviours and customs goes beyond the scope of this study, it is enough to say that few native converts were able to assimilate the Portuguese culture as was so desired by the Portuguese administration. Their social environment prior to the Portuguese was so deeply ingrained, that few missionaries were successful in changing the culture, behaviour and lifestyles of the native converts. Likewise, as their presence in Cochin was limited and contested, the Portuguese would have to wait until their arrival in Goa before their aim of getting a 'cultural foothold' in India could be modestly realised. The evolution of Latin Catholics in Kerala does not resemble that of Goa but rather has followed a path which is inextricably linked to larger Keralan society and to the community's culture and society prior to the advent of the Portuguese.

It is hardly surprising, therefore, to find that few Goans decided to permanently settle in Cochin and most returned to their homeland. It is difficult to assess the cultural evolution of Goans in Cochin owing to the few families still residing in Cochin. From the aforementioned case studies and the social history of Kerala, several conclusions can be inferred regarding the Goan families in Cochin. First, owing to their small numbers, the type of communal establishments and social organisations existing in Bombay were absent in Cochin during the first migrations. As a consequence, migration to Cochin was more difficult and only those with sufficient resources to survive on their own had a chance of making a living. Second, as no community migrates into a vacuum, the Goans in Cochin migrated into a very traditional society where Latin Catholics did not receive the high regard which was awarded them in Goa. Kerala throughout its history has been very conservative regarding matters of caste and social records indicate that even in the 1800's harsh caste observances were strictly enforced. Thus, native Latin Catholics, far from being a progressive community as in Goa, were themselves very tradition-minded and caste conscious. These traditional forces were strong and as a whole were capable of overpowering the communal identity of the Goans. Those who were successful in adjusting to life in Kerala were compelled to give up their Goan identity in appearance, custom and language. Many intermarried with local Latin Catholics and were able to adapt to Keralan society. Those who grew up in Kerala found it much easier to adapt, whereas those who migrated themselves demonstrated adjustment difficulties. While Goan culture most resembled that of Anglo-Indians, they were not accepted by that society and neither did they feel in touch with the conservative and often economically backward Latin Catholics of Kerala. In general, they were a unique community in Kerala but were not readily accepted by other native societies. Many began to feel that their only real 'place' was in Goa and as a result many Goans have since gone back to their native place. Those who remained in Kerala while still maintaining a Goan identity feel and are treated as foreigners in their own place of residence. Not knowing Malayalam has isolated them, causing them to adhere to their roots as a source of communal comfort and pride. Unlike Bombay, which was a veritable cultural melting pot in its early years, the society of Kerala was ancient, rigidly stratified and traditional.

The example of the historical, cultural and political evolution of Fort Cochin enhances an understanding of Goan culture and identity in several ways. The example of the Syrian Christians in Kerala is important because it shows an alternate path of Christian evolution within the Indian cultural complex. Owing to the traditional social structure, habits and beliefs of the Brahmin converts, the religious rituals and social behaviours of the Syrian Christians resembled those of their Hindu brethren. Syrian Christianity was also maintained as an upper-caste religion which enabled the Brahmins to retain the social prestige so important in Keralan society. Syrian Christians were not compelled to adopt the culture of St.Thomas and since its inception Syrian Christianity in Kerala has become thoroughly Indian. The Syrians, owing to their origins in the upper castes, have remained wealthy and prominent over the centuries and continue to enjoy an elevated position in today's society, which relegated Latin (Portuguese) converts to a second-class status.

The example of the Latin Catholics in Cochin also sheds light on the development of Portuguese Catholicism in other areas of India impacted by the Portuguese empire. The Latin Catholics in Cochin originated from the lower socio-economic castes of society and few if any came from the educated, cultured strata of the Keralan community. As a consequence, the efforts of the church to educate the converts was largely futile and, thus, the clergy preferred to focus on indoctrination rather than education. Following the Portuguese rule, the Latin converts remained in backward condition and were further persecuted by the new Dutch administration. The natives and Rajas also repressed them, acts which at times culminated in eviction and murder. Whereas in Goa the Catholic population has and continues to enjoy a respected position in society, the native Latin Catholics in Cochin experienced a great deal of persecution for trying to improve their socio-economic conditions. They have remained depressed both educationally and economically, a reality which, therefore, exists in today's Latin Catholic community in Cochin.

Gowda Saraswat Brahman migration in Cochin serves as an example of successful community reformation. Their involvement in business and detachment from politics have enabled them to promote their economy and culture throughout successive administrations. Because they migrated in numbers and maintained a close-knit community, they were able to adjust successfully into Kerala's society, maintaining their own traditions while simultaneously becoming a prominent and upstanding section of society. Deep-seeded cultural pride and a sense of communal identity are the characteristics which have enabled the GSB's in Cochin to maintain their cultural heritage in the face of migration and ongoing change. Through their own efforts and values stressing the importance of education and community, the Gowda Saraswat Brahmins of Cochin exemplify a well-integrated community within the Indian context.

As in the case of GSB's entering Keralan society, Goan Catholic migrants in Cochin had to adopt strategies in order to survive in the culture of Kerala. Owing to the distance and low social status of Latin Catholics, few families made the decision to migrate as far as south Cochin during the 1900's. Thus, village clubs, schools and social welfare institutions the likes of those in Bombay were not created in Fort Cochin. The few who migrated at a young age or who were enthralled by the culture of Kerala often chose to relinquish their Goan identity for the one available in Kerala. Those who did not want to abdicate their identity became virtual outsiders in the society and often maintained a type of fantasy image of their homeland in Goa from which to renew their source of identity and pride.

REFERENCES

1. Bernard, K.L., *Flashes of Kerala History*, Cochin: Swaraj Printers, 1995, p. 11.

2. *Ibid.*, p. 11.
3. *Ibid.*, p. 12.
4. *Ibid.*
5. *Ibid.*, p. 13.
6. *Ibid.*, p. 14.
7. *Ibid.*, p. 17.
8. *Cochin Harbour was formed only in 1341 after a powerful monsoon which resulted in the change in flow of a river.
9. *Ibid.*, p. 18.
10. *In either case the Arab merchants were the main links between Europe and India.
11. Day, Francis, *The Land of the Permauls, or Cochin*, New Delhi: Asian Educational Services, 1995 (reprint) 1st published in 1900, p. 75.
12. *Ibid.*, p. 80.
13. *Ibid.*, p. 81.
14. *Ibid.*, p. 83.
15. *Ibid.*, p. 84.
16. *Ibid.*
17. *The next fleet dispatched from Portugal was captained by John de Nueva who, upon his arrival, discovered that the Moors had persuaded the native merchants not to trade with the Portuguese for their merchandise in both Cochin and Cannanore. Instead, they insisted upon ready money in exchange for spices, which the Portuguese in Cochin did not have in such great quantities.
18. *Ibid.*, p. 85.

    *Between August and October of 1502, da Gama bombarded the town of Calicut again before sailing on to Cannanore where a treaty of friendship and commerce was concluded with the Raja.
19. *While Vasco da Gama was at Cochin, the Syrian Christians at Cranganore requested that da Gama intercede with the Portuguese King to become their ruler and protector. From their own accounts, the Christians were suffering from oppression under their current ruler and if residing on temple property, were forced to attend Hindu religious festivals. Da Gama promised them assistance and protection and on the 1st of September, 1503, he returned to Portugal. (See *History of the Syrian Christians*)
20. *The Raja appealed for assistance to the remaining Portuguese Captain Vincente de Sodre, but he would not enter into war against the Samorin.
21. Day, Francis. *op. cit.*, p. 87.
22. *On Sept. 30th Alonso de Albuquerque arrived (the former's cousin) and advanced the speed of the construction.
23. Day, Francis, *op. cit.*, p. 91.
24. *This was probably the first Catholic Portuguese religious festival to occur on Indian soil.
25. *Duarte Pacheco was left in charge of Fort Cochin with four vessels and

90 men while the rest of the fleet left in an attempted return to Europe (They were never heard from again).

26. Day, Francis, *op. cit.*, p. 93.
27. *Ibid.*, p. 95.
28. *Around the same time Gonzalo Vaz destroyed a Moorish vessel off the coast of Cannanore, disregarding the Portuguese pass and murdering the entire crew. One of these bodies floated ashore after which the Raja of Cannanore approached the Samorin for help in evicting the Portuguese from their outposts in India. The atrocity was blamed on the commander of the Cannanore Fort, Lorenzo de Britto, who was attacked by the Raja. Fortunately for the Portuguese, reinforcements arrived from Cochin and routed the Raja's troops. (Fort Cannanore had been built in 1505 by Almeida while en route to Cochin.)
29. Day, Francis, *op. cit.*, p. 99.
30. *See *History of Goa.*
31. Day, Francis, *op. cit.*, p. 101.
32. *Ibid.*, p. 103.
33. *Ibid.*, p. 105.
34. *Ibid.*, p. 107.

    *Don Martin Alphonso de Souza arrived in Goa that same year and during his administration the Portuguese empire reached its zenith of power and glory.
35. *Also during 1550, the Portuguese built the Raja of Cochin a palace at Mattancherri.
36. *In 1557 the Santa Cruz Church of the Holy Cross was raised to the status of a cathedral by Pope Pius IV.
37. *In 1576 Don Diego de Menezes assumed the Viceroyalty in India. In 1578 Spain invaded Portugal and severely curtailed her activities. Affairs in India were neglected and the Portuguese claim that their decline began with this invasion.
38. Day, Francis, *op. cit.*, p. 119.
39. *Ibid.*, p. 120.
40. *The day after capitulation news arrived from Goa of the peace between the Dutch and the Portuguese, albeit 24-hours too late.
41. Day, Francis, *op. cit.*, p. 121.
42. *Ibid.*, p. 122.
43. *Aggression between Cochin and the Raja of Travancore resulted in sporadic attacks between the two and the Samorin harbouring desires of territorial expansion into the Cochin State. Further, the Raja of Cochin failed to maintain his end of the treaty with the Dutch regarding the export of Pepper.
44. Day, Francis, *op. cit.*, p. 125.
45. *In 1762, Hyder Ali in collusion with the Portuguese brought Onore, Barcelore and Mangalore under his fold. In the same year combined forces of the Travancore and Cochin Rajas routed the Samorin and prepared for

an attack against Hyder Ali. But in 1766 as Hyder was preparing an attack, word reached that a combined force of the Marathas and the Nizam were about to invade the capital of his Mysore empire in Srirangapatanam. He recalled his armies to Mysore, thus, abandoning his attack on the Cochin State.

46. *Ibid.*, p. 154.
47. *Ibid.*, p. 155.
48. *Ibid.*, p. 159. * This agreement was not long in place before the Raja of Cochin began to openly persecute the Christians, in some cases throwing them from their lands.
49. *Ibid.*, p. 170.
50. *Ibid.*, pp. 161-62.
51. *Ibid.*, p. 163.
52. *Ibid.*, p. 165.
53. *Ibid.*, p. 174.
54. *In 1814 the British administration in Cochin decided not to maintain jurisdiction over the native Christians who resided in territories of the Cochin Raja, though the Konkanies (Canarese) were still under the British Court, much like they had been during the Dutch period.
55. *The British officials escaped through a secret underground tunnel built 250 years ago by the Portuguese leading from the Residency to a hidden location 100 yards outside of the Fort.
56. Day, Francis, *op. cit.*, p. 320.
57. *Ibid.*, p. 323.
58. Bernard, K.L. *op. cit.*, p. 11.
59. Day, Francis, *op. cit.*, p. 340.
60. *Ibid.*, pp. 352-53.
61. *Ibid.*, p. 211.
62. *Ibid.*, p. 213.
63. *They were called Nestorians and acknowledged the duality of persons in the Saviour of the World.
64. *From 658 to 780 A.D., the Syrian Christians relied on direct apostolic succession from St. Thomas, after which time they again recognised the authority of Seleucia.
65. *Ibid.*, p. 215.

    *The power of these Brahmin Christians continued to increase and in time they raised a chief of their own sect to rule over territory inland from that of the Cochin Kingdom. The Christians were allowed to be governed by these chiefs until the 10th century when a childless chief adopted the King of Diamper's son as his successor, after which both came into the fold of the Hindu Raja of Cochin.

66. *Ibid.*, p. 216.
67. *Ibid.*, p. 219.
68. *Ibid.*, p. 218.

69. *Ibid.*
70. *It was further ascertained that many of the poor were not baptised as they could not afford the fees which the priest exacted for their services. This effectively kept the religion of the Syrians among the high caste and wealthy communities of Kerala.
71. *Ibid.*, p. 219.
72. *This is true even today, as this author attended the Church Feast of the Syrian Christians in Palayur, where the festivities lasted over a two-day period and closely resembled the structure and style of the Trichur Festival in Kerala. The latter is a Hindu temple celebration involving fireworks, processions and bands and takes place within the same week in the nearby city of Trichur.
73. *Ibid.*, p. 222.
74. *Ibid.*, p. 225.
75. *Ibid*, p. 230.
76. *Ibid.*, p. 569.
77. *Even in today's climate where education and economic opportunities are more readily available, 'Syrian Christian' denotes wealthy, land-owning and Brahmin, while 'Latin Christian' denotes economically backward, low caste and labourer.
78. *Ibid.*, p. 233.
79. *Ibid.*, p. 418.
80. *Ibid.*, p. 425.
81. *Ibid.*, p. 398.
82. *Ibid.*, p. 401.
83. *A visit to the St. Thomas Syrian Christian Church museum in Palayur by this author in April-May of 1997 provided this information.
84. Day, Francis. *op. cit.*, p. 423.
85. *Ibid.*, p. 427.
86. Vide Diwan's diary Vol. No. 47, No. 144/1858 dated 6-3-1858 preserved in the State Archives, Ernakulam.
87. Day, Francis, *op. cit.*, pp. 309-10.
88. Bernard, K.L. *op. cit.*, p. 98.
89. *This author visited Cochin and Mattancherry in April-May 1997.
90. **See History of the Dutch in Fort Cochin.*
91. *Ibid.*, p. 310.
92. *Ibid.*, pp. 568-69.
93. *possibly Kunbis.
94. *Ibid.*, p. 309.
95. Memorial of Van Anglebeck, 1793, p. 145.
96. Day, Francis, *op. cit.*, pp. 310-11.
97. GSB Samaj, Cochin Thirumala Devaswom and the Gowda Saraswat Brahmins. (Self-publication), pp. 3-4.

98. *Other accounts mention it was found in a well by the Swamiji from Kumbhakonam.

99. *Ibid.*, p. 4.

100. *Ibid.*, p. 5.

101. *This author visited Cochin and Mattancherry to gather information and conduct interviews in April-May 1997.

102. *The following section has been paraphrased from the pamphlet published by the trustees of the temple. It is entitled, the *Cochin Thirumala Devaswom and the Gowda Saraswath Brahmins,* published by themselves and I have spared few details in order to describe the joint finances held by the community.

103. *These same deities are also favourites among the Gowda Saraswat Brahmins of Goa.

104. *This author witnessed the Cochin 'Aratu' festival in April of 1997.

105. *Though beyond the scope of this study, it is interesting that the initial inhabitants of Bombay were 'Prabhus', followers of Bhimadeva, who after some time spoke what came to be known as 'Konkani in the northern dialect'. They disappeared at some point in history and in the annuls of the British, who were in the habit of documenting in detail the social conditions of any acquired territory, no mention was made of these communities brought in by Bhimadeva. (See *Origins of Bombay*).

106. *As the GSB community was an extension to my original work, I regret not having been able to assess any fundamental psychological differences within the GSB's in Goa and Kerala, though I would assume that some psychological evolution has occurred in accordance with the psychology prevailing in Kerala.

107. *There was found to be one additional Konkani-speaking community in the Cochin Fort, the Vaishyas from Maharashtra. A discussion of this community goes beyond the scope of this study, though it would make a fascinating topic for further inquiry.

108. *Although there are no Goan clubs, the 'Anglo-Indians' of Fort Cochin have a club where they maintain a rentable hall for wedding receptions, dances and Christmas celebrations. The Goa Carnival is celebrated with dances, a procession of floats and a singing competition. During the first week in October, a Novina is held for nine days to Our Lady of the Rosary. The 14th of September marks the Feast Day in Santa Cruz Cathedral. They identify with their European ancestry and consequently prefer to sit on the floor, white wedding gowns to saris, wedding bands instead of thalis and dances during most celebrations. The youth can be found in western-style clothing, including jeans and long T-shirts and they maintain their community through intermarriage and exclusive social functions. Thus, while their social culture closely resembles that of upper-class Roman Catholic Goans, including dances and the Goa Carnival, the latter were not fully accepted into their social circles owing to their relation with European blood.

CHAPTER 10

Daman

A Community with a 'Dated' Cultural Identity

The Union Territory of Daman offers an interesting portrait of a Catholic Indo-Portuguese community struggling to maintain its 'cultural identity'. *Unlike Goa, however, where the people 'realised' their own subjugation, the native Catholic community in Daman did not welcome Liberation from the Portuguese.* Rather, they enjoyed the social mobility and power they enjoyed under foreign rule and had identified culturally, politically and linguistically with their rulers. Thus, when the Portuguese left Daman following the war for Liberation, the remaining Indo-Portuguese native community was left with a cultural identity and way of life that no longer assumed importance under the new administration. *Unable to liberate themselves psychologically from their previous rulers, the community elders have continued to follow the cultural traditions which existed under the Portuguese and remain identified to them emotionally and even politically.*

Located on the West Coast of India bounded by the State of Gujarat on the north and east, Maharashtra to the south and the waters of the Arabian Sea to the west, Daman is one of the few surviving Union Territories in India which is a former Portuguese colony. Within its 72 square-mile radius, live over 70,000 people, the majority of whom follow the Hindu religion and speak Gujarati as their native tongue.[1] Daman is divided into three segments: Nani Daman (Small Daman) , Moti Daman (large Daman) and the outlying districts of Dadar and Nagar Haveli. The former two regions are primarily examined in this case study, as they include the ancient Fort area inhabited by the

Portuguese and native Catholics who converted to that religion under the Portuguese regime. It is within these walls where the Portuguese cultural influence had its greatest impact and where the majority of the native Catholics (7-8 per cent of the total population in today's Daman) reside.[2]

Historical Overview

The ancient history of Daman is not unlike that of Bassein and Goa and, thus, will be only briefly mentioned in this case study. Initially, mostly tribal communities of fishermen and agriculturists occupied the tract of land known today as Daman. These communities still exist in Daman today and speak a language known as Konkani. According to locals it is a language similar to Marathi and is probably the early Konkani dialect of the north documented by early Portuguese missionaries in Bassein and Chaul. Only 190 km's from Bombay, the area of Daman has experienced many of the same political and religious influences as did both Bombay and Bassein, including the influences of Jainism, Buddhism, the Muslim invasions and the Portuguese conquest. Daman was included in the region known as the north Konkan prior to the Muslim invasions and, thus, was under the sway of the Mauryas, the Satavahanas, the western Chalukyas of Badami and the Rashtrakutas.[3] Prior to the 8th century, historians believe that Bassein was an important commercial trading centre of the Chalukya kingdom owing to its prime location at the mouth of a well-protected in-land river. The proximity of this city to Daman must have had affects on the culture and development of the latter area as well. As early as 696 copper-plate inscriptions mention Kalyana (in the district of Thana) as the opulent capital of the empire of the Solanki Kings.

Between the years 810 to 1260, roughly 20 Shilaharan Kings ruled over the north Konkan from their capital cities which were relocated from time to time. Gharapuri (Elephanta Island), located off the coast of modern-day Colaba district in Bombay, was one of these early capitals. Shristhanaka (Thana) was another ancient city close to the Bassein district which rose to prominence as the commercial and administrative capital of the Shilaharas.[4] The Shilaharas were local kingdoms who owed fidelity to the Rashtrakutas. From 1008 until 1100, the Kadamba King Shastadeva II exploited the civil animosities between the northern and southern

Shilaharas and made the northern Shilaharas his mandalikas (feudatories). During the reign of Guhalladeva II the Kadambas attacked and reconquered their lost northern territories, but during the reign of Jayakesi II (1104-1147-8), the Shilahara Malikarjuna regained the northern territories. During the rule of Someshwara, the last King of the Shilahara dynasty, the north Konkan was conquered by the Yadava King Mahadeva, the latter who ruled between 1260 and 1271. He was succeeded by his nephew Ramadeva (1272-1290), the latter who appointed Achuta Nayak as the Governor of north Konkan.[5] Krishnadeva succeeded Nayak in 1290 and the Yadavas continued to rule over the north Konkan (which at that time included the Thana district and the southern tip of Gujarat) until 1312. Until 1558 the area, including Gujarat and Daman fell under Muslim rule, including that of All-a-udin who descended from the north and also conquered Kalyana during the 1300's.

The region of Daman was under the control of the Gujarati King (The Bahadur Sultan) prior to its capture by the Portuguese. During this time forceful conversions to Islam occurred en masse and many mosques were constructed, some of which were later destroyed by the Portuguese missionary fanatics. It was the regional Gujarati culture influenced by Islam, which was flourishing at the time of conquest and the regional language was also the Gujarati dialect.

During the years when the Portuguese power was at its height and the territories of Ormuz and Malacca had been annexed to their Indian Empire, the Portuguese continued to be harassed by ships originating in the Ports belonging to the Sultan of Gujarat. The Sultan, after receiving Portuguese help against the invading Mughal armies, gifted the Portuguese vast areas of land, including Bombay, Bassein and Daman in 1531. The then Ethiopian governor representing the Sultan of Gujarat refused to relinquish the gifted territories to the Portuguese, and occupied the territory with the Sultan's men. In 1556 a Fort in Daman was constructed by the Bahadurshah and war ensued when the latter refused to abandon the territory to its rightful owners, the Portuguese. Diu was also captured by the Portuguese in 1531 following a fierce battle wherein the combined forces of the Turkish navy were destroyed.[6]

Daman under the Portuguese

When the Ethiopian general representing the Sultan of Gujarat refused to abandon the Daman territory to the Portuguese, the latter decided that it was necessary to occupy the region and establish a settlement. It might have taken years to convert the natives, thus, the Portuguese, in addition to sending their own clergy members, also invited individuals and families from the other settlements to occupy the Daman region. Those who migrated to Daman in those early years, therefore, came in small numbers from scattered places throughout the Portuguese settlements. They belonged to different castes and occupations and became a separate community which was probably also given land grants and Government posts in exchange for agreeing to occupy the territory. Owing to the small numbers which came, the successful teachings of the Portuguese missionaries, and the wealth which convests received, the caste system which prevailed even in Goa larger India did not develop among these Catholic converts in Daman. They eventually formed their own community, however, wherein complete identification with the Portuguese culture evolved and the old system was basically eradicated. Among the new converts from among the native inhabitants of the former Gujarati province, however, (fishing and farming tribals and those of the low caste) the caste system continued in its earlier form. They were not accepted into the new 'Portuguese society' as both poverty and prior traditions prevented them from assimilating to the same extent as the Catholic converts who migrated into Daman. The Goans who migrated in later years also felt the presence of a caste system whereby the Indo-Portuguese-Catholics in Daman kept to themselves and did not see fit to mingle with the 'shippies' from Goa. Thus, the Portuguese-Daman native migrant Catholics effectively created their own caste which distinguished itself from both Goans and converted Catholics of the indigenous communities in Daman.

In 1558 Daman was captured from the Gujarati Sultan and occupied under the leadership of Dom Constantino de Braganca, who arrived that same year to the Indian West Coast as the Viceroy of Portuguese India.[7] The latter fortified the existing Forts and allowed only the native converts and the Portuguese to live within the walls of the Portuguese under their protection. The Portuguese population at that time hovered around one million only and, thus, the majority of the people were involved in the maintenance and hold over the Portuguese colonies. They were mainly involved in naval transport and did little to improve the infrastructure or introduce industry to Daman during the years of their occupation.

Following the occupation of Daman by the Portuguese, the clergy also felt compelled to disrupt the existing social system in order to establish their own cultural foundations in society. Foreign Catholics in India at that time were considered almost as untouchables by the larger society, owing to European concept of hygiene and food habits juxtaposed with Brahmanical notions of purity and pollution. Polluting elements, such as the meat from cows, were thrown into the well water which forced many to convert to Christianity. The same laws and activities which occurred in Goa and Bassein likewise occurred in Daman. These three areas had extensive relations under the Portuguese rule and people and goods constantly trafficked between the areas. So much so that both Bassein and Daman claim the only Indo-Portuguese Saint, Gonsal Garcia. Born in Bassein, he was educated in Daman in the monastery of '1,000 Virgins' and was martyred in Japan in 1595. The Portuguese education was imparted by the different religious societies was dominated by the Jesuit clergy. In addition to reading, writing and arithmetic, the Portuguese taught the subjects of music and bread-making, the latter which eventually led to their nick-name in Bombay and other areas as pao-wallahs.

While under the Portuguese who now had an alliance with the Sultan (King) of Gujarat and they paid a tax (chot) to the Maharaja of Dharanpur for protection of Daman against outside invaders. This was a wise decision, as the Moghuls attacked Daman on three separate occasions, all of which were successfully defended by the allied forces. In 1581 during the reign of Akbar, in 1681 under that of Aurangzeb and in 1619 under the leadership of Shah Jahan the territory of Portuguese Daman was attacked by the Moghul troops. These attacks resulted from the piracy of the Portuguese on the open seas which prevented the Muslim ships from passing safely through the Arabian Sea on their way to pilgrimage at Mecca. The Portuguese pirates would attack and rob those ships on their way to Mecca and commit other atrocities as well.

Daman was firmly under the Portuguese control and divided into 3 territorial units, 2 administrative and the third known as Dadra and Nagar Haveli. However, several additional attempts were made to oust the Portuguese from their Damao possession. In 1668 the Maratha leader Shivaji invaded the area of Gujarat and occupied the villages of Dadra and Nagar Haveli, encroaching until the boundaries of the Daman Fort. They then demanded Chautai (tax) from the Portuguese at Daman, which the latter refused to pay. In 1683 the Portuguese did not allow Sambhaji to proceed through Daman to attack the Siddi ruler of Janjira, fearing that the Marathas would only conquer and capture Daman while on their way to their final war destination. Further, in 1739 the Marathas attacked and seized all Portuguese settlements north of Goa excluding Daman and Diu. It was at this time that Bassein, the 'North Court' of the Portuguese nobility, was likewise seized and occupied. Goa also was fully occupied by the Maratha troops excepting the Portuguese Panjim capital and might have been lost to the Maratha armies had not the Muslim invasions of Hyder Ali and Tippu Sultan encroached on the Maratha's northern territories, forcing them to halt their conquest and defend their territories now under seizure.

Daman consisted of only 72 sq. kilometres until the end of the 1700's. At that time, however, the Maratha armies sank two Portuguese ships which caused great loss to the Portuguese maritime activities. In retaliation, the Portuguese threatened for war and the Marathas, in order to appease their enemy, offered the areas of Dadar and Nagar Haveli in compensation. The areas consisted of 70 villages mostly populated by agrarian tribal communities from which the Portuguese extracted revenue in the form of land taxes. During this same time the British troops in 1779, under the leadership of Colonel Goddard, occupied Ahmedabad and most of the Gujarati territory which had been annexed by the Maratha troops. The Marathas feared for their empire, consequently and did not want to add Portugal to their list of enemies right away. Towards the end of that same year, however, the British troops were forced to retreat owing to the combined armies of Hyder Ali, Nana Fadnavis and Govindrao which swept in from the north-east.

Culture of 'Damao' under the Portuguese

After the conquest of the territory, previously under the control of the Gujarati King, the Portuguese inherited the recently constructed Forts which were separated by a wide river. The Portuguese renamed the region 'Damao' and fortified the existing fortresses. The Daman-Ganga bridge was built to connect the two, whereas previously a ferry was employed to cross from one Fort to the other. *Within the walls of the two forts the Portuguese officials and native Catholics had their residences and it is here where the cultural transformation, that would create a native community identified culturally, linguistically and politically with the Portuguese, occurred.* Prior to the Portuguese occupation, the native culture had been virtually identical to the neighbouring areas and had experienced the same historical flows as had the whole region of the northern Konkan. Situated across the border between Maharashtra and Gujarat and only 3 hours from Bombay, Daman's culture, identity and history prior to the Portuguese was inextricably linked to larger India's.

Under the Portuguese Indian empire, Daman became a part of the Territory of Goa, Daman and Diu. Those in Daman were subjected to the same laws as those in Goa and underwent the same process of enculturation with only slight modifications. The intellectuals in Daman also identified with the Portuguese and under the latter's administration there was peace, law, order and the consideration of complaints. Priests from Goa were often relocated there and the Portuguese trade empire, including the importation of slaves and Arabian horses also occurred in Damao. Hindus, Muslims, Parsees and Catholics lived in the Daman surrounds, though only the native converts were permitted to reside within the walls of the Fort. The social structure of Daman likewise resembled that of Goa, excepting the composition of the elite indigenous neo-Catholic class which in Daman arose from a variety of cultivating and artisan communities. As in Goa, these new upper-class converts learnt Portuguese, studied in Catholic schools and identified themselves as Portuguese citizens.

Likewise, they adopted all of the habits, customs, home furnishings and rituals of the Portuguese and moulded their culture entirely after that of the Europeans. Even the low caste converts and Hindus (in later years) began to observe some Portuguese social customs in public and dressed according to

Portuguese law. The people celebrated Christmas, New Years, Carnival, the Feasts of St. Francis Xavier and the Immaculate Conception, Maundy Thursday, Good Friday, Easter, Sunday and the basic Catholic sacraments. The Carnival was celebrated for four days with dances and revelry and Catholics would even come from Bombay in order to participate in the festivities. Women would wear fancy dresses in the Portuguese style of the day and both men and women would go about in masks. Street parades with floats and bands were also in vogue, but this celebration was eventually stopped by the Church in their attempts to improve the moral behaviour of the Portuguese. During Christmas families would go from door to door singing Christmas carols and social organisations would organise singing, crib, athletic and magical shows and competitions. These would take place in the general Halls located on the church premises and such activities still occur today among the remaining Indo-Portuguese Catholics in Daman.

Within the walls of the Fort, as in Bassein, several churches, a hospital, administrative buildings and Portuguese-style villas were constructed, much in the manner of Bassein. Our Lady of Rosary Chapel in Moti Daman, Our Lady of Sea Church in Nani Daman and Our Lady of Remedies outside the Fort's walls are just three of many churches existing during the Portuguese Indian empire. Four libraries were also established; two in Moti Daman and two in Nani Daman.

However, the administration in Daman suffered from the lax morals which characterised the Portuguese during the heyday of their empire. Corruption was rampant and even the high officials were engaged in non-sanctioned trade activities. While Bassein was known as the 'Corte do Norte', Daman was rather the entrepot for all of the corrupt Portuguese officials and others who were banished from Goa for accepting bribes during public office. The Catholic families in Daman were, thus, the 'tarnished' ones. An official transferral to Daman, therefore, was a hefty punishment for white-collar crimes. They continued their illegal activities even in Daman, however and the authorities in Goa left them basically alone.

The Liberation Years

Between 1954 and 1961 during the agitation for Liberation, the Indian Government in New Delhi employed the tactic of economic strangulation on the Portuguese through a territorial blockade of Goa, Daman and Diu. Many people from the border regions who used to work in làrger India were displaced during those years, especially toddy-tappers and daily labourers. In addition, the economic blockade was the cause which instigated the smuggling activities currently pervasive in Daman. Cut off from previous sources of revenue within India, the shipping trawlers began making three and five-day trips to the Gulf ports in order to purchase indispensible goods not produced in Daman. These goods were then illegally shuttled and sold across the Daman-Indian border to prop up Daman's sagging economy and provide a livelihood for those displaced by the war efforts. Some even disguised themselves as 'freedom fighters' during the border Satyagrahas and transported smuggled goods into India from Daman. These same individuals then reaped the benefits of having participated in the freedom wars.

Unlike the majority of the people of Goa, the Catholic natives of Daman were not fighting for their Liberation. Satyagrahis were performed mostly by people in neighbouring territories surrounding Damao and not by the clergy or native Catholics themselves. Even during the Liberation wars, the Damanese Army put up a fight before finally capitulating to the Indian Army troops. Following Liberation, many natives evacuated the region along with the Portuguese nationals and eventually settled in Portugal. They retained their Portuguese citizenship and within the year following Liberation more families decided to abandon their homelands and settle in the country to which they had identified and given their allegiance. Daman's native Catholic population, unlike that of Goa's, was fairly contented during the Portuguese regime. The strict laws and prejudices which were more emphasised in Goa did not have such a major effect in Daman. The people enjoyed their lifestyles and privileges under the Portuguese and did not welcome the freedom fighters. They derived their source of cultural pride based on the proximity they reached with Portuguese culture and felt themselves as citizens of Portugal. Other communities who suffered under the Portuguese policies felt differently, and it was with their help that Daman was liberated along with Goa in 1961.

The Gama family remembers the day when the Indian Army invaded Daman, as their house is situated opposite the military battery. At 4 am on the morning of 18th December 1961, the family could see fire outside the house and at 8 am planes bombarded the Fort. Shrapnel splintered the doors of their house and one child was killed while trying to hide in the safety of the convent. All of the native Catholic families which had not been evacuated in time sought shelter in the largest house in Nani Daman. The soldiers resisted the incursion and fought against the advancing Indian Army. The elders remember that people were praying, crying and the wounded were brought into one side of the house for emergency medical care. Outside, the sound of machine-gun firing was heard throughout the day, but by the following morning all was finished and the Portuguese army capitulated. The soldiers and natives within the Fort fought valiantly and in the end native Catholics were disappointed with this unsolicited 'freedom'.

Following Liberation, many Catholic families were confused as to how to proceed. Most did not have adequate English education and had made their livelihoods employed in the Portuguese administration. Consequently, many employed in high positions under the Portuguese, left Daman for Portugal where they continued in official positions. A tea party held at the Palace to celebrate Liberation consisted of typical north Indian cuisine and excluded all dishes introduced by the Portuguese and Indianised by the native Catholics. The Governor General even ate with his hands, the Gama family recalls, rather than using utensils as was Portuguese custom. For the native Catholics in Daman, this social gathering symbolised the end of their cultural recognition and the dismissal of their cultural heritage.

Daman as a Union Territory

The question was then raised as to how to integrate Daman into larger India. Merger with Gujarat was rejected unanimously, partially owing to Gujarat's enforcement of 'dry-State' laws which forbade the sale and purchase of alcoholic beverages. The people in Gujarat likewise rejected the idea of a merger as they looked to Daman as a vacation spot where they could indulge in the use of alcohol. Seven liquor factories also existed in Daman and their livelihood depended on the continuance of the 'wet' policies of the territory.

Thus, after Liberation the territories of Daman, Goa and Diu were incorporated into the Indian Republic as Union Territories. The possibility of the formation of a separate State was rejected by the Indian Government owing to the small size of Daman and the relatively small remaining Catholic population. At the time of liberation, the total population of Daman hovered around 40-50,000 people, a number which has increased to 70-75,000 in 1997. Therefore, when Goa decided to form itself into a separate State along cultural and territorial lines, the territory of Daman, only 72 square miles, remained as a Union Territory, which status still holds today.

As a Union Territory Daman receives special privileges which go beyond those awarded to regular States under the Indian Republic. They are given the same privileges as State governments in terms of policy making and local autonomy, all of which are under local discretion, including the distribution of alcohol. The salaries of Government employees are the same as those within the Central Government; almost double the salaries of State employees. The local administration collects its own taxes and the rest of the budget comes from the Central Government. As a result, taxation in Daman is low because revenue comes from the Central Government itself. Special reservations for seats in medical, engineering and technical colleges are available in Goa. Large amounts of financial aid are given by the Central Government for Daman's water supply, public and maintenance works, industrial development and infrastructure. Until 1987 Daman was administered from Goa under this administrative structure. Following the creation of the State of Goa, Daman was held accountable to New Delhi directly.

Following Liberation in 1961, the Archaeological Survey of India took an interest in the maintenance of the old Portuguese Forts. They passed a regulation whereby nothing could be erected within and around 500 meters of Nani and Moti Forts. Among the residential areas, houses are allowed only to be maintained and renovated in accordance with the Portuguese motif. The churches are looked after by the Archaeological Survey of India though many remain closed throughout the week and open only on special occasions. Industry, infrastructure and educational facilities have likewise entered Daman of late in addition to that required for the production of liquor.

Daman Today

The Daman territory today is an eclectic community of aboriginal tribals, Muslims, Hindus and Catholic communities who are all endogamous groups which tend to reside near members of their own communities. Structurally, tapped water is available to all, in Daman, the roads have been improved, two new hospitals and over 20 doctors are available and the local Government has drafted policies to encourage the development of industry (exemption from taxes, etc.). The rate of unemployment is at its lowest and the literacy rates have improved although they still lag behind Goa. Smuggling is a lucrative activity which continues in Daman to the knowledge of all the locals and boosts the economy of the region. Several electronic stores can be found in Daman which display the latest in media and home technologies.

The Gama family of Daman is one such family whose experiences illuminate the feelings of many native Catholics following Liberation. Their native language is Portuguese and the family studied through the Portuguese medium schools in Daman. They recall that there were no English-medium schools during those years (1930's) and in order to study beyond SCC students had to go to Goa. Daman's students were given scholarships to study in Goa if they achieved exemplary marks. Today there are technical universities and other schools in the Daman surrounds which people are allowed to attend. The Gama family consumes all types of food but cooks Portuguese specialities at home. The Gama family has several relatives in Goa and many in Portugal as well. They listen to Portuguese and English music and are fluent in the latter language as well. They attend mass at Our Lady of the Sea and on occasion visit the church of the Infant Jesus. Their son is a dentist and studied in London. The house inhabited by the Gama family is a 200-year-old Portuguese villa in Nani Daman. It was bought by the grandparents of the eldest living generation and was renovated from mud and stones to the spacious Portuguese villa that it is today. The large wooden doors extending to the ceiling originate from the early Portuguese days and the woodwork in the house has been imported from Portugal.

Many of the Catholics left Daman for Portugal following

liberation but some families, such as the Gamas, did not want to leave their homelands. The Catholics under the Portuguese, though in a minority position (10%), enjoyed the most privilege and power of all the communities. During the Portuguese regime, however, the Gama family admits that little progress was made in the development of infrastructure and electricity, which was the one positive change following Liberation.

Regarding the difference between the culture of Catholic Daman and that of Catholic Goa, the Gama family feels that there are some slight differences. The native language is one; Konkani is the mother tongue of both Hindu and Catholic Goans, whereas the Catholic upper-class in Daman use Portuguese and do not even know Gujarati. Also, the Indo-Portuguese Catholic community in Daman is much smaller than that of Goa, where in the former both the churches and convents are active agents in keeping the Portuguese culture alive among the Catholic community in Daman.

Issues of Reidentification

In today's generation the youth whose parents spoke Portuguese have learned to speak the language, but they do not study the language formally nor do they know to read and write in Portuguese. Unlike Goa, where the Konkani language remained as the local language of the people, Gujarati was abolished as the native tongue of the Catholic community whose people culturally identified themselves with the Portuguese. Though today's generation speaks Hindi and can understand some Gujarati owing to the professional and educational mixing which has occurred, previous generations of Catholic natives did not know either of these languages. *The loss of their Indian language as the community's mother tongue and the adoption of Portuguese in its stead had significant impact on the strength of the cultural identification of this Catholic community with that of Portuguese culture.* As a consequence of this near-total identification, this community following Liberation had very few cultural ties with their Indian ancestors and considered themselves Portuguese people. Weddings and other Catholic festivals were likewise celebrated by the native converts and the Portuguese together.

Among the Churches still exhibiting life, St. Anthony's Chapel draws a large crowd on Tuesdays. Our Lady of Remedies celebrates a feast in April, Our Lady of Augustias in September and in October Our Lady of the Rosary celebrates a feast similar to those in churches all over Goa. In early December at the ruins of Our Lady of the Sea, a feast is likewise held. On the 24th of July the Catholic community converges on the seashore and has a bath in the sea in symbolic remembrance of St. John the Baptist. There is a daily mass and Sunday Mass in Portuguese and on Sundays mass is also held in English. Many of the priests in Daman are from Goa and educated in the seminary at Pilar. However, they do not know Portuguese when they first come to Daman and learn to read the scriptures in that language during the first months of their post in Daman.

Education in Daman: Our Lady of Fatima School

Under the Portuguese regime few students attended school and of them the majority were from the Catholic community, Daman today has 15,000 students enrolled in primary schools. There are over 1,000 teachers in the Union Territory of Daman in addition to a college of arts and sciences and a poly-technical school (for engineering and chemical science). The Institute of Our Lady of Fatima is the best known school in Daman and one that receives the largest number of applicants. It is one of the only English-medium schools in the area and is run by the Catholic clergy. Following Liberation the school became a Government school which received funding from the Central Government in exchange for opening its doors to all communities in addition to Catholic students. The Portuguese language ceased to be taught following the decision of the Board of Education in 1992. Space was made available whereby a 'special' Portuguese class could be taught, but neither parents nor students showed an interest in such a non-credit class.[8]

This year matriculated 161 students from the Catholic community and 629 students combined from the Hindu and Muslim communities in the primary grades. There are 200 students in the junior classes and 175 classified as seniors. It is the only convent school in Daman and was at one time open to girls only. It gained repute over the years and in 1929 owing to pressure from the community the school was expanded to admit male students. First preference remains for girls, however, as the school was originally opened to encourage the education of women which had been neglected prior to and during the early years of the Portuguese regime. Our Lady of Fatima Convent is the oldest school in Daman and one of the four English medium schools in the area; the rest teach students through the Gujarati medium.

In addition to the positive contributions which the Portuguese culture had on Daman, the society left behind some character flaws as well. Most of the educated Catholics left Daman following Liberation and went to Portugal, London, or Goa, leaving behind a population with little experience in administration, education and social welfare. The easy life and assurance of Government posts under the Portuguese administration deemphasised the importance of academics. Parents, predominantly those among the Catholic community, often try to bribe the teachers and the headmaster to pass their children when they were not upto the mark. Bribe taking is originate prevalent among all the communities of Catholics and some teachers owing to the delayed or absent payment of Government salaries, will accept the bribes, with the result that some children reach the 10th standard who cannot read nor write in English, the very language of instruction. As a result, 20 per cent of each 10th standard student will fail in English. Teachers are also given private tuition to earn extra money outside of class, as a result less attention is paid to individual students in the formal class setting.

Among the poorer Catholic communities where alcoholism is spreading like an epidemic, some parents even removed their children from school rather than pay the required fees; money which they can then spend on alcohol. The mothers of these same children sit idle at home and refuse work as it is beneath their dignity to perform the jobs (such as sweeping, cleaning, laundry) for which they are qualified. When the women do attempt to work, the other community members taunt them as inferior and the result is that both women and children go hungry. Only one or two Catholics of late have actually been appointed to high Government posts and in general the non-Catholics scored better than Catholic students on exams and gave better overall performance. In 1996 alone only one Catholic was eligible for a certificate of general proficiency. All these difficulties may be due in large part to the Government quotas which exist for middle and low socio-economic classes at the convent school. These students are accepted equally if not more than qualified students from high income brackets are not admitted. Recently these schools have established a small computer centre with the aim of teaching students computer. Even this attempt was met with strong resistance from the lower class communities who argue they are too poor to afford computer education for their children. However, whereas it costs them Rs 80 per year at Our Lady of Fatima, outside it costs over Rs 7,000 for the same basic training in computers. However, among the upper-class Portuguese Catholics in Daman whose parents work in official Government jobs, pains are taken for educating their children.

Tourism Trends in Daman

Following Liberation and subsequent immigration of a large number of Gujaratis from neighbouring States, the idea arose to increase tourism in Daman. While the Archaeological Survey of India protects and maintains the old Portuguese churches, the local business entrepreneurs are busy thinking up novel ways to attract tourists into the region. Hotels and restaurants in dozens, though not one specialises in Indo-Portuguese cuisine of the native Catholic community. The coastal areas are slowly developing into upper-end tourist resorts promising a relaxing, laid-back weekend away from the noise and pollution of nearby Bombay. Daman has also become a weekend haven for the wealthy Bombay crowd who escape to Daman's pleasant, pollution-free surroundings after a hectic work week in the over-crowded cement jungle of Bombay. The tourist industry is also keen to promote the cultural identity of Daman as an Indo-Portuguese enclave ripe with a unique culture and landscape separate from neighbouring Gujarat. To present this image, during the Christmas season cultural dances and shows reminiscent of the Portuguese days are also sponsored in an attempt to draw in more tourists.

The high season for tourism begins in mid-December and continues through January, with the majority of tourists arriving from the neighbouring State of Gujarat. The flow of alcohol in the region is likewise emphasised, with the result that Gujarati youth flock to Daman for vacations where they can indulge in activities prohibited in their own State. During a high-season weekend in Daman, the hotels will be completely full and the beaches crowded with weekenders from Gujarat and the nearby metropolis of Bombay. Liquor prices in Daman are also significantly cheaper than those in Bombay, another attractive point which funnels many young tourists to Daman.

Daman's decision to remain a territory, especially a 'wet' one, has brought both the blessings and evils of tourism. Like Goa, Daman is seen by tourists, especially those from neighbouring Gujarat, as the place to go for a weekend of relaxation and revelry. The beaches, though far less captivating than those of Goa, are still a welcome break from fast-paced urban life. Only three hours from Bombay and offering attractive well-preserved historic sites in addition to bars and beaches, Daman seems destined to expand as a popular tourist destination in India. The influx of local tourists, however, has already influenced the youth culture of Daman. Forgetting that tourists are just that, people seeking an escape and a break from the monotony of their daily working lives, many youth in Daman wish to imitate the lifestyle that they see others enjoying. What they do not see are the long hours behind a desk, the years of education and the hard work which enables such a break in the routine. Tourism, thus, affects all communities in Daman, but especially those among the Catholics whose cultural history is directly linked to the Portuguese and the culture of 'sussegad' (without hurry) and alegria which they once enjoyed.

The Solidification of a Cultural Identity

With the Portuguese presence in Daman a reality of the past, the community's cultural evolution along those lines was halted following Liberation. The removal of the native Catholic community's cultural source seriously affected the existing culture of the indigenous Catholics whose native tongue was Portuguese. Its evolution had seemingly ceased on the day of Liberation. Portuguese Catholic culture became ill-fated, outdated and unrelated to the current socio-cultural environment of Daman which called for cultural adaptation and tolerance.

Today's adherents to the Portuguese cultural tradition are in an unusual psychological crisis different from that of Goa. The older generation follows the same patterns as did their ancestors prior to Liberation but the culture itself has become crystallised. Rejecting Indian-Gujarati culture while simultaneously isolated from the current trends in Portugal, this small community has entered into a period which can be classified as cultural stagnation and solidification. Even the Portuguese which the cultural adherents speak at home is an archaic Portuguese which is no longer in vogue in Portugal.[9]

Of late, the use of the Portuguese language in Church has likewise of late come under serious criticism. The study of Portuguese was stopped in primary and secondary schools following a school board decision in 1992 and since then only the young generations whose parents speak it at home have learned the language in its archaic oral form. Children in both public and private Government schools are now learning English, Gujarati and Hindi. Portuguese was once taught as an extracurricular class, but such non-credit additional course-work pleased neither the students nor their parents. In Daman today, the majority of the Catholics and especially those from the lower socio-economic communities do not have a working knowledge of the language. Influential elders within the upper-class community, however, insist on keeping Portuguese as the lingua franca of Church mass. Portuguese mass is, therefore, held on a daily basis, with English mass occurring only once a week on Sundays. Catechism class is likewise taught in both Portuguese and English as a majority of the children do not understand the former language. The religious foundation of the community, likewise, has suffered in consequence owing to these masses which are mostly held in Portuguese but which few members of the community understand. The messages are, thus, lost amongst the young, leaving them without the strong religious foundation characteristic of the earlier generations.

An interesting case study was done on the family of Maria.** A visit to her home was like a step back in time to the Portuguese era of the 1930's and 40's. Imported wooden furniture, porcelain vases and white crocheted lace table covers decorated the sitting room.

Maria's native tongue is Portuguese and her family follows the Portuguese habits and customs, including the time and content of meals. She feels that once the Portuguese left following the 'invasion' of Daman, the lifestyle enjoyed by her community ceased and most things became ill-fated. It was like watching the cessation of her cultural heritage which under the Portuguese had been a sense of pride and belonging. Now, it seems, their adherence to the Portuguese culture which was her cultural heritage prevents her and others of the elder community from identifying with larger India. Rather, a sense of isolation and 'foreignness' pervades the atmosphere of the community and celebrations occur on a level greatly scaled-down from pre-Liberation years.

In Daman unlike Goa, Maria and others argue that the Indian cultural surroundings have not 'diluted' Portuguese cultural traditions among members of her generation. Yet shame seems to emerge when the question of her Hindu ancestors arises, owing possibly to the Portuguese emphasis on the 'backwardness' of the Hindu community. Among the elder generation, their habits, behaviours and beliefs stemming from the Portuguese culture have been frozen in time and not permitted to evolve and adapt to the existing cultural environment of larger India.

This applies to the elder generation, however, as the younger generation has greater interaction and identification with larger India and was born into the post-Liberation society. The children of these Portuguese parents have grown up in a multi-ethnic school society where Hindu and Muslim children are in the majority. They have studied through the English medium and most have learned neither to read nor write in Portuguese. They have also been socialised and exposed to the various belief systems prevalent in modern Daman and consequently their adherence to their Portuguese cultural heritage is much less. The Catholic youth of today are well-versed in both English and Hindi and share many of the same attitudes and aims as their non-Catholic brethren. Some even view the elder's insistence on maintaining strict Portuguese practises as futile and quasi-neurotic. The younger group, who lives in a pro-Indian nationalist environment, demonstrates a psychological need to identify with larger India politically and culturally to some extent. Today's current political emphasis on Hindu India further exacerbates this psychological need to the extent that Catholic youth downplay their religious denomination in unconscious attempts to identify with today's cultural ideals. The cultural rigidity of the elders contrasted with the younger generations tolerance and need for identification with larger India have widened the generation gap among members of this community. Unless a major revival of the Portuguese language and culture occurs among the youth, these trends indicate that the future culture of Daman will undergo the process of 'Indianisation' wherein their heritage will be nostalgia of the past and their lifestyles will be modelled after current cultural trends in neighbouring areas.

In order to reach out to the larger community and preserve the Indo-Portuguese culture of Daman, Maria has organised a travelling 'folk-lore' group which performs old Portuguese dances around the world in former Portuguese colonies. The Corrodinho and the Mando among others are performed in the Portuguese-Daman dialect (archaic Portuguese) and the troupe recently performed in Macao, (a former Portuguese colony in China near Hong Kong). The folklore group also travels throughout India, bringing the unique cultural heritage of Daman to the attention of the Indian community in a way which is patterned after other folklore groups within the larger sub-continent. They often travel with a similar group which performs Gujarati dances at the same time.

What is 'left' of the Portuguese cultural traditions are mainly found in the folklore, religion and cuisine at the few families in Daman who adhere to their former culture. Even in such families, few know that the older dances and English music has pervaded the youth culture in Daman as it has in most adolescent communities in Goa. Among the cuisine, however, much of the Portuguese culture has remained. Breakfast followed by tea time were observed as in Goa during the Portuguese era and among the retired elderly Catholics this practise is still in vogue. Lunch consists of sorpatel, beef masala, vegetables and standard items which also form a part of Goan cuisine.

Some differences at the night meal, ***apash,*** is used, a non-fermented roti which is eaten with the hands rather than cutlery. Last sentence did exist between Goan and Daman cuisine, for example during the Portuguese era in Daman it was customary not to repeat the lunch meal in the night, as it was considered a sign of wealth to have three individual meals. ***Ishpatar*** is another dish unique to Daman and not found in the other Portuguese colonies. It is a special barbecue preparation made at home using spiced pork and cannot be bought in the market. Also different from Goan cuisine, where rice tends to be boiled twice, Daman cuisine utilises only fine white rice which is only boiled once.

The Goan Community in Daman

During the Portuguese era many Goan families were posted in Daman. Many of them, like other Portuguese officials, were moved to Daman as punishment for taking bribes in Goa. In 1961 following Liberation, Goan families were given the option to either return to Goa or remain in Daman. The majority returned to Goa and, thus, only a handful of families have remained in Daman. In addition to those coming directly from Goa, several Goans who were stationed in Bombay also have made Daman their home.

Mr Fernandes is one such Goan who runs a *Goan Pilsner Beer* wholesale business in Daman. He also imports feni from Goa to cater to some palates in Daman. Born in Aldona, he migrated to Bombay through the Aldona Village Boys' Club (Chira Bazaar) and worked in Bombay for 14 years. His two children were likewise living in Bombay with him and his wife, but they returned to Goa for primary schooling owing to the language problem they faced with Hindi and English-medium schools. Mr Fernandes returns only twice a year to Goa, once for the Christmas holidays and again for the month of May. He hopes to settle there, however as his ancestral home and relatives are there. The cost of living is also cheaper compared to Goa, as Daman has a larger number of small fishermen these people bring down the market price for fish and other commodities. Four years have passed since he has resided in Daman and as a result is now able to understand Portuguese and Gujarati, though he cannot speak the languages himself. With other Catholics he prefers to speak either English or Hindi. He continues to eat fish-curry-rice as a staple meal but mentions that in Daman they do not use coconut in their curry. The majority of Catholics are in Government service and a very few have their own businesses or have entered the medical and other professional fields.

According to Mr Fernandes, only 14 or 15 Goan families are living in Daman and he finds that there are several differences between the Goans and the Catholics from Daman. While Goans are friendly, the Daman Catholics tend to be rather community-oriented and prefer to mingle socially with 'their people only', excluding some Goans. They are more reserved and maintain a superiority complex because they feel it was 'we Portuguese' that brought the high culture and 'good things' into Daman. At social gatherings the Daman Catholics still say 'Viva Portugal!' and adhere fully to Portuguese cultural traditions.

Mr Tandel is the protagonist of our second case study. Born in 1951 in Daman, he moved to Goa when he was eight years old and commenced schooling in Betim. His father worked for a Government ship and was stationed in Goa prior to the Liberation War. Following Liberation in 1961, the family returned to Daman, where Mr Tandel has remained with his wife and two sons. As a result of this migration, he speaks Konkani, Gujarati and Hindi fluently. When first asked about his Goan roots he denied having any, though, later was able to fully communicate in Konkani. He speaks Konkani with his two brothers but his children do not speak the language. Mr Tandel is a member of the Hindu religious community and is a fisherman in Nani Daman. His parents are from Daman and, thus, he considers himself a 'Gujarati Hindu'. He works on his brother's fishing boat which goes out to the sea for as long as 8-12 days with a crew of 8 men. His other brother lives in Mapsa, Goa and operates his own business. His third brother is a ticket-collector on a ferry boat crossing in Panjim. Mr Tandel himself visits Goa twice a year.

Mr Tandel comments that in Daman there are no Hindu-Muslim-Catholic rifts. Inter-religious love marriages between Hindus and Catholic occur and argues that there is a caste system in Daman as in Goa among both Hindus and Catholics. He also feels that the Portuguese culture in Daman has died out and that even those people who speak the language do not know how to read and write it. Whereas in those days laws were passed prohibiting the use of traditional dress, (which often distinguished one's caste, a practise disapproved of by the Portuguese) today his wife can once again wear traditional fisherwomen's clothing. Otherwise, Mr Tandel himself has not perceived many changes following the liberation of Daman.

Dr Rachael Soreiro Brito is an interesting case-study of a Portuguese-Daman native still living in the Union Territory of Daman. A cordial man of keen intellect, Dr Brito has led an accomplished life and contributed to the community of Daman in several areas. It is in gratitude to him that I write his brief biography today. Walking into his house was like taking a step back in time to the Portuguese era where splendid Portuguese-style villas, grand wrapping porches and elegantly-carved wooden furniture were necessary components of wealthy homes. His house is reminiscent of those villas in Goa, as are many of the churches and buildings in Portuguese Daman.

Born in Daman in 1918, Dr Brito studied the Portuguese medium in primary and secondary schools until the age of 22. By 1945 he completed his Master of Laws (LLM) from the Bombay University and in 1949 completed a second Master of Arts in Eastern Politics. He wrote an extensive thesis on the Portuguese Empire in Asia but was unable to finish owing to family and property problems which arose in his final year. Dr Brito's wife was the direct ancestor to Domingo Mascarenas (originally from Bassein) who took possession of Nagar Haveli for the Portuguese in 1783. Mascarenas also purchased the village of Dabel which encompassed a total of 1,500 acres. Dr Brito himself has three daughters; one living in Portugal, second a surgeon in Brazil and the third working in a bank in Bombay. They studied in Portuguese in Daman and went on to study English in Sophia Women's College in Bombay.

In 1973 Dr Brito was invited to write an article on Daman to present to the Ministers, as he was the pre-eminent scholar on Portuguese-Daman during those days. His article discusses the revival and preservation of Portuguese culture in Daman, which influenced the Minister of Education who later felt that the Portuguese culture and language should be preserved in the Portuguese territories. Dr Brito concludes that Daman would be the best place where such preservation efforts would meet with success as there was a well-integrated nucleus of Portuguese-speaking families in Daman willing to take on such efforts. The article was presented in 1974 to an audience in Goa, including Mario Soares (the then Foreign Minister of Portugal and later the President), who later expressed his gratitude to Dr Brito for writing such an article in favour of the Portuguese culture. Today Dr Brito is 79 and retired in his old villa on the outskirts of Moti Daman.

Conclusion

Prior to Liberation in 1961, Daman was under the Portuguese rule administered from Goa. Over four centuries ago, the Portuguese had taken the Nani and Moti Daman Forts built by the Muslim army just two years before. As in Goa, many conversions to Catholicism took place and those people began to identify with Portuguese culture and customs. The mother tongue of this new Roman Catholic community became Portuguese and the eating habits, wedding celebrations, manners, clothing, etc., all replicated that of the Portuguese people stationed in Daman. Over the generations this community of migrated Catholic natives developed into an elite class which completely identified with the Portuguese; indeed sharing as well their same attitudes of Portuguese cultural superiority. They considered themselves 'Portuguese' in all sense of the word and derived much of their sense of identity and pride from this culture.

However, for the elite Catholic community living in Daman, the 1961 Liberation produced a serious identity crisis. The Portuguese rapidly returned to Portugal, taking their authority and influence with them. Many educated native families also took advantage of their Portuguese passports and fled to Portugal. Those Indo-Portuguese families who remained in Daman met with some difficulty as few had studied English or the language of the majority, Gujarati. Suddenly their new mother tongue was useless and their ways of life was considered foreign. They were perceived as converts and outsiders in their own land, especially as the wave of Indian 'nationalism' swept across Daman and the whole sub-continent.

This external pressure resulted in even stronger adherence to the Portuguese culture in which the Catholic community was raised. The elders of the community are particularly noticeable for this behaviour and have virtually 'fixed' their cultural forms to the date of the Portuguese departure. They define rigid characteristics and customs and even 'proper' home furnishings and eating habits, all which date to the long Portuguese rule in Daman. These same elders insist upon mass in Portuguese in attempts to promote the language, which causes the meaning of the church service to be lost by the youth who are not able to fully understand Portuguese. Many still identify themselves as 'we Portuguese' and at certain celebrations the crowd will cheer 'Viva Portugal' out of allegiance to their former country.

Yet beneath this outward show of pride exists an underlying sense of insecurity regarding their cultural identity due to the loss of their power and prestige with the departure of the Portuguese. Recognising their minority status and fast diminishing authoritative influence, the elders in the community seem to have reacted by erecting a wall of cultural superiority and elitism around their community, even to the exclusion of migrated Goans! This all has had destructive effects and the community seems poised for yet another identity crisis as the youth look towards India and Euro-American culture for cues and the formation of identity.

The very act of trying to define and confine Indo-Portuguese culture in Daman seems to have increased the speed of its demise, especially among the younger generation seeking to fit in and establish links with larger society. Once a culture becomes crystallised and rigidly defined, it ceases to live, adapt and assimilate the various other forces coexisting in society. As a consequence, a culture becomes antiquated and no longer harmonises with nor provides coping measures for modern generations. The results are clear in Daman, where the effect of the Portuguese Church Mass understood by only a few has resulted in a break in the transmission of cultural values to the younger generations. Further, the development of a protective superiority complex has led to isolation from the larger community which in turn creates an inferiority complex and a tendency to long for identification with larger society.

Lack of support combined with self-isolation from the larger community further exacerbates the process of cultural crystallisation among the Indo-Portuguese community in Daman. When Goa became a recognised State in the Indian Republic in 1987, the Catholic community in Daman felt betrayed as if the Goans had given in to pressure from larger India and abandoned their political identification with Portugal. Subsequently, the elite Catholic community in Daman withdrew into itself, beginning its long process of decline. Whereas Goans decided to identify with the Indian nation, the Catholic community in Daman continued to identify with Portugal (owing to their native language,

Portuguese), an attachment which has continued ever since, giving rise to some psychological sufferings among members of the older generation.

The future of Daman's cultural evolution and the psychological health of her Indo-Portuguese community is still an unwritten book, however. Trends among the youth indicate an increasing identification with the youth culture and with larger India, the latter at least politically. The younger generation do not feel themselves to be 'Portuguese' and they interact fluently with people from other communities in Daman. Thus, the adherents of Portuguese culture will most likely die out with the current elder generation and this generation's youth along with future generations will more closely resemble the culture of Goa; a combination of both the Catholic West and the traditional East Indians. What will remain among members of the community will do so in religion, folklore, music and the Portuguese language. (The latter as a marker of descendency from the elite indigenous community that once flourished and held cultural superiority over other communities in Daman.) Tourism will also have the desire effect of maintaining and recreating the 'cultural identity of Daman'. For while the population is over 90 per cent non-Catholic, Daman like Goa will for some time be portrayed as a western Catholic enclave flourishing in the Indian sub-continent. This will be an endeavour also supported by the business communities in Daman which stand to profit from an increase in tourism. It will, thus, unintentionally keep the Portuguese spirit alive in Daman which might otherwise die out among her former adherents in the younger generations who would prefer to adapt their lifestyles to those of their fellow Indian citizens.

Although fixing and confining a cultural identity has its negative effects, it can, if harnessed can lead to the generation of something positive. The beauty of a crisis, be it one of identity or otherwise, lies in its inherent possibility for innovation and creation. Rather than criticising the Catholic community in Daman for their cultural integrity, however, this author also would like to applaud and encourage them for their efforts to maintain what they feel is an important moment in historical time.

REFERENCES

1. Department of Tourism, Daman & Diu, New Delhi: Cross Publications, 1992, p. 7.
2. The information for this study was collected from personal field research in Daman in January, 1997.
3. See Chapter 2, History of the Konkan Territory known as Goa.
4. Kudva, V.N., *History of the Dakshinatya Saraswats*, Madras: Samykta Gowda Saraswats, 1972, p. 57.
5. *Ibid.*, p. 58.
6. Because of this victory the Turks lost their domination of the Indian Ocean and hence their economy, which had been fuelled by this trade. At this point in world history the Ottoman Turkish empire, one of the most powerful, had been making inroads into Europe with the aim of conquering the entire European continent. The defeat of the Turkish empire in the Arabian Sea marked a turning-point in world history as it halted the supremacy of the Turks on the seas. The Portuguese assumed power in their stead and destroyed their Arabian sea-borne empire, which compelled the Turks to halt their advances on the European continent and return to addressing pressing issues at home. Their empire went into decline from this point onwards, which then saved Europe from conquest of the Ottoman Turks and gave rise to the subsequent Christian era of our time.
7. Kudva, V.N., *op. cit.*, p. 43.
8. The information which follows was provided by the headmaster of the school who has worked in Our Lady of Fatima for the past five years. This case study highlights the concerns which some educators in Daman express regarding the educational trends in their region.
9. At first, owing to the language discrepancies, some chastised that the Damanese Portuguese was incorrect owing to improper learning. Historians cleared up the issue which aimed right at the core of Indo-Portuguese pride by stating that their Portuguese was in fact correct, only it was an obsolete form which had since evolved on the Portuguese mainland.

CHAPTER 11

Bassein Fort Area

A Synthesis of History in Cultural Forms

The story of Bassein is ancient and its history is a mini-version of Goa which parallels the aboriginal inhabitants, the beginnings of Hinduism, the Muslim invasions and the rise and fall of the Portuguese empire. Surrounded by a series of inland rivers which were once deep and perfectly suited for the creation of an inland harbour, today's Bassein Fort bears little resemblance to the international emporium and noble residential area which it once claimed. Today the massive stone buildings of Bassein Fort and surrounds are crumbling owing to neglect and the jungle has reclaimed much of the earth which was once moulded into splendid churches and double story bungalows with balconies. Petty thieves now roam the ruins of this once prosperous city and ghosts are believed to wander about the ruins at night.

Yet Bassein Fort is the story of an area which once displayed the opulence of the east and west combined and which has now returned to its origins as a small fishing settlement on the West Coast of India. Yet within the magnificent, crumbling ruins of the Bassein Fort lives a community whose people have withstood the test of time and whose culture demonstrates the various historical layers which passed through this piece of land only 29 miles from Bombay. Though their history is forgotten and the buildings have crumbled, the culture of today's people inhabiting Bassein Fort reveals these historical layers and provides a multitude of insights into the cultural evolution of a people influenced by foreign rule and the aftermath of such cultural influence.

History of Bassein Fort

Bassein Fort is located on the southern point of the Island of Bassein which is 11 miles long and 5 miles wide, with a total radius of 35 square miles. It was originally known as 'Vasai', which has probably derived from the Sanskrit word *'vas'*, meaning 'to dwell'.[1] Later under the Mohamedans it became known as Basai and during the Portuguese regime that name evolved into Bacaim. Under the English the area was known as Bassein, which is still its identity around the world and in history, though in recent years the name has once again returned to the original Vasai. Like the evolution of its name, the land and people of Fort Bassein have likewise undergone a series of evolution which ebb and flow in accordance with the region's historical patterns.

In its early days, Bassein was a densely wooded area with many creeks and lakes and was connected to the ancient religious pilgrimage sites of Vaitarani and Tungari. In ancient Hindu records Bassein island was connected to the seven divisions of Parasurama Kshetra and was known as 'Varar' (also a possible name-origin).[2] The Viatarai River was considered sacred during the time of the Puranas and all those who bathed in her were absolved of their sins. In the Mahabharata the Vaitarni is also mentioned as one of the four sacred streams. In addition to the sacred rivers, there were several Tirthas, or sacred water tanks constructed for the purpose of religious ritual, located on the island and mentioned in the Puranas. One such tirtha, the Nirmala Tirtha, was located on the island and became a celebrated place of pilgrimage for Hindu devotees. As stated in the Skanda Purana, "The Nirmala Tirtha, which is the best of all tirthas, is the seat of perfection, yielding fruit seven crore times. He who repeats a mantra 'thereat' and abstains from sin acquires perfection seven crore times. He who lives there in sanctity is sure of obtaining supreme happiness."[3] Thus, in ancient days, the island of Bassein was a sacred place void of major human settlements whose natural beauty was guarded and praised.

In the 7th century A.D. Bassein is thought to have been a great commercial centre under the Chalukya kingdom of the Deccan.[4] It's location at the mouth of an inland river enabled ships to travel to inland ports and distribute their produce.

Records from 696 A.D. indicate that while Bassein was a virtually uninhabited island devoted to religious pilgrimage, the nearby city of Kalyana was the capital of the empire of the Solanki Kings and, thus, the area enjoyed commercial prosperity owing to the evolution of this and the later sacred site of Sristhanka. Kalyana city at that time is described as "filled with spoils of conquered foes, with camels, horses, carts, elephants, jewellers, cloth-makers, chariot builders; makers of ornamental vessels reside there and the walls of the houses are covered with coloured pictures."[5] Kalayana was also the capital of the ruling dynasty in Maharashtra in 600 A.D.

From the 8th century A.D. to the beginning of the 13th century historians surmise that Bassein was under the control of the Shilahara dynasty and later was transferred to the Yadavas of Devagiri who conquered the area from the former.[6] Following the Yadavas, the Muslims, the Bhimraja of Mahim, Ramadeva of Devagada and other petty chiefs assumed control over the region at various times. Ramadeva was defeated in 1294 by All-a-udin and the Muslims had control of the area at which time they constructed the Fort of Basai.[7] The Muslims also conquered Kalyana in the 1300's.

Portuguese Beginnings

The Coast of Bassein was first visited by the Portuguese in 1509 by Captain Don Frnacisco d'Almeida on his way to Diu.[8] Bassein at this time was under the control of the Muslim ruler 'Baxay' who has built a Fort on the island and was engaged in a prosperous international trade. The rivers surrounding Bassein island were at this time deep and easily navigable, creating an excellent seaport. In 1528 Lopo Vas de Sampaio fought the Muslims at this fort but was unable to conquer the area.[9] In 1530 the Portuguese invaded Bassein and neighbouring cities of Thana and Kalyana, compelling the villages to pay taxes to the Portuguese, their new rulers.[10] Antonio de Silveira invaded Bassein, burnt down the existing town and plundered its wealth. He continued his winning streak in Thana but was offered both Mahim and Bombay by the King of Thana before he could take that city.[11] In 1531 Bassein was again invaded and pillaged by the Portuguese under Antonio de Saldanha who wished to punish the Bahadur Sultan and recover his losses from him, the King of

Gujarat. Bahadur Shah, the then King of Gujarat, was in possession of the island and did not want to sell it to the Portuguese.[12] The Muslims under Malik Tokan (son of the then Governor of Diu) again constructed a massive fort at Bassein with 15,000 troops, a naval fleet and horses to protect their possessions against their arch enemies, the Portuguese. In addition to the fortification of this military stronghold, Malik Tokan also established commercial buildings which attracted the native population and increased the size and prominence of the Basai Fort.[13]

Nunho da Cunha, wishing to arrest this military build-up, set sail to Bassein with 150 ships and 4,000 men with the intention of war. This third Portuguese attack on Bassein Fort took place in January of 1533 and the Portuguese were victorious.[14] Bahadur Shah, owing to his isolated position and loss of alliances, ceded Bassein to the Portuguese that same year and General Nunho da Cunha returned to Goa with the spoils of war and Muslim slaves. Later, in a renewed treaty between the two parties, the Portuguese confirmed the cession of Daman and Bassein and were further given permission to build a Fort at Diu. In return, the Portuguese were compelled to offer the Bahadur Shah protection and military aid in any ensuing wars against the Emperor Humayun.[15]

In 1535 the Portuguese decided to occupy the territory themselves because the Gujarati King once again set his sights on retaining the territory of Bassein. Garcia de Sa became the first captain of the Fort and in 1536 the Bassai Fort was re-christened the 'Bacaim Fort' by Nuno da Cunha who fortified the existing structure that had been built by the Bahadur Shah only a few years previously.[16] In 1540, however, the King of Gujarat besieged the Bacaim Fort under the Portuguese in an unsuccessful attempt to regain his lost territory.[17] In 1548 George Cabral replaced Garcia de Sa as Captain of Fort Bacaim, the latter who became the Governor of Portuguese India in that same year. From 1540, the Portuguese would command Fort Bassein for over two centuries with virtually no contest until the arrival of the Maratha Army in 1739.

Bacaim (Bassein) Fort under the Portuguese

The Portuguese were able to seize the Bassein Fort owing to the help of the native Bhandari community who were dissatisfied with the Muslim domination over the area. Under the latter, the Bhandaris had lost their prestige and position and wished to regain such rights following the Portuguese conquest.[18] Following the Portuguese occupation, the Fort of Bascaim rose to prominence as an international trading emporium and opulent city. Many industrious traders from the Saraswat Brahman community had relocated to Bassein from the neighbouring areas and served under the Portuguese administration as they had served under the Yadavas and Shilaharas before them. Though they served in the administration and in high official positions, they were just barely able to escape the religious conversion zeal of the Portuguese clergy.[19]

Bassein was divided into eight districts, each with its own church, convent, military fortifications and village hamlets. In order to establish both social and administrative control over these districts, the Portuguese continued the practise of religious persecution against the indigenous Hindu community.[20] The ancient religious tirthas which had existed since the earliest recorded history of Bassein were filled in with soil and their neighbouring temple complexes destroyed and plundered. As Goez writes in 1603, "When the Portuguese find an idol they burn or break it; they destroyed a tank at Bassein where the Hindus used to bathe for the remission of their sins; (and) the persecution of the Portuguese had made many Hindus, Muslims and Parsis abandon their homes and live in the dominion of the Shah Jehan."[21] For example, the Hindu community would normally celebrate an annual Zatra (religious festival and fair) at the temple tirthas whose waters were thought to be medicinal to both mind and body. At the climax of the Zatra, an occasional zealous devotee would throw himself from a height to his death in the water below.[22]

When the Portuguese Jesuits observed this Zatra they filled in the tank, raised the temple to the ground and from its remains constructed a chapel dedicated to the Holy Cross. The Hindu community found another healing tirtha which the Portuguese clergy then polluted by throwing into its waters the remains of a dead cow. However, the latter soon discovered that this water tank did have healing effects, wherein they constructed a church nearby and maintained the tirtha as church property usable only by Catholics and converts to the Catholic religion.[23] By these measures the clergy were able to construct churches from the ruined temples in the surrounding areas and convert many natives to the Roman Catholic religion. Nossa Senhora das Merces, Monte Calvario, Nossa Senhora da Vida and the Capel da Anunciada were also built by the Portuguese, as were the churches of Nossa Senhora da Graca, Sao Thome, Sao Thiago Maior and Espirito Santo.[24] Within Bassein Fort a large library was also built which housed an extensive collection of European literature.

Though Bassein remained firmly in the hands of the Portuguese for over two centuries, sporadic attacks continued by the Muslims and later the Marathas. In 1540 a Muslim invasion under Kacaji (under Akbar) destroyed the church of 'Nossa Senhora dos Remedios' and burnt many villages in the several districts.[25] The church was rebuilt in 1695, in the style similar to the first construction. Likewise, in 1535 the Portuguese missionaries constructed an orphanage dedicated to Nossa Senhora da Luz on Agasi Island. Many children who would have been sold as slaves to the Muslims of outlying regions were bought by the Christians and raised and educated as Roman Catholics. The same Muslim invasion destroyed this edifice and martyred five Catholics who refused to convert by the sword to Islam.[26] In addition to the Muslim attacks, in 1674 Moro Pandit, in an avenging attack against the Portuguese, descended from the Konkan with an army of 10,000 men and captured and fortified the ancient city of Kalyana.[27] The attack was instigated following the murder of several Maratha Hindus residing within Portuguese territory who had refused to convert to Christianity. It was unsuccessful, however, though this event marks the beginning of the Maratha attacks against the Portuguese in Bassein.

In the year 1573 alone the Jesuits baptised over 1,600 natives in the Church of Bacaim.[28] In previous years the converts had converted in hundreds, but never had so many converted at once. This was owing to the conversion of a high caste Brahmin native, whose baptism ceremony was undertaken with great pomp and circumstance. "They held a grand procession in his honour with the assistance of the Governor, Portuguese nobility and gentry of Fort Bassein",[29] finishing the ceremony with an opulent feast for all participants. This tactic worked and Hindus from all castes came forward wishing to undergo conversion. Such public Christenings continued and by 1588 over 9,400 Hindus in Portuguese Fort Bassein were converted by the Jesuits.[30] As the number of converts increased, so the number of churches in the districts grew so that eventually there were more churches than the inhabitants could fill!

The religious zeal of the Portuguese clergy and their influence on the converts also manifested in Bassein Fort area. For instance, the passion play known as 'Santos Passos' was performed in Bassein during the mid-1500 to late 1500 and depicted the life of Jesus Christ, including the Crucifixion.[31] A Jesuit priest by the name of Gaspar Berzeo, in order to incite his native audience to devotional emotional states, would deploy several native converts as 'disciplinantes' who would chastise and punish themselves during Berezeo's emotional speech. Slashing themselves with whips and small blades, the disciplinantes would inflict pain upon themselves in accordance with the pain of Jesus Christ, arousing the native audience to a similar emotional state. The entire crowd would work itself into a frenzy and begin punishing themselves as well.[32] This first performance in 1551 was very popular in its initial years, but later the enthusiasm for self-inflicting wounds dissipated and only the passion play was performed by the officiating priest, followed by a procession of Jesus Christ carrying the Cross.

St. Francis Xavier, a favourite among Portuguese Catholic converts, also made his appearance in Bassein, visiting the area in 1544 and twice in 1548, encouraging the conversion of the native population.[33] Goncalo Garcia was the Saint to hail from Bassein. During a proselytising journey to Japan, Garcia was martyred by the Japanese and was elevated to the status of a Saint by the Native Christians of Bassein.[34]

A hospital was also erected in the city though even trained professionals could do little to alter the course of the plagues that ravished the Fort on occasion. In 1695 alone 30 per cent of the population of city died from plague.[35] The plagues which affected Bassein were particularly strong and could destroy entire families within days, owing partially to the lack of ventilation which entered the city despite the four large wooden doors which allowed the entry of the four 'winds'.

Along with the Portuguese, Catholicism and international recognition, however, came the Inquisition, which did not leave the Bassein Fort area unscathed. By 1560 the Inquisition was established here as in Goa and all told over 1,250 people were martyred by this institution. Often the wealthy people were the chosen victims of the Inquisition as their lands and property were confiscated and transferred to the Church.[36] Many 'offenders' were often sent to Goa where the headquarters of the Inquisition was located. In 1603 the persecution of Hindus and Muslims took place to such an extent that many were compelled to leave their homelands and migrate to the area under the control of Shah Jehan. The same restrictions and proscriptions which outlined 'proper' Catholic convert behaviour in Goa also applied to those living in Bassein. For example, Christians were prohibited from employing any upper-class Hindus for their services and all converts were compelled the by law to attend mass on every Sunday at their parish church.[37]

A Corte do Norte (The North Court)

Bassein Fort Area was nick-named as 'A Corte do Norte' (The North Court) when compared with Goa, owing to the heavy concentration of Portuguese nobles residing there. Within and round Fort Bassein were 5 convents, 13 churches, an orphanage, an asylum for ladies (A Casa de Misercordia) and stately homes of the nobility.[38] In 1607 Francois Pyrard, a French traveller writes, "from Bassein is exported the best timber for the building of houses and ships, the greater part of which the latter is built here; it also yields a building stone that is fine and is as hard as granite and I never saw columns and pillars of entire stone so large as in this place. All the churches and sumptuous places are built of this stone."[39]

The city's circumference was surrounded by a high stone wall which allowed for ventilation from large doors opened to the north, south, east and west. Inside the Fort the city was designed with wide straight avenues and an open central market place.[40] Only Catholics, Prabhu merchants (Saraswat Brahmins) and converts were allowed to live protected within the walls of the Fort. Outside the city walls, the Christian, Hindu and Muslim peasants were gainfully employed in agriculture. The fields were continuously plowed and harvested; the produce a part of the international trade.[41]

Social life and culture in Bassein was defined by these stately Europeans and they resembled that of Goa in many respects. Wealth was displayed through the number of slaves, decorated parasols and fancy attire which nobles would adorn themselves with when moving about in public.[42] Church celebrations were observed with much pomp and splendour and the upper classes maintained strict European etiquette at the dining table and in their daily mannerisms. Ladies in Bassein would not walk in the streets unless they were provided with carpets and they entered churches through private doorways for fear of 'pollution' by the natives.[43] The ladies also contributed to the construction of a combined monastery and convent built in Goa and dedicated to St. Clara and St. Francis d'Assisi.

Wealthy Portuguese fidalgos of Bassein would maintain houses in the nearby village of Thana, a practise which increased as the population of Bassein crowded the area within the walls of the Fort.[44] They would return there after a day's work or on weekends in order to escape the urban crowd, as the ancient city of Thana had been surpassed by both Bassein and later Bombay. In this quiet area the wealthy people would reside in Portuguese villas surrounded by large gardens and orchards. As in Goa, the middle and lower classes tried to imitate the upper through similar lavish displays of wealth and country bungalows.

In 1634 there were 400 Europeans and 200 native Catholic converts living within the walls of Bassein Fort and each had several African slaves at his disposal.[45] Every fidalgo (nobleman) guarded his bungalow with several soldiers and in the event of an attack over 2,400 men could be mustered to defend the Fort. In that same year 21 armed frigates rested in the Port of Bassein, ready to defend as well as conduct trade and transport services.

Though the Portuguese nobility resided in Bassein, their moral behaviour has been described as less than first class.[46] The captaincy of Bassein Fort was a hereditary office assumed by a particular line of Portuguese nobles who rotated after three years of service and, thus, was expected by right rather than earned through deed. Corruption was pervasive and even the Fort captains' were engaged in non-sanctioned forms of trade. The manners and behaviours of the ladies were equally striking from a western perspective, as many of the Portuguese women in Bassein had taken up the habit of chewing areca nut and betel leaf, which was a Hindu practice done to redden a woman's lips and teeth.[47] The sexual license of the Portuguese was likewise shocking and the mesticos and mulattoes appeared in Bassein as well as in Goa. By 1695 records indicated that Bassein had lost its importance as a trading centre due to the behaviour of this local administration.[48]

Thus, the same 'historical accident' of the Portuguese likewise occurred in Bassein Fort and led the communities affected down similar bifurcated paths. As most Catholic converted natives resided within the walls of the Fort, they were effectively isolated from their Hindu brethren and further inculcated into the Portuguese lifestyle. Once some Prabhu Brahmin families converted to Catholicism, the conversion of natives accelerated and by 1720 the population inside Fort Bassein was roughly 58,000 Catholic natives and 2,000 Europeans.[49] As in Goa, converts were offered financial support, military protection and exalted status under the Portuguese administration. The high culture was considered that displayed by the wealthy Portuguese and members from all levels of society tried to emulate the nobility as much as possible. Within the walls of Bassein Fort and surrounds, the Catholic community was given a new identity and a source of pride. Their Hindu brethren suffered under the Portuguese policies and were treated as second class citizens. The few Muslims that dared to live in the area were treated equally bad.

For over two centuries this island on the West Coast promoted a cultural identity similar to that of the Portuguese and most of the converts, at least their second generation offspring, identified politically with the Portuguese administration. Many converts, especially those from the higher castes, learned the Portuguese language and took up employment under the Bassein nobility.[50] Uneducated converts could likewise find gainful employment as servants, gardeners and army troops within Fort Bassein. Like Goa, Fort Bassein was its own cultural enclave whose native population exalted Portuguese culture while simultaneously adhering to roots and traditional practises which could not be erased by mere political conquest. The laws and practises within Fort Bassein were the same as those enforced in Goa and the administrative personnel likewise made frequent journeys and switches between the two areas. The people were so identified with the Portuguese that following the initial Maratha invasions, they too fled aboard ships out of fear of the Maratha armies.[51]

The Coming of the Marathas

This tiny albeit internationally powerful and significant enclave and community was not to last, however. The Marathas had been plotting to conquer Bassein for years, owing to the martyrdom of several Hindu brethren. They waited until an advantageous time and as the Bhonsles were attacking and making strong inroads into the northern Goa territory and the British declining to lend assistance, the Maratha general Chimnaji Appa conquered the Bassein Fort and its surrounds on February 17th, 1739.[52] Both sides fought valiantly for days and nights and the final attack culminated with the Portuguese surrender. In all, 10,000 Maratha warriors and 800 Portuguese troops were lost. A simultaneous blockade of Daman, the ongoing attack on Goa and the lack of reinforcements led to the final capitulation of the Portuguese, which has gone down in Indo-Portuguese history as the greatest battle second to the successful attack on the Zamorin of Calicut.[53] In the final treaty all the military and civilian inhabitants of the Fort were allowed "to march out of the town with all the honours of war, whilst eight days are allowed to those of the inhabitants who so wished, to leave it with all of their moveable property."[54]

The Marathas, unlike their Portuguese predecessors, did not destroy the city of Bassein after its occupation by the troops. Rather, it was converted into a Sar Subha (administrative city) owing to its location, opulence and easily defensible ramparts.[55] However, "after the city was captured by the Marathas, all of the artillery and mortars were confiscated..." and the Fort was neither renovated nor substantially improved though inhabited by the administration.[56] They built two temples inside the Fort and purified the Tirtha in front of Nossa Senhora dos Remedios church and other tirthas in the outlying regions which had fallen into Portuguese hands. Many of the once splendid white-washed churches had already been destroyed by the prolonged attack. Under the Portuguese, all but the Saraswat Brahman traders had left the city and upon the conquest by the Marathas the former fled in fear of repercussion stemming from their allegiance to the Portuguese regime.

The General Madhavarao Peshwa, however, offered financial support and land grants to all Brahmins willing to relocate to the city and many Brahmans, mostly the Saraswats, returned to Bassein from Maharashtra and Gujarat.[57] The Marathas also established a tax in favour of the Brahmans, whom regarded the converts as polluted, in order to purify the latter and bring them once again under the Hindu fold in their former castes.[58]

Bassein under the British Empire

In 1768, less than 30 years later, the British East India Company became interested in the acquisition of Bassein following their annexation of the island of Bombay in 1665. When in 1774 a Portuguese army of 12,000 men arrived from Brazil with the intent to recapture Bassein and other lost possessions, the British offered to protect the Marathas against the Portuguese in exchange for the island of Bassein and other neighbouring territories once belonging to the Portuguese.[59] The British then stationed themselves off of the Goa Coast on March 6th, 1774 in an attempt to dissuade the Portuguese from their attack and prove their word to the Maratha forces. However, the Maratha ministry did not succumb to the temptation and in the final analysis General Goddard fought and captured Bassein from the Maratha forces in 1780 after an attack which lasted for twelve days.[60]

Where the Portuguese burnt and looted the Fort and the Marathas inhabited the area of Bassein, the British did neither. They had already decided to make Bombay island (3 hours south by train) into their main trading centre and, thus, left the Fort itself to be reclaimed by the jungle and inhabited by the locals. In 1840 a bridge was constructed to connect the mainland to

Bassein and later the railroad was extended to connect Bassein to Bombay.[61]

In 1870 when British historians visited the ruins, they discovered that the area was a prosperous taluka owing to the cultivation of rice, areca nut, bananas and sugar cane.[62] The name had been changed to "Bajipura",[63] Marathi for *The City of Baji Rao* and the district was divided into 161 villages. Papari, a village neighbouring the Bassein area, was inhabited by Chitpawan, Karada and Deshastha Brahmins,[64] Sonars (goldsmiths) and other inferior agricultural and artisan castes also inhabited the outlying areas.

Following the capture of Fort Bassein by the Marathas, not everyone who had converted to Catholicism returned to the Hindu fold. Though the majority of the Brahmans reconverted, many from the original inhabitants of the islands, especially the Bhandaris and Kolis, continued in the Catholic religion which was their religion at birth. Whether they feared persecution under the Hindus, were persuaded with financial gains by the remaining Portuguese to live among them, or psychologically unable to make the change from their traditions of old remains a matter of speculation. Most likely it was a combination of these forces and others which bound them to the Catholic tradition of their ancestors.

Consequently, in 1825 when the British explored their newly annexed territories in Bassein they discovered that the nearby city of Thana was inhabited primarily by Roman Catholics, both natives and Portuguese and that the latter closely resembled the natives in both skin colour and custom.[65] Ethnically they were distinguishable and consisted of alliances between Portuguese soldiers and low caste women and their subsequent offspring. These native Catholics of Bassein, indiscriminately labelled as Christians by the Britishers, were mostly the Bhandaris (musicians) and Kolis (indigenous fishermen).[66] Though they were seemingly devout, they were largely uneducated and ill-mannered ignorant of western etiquette. In 1870 historian da Cunha had written: "the Catholic culture in Bassein left over among the Kolis and Bhandaris is a mixture of Catholic doctrine and Hindu ritual, of Roman Catholic liturgy and Hindu ceremony."[67] Individuals within the community were unable to distinguish Catholic practises from Hindu ones and practised both as if they were of the same origin. Some living within the crumbling walls of the Fort had reconverted to Hinduism, only to revert back to Catholicism which was the religion of their family prior to the Maratha conquest.[68] Thus, a villager would have a typically Hindu name, but those of his grandparents or parents would be of Portuguese extraction such as da Silva and Fernandes. Socially, the Hindus and other communities considered them as outcasts and described them as having a 'low moral character' as had the Portuguese Catholics during the days of their rule.[69]

Though the area was explored and documented by the British in the mid to late 1800's, the city went into steep decline following its conquest in 1780. The Marathas and the Portuguese had abandoned the area and the Britisher did not care for its maintenance. As a consequence, the once opulent buildings and stone fortifications were slowly reclaimed by the jungle and inhabited by the indigenous population. Graves of Portuguese nobles were looted and all the valuables were removed. In 1818 the then British captain initiated plans to convert Bassein Fort into a jail, but these were abandoned.[70] By 1825 the Fort was completely uninhabited, doors locked and guarded by an English watchman. It is of little surprise, therefore, when in 1838 a British visitor to Bassein by name of Mrs Heber writes: "The city of Bassein has long been forsaken; except for a few fishermen and hunters who alone now occupy a spot once replete with luxury and power and still containing magnificent evidences of taste in the application of great national wealth."[71] In 1870 historian da Cunha, following his own visit to Bassein, records that the churches, convents, colleges, palaces and old villas are scattered about in pieces and the atmosphere was filled with 'silence and gloom'.[72] The scene in 1997 looked much the same.

Bassein Fort Today

Today's Fort of Bassein, now known as Kilabunder / Vasai Fort, resembles more or less that described by da Cunha in 1870.[73] Though the area has been declared a 'National Historic Site' by the Indian Archaeology Department, few repairs or restorations have taken place. Currently no guided tours, brochures, or attempts at tourism exist in the area. Rather, the forest has further reclaimed the stone walls and residents remark that during heavy storms additional deterioration occurs. Massive church skeletons stand covered in moss, groaning under the weight of centuries and virtual neglect. A silent and somewhat eerie atmosphere pervades the Fort and old grave stones written in archaic Portuguese remind the visitor of the opulence that once was.

As the name of Bassein once again referred by its ancient Sanskrit name 'Vasai', so the community predominantly inhabiting the land is once again the aboriginal tribe which became known as the Koli fishing class in the Vedic system. Their boats still line the beaches and fishing is, as it was during ancient days, the mainstay of the people. Education has improved somewhat and most young men complete the 6th standard, but as fishing remains the traditional occupation importance is not placed on formal education. In the past as in the present, the community speaks Marathi which predates the formal Marathi language and has many words which are also found in the Konkani language.[74] Likewise, the same Bassein tirthas are once again visited by devout Hindu pilgrims and the annual Zatra (temple festival) continues as if part of an unbroken chain of events from time immemorial.

Though the outer areas of the Fort seemed lifeless and degenerated, once the visitor passes through the western archway a different environment emerges. Hidden between the crumbling Bassein Fort and the sea face lies a small Koli fishing hamlet whose community and culture is very much alive. Isolated from larger society though only three hours train journey to Bombay, this community has, like other Christian communities in Bombay and surrounds, come to be classified generally as east Indians. In a unique cultural synthesis and evolution all its own, this community has incorporated within and kept alive the layers of historical evolution which have occurred within this small area known as Bassein Fort.[75]

Vasai (Bassein) village itself lies within the crumbling walls of the Bassein Fort, now over 450-year-old. The village extends onto the seashore, where large colourfully painted wooden boats are kept between high tides. Most residents are self-employed fishermen or work for a larger fishing company. Fishing and all the associated work usually delegated to women such as drying, cutting, cooking and selling, have been timeless occupations of the villagers employing all members of the family. The older generations are, thus, mostly illiterate because this relatively high income from the fishing trade discouraged the need to seek outside employment which would require higher education. The majority of today's youth study until the 5th or 6th standard, a small percentage reach the 10th standard and an exceptional family member will study beyond that, hoping to work in Bombay or abroad. The need for education, when fishing has been and continues to be a lucrative trade, was not recognised until this generation, where it is slowly seeping into the collective consciousness.

Though the Portuguese themselves were ousted after 1740, this predominantly fishing village today is still 95 per cent Catholic. A Marathi dialect reminiscent of an age-old Konkani is their mother tongue, Hindi is known to many owing to the popularity of films and pop music and English is known to a select few who have studied in English-medium schools beyond the 8th standard. No one knows a word of Portuguese. Though the ancient stone walls and churches linger like skeletons around the perimeters of the village, the place of worship currently in vogue is a typically Goan-style church painted yellow and white outside the fortress remains. The Mass was conducted in Marathi language and all the villagers attend the same Sunday services. Scattered throughout the village are crosses decorated with flower offerings and placed above most doors one finds a cross and a variety of pictorial images of Jesus. The villagers did not know that the church is similar to those seen in Goa and neither do they realised that their community is historically linked to that tiny neighbouring State.

In the village within Bassein Fort, the villagers themselves ascribe the origin of their particular customs and traditions to "our forefathers", who were simply those men "here before us."[76] The common villager does recognise that his village was under the control of the British at one point in time and prior to that the Hindu Marathas, but beyond that a substantial amount of communal memory loss has occurred. They do not even know how they became Catholics, nor does the community living within the walls of the Bassein Fort know the history of the Portuguese. Likewise, they are unable to distinguish Catholic customs from Hindu ones during their festivals and perform a variety of ritual and custom out of adherence to tradition. This psychology is most likely the cause which explains how the unique culture existing in Bassein Fort has evolved in a manner best described as 'pure fusion'. Yet the evidence of their multi-layered history surrounds the village outskirts and manifests in physical realities from old Portuguese churches with archaic Luso-Roman script to silver and red-velvet Maharaja chairs ready and waiting to receive the newly married Catholic couples. The community inhabiting Gorai Island is a similar fishing community which had undergone the same cultural-historical experiences. Though they would be broadly classified as east Indians, they do not fully understand the history behind this name designation nor do they identify themselves as 'east Indians', probably owing to some cultural and marital distinctions.

It was already discovered that the communities which laid the foundations for the various historical layers in Bassein are a blend throughout history of Gujarati and Maharashtrian Rajputs, Portuguese soldiers, Jesuit missionaries and British rulers. To review in brief, the original Bassein Fort was completed by the Sultan of Gujarat, Bahadurshah, in 1537; only to be taken by the Portuguese two years later in 1539. For the next 200 years Bassein Fort was a fine and prosperous walled city, complete with churches and richly ornamented buildings. During these two centuries much of the pre-existing population was converted to Catholicism due to the activity of the Jesuit missionaries. By 1695, however, the community, owing to pervasive corruption and opulent lifestyles, had begun to decline and diminish in importance as an international trading centre. In 1739, the harassment of these zealots in trying to covert the most prominent Hindus of Bassein made them to complain to the Maharaja King. His General, Sriman Chimaji Appa, stormed the San Sebastios Bastion, capturing the city of Bassein Fort. From 1740 until 1802, the city was under the control of the Maharashtrians, who then ceded it to the Britishers under the Treaty of Bassein in 1802. By 1818 it became incorporated into the Bombay province, under whose direction it existed before the National Liberation of India in 1947. Following Liberation, the ruins of Fort Bassein became government property transferred to the Archaeology Society of India, in whose possession it remains today.

The Day of 41 Weddings

When I visited Bassein, I arrived just in time to observe the most celebrated day of the year, *The Day of 41 Weddings.* Forty-one newlywed couples would soon be returning from the church to commence a lively procession throughout the village followed by at least five days of festivities. The marriage alliances were endogamous within this community and were formalised through negotiated proposals between members of this community and a few others in the neighbouring islands who share their culture, history and linguistic dialect.

Of importance to this study, this wedding celebration in the village of Bassein reveals a rare form of fusion and cultural synthesis within Catholic and Hindu cultural traditions. The annual celebration begins on a Sunday in early February during low tide which allows men, women and children to participate freely in the festivities and break from the monotony of daily life. After the nuptials in the church, all 41 couples march in lively procession through the entrance of the old walled fort. The procession of each couple is preceded by a group of young men dancing in western style clothes to a band following behind. The music played is both traditional and 'pop' on trumpets, tubas, French horns, snare and base drums, as well as several variants, including clarinets, saxophones, tambourines and even bagpipes! Each bride's family hires a band from the Bhandari community which performs throughout the marriage ceremony. Though the instruments are western, most songs are of Indian origin, culminating in the intense drumming characteristic of Hindu festivals. The procession stops after every few minutes when the drums reach a crescendo, the group of dancers reach a frenzy and everyone admires the newly married couple.

Behind the band, the groom wears a black suit, stark white shirt, gloves and maintains a serious countenance throughout the procession. The bride wears either a white and gold-trimmed sari or a lace white western-style wedding gown, the choice of which is hers. In both cases she also wears a small white veil, white lace gloves and a black-beaded chain ending in a gold pendant, (mangalsutra) which is the traditional mark of marriage in the Hindu community. Each couple is shielded from the sun by a beautiful red and gold decorated parasol which is held from behind by an attendant and spun time to the tune of drum beats. Behind the couple follows several ladies dressed in green and gold saris, with silver bows in their hair that reflect the sun's rays. The women carry special vessels on their heads made of silver and gold which are the gifts which the groom's family gives to the bride's on the day of the wedding. The procession fills the village lanes as each couple slowly marches towards the respective bride's house, where the family is busily preparing to receive the newlyweds and their entourage for lunch and well-wishing.

Once inside, delicacies similar to that found in Goan villages are prepared, including fish-curry-rice, mutton and beef curry, fried fish and cucumber-tomato salads. Unlike typical Goan Catholic cuisine, the sannas were thinner and made of rice, semi-sweet deep fried rice balls accompanied the meal and the fried fish was prepared using a special masala characteristic of Maharashtran fishing communities on the Konkan coast. Liquor as well as soft-drinks are served and many of the men since the early afternoon had made the most of the day's festivities to indulge in their favourite spirits.

After lunch each couple sat on black wooden and red velvet Maharaja chairs outside the bride's house under a pandal, while the green-saried ladies danced in slow, rhythmic circles to the music of the band. As evening sets in, the bride visits the houses of her friends and relatives for a final well-wishing often accompanied by the exchange of heart-felt greetings. The couple's entourage began its onward march to the house of the groom, this time accompanied by a decorated trunk containing the bride's dowry. For that bride whose groom lives in another village, the parting was a bit more emotional as she would leave her family to take up residence with her new in-laws. However, the difficulty of this initial parting was lessened by the return trip to her village expected on the following day. These return trips and the ensuing festivities continues for as many as 5 days, as the men on shore who would normally return to the seas to enjoy the break to its fullest.

The origin of this wedding customs are lost to antiquity,

though in structure they resemble the group marriage celebrations which prevailed in Hindu fishing communities where separate weddings caused financial difficulties. Thus, such customs may have had its origin prior to 1540, the arrival of the Portuguese, or after 1740, the reconquest of the Fort by the Hindu Marathas. Conversely, some historical research suggests that the Portuguese practised communal weddings when they indulged into intermarriage en masse with the local women. The women would convert to Catholicism on their wedding day, their inheritance would then go to their husbands as dowry and the women will be assured of financial wealth and social benefits. This tactic was practised by the Portuguese in Goa as they recognised the need to own land in order to gain access to the political mechanisms preexistent in the village. Most likely these particular customs are unique syntheses which have incorporated the various influences that have shaped the history of Fort Bassein.

Conclusion

Subsequent to 1739, many of the Hindu cultural forms existent prior to the Portuguese and pervasive following the Portuguese rule have become incorporated into the rituals and celebrations of these new Catholic communities, exemplified by the village of Vasai (Kilabunder). A cultural and religious identity which once held them exalted and privileged now made them virtual outcasts in larger society and abandoned by the Portuguese to whom they looked for cultural cues. Following the capture of Bassein Fort by the Marathas, the fishing village in Bassein has evolved owing to cultural diffusion occuring with other neighbouring communities. *Though they still piously attend church and mass, members of this community show little trace of the Portuguese culture other than their religion.* Even religious observance is performed in ways which are more Hindu-Indian than European, as none of the earlier religious restrictions placed on converts are applicable today. Eating habits closely resemble those of Goans, especially in the consumption of beef, chicken and fish.

Thus, it seems that over the generations, members of the community retained certain traditions that they liked (such as the use of a white lace wedding dress and formal suit at weddings, western instruments, consumption of meat) and discontinued those from the Portuguese era which they did not condone (ladies' western dresses, Portuguese morals, the Portuguese language as mother tongue, etc.). Further, they re-introduced cultural elements which stemmed from their past (communal weddings) and adopted different cultural elements which filtered in the community from outside sources. (Maharaja Chairs, Hindi pop music, baseball caps.) No one among the villagers distinguishes among these traditions; they only know that certain rituals are necessary, traditional and originated among their forefathers. Psychologically, therefore, members of this community today seem relatively content with the understanding that they are 'Christians' who have evolved special cultural traditions similar to those neighbouring island communities with whom they come into intimate contact. Though less than three hours away from India's largest city of Bombay, this community is both inextricably linked and paradoxically isolated from the rigour of modern urban existence.

In the previous discussion concerning Daman, it was suggested that the Portuguese Catholic culture is dying out because of the elders' resistance to change and insistence upon fixed, rigid cultural forms. While their attempts effectively solidify identity and document history, they as effectively relegate a culture to a specific historical time period, thus, preventing it from evolving and adapting to the changing needs of modern generations. The result is a marked feeling of being an 'outsider' in larger society; of living in a particular historical moment with which they do not identify. *The village of Bassein Fort, in marked contrast, seems to offer a more flexible solution, whereby what is a traditional "Hindu" custom has been freely incorporated into traditional Catholic ritual.* The villagers themselves seem not to perceive difference regarding the archaic origins of things such as the white lace wedding gowns, church nuptials, village processions, drum circles and Maharaja chairs. Rather, the community has embraced transformation and fusion rather than erecting barriers to these natural forces.

Why Bassein has been successful when most communities around the world suffer during periods of transformation still remains an interesting anthropological question. Perhaps a certain amount of 'memory loss' is necessary in order for a community and or communities to find a balance between tradition and transformation. When a community is more concerned about living in the present than preserving the past, it evolves naturally, without the pain of loss and nostalgia for the bygone days. This is not to say that tradition should be discarded and all things new fully embraced. Tradition and culture are beautiful and necessary things when they are harnessed to empower individuals, to celebrate life, family and God, as well as to form strong bonds between people. *What this case study intends to illustrate is that the village of Bassein has discovered how to successfully balance tradition with evolution through a 'pure' and unintentional cultural fusion which harmonises her various historical pasts. Whatever their origins, like the ancient awe-inspiring, crumbling fortress walls that surround it, the cultural traditions of Bassein village have gracefully flowed and adapted to the sands of time, expressing themselves with beauty and pride for what they are in this historical moment.*

The Cultural Relevance of Bassein to the Future of Goan Cultural Evolution

There are both similarities and differences between Goa and Bassein when examining the pre, post and current cultural evolution of these areas. Goa and Bassein prior to the Portuguese rule had a similar socio-cultural history, including the various overlords who brought Hindu, Buddhist and Jain influences into these regions. The inhabitants of these two regions were likewise similar, including the fishing and agricultural aboriginal tribes (Kolis and Kunbis respectively) and the Dravidian Chittapavan, Karada and Deshastha Brahmins from the southern region. Likewise the Saraswat Brahmins migrated into both Goa and the Bassein/Bombay regions and established trade links and Aryan Vedic culture. As in Goa, Bassein was invaded and conquered by the Muslim invasions prior to the advent of the Portuguese, who then brought the European culture and traditions to plant in Indian soil. The culture and society of Bassein was, therefore, virtually identical to that of Goa except that the former stronghold had a higher concentration of Portuguese nobility. Their language was likewise similar, a Marathi 'dialect' (early Konkani) which later was discovered to be the precursor to Marathi. In both regions the Marathas first under Shivaji and then under Sambhaji attempted to liberate the areas from Portuguese conquest and while they succeeded and Bassein fell in 1739 it would be another 250 years before Goa was liberated from the grip of Portugal.

The year 1739, therefore, marks the year in which the historical evolution of the regions of Goa and Bassein diverged for the first time in recorded history. While the former continued under the Portuguese administration, the latter area was liberated by the Maratha armies and the Hindu community once again enjoyed the favour of the ruling administration. The Catholic converts either reconverted to Hinduism or fled the city and settled in smaller, humble settlements in and around Thana. Many of the poor, uneducated Catholic converts like the above fishing community outside the walls of Bassein were 'purified' and taken back into the Hindu fold. After some time, however, owing to their adherence to tradition of their forefathers and to tradition, several of these communities reconverted and once again maintained what were for them the then traditional Catholic beliefs of their ancestors. Yet so strong was Phase I of the inculturation process among the native Catholic community, so minimal their understanding of religious doctrine and so outcast they became when they tried to return to the Hindu fold, that the members felt compelled to return to their previous belief system.

The similarities in the histories until 1739 raise the question of the future of Goan Catholic cultural evolution. Removed from the source which instigated these cultural trends, Catholic communities in Goa may eventually express again and further absorb many of the Hindu practises and customs as did those in Bassein, though it will take at least another 50 years before such practises manifest among the upper-class Catholics. Already, 80 per cent of the Portuguese culture is lost except for the Catholic religion, which is slowly evolving unique, Indianed forms of ritual and worship. Psychologically, while a few in Goa are staunch proponents of Portuguese culture and lifestyle, others are readily adapting to the trends in modern society and accepting that some amalgamation will occur in a State where in fact, 60 per cent of the population follows a Hindu way of life.

As the Portuguese clergy tried bring into fore Catholicism

to the surrounding cultural environment, the Goan Catholics now identified with larger India, eventually tried to identify their cultural traditions with those of their neighbours. Similarly, the extent to which the Goan Catholics seek an identification with the modern Euro-American culture or to that of their traditional Indian roots will also shape the direction of future cultural evolution.[77]

In the final analysis, it may be a question of perspective. Will others in Goa, as in the politically charged Bombay, regard the Catholic community as a foreign and converted people? Will those who cling to a past identity suffer from its 'pollution' by more modern influences as in Daman? Or might fusion and syntheses be regarded not as 'polluting', 'diluting', 'destructive' forces but as 'generative', 'creative' and 'natural' ones as in Bassein.

Anyone who has ever sat and watched a sun set over the Arabian Sea can testify to its unique and transforming beauty; watching as the emerging red, orange and pink hues paint the slowly moving clouds in an inspiring process of creation, destruction and evolution.

REFERENCES

1. Da Cunha, Gerson J., *Notes on the Antiquities of Chaul and Bassein*, New Delhi: Asian Educational Services, 1993, p. 217.
2. *Ibid.*, p. 125.
3. *Ibid.*, pp. 126-27, Includes preceding paragraph.
4. *Ibid.*, p. 130.
5. *Ibid.*, p. 168.
6. *Ibid.*, p. 131.
7. *Ibid.*
8. *Ibid.*, p. 132.
9. *Ibid.*
10. *Ibid.*, p. 133.
11. *Ibid.*
12. *Ibid.*
13. *Ibid.*, pp. 134-36.
14. *Ibid.*, p. 136.
15. *Ibid.*, p. 137.
16. *Ibid.*, pp. 137-38.
17. *Ibid.*, p. 138.

18. *Ibid.*, p. 170.
19. Kudva, V.N., *History of the Dakshinatya Saraswats*, Madras: Samyukta Gowda Saraswata Sabha, 1972, pp. 58-60.
20. Da Cunha, Gerson J., *op. cit.*, p. 144.
21. *Ibid.*, p. 143.
22. *Ibid.*, pp. 126-29.
23. *Ibid.*, p. 163.
24. *Ibid.*, p. 161.
25. *Ibid.*, p. 165.
26. *Ibid.*
27. *Ibid.*, p. 147.
28. *Ibid.*, p. 234.
29. *Ibid.*
30. *Ibid.*
31. *Ibid.*, p. 249.
32. *Interestingly, there was a Hindu ritual in vogue at that time wherein people underwent similar self-inflicted torment by poking steaks through their skin or walking over hot coals.
33. Da Cunha, Gerson J., *op. cit.*, pp. 246-49.
34. *Ibid.*, p. 241.
35. *Ibid.*, pp. 140-41.
36. *Ibid.*, pp. 235-40.
37. *Ibid.*, p. 144.
38. *Ibid.*, p. 139.
39. *Ibid.*, p. 140. Quote from Viagem de Francisco Pyrard, vol. II, pp. 226-27.
40. *Ibid.*, pp. 141-42.
41. *Ibid.*, p. 145.
42. *Ibid.*, p. 223.
43. *Ibid.*, p. 246.
44. *Ibid.*, p. 223.
45. *Ibid.*, p. 209.
46. *Ibid.*, p. 224.
47. *Ibid.*, p. 248.
48. *Ibid.*, p. 251.
49. *Ibid.*, p. 146.
50. *Ibid.*, pp. 150-52.
51. *Ibid.*, pp. 148-49.
52. *Ibid.*, pp. 149-50.
53. *Ibid.*, p. 149. For more information, see the Cochin Case-study.
54. *Ibid.*, p. 149.
55. *Ibid.*, p. 150.

56. *Ibid.*, p. 209.
57. *Ibid.*, p. 150.
58. *Ibid.*
59. *Ibid.*
60. *Ibid.*, pp. 150-51. Includes preceding paragraph.
61. *Ibid.*, p. 150.
62. *Ibid.*, p. 247.
63. *Ibid.*
64. *These Brahmans were of the same Dravida-Brahmin sub-groups from the south which also inhabited the Konkan territory, including the region of Goa prior to the settlements of Aryan Brahmins.
65. Da Cunha, Gerson J., *op. cit.*, p. 185.
66. *Ibid.*, p. 248.
67. *Ibid.*
68. *Ibid.*
69. *Ibid.*, p. 250.
70. *Ibid.*, p. 211.
71. *Ibid.*, p. 212.
72. *Ibid.*
73. A trip was made to Bassein Fort Area by this author in February of 1997.
74. Konkani in the north dialect, as a point to remember, was documented by one of the Portuguese priests who lived in Bassein and compiled this early language.
75. What impressed me as a cultural anthropologist is how the variety of customs from at least 4 different cultures have been fused to the extent that the participants themselves do not know from which culture the various components have arisen. Cultural systems are everywhere in constant flux. Like identities, they adjust and adapt to changing social, economic and environmental conditions. Though the characteristics that distinguish a particular culture are often ambiguous over time and space, they do create real differences in the way that people perceive themselves and behave in their worlds. In the context of the cultural evolution which has occurred in Bassein Fort, what this means is that the current customs and knowledge of communal history circulating within this community are most relevant to my research; for out of them people formulate opinions, make choices and complete actions. Consequently, like a detective, I visited Fort Bassein prior to conducting in-depth historical research with the aim of perceiving the community through the eyes of her inhabitants as an experimental technique designed to enlighten my examination of processes of cultural evolution in Portuguese India.
76. The information in The Village of Bassein is, therefore, collected from first hand, on-location research which was gleaned from stories and 'facts passed along to me from the villagers, names and numbers etched in the fort ruins, an informative sign posted by the Indian Archaeological Society and keen observation. The Tapeli family, prominent residents of Vasai, were instrumental to my understanding of the cultural practises which I

witnessed, the general information about the village and the perceptions of the people as perceived by their own members.

77. This further depends, however, on which countries and cultures will rise to prominence in the next millennium. As the decline of Euro-American culture increases owing to creative stagnation, over indulgence and materialistic values assuming precedence over spiritual and social concerns, a new region will emerge whose values may not necessarily be those of their predecessors. Though India will in time come full circle and rise again to prominence, other countries in the meanwhile are poised and ready to exert their cultural superiority around the world.

CHAPTER 12

Conclusion

In Part I of this work we explored the concept of 'culture', the ancient and modern history of Goa and the creation of the modern political entity known today as the Indian State of Goa. Chapter 5 of Part I, therefore, is really the culmination of Goa's history in human terms as it relates to its previous chapters. If we now can view culture as a process of evolution and Goa as one particular process as outlined by chapters 2, 3 and 4, then Chapter 5 is the logical conclusion of the past and such diversity and varied cultural elements are expected. Part I also illuminates the idea that Goa is quite representative of the process of cultural evolution which occurs the world over. She is a microcosm of which is restricted neither by people nor by nation. Yet Goa is unique, owing to its specific patterning, historical accidents, selective absorption, reinterpretation and value-orientation of her people.

Part I also attempts to address the question of what is Goa and what is Goan cultural identity. Though 'Goan identity' is still represented by its post-Liberation characteristics, hopefully this work has demonstrated that only a certain number of people living in Goa will exhibit all of those characteristics and a significant percentage had very limited contact with the cultural elements which are still used to characterise all Goans in general. However, the identity of a people or a place is not meant to reflect everything at once and identities, like cultures and communities, grow and evolve over time to adapt to the changing needs of people. As arguments are continually put forth challenging the currently accepted identity of Goa, it will change and include those communities formerly left out of the typical

'Goan identity'. But before a more inclusive definition of Goan identity can arise, their communities who have so long been separated by forces both internal and external must come together peacefully and respectfully to address both similarities and differences. Only when the psychological skirmish are exhausted and people are willing to listen to and accept the opinions of the other, a more complete picture of Goa will emerge which remains true to itself. And only when many communities are equally recognised as having significant contributions to the history and culture of Goa, their voices and cultural elements will find inclusion in the cultural identity of Goa.

The question of what is the culture of Goa can be taken more broadly, however, to include all of the major communities and their interactions with one another. Taken in the broad sense, Goa and people of Goa are a blend of the many cultural and historical elements which have landed upon her shores over thousands of years. A large number of tribal communities who had lived in Goa long before the arrival of the Hindu religion and Aryans still adhere to the ancient customs and traditions of their forefathers. Likewise, the Saraswat Brahmin community spread throughout larger India has some of its most famous temples and places of religious pilgrimage located in Goa and they have also inculcated many cultural elements into the Hindu culture of Goa. Clearly, the tribal and Hindu communities living in Goa are as 'Goan' and integral to the culture of Goa as are the Catholic communities which arose during the Portuguese era. Likewise, the Catholic Goans and tribals adhering to their ancient belief system are no less Indian simply because they do not profess Hinduism.

Possibly Konkani, is one of the few elements which truly crosses all other barriers and unites this diverse group of people. Konkani is an ancient language in Goa and one which flourished along the West Coast of India, as North as Daman and Bassein and as South as the state of Karnataka. That it is an indigenous langauge is obvious from the simple fact that even the illiterate populace of Goa speaks Konkani. Explorers arriving as early as the 1400's have mentioned the existence of the language and it was the Portuguese missionaries who documented and first formalised the language, using the Roman script to create a written form which did not previously exist. Originally an oral language whose roots are lost to antiquity, it has since evolved and adapted, like the people of Goa, to include first Marathi and Sanskrit, then Portuguese and most recently English in its vocabulary.

Part II next explores the process of rural-urban migration, a world-wide phenomenon with particular relevance to the economic and social development of Goa. Chapter 6 explored the processes of rural-urban migration in India, as well as the consequences of such migration trends in both the cities where migration occurred and homelands were vacated. Chapters 7 and 8 then examined three cities as case studies: Bombay, Bangalore and Mangalore and the varying degrees and results of such migration in terms of community reformation and creation and maintenance of identity.

Bombay had the largest number of Goan immigrants, many of whom arrived in the early years and have since enjoyed a substantial increase in their material well-being and social prestige. As large numbers of Goan Catholics migrated and reformed large Goan neighbourhoods within the city, stereotypes of Goan cultural identity solidified and spread throughout larger India. Several 'Goan clubs' and 'Goan neighbourhoods' which arose in Bombay, further contributed to enhance Goan identity which incorporated to a large extent the cultural ideal of the current ruling party; the Portuguese. Thus, while other communities from Goa blended more easily into their surrounding environment, the Goans who identified with the Portuguese-Catholics celebrated their culture under the conducive British empire and helped to establish the well-known 'Goan identity'.

In contrast to this strong identification and celebration of the Indo-Portuguese culture of Goan immigrants in Bombay, the migration of many Goans into Mangalore resulted in the creation of a new, separate identity. Agricultural records from the 1500's indicate that skilled cultivators of coconuts and their religious affiliates were invited to Mangalore and received land and earnings in exchange for the cultivation of coconuts. Probably owing to their higher status as landowners, Goan descendants in Mangalore today have disassociated themselves from their roots and collectively remember only their 'Mangalorean' heritage. They have assumed a different identity, owing also to centuries of separation from their homelands. This identification Continues even though their mother tongue is Konkani, their folk-arts include the Kunbi harvest dance, they profess the Catholic religion and they cook a typically Portuguese dish named Pork Sorpotel.

Bangalore is also mentioned as a case study, though only a few thousand Goans have actually migrated there over the years. Mangaloreans are many, however, in this city where the two cultures are again in the same geographic space and continue in a friendly rivalry. Of late, Bangalore has become one of Asia's fastest growing cities and more migration to Bangalore is expected in the coming years. Part II demonstrates that the migration of people from Goa has played an important role throughout their history and that different groups have maintained strong or weak ties depending on their particular set of historical circumstances.

Part III briefly examines three other areas along the West Coast of India which were also influenced by the historical presence of the Portuguese. These demonstrate varying degrees of cultural evolution following the Portuguese influence owing, to their unique set of historical circumstances prior to, during and following the Portuguese presence. The case studies of Cochin, Daman and Bassein have been included in this research work because, they present three different cases where the Portuguese influence took root and present excellent means for comparison. How these different areas have acted and reacted to the introduction, maintenance and removal of the Portuguese influence illuminates the larger trends occuring along the West Coast during those years as well as the unique historical circumstances surrounding each and the consequent patterns of evolution.

Fort Cochin, the first 'bastion' of the Portuguese empire, is an interesting example which demonstrates the selective conversion of a local community and the way in which the existing cultural elements can effect the introduction of a new, competing element. The ancient kingdom known today as Kerala, was a very conservative society whose class and caste barriers were rigidly enforced. In Cochin, due to the strength of the existing cultural system, those who converted remained bound to these same caste divisions and did not reap material and social benefits outside of the Portuguese community. As a result, most of the converts continued their previous mannerisms even to the extent of sitting on the floor while in church. The history of Cochin was also included in this case study as the difficulties which the Portuguese encountered there spurred the movement North, which eventually strengthened the selection of Goa and Bassein as the foundations of sustained colonialisation.

Daman, in contrast to Cochin, was a city won from the Muslim forces. It was a vacant space won in a just war and was much more permeable to the influence of the Portuguese. Those who converted to Catholicism in Daman were able to increase their wealth and social standing, gaining both financial and political stature. Among the converts the earlier caste system was absolved and the people enjoyed lasting benefits following conversion. As a result, Daman exemplified the full absorption of the Portuguese cultural elements into a particular community, placing Portuguese in its stead. Most other elements of Portuguese culture, including home furnishings, eating habits and social events, were also fully absorbed into the culture of this community, erasing previous cultural practises. Communities similar to Daman which benefitted significantly from the Portuguese, most fully identified with her culture and people. Following Liberation, they experienced a crisis of identity and have since shown reluctance to practise the culture of the larger population, still maintaining identity links to their former colonial rulers.

Chapter 11 examines the history and culture of Fort Bassein, a small fishing village which rose to international prominence and importance with the rise of the Portuguese and then fell following the battle which defeated the Portuguese power. This small village, which became the 'North Court' of the Portuguese nobility was reduced little more than crumbling stone walls nestled close to the seashore. Yet the culture which flourished within the village demonstrates centuries of cultural absorption from a variety of influences, both ancient and modern. All are blended harmoniously together and are visible during village celebrations. Yet those who practise these traditions are oblivious to the various origins and perceive the synthesis simply as the 'culture' of their forefathers. Part III, therefore, demonstrates that a similar group of elements, when inserted into even slightly different environments, can evolve in markedly different ways depending on the unique set of historical circumstances before, during and after its insertion.

The future of Goa, Goan culture and the Goan identity remains to be seen. New unpredictable elements will emerge and find their way into the community, new policies will change the course of social and economic development and new communities will immigrate into and migrate away from Goa. The process is a continuous one which has neither beginning nor an end and is always modified, only illusively controlled and constantly moving in rhythmic cycles like ebb and flow of the ocean's tides. Likewise, world sentiment and activities taking place in larger India will continue to have an impact on the evolution of Goa. Yet, Goa is not entirely vulnerable to these forces and does exhibit some control over her future. Goa, is truly a microcosm of activities, processes and changes which occur throughout the world. Goa herself is a process, one of constant change, adaptation, insight and evolution. This process of change is not uniform, however, because some elements of society evolve faster than others, as can be seen in Goa's classic juxtaposition of the old and the new; of cellular phones and bullock carts. She is as unique and different as she is similar and connected to other cultures and collective human experience.

A Sketch Map
of
PORTUGUESE ACQUISITION OF TERRITORY IN GOA
GOA-TALUKS

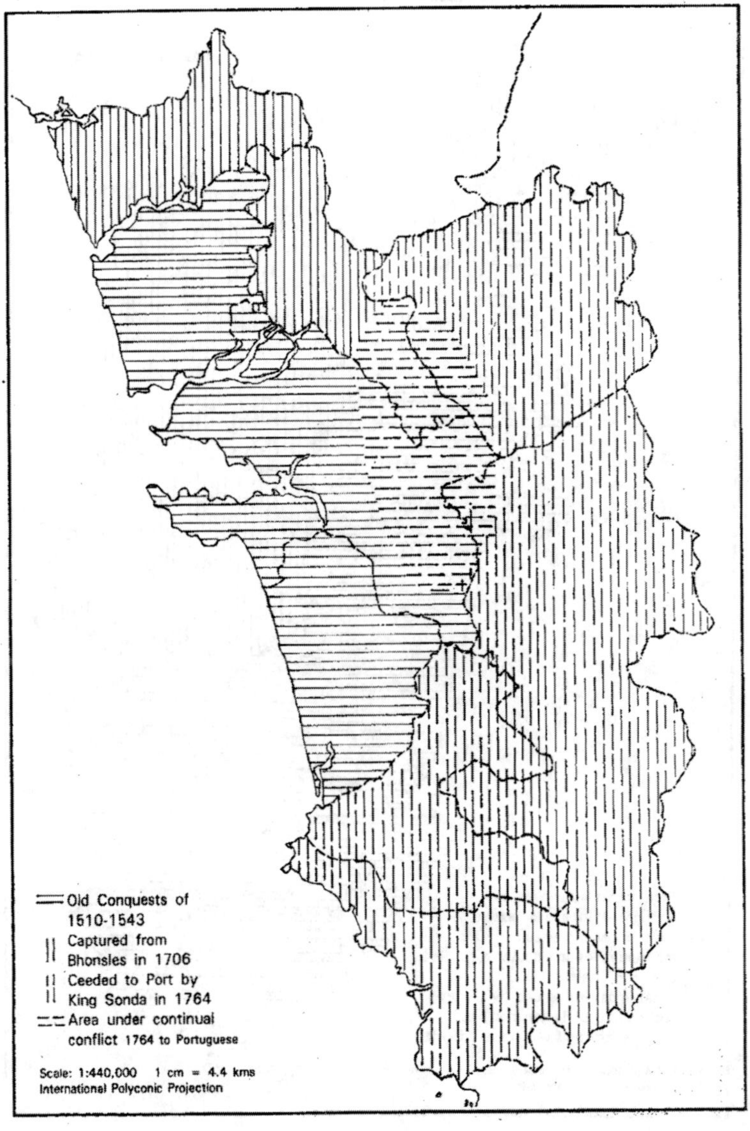

A Sketch Map

of

AREAS OF CULTURAL INFLUENCE: 1510-1961

GOA-TALUKS

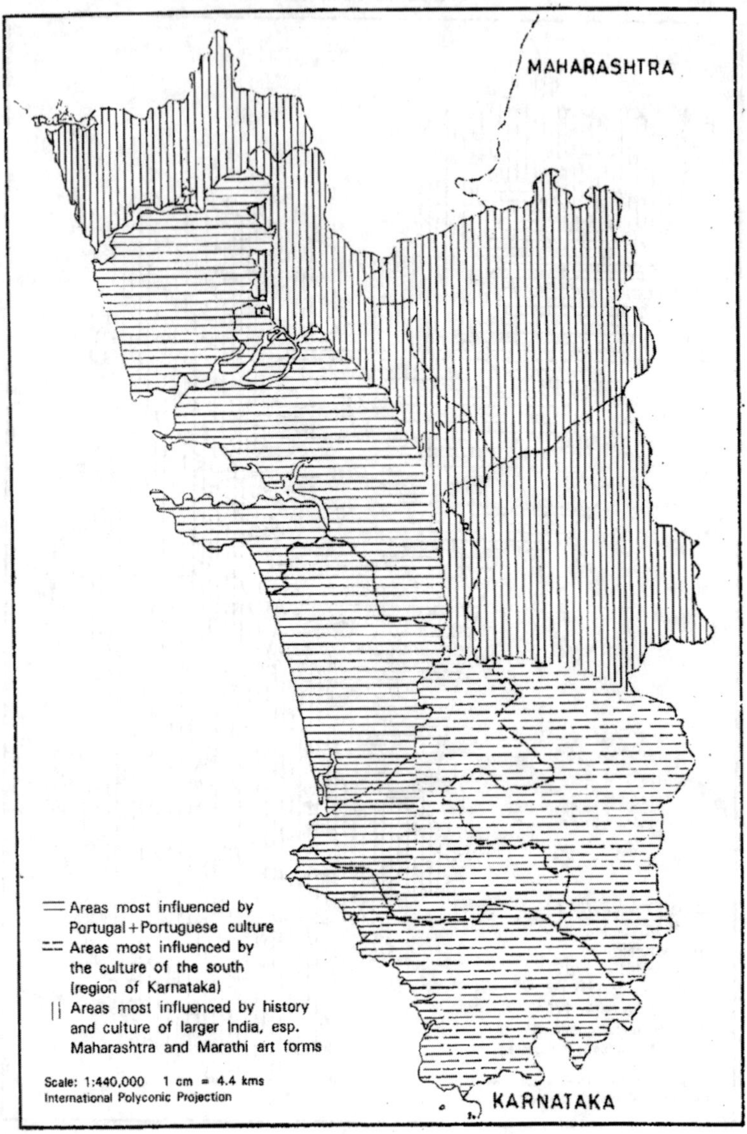

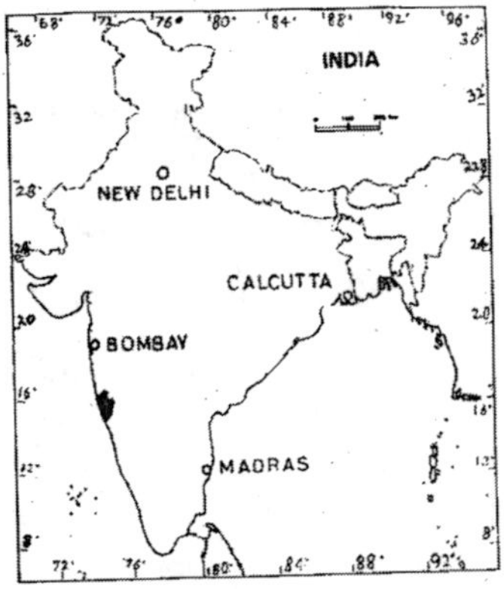

A Sketch Map
of
GOA—TALUKS

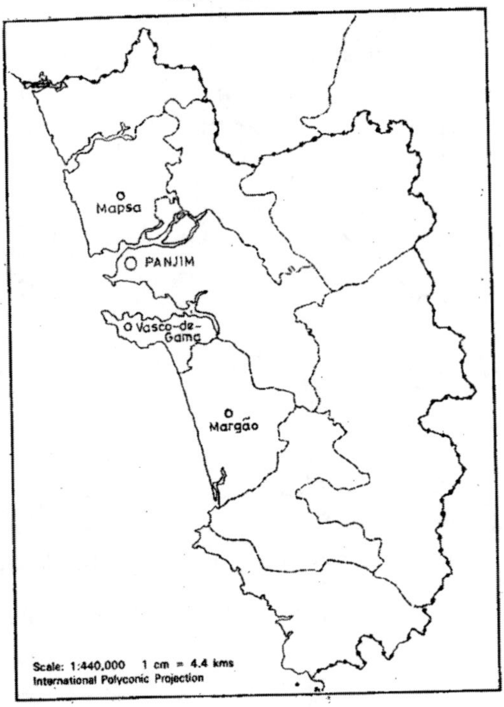

A Sketch Map

of

AREA OF PORTUGUESE INFLUENCE IN INDIA 1510-1961

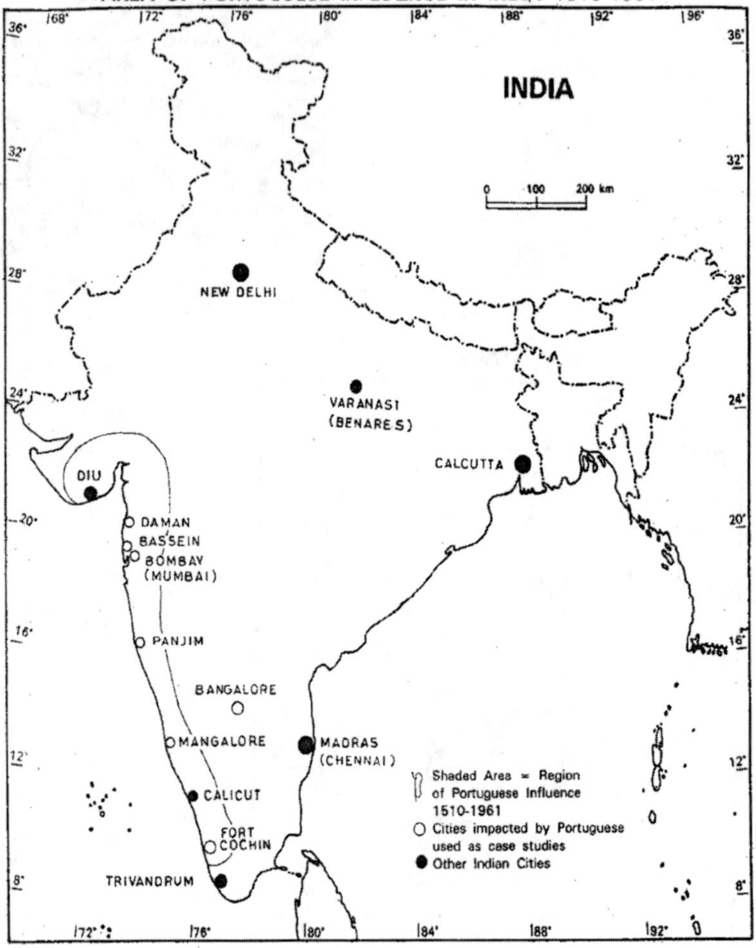

Sujata

A Sketch Map
of
VILLAGE CASE STUDIES
GOA-TALUKS

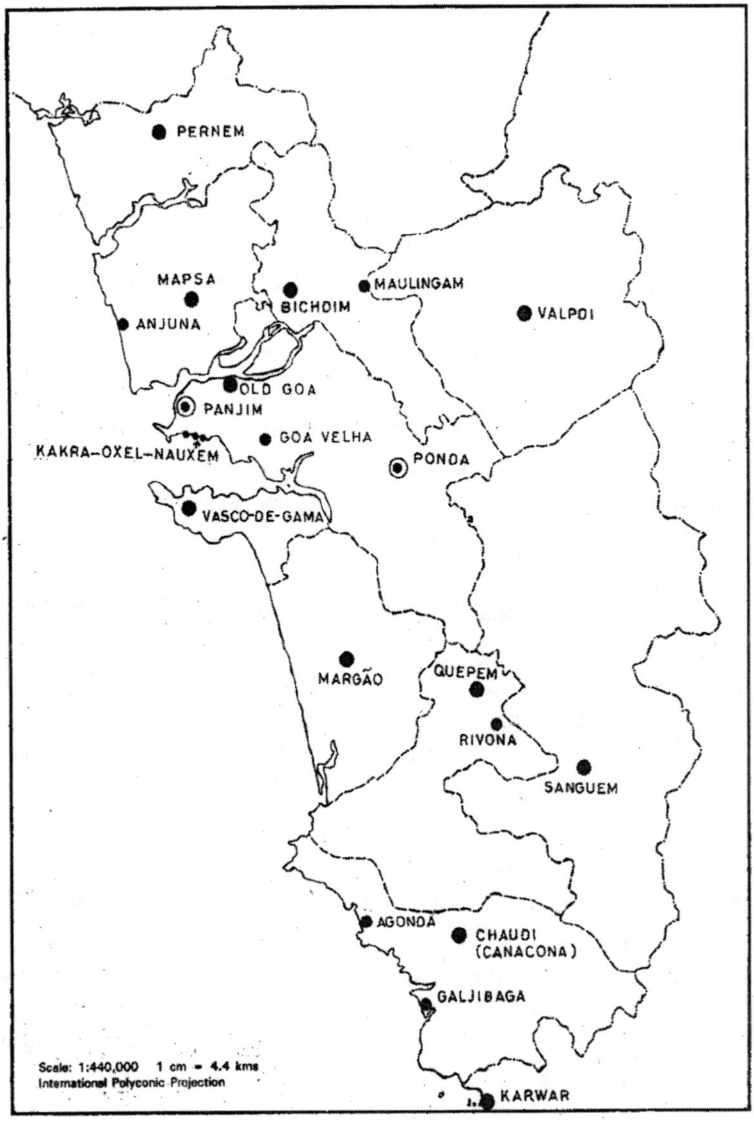

Bibliography

Abram, David, *Goa: The Rough Guide,* London: Penguin Books, 1995.

Almeida, S.J. Matthew, *Konkani Basic Course,* Panjim: Thomas Stephens Konkani Kendra, 1991.

Angle, Prabhakar S., *Goa: Concepts and Misconcepts,* Bombay: Goan Hindu Association, 1994.

Bernard, K.L., *Flashes of Kerala History,* Cochin: Swaraj Printers, 1995.

DaCunha, Gerson J., *Notes on the Antiquities of Chaul and Bassein* New Delhi: Asian Educational Services, 1993.

DaCunha, Gerson J., *Origin of Bombay,* New Delhi: Asian Educational Services, 1990. (reprint, 1st publication in 1900)

Day, Francis, *The Land of the Permauls, or Cochin,* New Delhi: Asian Educational Services, 1995. (reprint, 1st published 1900)

Department of Tourism, *Daman and Diu: The New Destination,* New Delhi: Cross Section Publications, 1992.

Department of Tourism, *Daman and Diu,* New Delhi: Cross Publications, 1992.

Department of Information and Tourism, *Ten Years of Liberation,* Panjim: Government Printing Press, 1971.

DeSouza, Teotonio R., *Medieval Goa,* New Delhi: Concept Publishing Co., 1979.

Dhume, Anant Ramkrishna Sinai, *The Cultural History of Goa from 10,000 B.C.-1352 A.D.,* Panjim: Map Printers, 1985.

Directorate of Tourism, *Goa: Tourist Directory,* Panji: Government of Goa, 1987.

Directorate of Tourism, Goa Yatra, Panji: Government of Goa, 1987.

Directorate of Tourism, Hello Goa!, Panjim: Government of Goa, 1996.

Discover India: Destination Goa, May 1994, Vol. 7, 5. Hong Kong: Media Transasia.

"Education Super-Bazar," *Mangalore Today,* Vol. I, Issue 5, April 1997.

Ferreira, Eduardo deSouza, *Portuguese Colonialism in Africa,* Paris: The Unesco Press, 1974.

Furtado, A.D., *Goa: Yesterday, Today, and Tomorrow,* Panjim: Furtado's Enterprises at Priya Prints, 1981.

Gaitonde, P.D., *The Liberation of Goa,* New Delhi: Oxford University Press, 1987.

Goa Today, April 1996. (various articles within the issue)

Goa Today, January 1997. (various articles within the issue)

Goa Today, March 1997. (various articles within the issue)

Goa Today, April 1997. (various articles within the issue)

Gomes, Olivinho, J.F., *Village Goa,* New Delhi: S. Chand & Co., 1996.

Gowda Saraswat Saman, "41st Annual Report", Bangalore: Gowda Saraswat Samaj, 1996.

Gowda Saraswat Samaj, "36th Annual Report", Bangalore: Gowda Saraswat Samaj, 1991.

Gracias, Fatima de Silva, *Health and Hygiene in Colonial Goa: 1510-1961,* New Delhi: Concept Publishing Co., 1994.

GSB Samaj, *Cochin Thirumala Devaswom and the Gowda Saraswat Brahmins,* Cochin: GSB Samaj.

Gune, V.T., *Gazetter of the Union Territory of Goa, Daman and Diu, Parts I, II and III,* Bombay: Government Central Press, 1979.

Herskovits, Melville J., *Cultural Dynamics,* (Abridged from Cultural Anthropology), New York: Alfred A. Knopf, Inc., 1964.

Hinsie, M.D. and Campbell, M.D. *Psychiatric Dictionary,* 4th Edition. New York: Oxford University Press, 1970.

Honigmann, John J., *Personality in Culture,* New York: Harper and Row Publishers, 1967.

Jungblut, Fr. Leon J., *Our Lady of the Mount,* Bombay: Institute on Indian Culture.

Karunan, Victor J.R., *History of St. Mary's Basilica,* Bangalore: St. Mary's Basilica, 1974.

Kinatukara, Paul Fr., *St. Mary's Basilica,* Bangalore: St. Mary's Basilica, 1974.

Krishnamurthy, V., The Soul of Mangalore, *Mangalore Today,* April 1997. Vol. I, Issue. 5.

Kudva, V.N., *History of the Dakshinatya Saraswats,* Madras: Samykta Gowda Saraswats, 1972.

Madhava, Dr. K.G., Vasantha, *Agrarian Relations of Western Karnataka; A.D. 1500-1800.* New Delhi: Naurang Inc. 1991.

Mangalore Today, "The Turbulent History of a Vibrant City", March 1997, Vol. I, Issue 4.

Mangalore Today, "Industries: A Real Threat to the Environment" March 1997, Vol. I, Issue 4.

MCH and Family Planning, *National Family Health Survey: Goa 1992-93,* Bombay: International Institute for Population Sciences, 1995.

Migdal, Joel S., *Strong Societies and Weak States,* Princeton: Princeton Univ. Press, 1988.

Oberai, A.S. and H.K. Manmohan Singh, *Causes and Consequences of Internal Migration: A Study in the Indian Punjab,* Jaipur: Rawat Publications, 1992.

Pinto, Celsa, *Trade and Finance in Portuguese India: A Study of the Portuguese Country Trade,* New Delhi: Concept Publishing Co., 1994.

Pissurlencar, Panduronga S.S., *Roteiro dos Arquivos da India Portuguesa,* Bastora: Tipografia Rangel, 1955.

Roa, Navin Kumar, "A Dubai Round-up" *Mangalore Today,* April 1997, Vol. I, Issue 5.

Rao, R.P. *Portuguese Rule in Goa, 1510-1961.* Bombay: Asia Publishing House, 1963.

Rubinoff, Arthur G., "Goa's Attainment of Statehood," *Asian Survey,* May 1992, Vol. XXXII, No. 5.

Shevgoor, Bharati, "A Season for Self-Analysis", *Mangalore Today,* Vol. I, Issue 5, April 1997.

Shirodkar, P.P. (ed.) *Goa: Cultural Trends,* Seminar Papers, Panjim: Director of Archives, Archaeology, and Museum, 1988.

Shrine of the Holy Cross of Bambolim-Souvenir Issue-Inauguration and Blessing. Panjim: New Age Printers, 1996.

"The Chariots of the Gods", *Mangalore Today,* Vol. I, Issue 4, March 1997.

The Economist, "A Safe Place in India", Dec. 7th, 1991.

UT Administration, *Daman: Where Time Stands Still,* Nani Daman: Tourism Deptt.

Varde, Dr. P.S., *History of Education in Goa from 1510 to the Present Day,* Bombay: Somaiya Publications, 1977.

Xavier, P.D., *Goa: A Social History from 1540 to 1680.,* Panjim: P.D. Xavier, 1993.

"Yugadi: Ringing in the New", *Mangalore Today,* Vol. I, Issue 5, April 1997.

Index